Cantonese

CANTONESE
SINCE THE 19TH CENTURY

Hung-nin Samuel Cheung

The Chinese University of Hong Kong Press

Cantonese: Since the 19th Century
  By Hung-nin Samuel Cheung

© The Chinese University of Hong Kong 2023
All Rights Reserved. No part of this publication may
be reproduced or transmitted in any form or by any
means, electronic or mechanical, including photocopying,
recording, or any information storage and retrieval
system, without permission in writing from
The Chinese University of Hong Kong.

ISBN: 978-988-237-253-5

Published by The Chinese University of Hong Kong Press
    The Chinese University of Hong Kong
    Sha Tin, N.T., Hong Kong
    Fax: +852 2603 7355
    Email: cup@cuhk.edu.hk
    Website: cup.cuhk.edu.hk

Printed in Hong Kong

Contents

Foreword vii

One Language, Two Systems: A Phonological Study of
  Two Cantonese Language Manuals of 1888 1

Cantonese Phonology as Reconstructed from Popular Songs 33

Completing the Completive:
  Reconstructing Early Cantonese Grammar 75

The Interrogative Construction:
  (Re-)constructing Early Cantonese Grammar 109

The Pretransitive in Cantonese 151

Naming the City: Language Complexity in the Making of
  an 1866 Map of Hong Kong 209

Terms of Address in Cantonese 247

A Study of *Xiehouyu* Expressions in Cantonese 287

Appendix: Chinese Abstracts 357

Foreword

I was born in Shanghai in 1946, the youngest son to parents who were natives of Zhenjiang 鎮江, a city to the north of the Yangtze River. I grew up in Hong Kong speaking a variety of dialects, vastly different dialects. Seemingly an impossible task, but, to a kid, it was a simple matter of matching different sounds to different faces. My mother spoke to us only in the Zhenjiang dialect, a member of the southern Mandarin family, which was truly my mother tongue. My siblings spoke with each other mostly in Shanghainese, a Wu 吳 dialect. I was never conversant with that Shanghai accent, and it wasn't until I came to the San Francisco Bay Area in the late 1960s that I began to realize those buzzing apical sounds, which I used to find so conceitedly unnatural, had always been in my language repertoire; when I hung around friends who had come from the old Shanghai, I spoke almost like a (semi-)native. And, of course, as I went to school in Hong Kong, from kindergarten to graduate school, Cantonese was by default my second native, and most fluent, language. But, for whatever inexplicable reasons, however proficient I may seem to have mastered these dialects I grew up with, I often speak with a little accent, which natives can easily detect—and I am not one of them.

I started Mandarin in school when I was seven or eight years old. Thanks to the teachers I had since then, especially those who came from Beiping 北平 in the 1940s, I acquired a rather competent command of this northern dialect. I began teaching Mandarin at Berkeley as a teaching assistant in 1970, and I continued my work in language pedagogy for the next thirty years. People were always surprised that I was from Hong

Kong. "Where did you learn to roll your tongue and acquire that beautiful Peking accent?" A flattering remark that never failed to boost my pride as a language virtuoso. That was until one day when I went into a store where the storeowner was an old Beijing gentleman. Perhaps out of curiosity, he asked, "Where are you from?" And, with a mischievous grin I answered, "Beijing." He paused, and then curtly remarked, "You must have been away for quite some years." I got similar feedback on my Shanghainese and even Cantonese—my tones always seem a teeny tiny bit off key. When I visited Yangzhou 揚州, a neighboring city of Zhenjiang, the people in town refused to talk to me in the dialect I felt most intimate with. Either my command of words was strangely deficient, or my intonation was perceptibly odd. One of the first linguistic terms I learned when I came to Berkeley to do linguistics was "SWONL"—an acronym for "a speaker without a native language." In simple terms, I am a good example of SWONL competence. English came to me as a foreign language. But, growing up and going to school in Hong Kong and having been living in the United States for decades, I have had more than plentiful chances to work on and polish my English. When I was in England in the late 1970s, I was on a train going to Portsmouth. I struck up a short conversation with the ticket conductor. The first response I got from him was, "Are you from America?" Apparently, I was speaking with a Californian accent. It took me years of hard effort to switch from the British rounded *o* [ɒ] to the American unrounded *o* [ɑ] as in the name Bob, or the vowel sound of *ey* to *e* as in the word "again." But, has anyone ever mistaken me as an America-born Chinese? No. Another proof of my SWONL identity.

Did I ever feel discouraged by my less-than-competent performance in language? Perhaps in the early years when I realized that my faulty command was hopelessly beyond repair. Nonetheless, when I was in college, a professor offered me these words of encouragement. "A great pianist," he said, "aspires to sounds that could be very different from the kind of notes that engages the mind and imagination of a musicologist." In other words, he concluded, "A polyglot does not necessarily make a good scholar of language." So, what's wrong if I am not blessed with the gift from the Babel Tower? I could still pursue my interest in language by exploring its immense domain in words and sounds.

    I took two linguistics classes as an undergraduate, one in general linguistics and one in historical Chinese phonology. The classes were vastly different in their coverage and research methodology. But what I learned from one class bore significantly on what I took in the other. Language-specific examinations helped me understand how Bloomfield and Chomsky would arrive at their general characterizations of language, and the theoretical input made me wonder how I could approach Chinese with a different perspective. In 1967, I decided to pursue further training under the tutelage of Professor Chou Fa-kao 周法高 in the postgraduate program at The Chinese University of Hong Kong (CUHK). Aside from attending his lectures, I was entrusted with two additional assignments: to translate B. Karlgren's *Compendium of Phonetics in Ancient and Archaic Chinese* (1954), and to assist in another translation project of Y. R. Chao's 趙元任 *A Grammar of Spoken Chinese* (1968). Both projects, demanding as can be imagined, gave me the extra advantage not only to keep abreast with the most current developments in the fields, but also to plough through the writings by two great minds, page by page and word by word. I began to appreciate how their thoughts came together from data, and how their arguments were constructed with implications far beyond the scope that the pages covered. At the end of my first year in the MA program, I wrote an article on the use of aspectual markers in Cantonese, which Professor Chou recommended for publication.[1] It was indeed a huge vote of confidence on what I was trying to explore, and with his further encouragement, I began to work on my Master's thesis, a study of Cantonese grammar. I was able to gain access to a rather extensive corpus of raw data, including 15 hours of recording of a radio soap opera, which I transcribed and examined with painstaking care. Following Chao's theoretical model, I made an attempt to analyze the way how Cantonese

---

[1] "Some Common Predicative Suffixes in Cantonese" (in Chinese), *Journal of The Institute of Chinese Studies of The Chinese University of Hong Kong*, 3.2 (1970): 459–487.

behaved in a structuralist framework. The thesis was eventually published in 1972. In the same year, my translation of Karlgren's phonology came out in Taiwan.

When I embarked on my doctoral studies at the University of California, Berkeley, I had the great privilege to work under Professor Kun Chang 張琨 on Chinese phonology, dialectology, and historical grammar. I decided to choose grammar as the focus of my research and took on a corpus of medieval manuscripts, generally known as the *bianwen* 變文, as my data for looking into early Chinese grammar. The dissertation was filed in 1974. For the next decade or so, during my early years of teaching at Berkeley, I was primarily engaged in language pedagogy and literary studies, and it was not until the 1980s that I began to gradually return to my initial interest in Cantonese. With a lapse in time of many years, and physically living in an English-speaking world, my understanding of Cantonese was essentially limited to what I knew of it in the late 1960s. To make up for what was lacking, I concentrated on what I could find in printed materials and what I could gather from informants, admittedly rather small in number, in the Bay Area, looking for language phenomena that might have escaped my attention in the past. The more I ventured out, the more piqued was my curiosity. One of the first articles I published during that period was based on an investigation of more than three hundred *xiehouyu* 歇後語 expressions, witty and often enigmatic folk sayings, which I examined with a specific focus on the structural principles and the intricate linguistic mechanisms involved in the construction of these colloquial idioms. Another project just as challenging was one on kinship terms; I collected a rich stock of familial terms in Cantonese, both designative and vocative, across a span of five generations, and I reported on the various linguistic operations responsible for the making and (the) use of these monikers, including phonological variation, morphological modification, semantic shift, and social borrowing. My articles on the measure words and the pretransitive in Cantonese allowed me to compare Cantonese with Mandarin in their use of grammatical patterns which they seem to share, but actually with many subtle and intrinsic typological differences between the two dialects. These research projects, tricky and time-consuming during the process, proved not only rewarding in what I had to offer; the efforts were particularly gratifying to me on a personal level—I felt like coming home as a prodigal son.

It was during the 1990s when I took a radical turn, almost by accident, from where my work had been headed all along. From my fascination with the contemporary language, I turned to diachronic investigation. One day, on one of my regular visits to the East Asian Library at Berkeley, I came across an old volume, a bit dusty, hiding between hard-bound publications, a book on Cantonese published in the late 19th century. I took a quick look under the dim light at the stack, and I quickly checked it out—for the rest of the semester. It was a language manual, in both Chinese characters and romanization, designed for teaching Westerners a language often considered almost impossible to decipher, let alone to acquire. Lessons after lessons, the texts were full of surprises for a 20th-century reader. There were sounds and words that I failed to recognize, and strangely constructed sentences on almost every other page. Like the spell that opened the cave in the Arabian story, this mysterious volume unlocked a gate for me to venture into an unchartered land; it gave me a privileged vantage point to look at the past of a language that had not seemed to have much of a history of its own. The article I published in 1997, "Completing the Completive," marked the beginning of my next phase of linguistic pursuit, a historical project to reconstruct early Cantonese grammar.

I returned to Hong Kong at the end of the 1990s to take up new teaching appointments, initially at the Hong Kong University of Science and Technology (HKUST) and then at CUHK, my alma mater, until my retirement in 2010. For almost two decades, I focused my efforts primarily on old Cantonese. Through generous supports of both universities and also of the Research Grants Council in Hong Kong, I was able to conduct intensive search for language materials of the 19th and early 20th centuries. Also through the help of many friends who shared my interests, I put together a good collection of early writings of various kinds, including language manuals, Bible translations, and maps of Hong

Kong. Some of the titles were included in a database I built, entitled *Early Cantonese Colloquial Texts: A Database*, now available online.[2] A number of new databases have been introduced by other scholars in recent years, constituting an enviably rich pool of raw materials awaiting exploration.

When faced with piles of pages from old documents and thousands of entries online, I often wonder: where do we begin our search and research? Many of the words we find in the data are strangely familiar—yes, we seem to recognize the characters and/or the spelling, but the meanings and usages seem to evade our comprehension. Many a time, I would dismiss what I could not decipher as textual errors—and, in fact, there are quite a few graphic and spelling mishaps in the texts. For example, one of the earliest texts, Morrison's *Vocabulary of the Canton Dialect* (1828), did not include tone marking in its romanization. Could it be an indication that the language was atonal in the early 19th century, or was it simply a deliberate omission so as to facilitate the transcription? Consultation with other texts around the same period readily relieved our concerns—tones were left out by design. Oftentimes when I was hesitant with a quandary, I would recall what Professor Chang used to say about the use of data from ancient documents: let the data speak to you before you speak on behalf of the data. His words rang a bell and I would then studiously double check the suspicious items against what other sources might have before I would pronounce what they were. Were they recorded by mistake? Or, they could represent features of an early language that were no longer active in current usage. A good example of this baffling phenomenon is the use of *hiu* 曉 as a marker for the perfective aspect in early Cantonese. The first time I spotted the form, I did not recognize the character, and I was appalled by its given pronunciation, which sounded to me more like a curse word with obscene innuendo. Upon further search, however, I found *hiu* popping up in almost every old text, and it was not until the 1930s that the marking was eventually replaced by a new suffix, *jo* 咗, a grammatical form that we still use today. Or, an example from phonology. The deictic marker, *go* 個 or 嗰 ("that") was marked with a

---

[2] See https://database.shss.hkust.edu.hk/Candbase/.

level tone in all early materials, making it completely identical with the classifier *go* 個, in writing as well as in pronunciation. The first time *gogo* 個個, meaning "that item," appeared in my data; the combination struck me as a clear typo where the deictic was wrongly marked in tone. No, again, it wasn't. The deictic *go* retained its level tone till much later when it underwent a tonal modification, a process that was convoluted but clearly documented in the texts.

From those early blundering trials, I learned that whenever I came across a feature that looked unusual, I would pause before hurriedly declaring it fake or wrong, and my mind would start to look for a possible and reasonable explanation. Sleuthing has indeed been such a rewarding challenge for me, a task that has enabled me to read between lines and to trace the changes across timelines. I have written a number of articles on early Cantonese, covering topics ranging from phonology to grammar and to lexicology. The texts inform us about the many subtleties in the old language that have disappeared over the years, and what we have learned from them has in turn helped us understand how language evolves often in paradigms that can be mapped out in clear terms. When I look at an old map of the 19th century, I will no longer be disturbed by the unfamiliar spelling of place names; they are clues to changes in the sound system, and, in addition, they could also be demographic markers for speakers of different dialects who settled in Hong Kong during the early years.

Not much was recorded in official documents or gazetteers about the early history of Hong Kong. Our knowledge of Cantonese is likewise quite limited except for occasional mentions of its culture and customs in writings here and there. For a long time, Cantonese was deemed a local dialect enjoying little prestige among the intellectuals. Its language and its origin remained much of a mystery until the mid-20th century when scholars started to accord it with increasing attention. The efforts were, however, primarily focused on contemporary Cantonese, its language system of sounds and grammar, its typological affiliation with other Yue 粵 dialects in South China, the role it played as the medium of instruction, and the political status it enjoyed vis-à-vis English and Mandarin during the colonial reign. What do we know about the past of the Cantonese language? Knowledge of the past requires access to bona-fide materials from the past. Language manuals of the 19th century have supplied the missing link.

Systematic preparation of language materials began with the missionaries and scholars who came to the Pearl River Delta for various reasons and who saw the need to learn the local language so as to facilitate their activities in official, religious, and commercial businesses. Instructional books were compiled, dictionaries were published. And, to cater to a Western audience, romanization was a necessary means to transliterate and record the speech of the locals. Grammatical notes were drawn up to explain how the language worked, and vocabulary projects were launched to collect and translate words of common usage. Pedagogical manuals also showed up overseas and, subsequently, Cantonese textbooks were prepared for dialect speakers around the Delta. Language learning became a vibrant enterprise at the turn of the 20th century, as a result of which some manuals went through several printings so as to meet the demand. *Cantonese Made Easy*, for example, saw its first publication in 1883 and was subsequently reissued in 1887, 1907, and 1924.

Thanks to the dedicated efforts of these early pedagogues for faithfully recording the language of the time, we are now blessed with a rich pool of firsthand materials that make it possible for a modern reader to go back in time and experience vicariously what it was like speaking a language that gave rise to modern Cantonese. If we were to eavesdrop on a chitchat at a street corner in the 19th-century Hong Kong, would we be able to follow their conversation? If possible, would we be able to partake in their discussion? According to what we could gather from the century-old materials, the language then was essentially the same as modern Cantonese. There are differences in sounds, in words and in grammar, but the overall ingredients and workings are characteristically Cantonese. Granted that general identification, how do we tell that the language is of an early period? What are the obvious features that would readily distinguish the old from our speech today?

As a first approximation, the following is a list of such distinctive features that I have gathered from my examination. By no means exhaustive or in great detail, the list provides a useful guide to distinguish the new from the old, with features that highlight not only some of the major developments of the language in recent times, but also the paths and pace that the language took in the process of becoming what it is today.

In terms of sounds:

(1) There was a set of apical affricates and fricative, *ts*, *ts'*, and *s*, that coexisted with their alveolar counterparts *tʃ*, *tʃ'*, and *ʃ* in early Cantonese. Words such as 資秋先 (of the first set) and words as 之醜扇 (of the second set) now share the same initial consonants.
(2) There was an apical vowel to accompany the apical consonants. A character like 資 was spelled as *tsz*, in contrast with 之 *chi*.
(3) There were two finals *om* and *op*, which eventually became *am* and *ap* in later development (e.g., 庵 *om* → *am*, and 合 *hop* → *hap*).
(4) The 陰平 tone was high-falling in pitch contour, with a possible high-level reading as a variant form. In modern Cantonese, high-level is the norm.

In terms of grammar:

(1) The *yes/no* question was formed with the construction V-NP+*mh*-V (e.g., 食飯唔食？) in early Cantonese, but the pattern was eventually replaced by V *mh*-VP (e.g., 食飯唔食？ → 食唔食飯？). The direction of deleting identical constituents has changed from forward to backward in application. A disyllabic compound XY such as 歡喜 formed its *yes/no* question with XY *mh*-XY, i.e., 歡喜唔歡喜, which has now followed the same pattern of backward deletion in modern Cantonese, namely, X *mh*-XY, to yield 歡唔歡喜.
(2) The perfective marker is *hiu* 曉 instead of *jo* 咗. For example, 食咗飯 would be 食曉飯 in early Cantonese.
(3) The deictic marker for *that* was *go* 個 or 嗰 with a mid-level tone, which later became high-rising.
(4) The adverbial marker 咁 was *gom* in pronunciation with a mid-level tone, which later became *gam* with a high-rising tone. The tonal change was accompanied by a change of the vowel from *o* to *a*.
(5) The negative imperative was marked by 莫個 *mogo*, a marker that eventually disappeared in later years.

In terms of vocabulary, words such as *gaoguan* 交關 (very much), a degree modifier, *shatshou* 實首 (truly), an adverbial modifier, and *fenggau* 風颶 (typhoon), were common terms in old Cantonese but have become obsolete in the 20th century. There is indeed a huge group of words, nouns and verbs, substantive and functional, in the data that deserves close lexicographic attention.

By early Cantonese, we refer to the language primarily of the 19th century, a timeline that may be extended to the 1930s, when changes began to crop up in our data. By the mid-20th century, with almost all the early phonological and grammatical features slipping into obscurity, Cantonese greeted its speakers with new sounds and revised grammar, and of course with many novel terms in circulation to capture the new culture of a modern era. If we were to be shown a text without a clear date of composition or publication, we could resort to its language and judge whether it was a work of which period, say, roughly before or after the turn of the 20th century. Or, as I once noted in another article, if we were to produce a movie about the revolutionary history in early Hong Kong or Canton, we would have to rely not only on the movie set or the costume design to create a credible period drama; a good script, with language devoid of modern sounds and word usages, would be just as crucial.

As I have worked on the Cantonese of the 1960s, I am quite aware of some of the changes that the language has undergone since then. Choice of diction of course accounts for the biggest change; loan words such as *shido* 士多 (store), *shidaam* 士擔 (postage stamp), or common terms at least in my speech such as *baakfo gungsi* 百貨公司 (department store), are no longer prevalent among the younger generation of speakers. A time expression such as the use of *gwat* 骨, a borrowing from "quarter (of an hour)," has dropped out in usage. The grammatical use of adjectival reduplication, such as *honghong* 紅紅 with a change tone (high-rising) on the first syllable "very, very red," has become a morphological process of the bygone years. Phonologically, aside from denasalizing *n-* to *l-* and *ng-* to zero initial, the tendency to palatalize dental obstruents (e.g., *ts* → *tɕ*) and the dropping of the final *-k* and *-ng* (e.g., *dang* → *dan*; *dak* → *dat*) have often been red-flagged as indications of a corrupted form of "lazy

Cantonese." Laziness or not, these pronunciations have come to define a new form of speech habits, a new setup that has in fact reconfigured the entire Cantonese phonological system, a paradigmatic change that I report in my article on the language of the 21st century.

In recent years, I have produced a number of articles on old Cantonese, with findings that I feel will be useful for our future efforts to trace the development of a language that has gone through many rounds of incredible and, at times dramatic, changes during the last two hundred years. Now that as I am in my seventies, I feel it is perhaps time for me to put together some of these findings into a collection for general reference. As the articles appear some in Chinese and some in English, the collection is to be in two volumes.[3] The present volume, entitled *Cantonese: Since the 19th Century*, contains a total of eight articles in English, four each on Old Cantonese and on Contemporary Cantonese. The articles appeared in various journals, each here properly acknowledged in the volume. Aside from some stylistic editing and amendments, little changes have been made to the content or the use of data.

I began this foreword by saying that I was a SWONL with no real native competence in any of the languages I speak or have studied. Having worked on Cantonese for more than fifty years, however, I have always known that Cantonese is the language most intimate to my mind and soul. I might have spoken with a slight accent, but I am sensitive to any change, however subtle, that may have happened to its sounds, words, or grammar. When I was working in Hong Kong, I took the public transport to and from work, and I often eavesdropped on what others were talking, either on the phone or to those next to them. Of course, it was the speech rather than its actual content that would catch my fancy. Ha, ha—this person speaks perfect Cantonese, and that person unabashedly is showing off his "lazy" accent. Inadvertent use of "incorrect" grammar? Or, a slip of tongue with some never-heard-of cursing slangs. Or, a random mix of English and Cantonese, a code-switching phenomenon quite common in

---

[3] The Chinese volume is titled 香港粵語：二百年滄桑探索 (*Cantonese in Hong Kong: An Exploration of the Past 200 Years*) (Hong Kong: The Chinese University of Hong Kong Press, 2021) and consists of 12 articles with 3 appendices.

Hong Kong. I took notes and wrote brief remarks about my observations. Many of these fortuitous observations would become anecdotal details in my lectures in class, exciting matters to discuss with colleagues over coffee or in workshops. I am hopeful that, someday, someone could take on a new project to decipher the language of today and determine the distinctive features of the 21st-century Cantonese. As my professor claims, knowing a language and knowing of a language are pursuits just as demanding and meaningful as each other. A linguist may not be talented in speaking a foreign tongue, and, likewise, a polyglot does not necessarily know the distinction between a *phone* and an *allophone*. Yes, that distinction may appear as a comforting reassurance to a SWONL; yet, I am also of the opinion that the fun of studying a foreign tongue is such an enjoyable and fulfilling experience that I would never forego. I strongly believe that the more languages you know, the more you will learn about your own language, and the better you will appreciate those around you who speak different tongues or with different accents. When I was working on the pretransitive in Cantonese, I relied on my Mandarin to redefine its use in Cantonese. When I was working on place names in an 1866 map of Hong Kong, I had to consult several other dialects to come to terms with names that were spelled drastically different from their Cantonese pronunciations. And, when I was trying to pick up a new dialect, I tried to figure out its phonological relationships to the dialects I already knew, so as to help me acquire a better and more efficient command of its sounds and tones. I truly believe that, while new findings in linguistics have much to bear on language pedagogy, learning to speak in a foreign tongue has just as much to contribute to our scientific study, empirical or theoretical, of the greatest gift that humans are ever blessed with, namely, *speech*.

I should take this chance to thank my professors, especially Professor Chou Fa-kao at CUHK and Professor Kun Chang, my mentor at UC Berkeley. I owe all of what I know about language and linguistics to their teaching and support. To my colleagues and many, many young friends whose passion for language has made it possible for us to cross paths and to work together in a fertile land for linguistic cultivation. What I have reaped is far more than I can ever imagine or deserve. Special thanks to The Chinese University of Hong Kong Press for its generous offer to publish the collection, taking care of every detail in the process, including obtaining approval from individual journals where my articles originally appeared. In particular, I wish to thank Mr. Brian Yu of the Press for his meticulous efforts in editing both Chinese and English volumes, and also Ms. Pauline Pang for her willingness and patience in helping me with reformatting and retyping some of the articles at the early stage.

My wife, Adaline, has been my greatest support throughout the years. She is my muse and my best companion, especially during the pandemic crisis when I was always in an absolutely lockdown mode working on the manuscript. Like me, Adaline grew up in Hong Kong; but unlike me, she was born in Canton to parents who are natives of the Canton region. For decades, she is my informant, and her Cantonese has always been my most appreciated source of information. If the Zhenjiang dialect is my mother tongue, then, without doubt, Cantonese is my wifey speech. To her, therefore, I dedicate this collection on Cantonese.

Hung-nin Samuel Cheung

One Language, Two Systems:
A Phonological Study of
Two Cantonese Language
Manuals of 1888

CANTONESE MADE EASY

A BOOK OF SIMPLE SENTENCES IN THE CANTONESE DIALECT, WITH
FREE AND LITERAL TRANSLATIONS, AND DIRECTIONS
FOR THE RENDERING OF ENGLISH GRAM-
MATICAL FORMS IN CHINESE.

SECOND EDITION.
REVISED AND ENLARGED.

By

J. DYER BALL, M.R.A.S., ETC.

OF HER MAJESTY'S CIVIL SERVICE, HONGKONG.

Author of "Easy Sentences in the Hakka Dialect with a Vocabulary,"
"the Cantonese Dialect with a Vocabulary," "The Cantonese-made
"An English-Cantonese Pocket Vocabulary
or Tonic Marks," &c.

Abstract: In 1888, two Cantonese teaching manuals were published, one in Hong Kong and one in the United States, both using characters and romanization to teach Westerners how to acquire a good command of a language so very different from their native tongues. Upon close examination, however, the sounds and tones as recorded in the books demonstrate some major differences that make it unlikely to conclude that they were based on the same Canton dialect, as the authors claimed. *Cantonese Made Easy* (CME), by Dyer Ball, a British government officer and a language pedagogue in Hong Kong, gives a sound system with 22 initials, 56 finals, and 9 tones. In contrast, the book published in the United States, *A Chinese and English Phrase Book in the Canton Dialect* (PB) by Thomas Stedman and K. P. Lee, offers 19 initials, 51 finals, and 8 tones. When compared with modern Cantonese, CME appears to be more in sync with what we know about the language of the 20th century. If CME is to be taken as an early version of Cantonese, then what would PB represent? A different variety of Cantonese? Studies of the neighboring dialects in the Pearl River Delta, including both early reports and modern dialect surveys, seem to point to Zhongshan as a possible base for the language in PB. It should also be noted that Lee, one of the two authors, was a native of Zhongshan.

Keywords: early Cantonese; historical phonology; dialectal pronunciations; language teaching manuals; *Cantonese Made Easy*; *A Chinese and English Phrase Book in the Canton Dialect*

1. Introduction

Any historical investigation begins with data. Data tell of the past by betraying secrets of change; they also help us gauge the direction of these changes and reconstruct the patterns in which the changes have taken place. Data, however, could also be misleading. Historical linguistics resorts to both modern idioms and ancient documents in its efforts to examine how languages evolve over time and to account for differentiation and assimilation between languages and language communities. Chinese, not being a phonetic language, is known for its inadequacy in capturing sounds or sound changes in its orthographic system. Early writings in dialects other than Mandarin were scarce, and the scarcity is even more pronounced in Cantonese. Unlike the Wu 吳 and Min 閩 dialects which saw some productions of fiction and drama in regional speech in as early as the 16th century,[1] the earliest extant work in Cantonese is a collection of folksongs that dates back to the early 19th century.[2] However, because of their composite style of mixing the vernacular with the classical, the songs do not necessarily reveal much about the actual happenings in the language. It was not until the 20th century, thanks to radio recordings and movie productions especially in Hong Kong, that colloquial Cantonese was recorded and preserved in its full gamut of styles and contents, a presentation that is crucial to any form of linguistic inquiry.

On the other hand, Cantonese has long been the focus of pedagogical attention since the 19th century. When the Manchu (Qing) government opened Canton to the West for trading in the early 1800s, and especially after Hong Kong was ceded to the British in 1842, there was a growing demand for Cantonese language instruction to meet the urgent needs of Western colonial officers, businessmen, and missionaries who came to the Canton–Hong Kong–Macao region where they had to interact with the

---

[1] For example, the earliest extant material for the Min dialect is *Lijing ji* 荔鏡記, a drama composed in the 16th century. Feng Menglong 馮夢龍 (1574–1646) compiled a collection of folksongs, entitled *Shan'ge* 山歌, written in a colloquial Wu dialect.

[2] *Yue'ou* 粵謳 was a collection of close to a hundred Cantonese love songs, produced by Jiu Jiyung (Zhao Ziyong 招子庸) in 1828.

locals while pursuing their activities. One of the first textbooks compiled was *Chinese Chrestomathy in the Canton Dialect* in 1841. In almost 700 pages, the author covered a wide range of linguistic and cultural topics written mostly in colloquial Cantonese. A series of other primers followed suit in subsequent years, both in China and abroad. The pool of teaching materials produced since then has been vast in quantity and varied in both pragmatic concerns and pedagogical devices. They provide a most valuable source of colloquial data that document how the language has changed in a span of almost two hundred years.[3]

Admittedly, the use of pedagogical materials for linguistic analysis has its shortcomings. As teaching materials in general are prescriptive by design and tend to use simple sentences and words in beginning chapters, the paradigms do not always represent or reflect the complexities in the actual language. On the other hand, as Cantonese textbooks are primarily written in romanization of one kind or another, the transcriptions preserve the colloquial flavor otherwise impossible to achieve in the regular writing system. By virtue of its phonetic make-up, a romanized text is more readily equipped to record and reflect sounds and sound changes than a character version. In this regard, the Cantonese pedagogical materials are richly informative, and critical to our efforts to look into the phonological past especially of the early days when neither radio nor video recordings were available.

The year 1888 saw the publication of two such Cantonese manuals, both designed for teaching English speakers how to study the Cantonese language. One was published in Hong Kong, with a preface actually dated 1887. The other came out in New York, with a Chinese title page showing 光緒十四年, i.e., 1888, as the year of publication.

> J. Dyer Ball. 1888. *Cantonese Made Easy: A Book of Simple Sentences in the Cantonese Dialect*. Hong Kong: China Mail Office.

> T. L. Stedman and K. P. Lee. 1888. *A Chinese and English Phrase Book in the Canton Dialect*. New York: William R. Jenkins.

---

[3] I have used some of these materials in my works on early Cantonese grammar. See, for example, Cheung (1997; 2001).

Hence, despite the vast distance between Asia and America, the two manuals were describing and teaching, so they claimed, essentially the same Canton dialect of the same period in time. They each have their own spelling systems to detail the phonological make-up of every character in the lessons.

The following are two excerpts from the manuals that pertain to similar topical contents.

Phrase Book (PB)
請醫生。
(1) 有乜病呀？
(2) 先生，我今日覺得唔爽快…
(3) 邊處覺得唔自然呢？
(4) 我頭好暈。
(5) 有食錯嘢黎嗎？(p. 105)

Cantonese Made Easy (CME)
(1) 呢位係醫生咯…
(2) 我今日唔多自然咯
(3) 你有乜嘢病呢？
(4) 頭痢呀…
(5) 我應食乜嘢藥呢？(p. 24)

The subject matter aside, even a cursory look at the style of the dialogues suggests that the two manuals are very much alike in their use of words and grammatical patterns. Those who are familiar with Cantonese can easily tell that the language these lessons teach is Cantonese—perhaps an older variety of Cantonese.

In phonology, however, the two manuals are not quite as collaborative with each other, either segmentally or in terms of tones. As the following numbers show, CME seems to have a larger inventory of initials, finals, and tones.

	PB	CME
Initials:	20 initials	22 initials
Finals:	55 finals	63 finals
Tones:	8 tones	9 tones + changed tones

The logical question to ask would be why there were two apparently very different sound systems for the same language in 1888. The answer could be that the systems were basically the same, the differences being merely a matter of transcription. Or, there could be phonological variants in the language, variations that were only partially recorded in the manuals. Or, the manuals could in fact represent different varieties of Cantonese in the late 19th century. Or, was there a standard form of Cantonese in circulation in the late 19th century? What I will do in the following pages is to compare and contrast the two language manuals, identify their discrepancies in sounds, sort through the materials, and seek to account for this intriguing story of "one language, two systems."

2. *Cantonese Made Easy*

2.1. *Cantonese Made Easy* (CME) was a work produced by a celebrated linguist, James Dyer Ball (1847–1919), an Englishman who was born and raised in China.[4] Admirably gifted with sounds, he spoke several southern Chinese dialects since childhood. He served as Chief Interpreter, among other official assignments, at the Hong Kong Civil Service for 35 years, and was the Editor of *China Review*, a journal in which he published many of his articles on the Chinese language. He compiled a series of Cantonese textbooks and several in-depth studies of southern dialects, including Dongguan 東莞, Xiangshan 香山, Xinhui 新會, Kejia 客家, etc.[5] *Cantonese Made Easy* was first published in 1883, and it underwent three rounds of revisions in 1888, 1907, and 1924. Evidently, the textbook received more than a warm welcome among students of Cantonese. Divided into 15 lessons, CME covers a wide variety of subjects, ranging from domestic living to nautical training, from monetary transactions to medical consultations, from ecclesiastical discussions to judicial hearings. Each lesson contains invariably 32 sentences, often cast in the form of a dialogue. Every lesson is given in (1) Chinese characters, and (2) romanization, accompanied by (3) a word-for-word rendition, and also (4) a free translation. With great pride as a language pedagogue, Ball pronounces that "nothing will be found amongst the fifteen lessons but pure good colloquial." (p. III) There is also a long section on grammar at the end of the book, followed by an index. The book begins with a 44-page introduction that focuses primarily on pronunciation.

---

[4] See *Who Was Who, 1916–1928* (London: Adam & Charles Black, 1947).
[5] For more of Ball's publications, see Cheung and Gan (1993).

2.2. CME shows a 22-initial system.[6]

p	p'	m	f		
t	t'	n		l	
ts	ts'		s		
ch	ch'		ch		y
k	k'	ng	h		
kw	kw'				w

Table 1. CME initials (22)

If a zero-initial is added to the list, the total is 23.

In both technical terms and simple explanatory notes, Ball gives a useful description of the distinction between aspirated and non-aspirated words (pp. xxxviii–xlii), a distinction that must have proven difficult for English-speaking students to master. Other than aspiration, Ball accords little attention to the articulatory characteristics of individual consonants, apparently assuming that his readers would be able to pick up the values and differences in sound from the orthographic signs. He claims that "the orthography adopted in this book represented by similar sounds in English, &c., when such sounds exist . . ." (p. xlvii). Accordingly, the initials can be rewritten, in the IPA system, as follows:

p	p'	m	f		
t	t'	n		l	
ts	*ts'*		s		
tʃ	*tʃ'*		ʃ		j
k	k'	ŋ	h		
k	kw'				w

Table 2. CME initials (22) (IPA)

To a 21st-century speaker of Cantonese, Ball's list of initials is unusual in that it contains two sets of affricates and fricatives: *ts/ts'/s* vs. *tʃ/tʃ'/ʃ*. In modern Standard Cantonese (SC), there is only one set, *ts/ts'/s*, as shown in the following table.[7]

---

[6] Syllables lacking a consonantal initial are generally referred to as having a zero-initial.

[7] There is a new development in modern-day Cantonese, where the affricates and fricatives have undergone palatalization when appearing in front of certain round vowels, e.g., [y], [o], [u]. See Cheung (2003).

p	p'	m	f		
t	t'	n		l	
ts	*ts'*		s		j
k	k'	ŋ	h		
kw	kw'				w

Table 3. Modern Cantonese initials (19)

While CME makes no real attempt to define the phonetic differences between the two sets, the orthography itself may suffice to betray the approximate nature of the sounds. The first set seems to be more towards the dental or the alveolar, while the latter more towards the palatal. Examples from CME are:

秋	ts'au	vs.	醜	ch'au
先	sin	vs.	扇	shin
歲	sui	vs.	水	shui
資	tsz	vs.	之	chi
私	sz	vs.	時	shi

In modern SC, both sets are pronounced with an alveolar. The coalescence, therefore, represents one major phonological development since the late 19th century. The dichotomy, nonetheless, was a reflection of an ancient phonological distinction,[8] a distinction that was recorded in many of the 19th century manuals on Cantonese, including an 1828 Cantonese-English dictionary by Robert Morrison, and an 1841 textbook, *Chinese Chrestomathy*, by E. C. Bridgman. The distinction may have disappeared in the language during the early 20th century. Even though some dictionaries of the 1950s maintained the distinction, it was admittedly an artificial differentiation not found in real speech.[9]

2.3. The final system in CME includes a total of 63 units, as listed in the following table. But, not all the finals listed are valid ones. A few of them are wrongly placed because of errors in romanization.

---

[8] There was a four-way distinction, in ancient Chinese, among initials generally referred to as 精, 莊, 知, and 章. Whereas the last one gave rise to *ch* in CME, the first three essentially combined into *ts*. The two new sets were further reduced to one in the 20th century. See Chan and Mok (1995).

[9] See, for example, Wong (1954).

	-i	-u	-m	-n	-ng	-p	-t	-k
á	ái	áu	ám	án	áng	áp	át	ák
a	ai	au	am	an	ang	ap	at	ak
	éi							
e					eng			ek
í		íu	ím	ín	íng	íp	ít	ík
i					ing			ik
z								
o	oi		om	on	ong		ot	ok
ò			òm	òn		òp	òt	
ö					öng			ök
		ui		un	ung		ut	uk
ú		úi		ún			út	
ü				ün			üt	
m		ng						

Table 4. CME finals (63)

For example, the table makes a distinction between a long *á* and a short *a*, as two separate finals. As noted elsewhere in the book, a short *a* does not constitute a full final in Cantonese, a phonotactic condition that explains why it should be removed from the table.[10] Similar observations can be made of a few other pairs, like the long *í* and the short *i*, the open *o* and the closed *ò*, etc., all due to errors in orthography. And, with all the incorrect items removed, the inventory is left with 56 finals, as shown in Table 5.

2.4. For each of the vowels in his transcription, Ball gives a phonetic approximation vis-à-vis its counterpart in English, a correspondence that enables us to convert the system into an IPA format. For example, the sound "*a*" is compared to *u* as in the English word *sun*, hence [ʌ] or [ɐ] in phonetic value. In contrast, the symbol "*á*" is described as *ah*, hence the long [a] in quality. When listed as an independent final, "*ng*" is referred to as *ng* as in *sing*, hence [ŋ].

---

[10] Only three examples are marked with a short *a* in CME, all of which are given alternate readings with a long *á*, e.g., 加 *á* (p. 12) vs. *a* (p. xxxiii).

	-i	-u	-m	-n	-ŋ	-p	-t	-k
a	ai	au	am	an	aŋ	ap	at	ak
	ɐi	ɐu	ɐm	ɐn	ɐŋ	ɐp	ɐt	ɐk
	ei							
ɛ					ɛŋ			ɛk
i		iu	im	in		ip	it	
					ɪŋ			ɪk
ɿ								
ɔ	ɔi			ɔn	ɔŋ		ɔt	ɔk
		ou	om			op		
œ					œŋ			œk
	ɵi			ɵn			ɵt	
u	ui			un			ut	
					ʊŋ			ʊk
y				yn			yt	
m	ŋ							

Table 5. CME finals (56) (IPA)

2.4.1. The revised system can now be compared with that of modern Standard Cantonese, with 53 finals, as shown in the following table. The three extra finals in CME are the apical final ɿ, transcribed as z, and the two finals om and op, transcribed with a long ó, in Table 4.

	-i	-u	-m	-n	-ŋ	-p	-t	-k
a	ai	au	am	an	aŋ	ap	at	ak
	ɐi	ɐu	ɐm	ɐn	ɐŋ	ɐp	ɐt	ɐk
ɛ					ɛŋ			ɛk
	ei							
i		iu	im	in		ip	it	
					ɪŋ			ɪk
ɔ	ɔi			ɔn	ɔŋ		ɔt	ɔk
		ou						
œ					œŋ			œk
	ɵi			ɵn			ɵt	
u	ui			un			ut	
					ʊŋ			ʊk
y				yn			yt	
m	ŋ							

Table 6. Modern Cantonese finals (53)

2.4.2. The apical final *z* in CME appears exclusively with the dental affricates and fricative, *ts*, *ts'*, and *s*. Its counterpart in SC is a simple [i]. Examples are:

	自	慈柿似	師死四
CME	tsz	ts'z	sz
SC	tsi	ts'i	si

The apical variety was at one time quite prevalent in Guangzhou, especially in the Xiguan 西關 area. Ball writes that while "even in the city of Canton itself, the seat and centre of pure Cantonese, more than one pronunciation of words is used; the standard, however, being the "Sai Kwan wa" (西關話, or West end speech), to which the learner should endeavor to assimilate his talk" (p. xv). Indeed, it was this pronunciation that Ball endeavors to give in CME, a standard that he sets up for Cantonese. The apical series subsequently lost its prominence, merging with the regular -*i* without exception.

2.4.3. The pair of finals with *ó*, namely *óm* [om] and *óp* [op], no longer exist in modern Standard Cantonese. Examples from CME are:

óm	甘敢噉咁紺含砍領憾
óp	合蛤

Historically, these *ó*-words were members of 咸攝 of the first division. In ancient Chinese, words were classified into four divisions (等) according to the quality of their vowels. Cantonese has been hailed as one of the few dialects that still maintain that vocalic distinction, especially between the first (一等) and the second divisions (二等). As shown below, words of 一等 are now pronounced with an open [ɔ] and those of 二等 with an [a].

	果假	蟹	山	宕梗		咸	
一等	歌	蓋	干	葛	剛	各	甘	合
	ɔ	ɔi	ɔn	ɔt	ɔŋ	ɔk	ɐm	ɐp
二等	家	佳	間	軋	更	格	監	甲
	a	ai	an	at	aŋ	ak	am	ap

In contrast with the other rime categories (攝), namely 果假蟹山宕梗, where there is a constant 等 differentiation between [o] and [a] in modern Standard Cantonese, 咸攝 shows [ɐ] for its 一等, a rather unusual rendition in terms of the symmetry across different 攝 categories. Yet, CME provides an [o] rendition, which could be easily traced to an [ɔ] in even earlier sources such as Bridgman's *Chrestomathy* of 1841.[11] In other words, just like its counterparts with other endings, 咸攝一等 was pronounced with an [ɔ] at one point in time. The change from [ɔ], via [o], to [ɐ] can be charted out as follows:

ɔm	→ om →	ɐm
Chrestomathy	CME	SC
1841	1888	20th century

As words of 咸攝 end with a bilabial *-m* ending, the unrounding development from [ɔ] to [ɐ] can be easily accounted for as a process of dissimilation.

2.4.4. All in all, except for the three additional finals, the CME system is essentially identical with what we find in modern Standard Cantonese.

2.5. In terms of tones, CME lists a total of nine tones, divided into two series: the upper and the lower registers. The tones are marked diacritically, with little half-circles placed at the four corners of a syllable. The lower series shows an additional stroke under the half-circle.

上平 ˖sín		下平 ˳sín
上上 ˚sín		下上 ˳sín
上去 sín˚		下去 sín˳
上入 sít˳	中入 sít˳	下入 sít˳

Table 7. CME tones (9)

Compared with other language pedagogues of his time, Ball should be credited for his unusual sensitivity to tones in Cantonese and for his extra efforts to teach them[12] and their variations with detailed notes and multiple tonic exercises. The following are the descriptions he provides for some of the tones on pages XXIV–XXVIII.

---

[11] See Cheung (2003).

[12] In his 1828 publication, *A Vocabulary of the Canton Dialect*, Robert Morrison did not include any tone marking in his romanization.

上平	a monotone, without elevation or depression
下平	an octave lower than 上平
上上	gradually ascending
下上	starts from a lower pitch, does not ascend so high
上去	a prolonged tone, diminishing while it is uttered
下去	nearer a monotone, not so gruff
入	peculiar abruptness in enunciation in these words that end in *k*, *p*, and *t*

While not much is said about the differences among the three kinds of 入, it is noted that most of the words having long vowels belong to 中入 and "the other as well as some words with long vowels belong to 上入 or 下入" (p. xxvii). Please note that 中入 is marked with a small circle on the lower right corner.

The nine-tone system remains almost intact in present-day Cantonese. Although Ball provides little concrete information about the actual pitch height or contour of any of the tones, his impressionistic descriptions as outlined in CME and elsewhere are very much the same as what we know about Standard Cantonese at least of the 20th century. On the other hand, Ball goes into great details about the use of changed tones in Cantonese, a situation that is too complex to delve into in this article. Again, what he reported about the changed tone then is still very much valid for characterizing the situation today.[13]

3. *Chinese and English Phrase Book*

We shall now turn to *Chinese and English Phrase Book* (PB), which according to the title was based upon the Canton dialect of the same period as CME. As mentioned before, the phonological system in PB is quite different from that in CME. To recapitulate, PB consists of 20 initials, 55 finals, and 8 tones. The following provides a more in-depth investigation of the PB phonology.

---

[13] For a detailed discussion of changed tones in CME, see Cheung (2000).

3.1. The initials in PB include:

p	pʻ	m	f		
t	tʻ	n		l	
ch	chʻ	sh	s		y
k	kʻ	ng	h		
kw	kwʻ				w

Table 8. PB initials (20)

3.1.1. Unlike CME, where there are two sets of affricates and fricatives, PB gives only one set, namely *ch*, *chʻ*, and *s*. There is only one occurrence of *sh*, which is most likely an error; hence, the contrast between *s* and *sh* is negligible. The manual notes that *ch*, when unaspirated, is pronounced more softly than in English, approaching closely the sound of *j* in *joint*. Likewise, for *s*, "instead of the hard sound of *s*, heard in the word *so*, . . . the sound heard is nearly as *show*" (p. 11). In other words, the set should be more like the palatals *ch-chʻ-sh* in CME than the dentals *ts-tsʻ-s*. The two-way distinction that is so prominent in CME disappears completely in PB, which is one of the major characteristic features of the PB sound system.

3.1.2. The PB initials can now be converted to the IPA system:

p	pʻ	m	f		
t	tʻ	n		l	
tʃ	tʃʻ		ʃ		j
k	kʻ	ŋ	h		
kw	kwʻ				w

Table 9. PB initials (19) (IPA)

3.1.3. Another characteristic feature of the PB language pertains to the velar initial *ŋ-*. The following are two lists of *ŋ*-words in PB and their correspondences in CME and in Standard Cantonese:

	PB	**CME**	**SC**
外我硬眼牛衙	ŋ-	ŋ-	ŋ-
魚月熱二而如	ŋ-	j-	j-

The first list are words, historically of the 疑 initial, that have retained ŋ- in all three forms of Cantonese speech. The second list includes words of both historical 疑 and 日 initials, but are pronounced with ŋ- only in PB. The situation in CME, which has been evidently inherited by modern Cantonese, represents a development in which ŋ- disappears before high front vowels.

ŋ- → 0 / __ high front vowel
→ ŋ-

The discrepancy appears so stunningly odd that we will have to ask: why is it that PB and CME of the same period exhibited two diverse developments, exclusive of each other? Had there been alternate readings found in the same text, that alternation could be construed as an indication of an ongoing sound change? But, there seems to be no exception and the readings in the two manuals are kept strictly apart.

3.1.4. The third feature pertains to a distinction between the velars and the labialized velars, i.e., *k-/kʻ* and *kw/kwʻ*. While both manuals seem to share the same sets, the distribution is not quite identical. Compare the following words:

	PB	**CME**
間	kan	kan
關	kwan	kwan
剛港講	kong	kong
光廣	kong	kwong
廓	kʻong	(kwʻong)
角	kok	kok
國	kok	kwok

While CME maintains a distinction between *k* and *kw* before both *a* and *o*, PB shuns that distinction before *o*. Evidently, a labialized velar *kw* becomes delabialized *k* in PB, when standing before the round vowel *o*.[14]

3.1.5. Between the two manuals, there are altogether three differences in the initial system. But, how do we account for the differences in the two

---

[14] A similar development is underway in contemporary Hong Kong Cantonese.

accounts that were supposedly based on the same language of the same period? Could they be considered phonological changes representing a new trend in development, the precursors of phenomena that would become prevalent in the following decades? Or, could PB in fact represent a different variety of Cantonese, which did not share the same phonology with CME?

3.2. On the finals, PB has a total of 55 finals, as listed below.

	-i	-u	-m	-n	-ng	-p	-t	-k
á	ái	áu	ám	án	áng	áp	át	ák
	ai	au	am	an	ang	ap	at	ak
e					eng			ek
ye								
eu					eung			euk
i		iu	im	in	ing	ip	it	ik
u	ui		um	un	ung		ut	uk
ü				ün			üt	
o	oi		om	on	ong		ot	ok
ó			óm			óp		ók
m	ng							

Table 10. PB finals (55)

3.2.1. Though not as detailed as in CME, the phonological notes in PB give us a general idea of what the vowels stand for in the language. For example, *a* pronounced as *u* in *fun*, hence [ʌ] or [ɐ]; and *á* as *a* in *father*, hence [a].[15] Based on this pronunciation guide, we can reproduce Table 10 in an IPA format. Three of the finals are questionable and will be removed from the inventory. They are: (1) *um*, with only one example (斟), whose pronunciation should have been *am*; (2) *om* with only one example (柑), whose pronunciation should have been *óm*; and (3) *ók*, though with 12 examples, which evidently was mixed up with *uk*. Most of the words marked with *ók* and *uk* are of the same historical origin, and are not

---

[15] For details, see pp. ɪɪ–ɪɪɪ. Some of the notes may require a bit of guessing. For example, "*eu* pronounced like vowel sounds in *person*, but with no stress on the first one and very rapidly so that the two sounds almost blend into one." Most likely, the vocalic *eu* stands for [œ], a sound that is wanting in the English vowel system.

distinguished in any of the Cantonese dialects. The revised system now includes a total of 51 finals, 5 fewer than that in CME. Aside from this inventory, there are also distributional differences between the two systems.

	-i	-u	-m	-n	-ŋ	-p	-t	-k
a	ai	au	am	an	aŋ	ap	at	ak
	ɐi	ɐu	ɐm	ɐn	ɐŋ	ɐp	ɐt	ɐk
ɛ					ɛŋ			
jɛ								
œ					œŋ			œk
i		iu	im	in	ıŋ	ip	it	ɪk
u	ui			un	ʊŋ		ut	ʊk
y				yn			yt	
ɔ	ɔi			ɔn	ɔŋ		ɔt	ɔk
		ou	om			op		
m	ŋ							

Table 11. PB finals (51) (IPA)

3.2.2. As PB contains no dental affricate or fricative, there is no apical *z* [ɿ] to form a matching final. As the following examples illustrate, the apical final in CME is replaced by a regular [i], as in modern Cantonese:

	PB	**CME**
資子字	chi	tsz
祠詞似	ch'i	ts'z
司死四	si	sz

3.2.3. One characteristic feature of the PB final system is its lack of the diphthong [ei], as found in CME and also in modern Standard Cantonese. All words with *ei* in CME are found to be pronounced with the vowel *i* [i].[16] Examples are:

	PB	**CME**	**SC**
俾皮美未 (p-)	i	ei	ei
地你利李 (t-)	i	ei	ei
幾企起氣 (k-)	i	ei	ei

---

[16] It should be noted that in earlier Cantonese records, such as Morrison (1828) and Bridgman (1841), *ei*-words were pronounced with *i*.

3.2.4. The final *ü* [y] in PB corresponds to two groups in CME:

	PB	CME	SC
(a) 書處樹豬珠主住如魚雨語寓 (ch-, 0)	y	y	y
(b) 句舉佢女去 (k-, n-, h-)	y	ɵi	ɵi

3.2.5. Similarly, the final *u* [u] in PB often contrasts with [ou] in CME. Its appearances correspond to essentially two groups of words in CME and SC:

	PB	CME	SC
(a) 夫苦咐父古壺 (f-, k-, w-)	u	u	u
(b) 舖務母都渡爐路做 (p-, t-, ts-)	u	ou	ou

Occasionally, there are words with dual readings, e.g., 霧: ***mu*** and ***mou***. Transliterations also offer interesting examples with an alternation between u and ou. For example, 布朗, for Brown, is romanized as both [**pou**-lɔŋ] (p. 83) and [**pu**-lɔŋ] (p. 109).

Based on the above examples, we may conclude that diphthongization is one major difference between the two sound systems. All three monothong finals *i*, *y*, and *u* in PB are rendered with a vowel split in CME, becoming *ei*, *ɵi*, and *ou*.

3.2.6. The final *oi* [ɔi] corresponds to two different finals in CME.

	PB	CME	SC
(a) 代檯耐來在再外開海愛 (t-, k-)	ɔi	ɔi	ɔi
(b) 水誰歲 (ch-)	ɔi	ɵi	ɵi

3.2.7. The final *ui* [ui] corresponds to two different finals in CME.

	PB	CME	SC
(a) 杯賠每灰回會 (p-, f-, 0)	ui	ui	ui
(b) 對雷稅吹 (t-, ch-)	ui	ɵi	ɵi

In other words, the three PB finals described above, namely [y], [ɔi], and [ui], each corresponds to two different finals in CME and SC, one being identical with the one in PB and the other, namely [ɵi], a final that does not exist in PB.

3.2.8. *an* [ɐn] and *at* [ɐt]

The final [ɐn] in PB corresponds to [ɐn] and [ɵn] in CME, and also in SC. Examples are:

	PB	CME	SC
(a) 濱文分吞申 伸身新晨神真珍 親緊銀軍裙人因	ɐn	ɐn	ɐn
(b) 噸頓信樽	ɐn	ɵn	ɵn

Words in (a) and (b), though both pronounced with [ɐn] in PB, are rendered differently in CME as well as in Standard Cantonese: (1) as [ɐn], and (2) as [ɵn]. Likewise, corresponding to [ɐt] in PB, there are two CME forms: [ɐt] and [ɵt]. Historically, the words were by and large of the same origin, namely 臻攝. The condition for the differentiation in CME is unclear.

	PB	CME	SC
(c) 七	ɐt	ɐt	ɐt
(d) 出	ɐt	ɵt	ɵt

3.2.9. *un* [un] and *ut* [ut]

Adding to the complexity of the preceding picture is that words of the [un] category in PB also fall into two groups, one corresponding to [un] in CME and SC, and the other to [ɵn]. Examples are:

	PB	CME	SC
(a) 搬滿官半 本門碗換	un	un	un
(b) 倫樽準春	un	ɵn	ɵn

There is only one example of [ut], which corresponds to [ɵt] in CME and SC.

	PB	CME	SC
(c) 律	ut	ɵt	ɵt

In other words, the dichotomy between [un]/[ut] and [ɐn]/[ɐt] in PB translates into a three-way distinction in CME and SC:

	PB				ɐn/ɐt
PB		un/ut			ɐn/ɐt
CME/SC	un/ut		ɵn/ɵt		ɐn/ɐt

Again, the conditions that allow the overlapping of the two groups of finals in CME remain to be worked out. A number of words in PB could have both readings of [un] and [ɐn], e.g., 樽, *chun* and *chan*. The corresponding form in CME is [ɵn].

3.2.10. *ang* [ɐŋ] and *ak* [ɐk]

The following words demonstrate pronunciations that are drastically different between PB and CME/SC.

	PB	**CME**	**SC**
請	ch'ɐŋ	tɛ'ıŋ, ts'ɛŋ	ts'ıŋ, ts'ɛŋ
等	tɐŋ, tɛŋ, tıŋ	tɐŋ	tɐŋ
力	lɐk	lık	lık
石	sɐk, sɛk	shɛk	sɛk
食	sɐk	shık	sık
識	sɐk	shık	sık

In CME, these words may have two sets of pronunciations, [ıŋ]/[ık] and [ɛŋ]/[ɛk], a distinction often referred to as that between the literary and the colloquial readings. That stylistic differentiation is quite apparent in CME. In PB, however, the dominant form of reading is neither [ıŋ]/[ık] nor [ɛŋ]/[ɛk], but rather [ɐŋ]/[ɐk]. It is interesting to note that the last name, *Black*, is transliterated as 布力 [pu-lɐk], a rendition that would be closer to the original English pronunciation than the reading [pu-lık] in the CME system.

3.2.11. *ye* [jɛ]

This is a very unusual final, with only two words: 些 and 寫. Romanized as *sye*, both words are probably pronounced like [siɛ], with a medial -*j*- or -*i*-. The inclusion of a medial -*i*- is non-existent in CME or in SC.

3.3. Tones

PB shows a rather simple tonal system, with a total of eight tones, four in a higher register and four in a lower register. The two registers are separated, according to the authors, by two or more full musical keys (p. xx). The first tone is described as an even monotone, the second tone a rising tone, the third tone with a dropping intonation, and the fourth tone with an abrupt termination. Tones are marked in the following manner:

> For the upper tones commas are used, and are placed at one of the angles of the word. . . . The lower tones are indicated in the same manner by a period at one of the four corners of the word. (p. iv)

There is no mention of or reference to changed tones in the language.

3.4. The above is a general description of the sound system in PB, a system that is indeed very different from what CME shows in its lessons. The differences in inventory are summarized below:

	PB	**CME**
Initials:	19	22
Finals:	51	56
Tones:	8	9 + changed tones

Table 12. Comparison between PB and CME

In section 2, we have observed a close resemblance between CME and modern Standard Cantonese, a resemblance that suggests a close relation, one probably of derivation, between the two systems. The relationship between PB and SC is, however, less apparent. If the two manuals, both of the same period, differ in a great many ways in their efforts to render Cantonese, then what was the speech that PB adopted as representing the city of Canton? The authors of PB claim:

> The language of the book is not the official Chinese, the so called Mandarin, but the dialect spoken by the natives of Canton and its vicinity, from which province come the greater number of the Chinese in America. (p. 1)

Stedman and Lee are evidently aware of the differences in pronunciation between what they give and what is taught elsewhere; nonetheless, they reiterate that

> ... the sound here given, however, both vowel and consonantal, are those given to the words by most of the Cantonese resident in New York. (p. 1)

At times, they admit that [ou] and [u], and also [oi] and [ui], are often interchangeable:

> A word having the *ó* (i.e., [ou]) sound in one village being pronounced *u* in another village, and the one in which the diphthongal sound *oi* (i.e., [ɔi]) being heard as *ui*. The same is true of *i* and *e* (i.e., [ei]).[17] (p. 11)

The reference to the village pronunciation might suggest a dialectal influence on the PB compilation, a factor that could have contributed to its phonology, thereby setting it apart from the kind of Cantonese as presented in CME.

3.5. To further examine the phonological nature of the PB language, we will first summarize the special features that distinguish it from that of CME:

(1)	ŋ- before high front vowel		二魚
(2)	k- instead of kw- before [ɔ]		光國
(3)	one set of ch- [tʃ], chʻ- [tʃʻ], and s- [ʃ]		
(4)	[i] instead of the apical z [ɿ]		資詞司
(5)	[i-] instead of [ei-]		氣美
(6)	[ɐn]/[ɐt] instead of [ɵn]/[ɵt]		信出
(7)	[un]/[ut] instead of [ɵn]/[ɵt]		春律
(8)	[ɐŋ]/[ɐk] instead of [ɪŋ]/[ɪk]		請力
(9)	ye [jɛ]		寫些
(10)	[u] instead of [ou]		舖做
(11)	[ɔi] instead of [ɵi]		水歲
(12)	[ui] instead of [ɵi]		對吹
(13)	[y] instead of [ɵi]		渠去
(14)	8 tones instead of 9 tones		

Table 13. Special features in PB

---

[17] The IPA forms are supplied by me.

We have taken each of these features and compared the pronunciations of the sample words in both PB and CME with their modern renditions in eleven major cities around Canton. Dialectal readings are based upon 珠江三角洲方言字音對照 (Zhan and Cheung 1987). The following are two examples of such a comparison. Tones are marked with tone letters.

3.5.1. Velar *ŋ-* vs. Zero-Initial

	二	月	語	業
廣州	ji²²	jyt²²	jy¹³	jip²²
番禺	ji²²	jyt²²	jy¹³	jip²²
南海	ji²²	jyt²²	jy¹³	jip²²
順德	ji²¹	jyt²¹	jy¹³	hip²¹
中山	ɲi³³	ɲyt³³	ɲy²¹³	ɲip³³
珠海	ɲi³³	yt³³	y¹³	ip³³
PB	**ŋi²²**	**ŋyt²²**	**ŋy¹³**	**ŋip²²**
斗門	ŋgi³¹	ŋgit²¹	ŋgi²¹	ŋgip²¹
江門	ji³¹	(j)iat²¹	ji²¹	(j)iap²¹
新會	ŋgi³¹	ŋgit²¹	ŋgi²¹	ŋgip²¹
台山	ŋgei³¹	ŋgut²¹	ŋgui²¹	ŋgiap²¹
東莞	zi³²	zøt²¹	zy¹³	zit²²

Table 14. Readings of *ŋ-* in PB and 11 modern Cantonese dialects

3.5.2. Labialized Velar *kw-* vs. Delabialized Velar *k-*

	光	國	廣
廣州	kuɔŋ⁵⁵	kuɔk³³	kuɔŋ³⁵
番禺	kuɔŋ⁵³	kuɔk³³	kuɔŋ³⁵
南海	kuɔŋ⁵⁵	kuɔk³³	kuɔg³⁵
順德	kuɔŋ⁵³	kuɔk³³	kuɔŋ²⁴
中山	kɔŋ⁵⁵	kɔk³³	kɔŋ²¹³
珠海	kɔŋ⁵⁵	kɔk³³	kɔŋ¹³
PB	**kɔŋ⁵⁵**	**kɔk³³**	**kɔŋ³⁵**
斗門	kɔŋ³³	kɔk⁵⁵	kɔŋ⁵⁵
江門	kuaŋ²³	kuak⁵⁵	kuaŋ⁴⁵
新會	kɔŋ²³	kɔk⁵⁵	kɔŋ⁴⁵
台山	kɔŋ³³	kɔk⁵⁵	kɔŋ⁵⁵
東莞	kuɔŋ⁵⁵	kuɔk²²⁴	kuɔŋ³⁵

Table 15. Readings of *kw-* in PB and 11 modern Cantonese dialects

The comparison yields interesting results. As expected, Guangzhou shows little resemblance to PB in most of the sound categories. The dialect that seems to bear the closest affinity to PB is the Zhongshan 中山 dialect, one of the major speeches in the Pearl River Delta, a dialect also spoken in Zhuhai 珠海 and Macao 澳門. The following table lists the behaviors of most of the special features noted above,[18] showing (1) the correspondences between PB and Zhongshan/Zhuhai, and (2) those between CME and Standard Cantonese spoken in Guangzhou / Hong Kong.[19] In addition, Taishan 台山 pronunciations are attached for comparison.

	PB	中山 / 珠海	CME	廣州 / 香港	台山
ŋ—0	ŋ	ŋ	0	0	ŋ
kw—k	k	k	kw	kw	k
i—ei	i	i	ei	ei	ei
y—ɵy	y	y	ɵy	ɵy	ɵy
u—ou	u	u	ou	ou	u
ui—ɵy	ui	ui	ɵy	ɵy	ui
un—ɵn	un	ɐn	ɵn	ɵn	un
ɐn—ɵn	ɐn	ɵn	ɵn	ɵn	in
ɔi—ɵy	ɔi	ɵy	ɵy	ɵy	ui
ɐŋ—iŋ	ɐŋ	ɐŋ	ɪŋ	ɪŋ	en

Table 16. Special PB features and their correspondences in other dialects

The table juxtaposes PB with Zhongshan/Zhuhai on the left, and CME and Guangzhou / Hong Kong on the right. The juxtaposition highlights the differences between PB and CME, differences that are reflected in the contrast between modern Zhongshan and Guangzhou. The juxtaposition also confirms our earlier speculation that the Guangzhou / Hong Kong Cantonese is a derivative of the CME system. Would it also suggest that

---

[18] Of the 14 features listed in Table 13, only ten prominent ones have been included in Table 16. None of the dialects surveyed exhibits a two-way contrast between dental and palatal affricates/fricatives, a lack that actually is characteristic of the PB language. And, because of the absence of a dental set of affricates/fricatives, none of the dialects possesses an apical vowel, a phenomenon that is found in PB. Like PB, a few dialects offer a medial [-j-], e.g., 寫 [sia] in Xinhui 新會; but the presence of [-j-] is very limited in PB. Lastly, because of the complications in tonal renditions, tone is not included in the comparison.

[19] Standard Cantonese in Hong Kong is essentially identical with that of Guangzhou.

PB represent not so much the language of Canton but rather a variety of the Zhongshan dialect of the 19th century?

3.6. As noted at the beginning of this article, PB was published in New York in 1888. As such, the language manual could reflect the local speech habit of the overseas Chinese community at that early period. According to recent studies of the history of Chinese immigration, a large number of the early settlers in New York were from the Siyi 四邑 area of the Pearl River Delta.[20] If that was the case, it would be the Taishan dialect, for example, that informed the compilation and not the Zhongshan dialect. "Zhongshanese were a majority in Hawaii, but not in the continental USA."[21] Table 16 displays, however, many differences between PB and the Taishan speech.

In 1897, Dyer Ball, author of CME, published a long article on the dialect of Zhongshan (ZS), formerly known as Hong Shan 香山 (HS). Entitled "The Höng Shán or Macao Dialect," the article provides a detailed description of the Zhongshan phonology and lists features that distinguish ZS from Cantonese. Many of these special features are characteristic of the PB language. They include:

(1) *kw-* dropped throughout the HS district
(2) *ŋ-* instead of the zero-initial in words such as 二
(3) HS *i* vs. Canton *ei*
(4) HS *eŋ* vs. Canton *iŋ*, e.g., 請
(5) HS *y* vs. Canton *oi*, e.g., 佢
(6) HS *ui* vs. Canton *oi*
(7) The inclusion of a medial *-i-*
(8) The *ch-ch'-s* series: the distinction between *ch-* and *ts-* is gone, and the *ts-* sound predominates in the Hong Shan dialect (p. 507); when standing before high front vowels, e.g., *i, e, y, ø*, the consonants may sound more like *ch-*
(9) An eight-tone system

---

[20] See, for example, Xinyang Wang, *Surveying the City: The Chinese Immigrant Experience in New York, 1890–1970* (2001).

[21] Xinyang Wang, personal communication.

Hence, both historically and also based on a comparison with other modern Cantonese dialects, our investigation clearly points to the Zhongshan language as the closest to the PB system.

3.7. A textbook designed to teach the Canton dialect, PB was compiled by two authors, T. L. Stedman and K. P. Lee. Who were they? What were their individual language backgrounds? Were they professional language pedagogues? That knowledge could prove crucial to our understanding of the phonological nature of their joint efforts. There was, however, little reference to either author in the manual. Other sources provide the following biographical sketches.

Stedman's full name is Thomas Lathrop Stedman (1853–1938).[22] Born in Cincinnati, he received his MD from Columbia University in 1877, and worked as a doctor in New York all his life. He was the author of a series of medical books and dictionaries, including *A Practical Medical Dictionary*, which is now in its 27th edition, also available on the web. Also an editor of a number of major reference handbooks in medical sciences, Stedman was exceptionally successful in his field. Adding to his academic credit was the 1888 language textbook, *A Chinese and English Phrase Book in the Canton Dialect*, which he co-authored with K. P. Lee. We do not know much about Stedman's language background, how much Cantonese he knew, when and where he studied Chinese, if any, and what prompted him to compile a textbook that seemed not so much to cater to the professional needs in the medical field as to the linguistic interests of a general readership. As stated in the preface of the manual, PB was originally

> ... conceived with the design of furnishing to the Chinese, residing in this country, the means of acquiring an elementary knowledge of English, such as would be of use to them in their intercourse with our own people. With this object in view the subjects have been those of everyday use and the sentences have been made as brief as possible and are expressed in

---

[22] See *Who Was Who in America: A Companion Volume to Who's Who in America, Volume 1: 1897–1942* (Chicago: Marquis Who's Who, 1962).

simple language. The pronunciation of everyday English word is indicated in Chinese characters placed immediately beneath it. (p. 1)

In other words, PB was initially intended to be an English language textbook for Chinese immigrants in the United States, a manual whose function was characterized by its Chinese title 英語不求人 (Self-Taught English). However, as the project was in progress, the authors came to realize that the manual might be "made serviceable to English speaking persons who, for commercial, missionary or philological purposes, desired to acquire some knowledge of Cantonese" (p. 1). And, for that reason, Roman characters were added to the Chinese translations as indication of the pronunciations in the Canton dialect.

The co-author, K. P. Lee 李桂攀, wrote a Chinese introduction to the manual, in which he highlighted the dual purposes of the book, a primer that taught English on paper as if in person, a primer that could also benefit the Westerners when they wished to study Chinese (p. v). According to the little biographical materials we have been able to gather (Qian and Hu 2003), Mr. Lee was on a government scholarship when he went to study in the United States at a young age. He was a fellow classmate of Zhan Tianyou 詹天佑, who would become the famous Chinese engineer of the late 19th century. Mr. Lee seemed to have gone back to China after graduation, but he subsequently returned to the US, where he resided in New York until his death. Our knowledge of his story ends here. We do not know where he went to school, what he did for a living, etc. But, we do have a piece of vitally important information that will help us decide on the linguistic nature of the language manual, information that may explain why the book does not seem to record a language that can be called the dialect of Canton. Mr. Lee was a man from Zhongshan. When the manual he took part to compile claimed to represent the dialect of the Chinese immigrants in New York, that representation could be more of the Zhongshan-speech community than the Canton dialect as stated in the book title.

So, on that note, we seem to have resolved the puzzle. The story, after all, is not about "one language, two systems"; rather, it pertains to "two dialects, two systems."

Our job, however, is not quite done yet. While PB seems to have included a large number of ZS features, it is not a genuine Zhongshan language. According to the study by Ball in 1897, there are many other important ZS features that are missing in PB, including:

(1) ZS has a six-tone system: 上平, 下平, 上去 (= 下去), 上上 (= 下上), 上入, and 下入. Recent studies also report a six-tone system.[23] PB, on the other hand, lists eight tones, with 平上去入 each divided into two.

(2) In ZS, *h*- takes the place of the initial *f*- in Cantonese when appearing before finals with a *u/ʊ* vowel. PB, however, behaves like CME and systematically shows an *f*- instead. Examples are:

	夫	歡	灰	風	福
ZS	hu	hun	hui	hʊng	hʊk
PH	fu	fun	fui	fʊng	fʊk
CME	f-	f-	f-	f-	f-

(3) According to Ball and Y. R. Chao (1948) who worked on ZS of the early 20th century, there was a medial -*i*- with a number of finals in ZS, e.g., *iɛu* (求), *iɛm* (金), *iaɛ* (請). PB shows no -*i*- in these readings. The only case in PB that may be taken as an example with a medial is the syllable *sye*, transcribed here as *sie*, for 些 and 寫. Both words are given an alternate reading without -*i*-. Modern ZS gives *se*, but Chao gives *sia*.

(4) Corresponding to *ŋ/ɪk* in Cantonese, Zhongshan shows *ɐŋ/ɐk*, which is a feature we have already noted above. Yet, PB often gives dual readings for these words, e.g.,

請早日再來坐	ch'ang	(p. 9)
我想再請一個	ch'ing	(p. 116)
來得我處食飯嗎？	sak	(p. 23)
我哋食便飯啫	sik	(p. 111)

Does the co-listing imply that PB, though an earlier publication than Ball's report, was already showing a change in the ZS pronunciation? Or, could it have recorded two different readings actually from different dialects, with *ŋ* being borrowed from Cantonese?

---

[23] For example, Zhan and Cheung (1987).

So, what language does PB represent? If we have to choose one dialect that closely matches what we have observed in the manual, without a doubt, that dialect would have to be Zhongshan. On the other hand, there are a few Cantonese features that seem to have crawled into that speech, giving it a flavor of the CME dialect, which on all counts is based upon the dialect of the city of Canton. In his work on the Hong Shan dialect, Ball suggests a lexical item as a test case that would distinguish ZS from Cantonese. For the word "who," ZS uses 邊誰, whereas Cantonese prefers 乜誰. In PB, both terms appear, but 邊誰 is used only once.

你想寫信去**邊誰**啞？　　(p. 39)
乜誰係傳道人呢？　　(p. 55)

Our project began with a query of the validity of two different phonological systems for the same language in Canton, a scenario that appears highly suspicious, if not at all impossible. After a much roundabout investigation and comparison, we seem to conclude that while CME might be genuinely Cantonese, PB probably represents a dialect that was most likely that of Zhongshan. Features of other dialects or Cantonese might have also left imprints on the make-up of this dialect. So, who were the true speakers of the PB language—乜誰 or 邊誰? Where were they from? What was their true linguistic identity?

4. Conclusion

By way of comparing two 1888 language manuals of a Canton dialect, this article hopes to demonstrate how very labor-intensive it is to conduct a textual cum historical study on an ancient language. We need to apply meticulous efforts to comb through the old materials if we are to use them as a gauge of the evolution, a window to the past. That window may have opened to a different scene or scenery, and not necessarily the one that we have hoped to look into. There could be a slight shift in time or space, and our observations could also be shifted in turn. The picture may not be of the space or time frame that we thought we had identified. Historical sources are not often as innocently reliable as they seem, and we must handle them with care and discretion. In this project, we have examined a book that claims to be based upon the Canton dialect and that indeed appears at least on the surface very Cantonese, and we conclude that it is in fact based most probably on a dialect or dialects other than Cantonese. We need to read and understand with a grain of salt, rub it in if necessary, and see what lies beneath the surface. Yes, it may hurt, but not as painful as we would otherwise find out if we were to build our entire theory on erroneous impressions or assumptions. We used to think that PB played just as important and valuable a role as CME in helping us reconstruct the past of the Cantonese language. We are not so sure anymore. But, to what extent do we know that our speculations about the linguistic background of PB are valid? We will have to rely on more materials and more critical studies of these materials to arrive at a conclusion, if any. Like any line of historical investigation, our work is both tempting and challenging, rewarding at times, and frustrating most of the time. The past is in the past, and we will never be able to bring that past fully to the present. Yet, as more materials surface, we strive forward, or backward in time, and we hope that our efforts will bring us another step closer to reconstructing that historical truth.

References

Ball, Dyer. 1888. *Cantonese Made Easy: A Book of Simple Sentences in the Cantonese Dialect, with Free and Literal Translations, and Directions for the Rendering of English Grammatical Forms in Chinese*. 2nd edition, revised and enlarged. Hong Kong: China Mail Office.

———. 1897. "The Höng Shán or Macao Dialect." *China Review*, 22.2: 501–531.

Bridgman, Elijah C. 1841. *Chinese Chrestomathy in the Canton Dialect*. Macao: S. Wells Williams.

Chan M. S. 陳萬成, and Oliva Mok 莫慧嫻. 1995. "Jindai Guangzhou hua 'si 私' 'shi 師' 'si 詩' san zu ziyin de yanbian" 近代廣州話「私」「師」「詩」三組字音的演變. *Zhongguo yuwen* 中國語文, 2: 118–122.

Chao Yuen Ren 趙元任. 1948. "Zhongshan fangyan" 中山方言. *The Bulletin of the Institute of History and Philology, Academia Sinica* 中央研究院歷史語言研究所集刊, 20: 49–73.

Cheung, Hung-nin Samuel 張洪年. 1997. "Completing the Completive: (Re-)constructing Early Cantonese Grammar." In *Studies on the History of Chinese Syntax*, ed. Sun Chaofen, pp. 134–165. *Journal of Chinese Linguistics*, Monography Series 10.

———. 2000. "Zaoqi Yueyu zhong de biandiao xianxiang" 早期粵語中的變調現象. *Fangyan* 方言, 4: 299–312.

———. 2001. "The Interrogative Construction: (Re)constructing Early Cantonese Grammar." In *Sinitic Grammar: Synchronic and Diachronic Perspectives*, ed. Hilary Chappell, pp. 191–231. Oxford; New York: Oxford University Press.

———. 2003. "21 shiji de Xianggang Yueyu: Yi ge xin yuyin xitong de xingcheng" 21世紀的香港粵語：一個新語音系統的形成. In *Di 8 jie guoji Yue fangyan yantaohui lunwenji* 第八屆國際粵方言研討會論文集, ed. Zhang Bohui 詹伯慧, pp. 129–152. Beijing: China Social Sciences Press 中國社會科學出版社.

Cheung Yat-shing 張日昇, and Gan Yu'en 甘于恩. 1993. *Yue fangyan yanjiu shumu* 粵方言研究書目. Hong Kong: The Linguistic Society of Hong Kong.

Morrison, Robert. 1828. *A Vocabulary of the Canton Dialect*. Macao: The Honorable East India Company's Press.

Qian Gang 錢鋼, and Hu Jingcao 胡勁草. 2003. *Da Qing liu Mei youtong ji* 大清留美幼童記. Hong Kong: Chung Hwa Book Company.

Stedman, Thomas L., and K. P. Lee. 1888. *A Chinese and English Phrase Book in the Canton Dialect*. New York: William R. Jenkins.

Wang, Xinyang. 2001. *Surviving the City: The Chinese Immigrant Experience in New York, 1890–1970*. Lanham, MD: Rowman & Littlefield.

Who Was Who, 1916–1928. 1947. London: Adam & Charles Black.

Who Was Who in America: A Companion Volume to Who's Who in America, Volume 1: 1897–1942. 1962. Chicago: Marquis Who's Who.

Wong Shik-ling 黃錫凌. 1954. *Yueyin yunhui* 粵音韻彙. Hong Kong: Chung Hwa Book Company.

Zhan Bohui 詹伯慧, and Cheung Yat-shing 張日昇. 1987. *A Survey of Dialects in the Pearl River Delta, Vol. 1: Comparative Morpheme-Syllabary* 珠江三角洲方言字音對照. Hong Kong: New Century Publishing House.

This article originally appeared in the *Bulletin of Chinese Linguistics*, 1.1: 171–199 (Li Fang-Kuei Society for Chinese Linguistics and Center for Chinese Linguistics, The Hong Kong University of Science and Technology, 2006).

Cantonese Phonology as Reconstructed from Popular Songs

Abstract: For many centuries, our knowledge of ancient Chinese phonology has relied primarily on the study of rhyming patterns in particular poetic corpuses. The effort is based upon the presumption that poets and lyricists share not only the same language, but also a common phonological awareness that allows them to choose rhyme words with the same or similar *yunmu* in their compositions. Any differences in practice may be construed as indicative of dialectal variations or of new developments in language. This article challenges that view by examining the rhyming practice in close to 500 popular Cantonese songs. The phonological system as reconstructed on the bases of thousands of rhyme words yields 24 finals, 19 short of what we find in the actual spoken language. The results are alarming. Close analysis reveals that while phonological identity remains a strong preference in rhyming, it is not the precluding factor. Many words rhyme because they share the same vowel even though they may differ in their consonantal endings. Others interact for historical reasons and do not reflect any phonological changes in modern pronunciations. Cross rhyming allows literary flexibility but can be misleading in terms of what it informs us about the language. The article also discusses the use of bilingual rhyming in lyrics that contain English words, a phenomenon that bespeaks the hybrid nature of speech in contemporary Cantonese.

Keywords: rhyming in Cantonese songs; Cantonese sounds and tones; cross rhyming between Chinese and English; the *xilian* approach to diachronic investigation

1. As Chinese characters are essentially morphemic in nature and do not necessarily inform the language of their pronunciations, the task of reconstructing ancient phonological systems has to rely on linguistic data other than the writing system itself. While it is true that the majority of Chinese characters are *xiesheng* 諧聲 compounds each of which contains a phonetic signifier, the phonetic correspondence, however, does not always remain constant or reliable as the language evolves. On the other hand, the long literary tradition in China has produced and preserved large collections of ancient writings that readily avail themselves for diachronic linguistic investigation. In particular, Chinese poetry which is characterized by a ubiquitous rhyming practice that makes it convenient to group words according to phonological affinities. If character X rhymes with character Y in a text, the two must have sounded identical to the author at least in terms of the last portion of the syllables. This last portion, generally referred to as *yunmu* 韻母 in Chinese, includes primarily the vocalic nucleus and, if there is one, the consonantal ending. When a series of rhyme words is established through meticulous research of verse materials of the same time period, a series that is readily distinguishable from other rhyme series in the same material, we can comfortably identify them as members of a rhyme category or *yunbu* 韻部. Even though the exact phonetic or phonemic value of the category has yet to be reconstructed through mediation of other materials such as modern dialects, the practice of *yunbu* categorization represents the first step towards a methodical analysis of the sound system of the past.

For centuries, our knowledge of ancient Chinese phonology has relied heavily on the study of rhyming patterns in poetic corpuses. Many important diachronic studies are products of these elaborate investigations, ranging in time period from the pre-Qin to the late imperial eras.[1] Presumably, speakers of the same language observe the same rhyming

---

[1] Most notable among the works of this nature are Luo Changpei and Zhou Zumo (1958), *Han Wei Jin Nanbeichao yunbu yanbian yanjiu*; and Ting Pang-hsin (1975a), *Chinese Phonology of the Wei-Chin Period: Reconstruction of the Finals as Reflected in Poetry*. In 1992, I worked on the reconstruction of ancient Suzhou phonology by examining the rhyming practice in a 17th-century collection of Wu folksongs.

principle when they write, namely the identity in *yunmu* among the rhyming words. When differences begin to show up in practice and form regular patterns of deviations, the discrepancies may be construed as results of dialectal variations or as indications of new developments in the language. Such a view, however, poses certain empirical dangers. First of all, is rhyming always an accurate reflection of actual linguistic behaviors? Could factors other than phonological identity contribute to the rhyming convention? Furthermore, when two words are chosen as a rhyming pair, do they have to share exactly the same *yunmu*? Is there any flexibility that allows for partial identity?[2] If so, do vowels or other segments in the finals play a deciding role in rhyming? These are some of the questions that we need to address in order to either confirm or reevaluate the validity of our efforts to reconstruct a sound system by way of *yunbu* categorization.

The project of utilizing rhyme words in a historical investigation invites a challenge, a challenge that is theoretically justifiable but, again, empirically rather difficult to confront. As a historical project involves a historical language, there is no living evidence to prove right or wrong what we conclude from a study based essentially on secondary materials. Unless what is observed has been reported by the contemporaries of that historical period, our analysis remains speculations, forever shy of capturing the actual happenings in the language. In the case of versification, when an ancient text displays a certain rhyming pattern, how do we verify whether the choice was phonologically motivated or if it was made for other reasons? As an alternative, we could look for historical proofs in the modern, living language, which represents after all an intermediary stage in the long process of linguistic evolution, a stage that is perhaps one or a few steps removed from the past. The present may reflect the past, but it does not necessarily speak for the past. The past can never be fully retrieved, a regrettable fact that, nonetheless, does not have to prevent us from using the modern language to test the validity

---

2   In his 1992 MA thesis entitled "Notes on Consonantal Cluster Endings in Archaic Chinese," Zev Handel proposes an *nd*-ending in his reconstruction for the rhyme category in Archaic Chinese and argues that *-and* and *-an* words, in spite of their slight difference in syllabic structure, could interact in the *Shijing* as rhyme words just as they do in English popular songs. See pp. 15–19.

of the long-standing understanding of rhyming in versification. For one thing, we can examine the rhyming practice by modern writers vis-à-vis the actual language that they speak. If we observe a strict correspondence between the rhyming system and the phonological system of the living language, the findings would confirm the validity of the traditional approach to *yunbu* categorization. If, on the other hand, we come to discover great discrepancies between the two systems, the results would call for a reconsideration of the traditional approach, hence, a further effort to seek for an explanation for the deviations. And, if rhyming does not adequately speak for linguistic realities, many diachronic issues examined in the past will have to be addressed again. In fact, the entire field of historical phonology will need to be reopened for further inquiry and exploration.

The following is a case study of the rhyming practice in contemporary Cantonese, a study which hopes to show the extent to which the literary convention matches the actual linguistic performance.[3] Upon a careful analysis of rhyming in close to 500 contemporary Cantonese songs, I will attempt to reconstruct a phonological system based upon rhyming, which I will then compare with the actual phonological system of the spoken language. Knowledge of the real language will help us determine whether rhyming is truly reliable in reflecting or recording what is happening in speech, or whether some form of poetic license has been applied to the rhyming practice when songs are composed. The implications of such a practice to change or modify strict rhyming are no small matters to our understanding of the past, especially when linguists are trying to bring the literary tradition to bear on their diachronic investigation.

2. The chief corpus of Cantonese materials under examination falls under the general category of songs. The reason why songs have been selected over poetry is simply that the former far outnumber the latter and hence represents a wider and more reliable database. As in all regional

---

[3] Paul Jen-kuei Li (1986) conducted a similar study on rhyming in Taiwanese. His examples, largely drawn from the oral tradition of folk songs and nursery rhymes, show that rhyming does not necessarily indicate all phonemic distinctions in the language.

dialects, Cantonese songs are written in rhyming lines, with but a few exceptions in blank verse. The rhyming patterns vary from song to song: some choose to observe a single rhyme scheme throughout the entire composition of many stanzas; some change rhymes regularly or even randomly from one section to another. Unlike classical poetry where repetition of words is strictly prohibited, in contemporary songs the same word may occur time and again, thereby forming its own rhyming unit. There are two major types of Cantonese songs included in this study, namely traditional operas and folk songs. Operatic lyrics are written in a semi-literary style and folk songs are often composed in modern colloquial Cantonese. This general characterization needs, however, some qualification. While operatic lyrics are highly eloquent in their choice of diction, they do at times accommodate common colloquial expressions. As for folk songs, the vernacular flavor was particularly prominent in lyrics composed in the 1960s; their use of colorful regional words may not be always comprehensible to speakers of a different dialect. During the last few decades, Cantonese folk songs have adopted a more refined mode of expression, primarily modeled after that of Mandarin. Colloquial forms are present but only in admixture with words from the standard lexicon. Regardless of style, the songs are all sung in Cantonese. Given this stylistic switch in lyrics since the 1960s, could there also be changes in pronunciation as reflected or recorded in singing? To address this possibility, I have grouped songs into the following four periods, each appended by the actual number of songs I have collected for that period:

(1) Pre-1980   230
(2) 1980–1985   74
(3) 1986–1990   117
(4) 1991–1994   51
                    ___
                    472

The division is admittedly arbitrary; in fact, the numbers seem a bit askew as the first period covers a much longer span than the other three periods combined. The distortion is due to a very simple reason, namely lack of sufficient data. My sources include a large number of audio cassette tapes produced in Hong Kong since 1980. Far from being exhaustive, the collection is nevertheless representative of various time periods, different singing styles, and mostly by major singers. Unfortunately, I do not possess any tapes or albums produced prior to 1980. However, I have a song anthology, entitled *Zhiyin ji* 知音集 in Chinese and *Let's Sing* (LS) in English, which contains among all sorts of musical pieces a large number of early Cantonese songs. Produced in Hong Kong in 1978, *Zhiyin ji* is my primary source for lyrics before 1980. As will become evident from the following pages of analysis, the rhyming patterns in Cantonese songs, operatic or otherwise, remain quite consistent over the last few decades.

3. Prior to offering a comprehensive analysis of the data, I will first present a brief description of the sound system in modern Cantonese. Traditionally, a Chinese syllable can be dissected into three components: the initial consonant (*shengmu* 聲母), the final (*yunmu* 韻母), and the tone (*shengdiao* 聲調). As this article is primarily concerned with the rhyming practice, a poetic convention that pertains little to the behavior of the initial consonants, I shall focus my attention on the final and the tone in the ensuing discussions. The following is the final system in standard Cantonese as spoken in Hong Kong and reported in various studies. The transcription follows that of the Yale system of romanization.

	V + (G)		V + N			V + C		
a	aai	aau	aam	aan	aang	aap	aat	aak
	ai	au	am	am	ang	ap	at	ak
e	ei				eng			ek
eu	eui			eun	eung		eut	euk
i		iu	im	in	ing	ip	it	ik
o	oi	ou		on	ong		ot	ok
u	ui			un	ung		ut	uk
yu				yun			yut	

Syllabic nasals: m̩, ng̩

Chart 1

There have been ongoing changes in the finals, a topic to which I will return when discussing the use of rhymes. One noticeable development, for example, is the develarization of the final consonant *-ng*. For some speakers, for example, the distinction between *-ang* and *-an* is absent, and *pahng* 朋

and *pahn* 貧 are both pronounced as *pahn*.[4] When *-eung* is pronounced as *-eun*, the change further involves introduction of a new phoneme into the system. Phonetically, *-eung* is [œŋ] and *-eun* is [ɵn], and since [œ] and [ɵ] are in complementary distribution, they are grouped together as one phoneme. However, as the process of develarization has altered this distributive condition, resulting in a distinct contrast between [œn] and [ɵn], the language at least for these speakers has acquired a new phoneme.[5]

Cantonese is well-known for its rich repertoire of tones. Historically, the Chinese language had four tones: *ping* 平, *shang* 上, *qu* 去, and *ru* 入, each of which underwent a split as conditioned by the voicing quality of the initial consonants of the syllables. In Cantonese, a further split occurred on the checked syllables, generally referred to as the *rusheng* 入聲, giving rise to three *ru* tones. Hence, Cantonese displays a nine-tone system as represented below both in tone letters and in Yale romanization.

ping	(1) *yinping*	陰平	55:/53:[6]	sī/sì
	(2) *yangping*	陽平	31:	sìh
shang	(3) *yinshang*	陰上	35:	sí
	(4) *yangshang*	陽上	13:	síh
qu	(5) *yinqu*	陰去	33:	si
	(6) *yangqu*	陽去	22:	sih
ru	(7) *shangru*	上入	5:	sīk
	(8) *zhongru*	中入	3:	sek
	(9) *xiaru*	下入	2:	sihk

Chart 2

Phonemically, the membership of Cantonese tones can be reduced to six since the *ru* syllables (tones 7, 8, and 9) are characteristically marked with obstruent endings and their pitch levels are identical to those of tones 1, 5, and 6 respectively. In other words, the *ru* tones may be treated as short versions of their non-checked counterparts. The tonal system, complex as

---

4 The *h* that appears after the vowel serves to mark that the syllable is of a lower tone register.

5 In his 1979 article "Alveolarization in Cantonese: A Case of Lexical Diffusion," Robert Bauer examines the process of alveolarization that has affected the Cantonese language since the late 19th century.

6 To avoid confusion, *yinping* will be marked as high-level (55:) in this article.

it may seem, has remained intact over the years, although individual words may have occasionally switched membership from one tonal category to another.

4. In traditional Chinese poetics, rhyming required not only identity of *yunmu* but also sameness in tone. Syllables like *dang* and *sang* may rhyme only when they belong to the same tonal category. Such a tonal requirement, however, became optional in subsequent forms of versification. With the exception of the *rusheng* words which are distinguished from other syllables by virtue of their stop endings, cross rhyming among *ping*, *shang*, and *qu* categories has become a standard practice in all song compositions. The following is an example of a Cantonese song that demonstrates this phenomenon.

(1) 我時常清風兩袖　　jauh (22)
　　吊兒郎當最自由　　yàuh (31)
　　但得有三餐足夠　　gau (33)
　　為人樂觀好少掛憂　yāu (55)
　　咪彈人貪新厭舊　　gauh (22)
　　愛情如海市蜃樓　　làuh (31)
　　問天賜幾許佳偶　　ngáuh (13)
　　離合悲歡定必有　　yáuh (13)
　　飲翻杯冰凍啤酒　　jáu (35)
　　高歌一曲氣量厚　　háuh (13)
　　無謂再去為情悔疚　gau (33)
　　你盞心罷得個嬲　　nāu (55)
　　我懷疑天邊宇宙　　jauh (22)
　　有神靈管轄地球　　kàuh (31)
　　實應要睇通睇透　　tau (33)
　　成敗得失莫追究　　gau (33)
　　大家要睇通睇透　　tau (33)
　　成敗得失莫追究　　gau (33)

—*Bei jiu dang ge* 杯酒當歌, Sam Hui 許冠傑, LS: 976 (pre-1980)[7]

---

[7] While song lyrics are romanized according to Cantonese, all titles and names are spelled according to Mandarin pronunciation. For each example, the bibliographical information is given in the following order: title of the song, singer, year of production and, if known, lyricist. If the song is cited from *Let's Sing* (*Zhiyin ji*), the page number follows LS, and the time period is noted as "pre-1980."

The above song contains 18 lines, all of which end with the same rhyme -*au*. Among the 18 rhyme words, two are *yinping*, three *yangping*, one *yinshang*, three *yangshang*, six *yinqu*, and three *yangqu*. The free association across tones betrays an important feature of the practice: rhyming is determined by the segmental rather than the supra-segmental component in a syllable. It is for this reason that we do not witness much interaction between the checked syllables and the non-checked counterparts even though their pitch values can be identical in Cantonese. However, we do observe some seeming anomalies, whose behaviors I will return to examine in a later section.

5. The collection of 472 Cantonese songs provides thousands of rhyme words, which I have categorized according to their rhyming association. The categorization follows the traditional method known as *xilian* 系聯. In brief terms, *xilian* places X, Y, and Z in the same rhyme category or *yunbu* if X rhymes with Y and Y rhymes with Z.[8] The results of this *xilian* classification are summarized below. The setup in the chart follows that of the Cantonese phonology as produced above. Where cross rhyming occurs, the finals are grouped together in a box. Please note that certain finals are missing in the song chart.

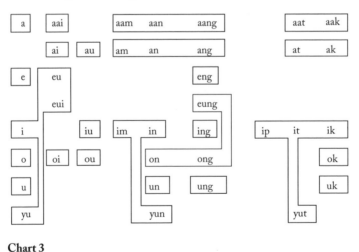

Chart 3

---

[8] The first scholar who proposed the practice of *xilian* in relation to diachronic investigation was Chen Li 陳澧 (1810–1882). For a brief discussion of his work, *Qieyun kao* 切韻考, see Dong Tonghe 董同龢 (1968), pp. 88–92.

5.1. Missing Finals

The finals missing in the chart are the two syllabic nasals (*m* and *ng*) and the following units:

aau		aap
		ap
		at
eu	eun	eut
		euk
		ot
ui		ut

The syllalbic *m* and *ng* are excluded from serving as rhyming words for obvious reasons. Being syllabic by themselves, they carry little audible vocalic resonance, hence not a good choice for effective rhyming particularly in songs.[9] The *rusheng* words are ignored probably on similar grounds. The implosive endings of the checked syllables, phonetically short and abrupt by nature, are difficult to enunciate and maintain in singing. There are in fact very few *rusheng* words utilized as rhyme words, and of those that do participate, many display unusual rhyming schemes, which I will discuss in section 5.4. The final *-eu* carries a very small group of words, which may explain why its limited members do not make it in our corpus.

As for the other missing finals, there seems to be no good explanation other than to claim that these gaps are unfortunate deficiencies in the data. As is, our collection of songs covers a rather extensive period of time and a great variety of subject matters, and we feel that these accidental absences would not affect our analysis in general or the arguments we are making in the following pages.

5.2. *Yinsheng yun*

Chinese syllables are traditionally classified into three types: those that conclude with nasals are *yangsheng yun* 陽聲韻 (nasal finals), those that end with stops are *rusheng yun* 入聲韻 (checked syllables), and those that consists of only vocalic elements are *yinsheng yun* 陰聲韻 (open syllables).

---

[9] The syllabic nasals represent a very small number of words, few of which occupy a sentence final position. This may be another reason why they are seldom used as rhymes.

As illustrated in Chart 1, Cantonese has under *yinsheng yun* seven finals with single vowels and ten finals with diphthongs. In other words, we would expect a total of 17 distinct *yunbu* groups for rhyming purposes. Yet, according to the grouping as shown in Chart 3, there are only 11 rhyme groups, with some of the original finals now coalescing into one large category. The following is a detailed examination of each of these 11 rhyme groups. Please note that, since all my pre-1980 songs are collected from *Let's Sing*, which gives no information other than the song titles, I will not be able to provide any further details, as I will do for those composed after 1980, regarding names of both the singers and the lyricists.

5.2.1. The final *-a* is a simple vocalic unit that represents about 40 rhyme words in 11 songs in our collection. The rhyming behavior of *-a* is straight and simple as illustrated in the following two examples, one from the pre-1980s period and one from afterwards.

(2) gwa 掛　　gá 假　　tā 他
　　háh 吓　　hah 下　　gwā 呱
　　pa 怕　　pàh 爬　　gā 家
　　hā 哈　　wah 話　　ba 吧
　　　　　　　　　　—*Wanxia la* 玩吓啦,
　　　　　　　　　　　LS: 870 (pre-1980)

(3) fā 花　　ga 價　　tā 他
　　hah 下　　wah 話　　ba 吧
　　fa 化　　mah 罵　　ga 嫁
　　　　　　　　　　—*Qu ba, qu ba* 去吧去吧,
　　　Jenny Tseng 甄妮 (1986), lyrics by Jimmy Lo 盧國沾

5.2.2. The final *-e* again constitutes a small rhyme category with only 19 members from a total of three songs. All three pieces are from the post-1980 period.

(4) jē 遮　　ché 扯　　se 瀉
　　chē 奢　　sē 些　　chē 車
　　yeh 夜　　yéh 野　　chèh 斜
　　seh 射　　je 借　　se 赦
　　sē 賒　　chèh 斜　　jeh 謝
　　jē 嗟

　　　　　　　　　　—*Xin ye ye* 心野夜,
　　Sandy Lam 林憶蓮 (1991), lyrics by Thomas Chow 周禮茂

5.2.3. The final -*o*, though relatively small in membership, is an active rhyme in Cantonese songs. About 20 songs are written in the -*o* scheme.

(5) dō 多   chó 楚   cho 錯
    gwó 果 hòh 何   bō 波
                    —*Wen wo* 問我,
                    LS: 850 (pre-1980)

(6) ngóh 我 chó 楚   tòh 陀
    bō 波   joh 助   woh 禍
    cho 錯   dō 多   po 破
    hòh 河   mòh 磨   gwo 過
                    —*Rensheng zhi ge* 人生之歌,
                    George Lam 林子祥 (1980)

It is interesting to note that -*o* also interacts with other rhymes that contain -*o* as their main vowel. As illustrated below, -*o* inter-rhymes with -*on*, -*ong*, and -*ok*. Examples are few, but the versatile behaviors provide a first glimpse of the phenomenon of cross rhyming in Cantonese songs.

<u>-o : -ong : -ok</u>

(7) ngóh 我   gok 角   gok 覺
    mohng 望
                    —*Wo ruhe zhidao ni ai wo* 我如何知道你愛我,
                    Dave Wang 王傑 (1989)

<u>-o : -on : -ong</u>

(8) dō 多   wóh 喎   doh 墮
    gō 哥   talk   gwo 過
    ngoh 餓 tō 拖   fong 放
    song 喪 gōn 干   dóng 擋
    ngon 案 dong 當   wóng 枉
    góng 講
                    —*Tiancai baichi, qian, qian, qian* 天才白痴錢錢錢,
                    Sam Hui, LS: 940 (pre-1980)

It is obvious that the vowel plays a crucial role in the rhyming game. The vocalic resonance of -*o*- creates a resounding effect in singing and hence becomes the distinctive and representative feature of all the syllables that carry this vowel. The most revealing evidence to prove that rhyming operates on -*o*- is the inclusion of the English word "talk" in example

(8). With an obstruent ending, "talk" operates like an -o- syllable in Cantonese, thereby qualifying itself for joining the rhyming scheme.

5.2.4. The final -u is represented by only four songs in the corpus. There is no cross rhyming between -u and other finals.

(9) wú 壺   fū 呼   wuh 戶
     fū 膚   fú 撫   fu 褲

—*Mou yitian* 某一天,
Anita Mui 梅艷芳 (1986), lyrics by Andrew Lam 林敏驄

One song, however, demonstrates interaction with English.

(10) fú 苦   fū 夫   fuh 乎
     you

—*Ni shi wo de nüren* 你是我的女人,
Alan Tam 譚詠麟 (1993), lyrics by Jolland Chan 向雪懷

5.2.5. The final -aai is another small rhyme category with 25 members appearing in five different songs. The rhyming is strictly among the -aai words.

(11) saai 曬   waaih 壞   jaai 債
     màaih 埋   gāai 階   gāai 街
     chàaih 柴 gwāai 乖   hàaih 鞋
     páai 牌   faai 快   gaai 戒

—*Xin duzai zi tan* 新賭仔自歎,
LS: 935 (pre-1980)

5.2.6. The final -ai represents 62 rhyme words in eight songs. No unusual rhyming behavior is observed.

(12) jai 制   sai 世   jaih 滯
     waih 謂   yáh 曳   laih 例
     dai 帝   kāi 稽

—*Guima shuangxing* 鬼馬雙星,
Sam Hui, LS: 900 (pre-1980)

(13) dāi 低   sai 世   làih 嚟
     chai 切 jāi 劑   dái 底
     jai 際   jái 仔   jai 制
     fāi 揮   láih 禮   gai 計

—*Stand Up*,
Leslie Cheung 張國榮 (1986)

5.2.7. The final -*oi* appears in six songs all rhyming within the same category.

(14) lòih 萊   joih 在   goi 蓋
      ngoih 外   noih 內   ngoi 愛
                              —*Hechu mi penglai* 何處覓蓬萊,
                              Sam Hui, LS: 912 (pre-1980)

(15) ngoi 愛   koi 概   gói 改
      lòih 來   ngōi 哀   doih 待
      chói 彩   ngoih 外   joih 在
                              —*Huozhe jiu shi dengdai* 活著就是等待,
                              Karen Tong 湯寶如 (1992), lyrics by Jolland Chan

Two other songs, one given below, demonstrates cross rhyming among -*oi*, -*o*, and -*ong*, a phenomenon that resembles the interaction beween -*o* and other related finals as discussed above.

(16) hói 海   hōi 開   gwo 過
      kwong 曠   mohng 望
                              —*Dahai yijiao* 大海一角,
                              Dave Wang (1989), lyrics by Dave Wang

5.2.8. The final -*au* is an important rhyme category in Cantonese songs. With about 60 members, it accounts for the composition of 22 songs in both pre- and post-1980 periods. Rhyming is exclusive to its membership.

(17) yàuh 遊   yàuh 悠   chàuh 酬
      làuh 流   sàuh 愁   sáuh 守
      háuh 厚   tàuh 頭   làuh 留
      sàuh 愁
                              —*Hao fuqi* 好福氣,
                              LS: 847 (pre-1980)

(18) sáu 手   dauh 竇   hauh 候
      sauh 受   yāu 憂   háu 口
      yáuh 有   làuh 流   jáu 酒
                              —*Neixin you menghua* 內心有夢話,
                              Liza Wang 汪明荃 (1981), lyrics by Jimmy Lo

5.2.9. The final -*ou* forms a rhyme category with about 50 words. Again, rhyming does not extend beyond membership.

(19) tou 兔   chóu 草   gou 告
      hóu 好   bóu 保   bouh 暴
      tòuh 陶

—*Xuyuan* 許願,
LS: 848 (pre-1980)

(20) louh 路   móuh 舞   sōu 騷
      tòuh 途   gōu 高   mouh 霧
      hóu 好   bouh 步

—*Yun shang chuang qian lu* 雲上創前路,
Jenny Tseng (1986), lyrics by James Wong 黃霑

5.2.10. The final *-iu* appears as the rhyme in nine songs, which all observe the general requirement of rhyming within the category.

(21) siu 笑   diuh 掉   tiu 跳
      chiu 俏   síu 小   miuh 妙
      jiu 照   yiuh 耀   yìuh 遙
      jīu 焦   kìuh 橋

—*Shijie zhen xixiao* 世界真細小,
LS: 925 (pre-1980)

(22) líuh 了   síu 少   liuh 料
      sīu 宵   pīu 飄   yiu 要
      yìuh 搖

—*Poxiao* 破曉,
Sandy Lam (1991), lyrics by Thomas Chow

5.2.11. If the discussion of Cantonese rhymes thus far appears simple and straightforward, the regularity is restricted to the above ten *yinsheng* finals. The next four finals, namely *-i*, *-yu*, *-ei*, and *-eui*, display a complex picture of rhyming interactions among members that are neither phonologically similar in structure nor acoustically close in effect. In fact, the high frequency of cross rhyming among the four finals seems to indicate the presence of some common features that would accordingly place them in the same *yunbu*. On the other hand, there are song compositions that strictly observe boundary restrictions, in which case the finals should be treated as different rhymes. The following are examples of both patterns: rhyming within group and rhyming across categories.

Exclusive use of -i

(23) jī   志   jī   姿   chìh 遲
      jī   枝   yíh   以   sī   思
      yìh 移   sī   絲   ci   次
      si   試   dī   啲   sìh   時

—*Qingchun nütan* 青春女探,
Tomi Wong 黃愷欣, LS: 883 (pre-1980)

(24) sih 事   chíh 始   sī   詩
      yi   意   ci   賜   si   試
      ci   次

—*Jiang kuaile yi shi* 將快樂一試,
Johnny Yip 葉振棠 (1982), lyrics by James Wong

Exclusive use of -ei

(25) néih 你   béi   比   héi   起
      hei 氣   deih 地   héi   喜
      leih 利   géi   幾   léih 理
      gēi 機   hei   戲   hēi   嘻
      béih 脾

—*Gongxi ni* 恭喜你,
LS: 874 (pre-1980)

(26) fēi 扉   néih 你   lèih 離
      géi 紀   mèih 微   héi   喜
      gei 記   méih 美   gēi   羈

—*Jiang yisheng song gei ni* 將一生送給你,
Karen Tong (1992), lyrics by Poon Wai Yuen 潘偉源

Exclusive use of -eui

(27) léuih 侶   sèuih 垂   héui 許
      kēui 軀   chèuih 隨   géui 舉
      néuih 女

—*Shendiao xialü* 神雕俠侶,
LS: 901 (pre-1980)

(28) heui 去   leuih 淚   jeui 醉
      seuih 睡   deui 對   léuih 裡
      jeuih 罪

—*Lai congcong shi gudan* 來匆匆是孤單,
Susanna Kwan 關菊英 (1985), lyrics by James Wong

Mixed use of -i and -yu

(29) yúh 雨   sī 詩   yi   意
      chī 痴   yúh 語   yíh 耳
      jih 字   jī 知   sih 事
      sī 思   ji 智   syuh 樹
      chyu 處

—*Yeban qing si yu* 夜半輕私語,
Sam Hui, LS: 929 (pre-1980)

(30) jyuh 住   yi 意   jih 稚
      sih 視   yih 義   jī 知
      syu 恕   sih 示   yíh 以
      si   試

—*Lei zhi ai* 淚之愛,
Susanna Kwan (1985), lyrics by Jolland Chan

Mixed use of -i and -ei

(31) jī 姿   jī 枝   sih 時
      hēi 稀   sī 思   meih 味
      bēi 悲   gei 記   yī   依
      fēi 飛

—*Yi shui ge tianya* 一水隔天涯,
Teresa Teng 鄧麗君, LS: 922 (pre-1980)

Mixed use of -ei and -eui

(32) néih 你   deih 地   léuih 裡
      hei 氣   gei 記   bēi   悲
      heui 去

—*Yongyuan dou shen ai ni* 永遠都深愛你,
Alan Tam (1993), lyrics by Poon Wai Yuen

Mixed use of -yu and -eui

(33) chyu 處   jyuh 住   léuih 裡
      jyu 注   yúh 雨   yúh   語
      geui 句

—*Xinyu* 心語,
Susanna Kwan (1985), lyrics by James Wong

Mixed use of -*i*, -*yu*, -*ei*, and -*eui*

(34) hei 氣   meih 味   néih 你
      kéuih 佢   jyuh 住   léih 理
      sih 事
                              —*Yiqi ge*, LS: 961 (pre-1980)

(35) jyuh 住   yī 漪   sìh 時
      yih 易   jyu 注   fēi 飛
      jeuih 聚   yi 意   héi 喜
      beih 避   leuih 慮   héi 起
      néih 你
                              —*Zuihou de meigui* 最後的玫瑰,
                   Jenny Tseng (1986), lyrics by Cheng Kwok Kong 鄭國江

(36) seuih 睡   léuih 裡   méih 美
      sī 詩   yih 義   yi 意
      yìh 疑   sih 示
                              —*Wo yuanyi* 我願意,
                                    Leslie Cheung (1987)

Interactions between -*i* and -*yu* are noticeably more frequent than those among the others. In fact, there is no example in which -*yu* constitutes its own rhyme. Both -*i* [i] and -*yu* [y] are high, front vowels, whose phonetic features might account for their rhyming association even though they are quite different in terms of lip rounding. Likewise, the association between -*i* and -*ei* might be explained in terms of their frontness, and that between -*yu* and -*eui* might be understood in terms of their roundness. However, the mixed use of all four finals defies any imaginable phonetic reasoning. Two of them are diphthongs and two are monothongs; two contain round vowels and two unround vowels. By virtue of their vocalic make-up, they are decidedly different from each other. To account for the phenomenon, it is necessary to look elsewhere and even beyond contemporary language for an explanation.[10] The principle of *xilian* which claims that all rhyming is based upon phonetic identity no longer applies in this Cantonese song.

---

[10] This cross rhyming phenomenon could be understood, as proposed by some Japanese scholars, in terms of phonetic closeness between the final elements, and not between the vowels, of the rhyme syllables. Whether they are monothongs or diphthongs, the four finals (*yunmu*) in question all end with a high front [-i] or [-y]. I am grateful to Dr. Cheung Kwan Hin, of the Hong Kong Polytechnic University, for calling my attention to this alternative analysis.

5.3. Yangsheng yun

5.3.1. As in traditional phonology, Cantonese displays a three-way contrast among its nasal finals. And, in most cases, the distinction is strictly kept in traditional Chinese poetics.

Vowel + m	:	Vowel + n	:	Vowel + ng
saam		saan		saang
sam		san		sang
tim		tin		ting

Chart 4

In Cantonese rhyming, however, the distinction seems to be disappearing, hence irrelevant. Of the 472 songs, very few observe the three-way distinction and keep rhyming within the confines of one particular nasal ending *yunbu*. Insofar as they share the same vowel, words can rhyme regardless of their final nasal components.[11] The following are a few examples.

Mixed use of *-aam, -aan,* and *-aang*

(37) sāam 衫   ngáahn 眼   wàahng 橫
      nàahm 喃   gāan 間   gaam 鑒
      paan 盼   naahn 難   wàahn 還
      sāan 山   láahng 冷   chàahn 殘
      hāan 慳   saan 散

—*Chun can meng duan* 春殘夢斷,
Liza Wang, LS: 908 (pre-1980)

(38) gāam 監   jaahm 暫   dāan 單
      fàahn 煩   nàahn 難   gāan 間
      láahng 冷   ngaahng 硬   wàahn 環
      dáan 彈   màahng 盲   fáan 返
      hàahng 行

—*Zhadan* 炸彈,
Jacky Cheung 張學友 (1986), lyrics by Poon Wai Yuen

---

[11] Li (1986) reports similar rhyming practice across different nasal endings in Taiwanese songs. See pp. 449–451.

Mixed use of -am, -an, and -ang

(39) hahn 恨   màhng 盟   fahn 份
      wàhn 魂   fān 分   wáhn 韻
      máhn 憫   gam 禁   fáhn 憤
      hàhn 痕   kwan 困   yàhn 人
      sān 新   mahn 問   sām 心

—*Yuanyangjiang yueye* 鴛鴦江月夜,
LS: 936 (pre-1980)

(40) dāng 燈   yàhn 人   fān 氛
      yám 飲   fáhn 奮   wáhn 韻
      máhn 吻   sam 滲   sām 心
      yān 欣   wān 溫   gahn 近
      ngam 暗

—*Haoqing ye* 豪情夜,
Alan Tam (1993), lyrics by Poon Wai Yuen

Mixed use of -im and -in

(41) pin 片   tīn 天   yihn 現
      bin 變   mihn 面   yīn 煙
      nihm 念   chín 淺   gin 見

—*Gumeng* 故夢,
LS: 845 (pre-1980)

(42) gīn 肩   nihm 念   gin 見
      tīn 天   yìhn 然   bīn 邊
      mihn 面   yim 厭   chīn 遷

—*Touxinzhe* 偷心者,
Jacky Cheung (1986), lyrics by Richard Lam 林振強

In speech, the three-way distinction is real and retained by most speakers. Yet, even after listening to the audio cassettes repeatedly and with great care, I was still not always able to tell whether the distinction was preserved in singing. Admittedly, the presence of nasality was clear in the rhyme words; and most of them sounded more like forms with *-n* than with *-m* or *-ng*. Nonetheless, cross rhyming is a prevalent phenomenon among nasal finals in song lyrics, and in accordance with the *xilian* practice it is possible to group most *-m*, *-n*, and *-ng* forms into one single category sharing the same vowels. In other words, the sound system as reconstructed from rhyming in Cantonese would yield only one kind of nasal final, those ending with an *n*-like coda, for the following groups *of yunmu*.

Speech	Rhyming
-aam, -aan, -aang	-aan
-am, -an, -ang	-an
-im, -in	-in

Please note that *-ing* does not coalesce with *-im* and *-in* in songs, which I will examine in a later section.

There exist in the corpus, as mentioned, a few compositions which seem to enforce the nasal distinction. The following is an example that makes an exclusive use of *-aan*.

(43)　laahn　爛　　haahn　限　　maahn　曼
　　　　maahn　漫　　gāan　　間　　waahn　幻
　　　　　　　　　　　　　　　　—*Qinghua kai* 情花開,
　　　　　　　Chan Tsai Chung 陳齊頌, LS: 875 (pre-1980)

However, as such examples are scarce in number, it is not apparent whether the exclusion was by intention or merely a coincidence.

5.3.2. Another nasal final that is ambiguous in status is *-yun* [yn]. The final *-yun* may form a rhyme category all by itself or it may rhyme freely with nasal finals *-in* and *-im*. The following are examples of its various rhyming patterns.

Exclusive use of *-yun*

(44)　syún　　選　　dyuhn　斷　　yùhn　　園
　　　　syùhn　船　　yuhn　　願　　gyun　　眷
　　　　lyuhn　亂　　jyūn　　尊　　chyun　　寸
　　　　chyùhn　泉　　yuhn　　怨
　　　　　　　　　　　　　　　—*Juezhan qianxi* 決戰前夕,
　　　　　　　Adam Cheng 鄭少秋, LS: 884 (pre-1980)

(45)　lyuhn　　亂　　syùhn　　旋　　hyún　　犬
　　　　yùhn　　緣　　chyùhn　存　　chyùhn　全
　　　　lyúhn　　戀　　hyūn　　圈　　syùhn　　船
　　　　yùhn　　完

　　　　　　　　　　　　　　　　　　—*Crazy Rock*,
　　　　　　　Leslie Cheung (1986), lyrics by Richard Lam

Mixed use of -*yun*, -*in*, and -*im*

(46) bīn 邊   tīn 天   yúhn 軟
      yìhn 言   gin 見   hīn 牽
      nìhn 年   yúhn 遠   dyuhn 斷
      chín 濺   nihm 念   bīn 邊
      pīn 篇   pin 遍   lìhn 連
      chīn 千   gyuhn 倦

—*Liuyue tian* 六月天,
LS: 806 (pre-1980)

(47) lyúhn 戀   tìhm 甜   yin 燕
      nìhn 年   yùhn 完   bin 變
      mìhn 綿   jyūn 專   míhn 勉
      yìhn 妍   yìhn 言   mihn 面
      syūn 飧   syūn 酸

—*Chu lian* 初戀,
LS: 848 (pre-1980)

(48) mihn 面   lyuhn 亂   yihn 現
      hīn 牽   pin 遍   tīn 天
      tìhm 甜   bīn 邊   chín 濺
      dihn 電   dím 點   nyúhn 暖

—*Anlian* 暗戀,
Shirley Kwan 關淑怡 (1989), lyrics by Andrew Lam

The ratio between the exclusive use of -*yun* and the mixed use of -*yun* with -*in*/-*im* is 1:5 in the data. The scale is tipped to such a degree that the three finals can be comfortably grouped together into one *yunbu*. The grouping does not disclaim the fact that in actual language there is no confusion between -*i*- and -*yu*-. And indeed, because of this actual phonetic difference, we could argue that the exclusive use of -*yun* in some lyrics, however few there may be, is not by accident. The writers are aware of the phonetic nature of -*yun*, the roundness of which distinctly sets it apart from -*in*/-*im*. On the other hand, as both -*i*- and -*yu*- are characteristically high front vowels, they must have felt equally justified to inter-rhyme between -*yun* and -*in*/-*im*.[12]

---

[12] Cross rhyming between /-in/ and /-yn/ is also a common practice in Mandarin songs.

5.3.3. In contrast with the coalescence of all three nasal endings after *-aa-* and *-a-*, only *-m* and *-n* merge in the presence of *-i-*. The fact that *-ing* remains in general a self-sustaining category might appear to be a strange phenomenon. The anomaly, however, could be readily accounted for in terms of an actual vocalic difference between the finals: the vowel before *-m* and *-n* is a high front [i], and the vowel before *-ng* is a lower and shorter [ɪ]. Acoustically, the two sounds are very different even though phonemically they can be considered allophones of the same unit. The following are two examples of the exclusive *-ing* pattern.

(49)　hīng　卿　　mihng　命　　sīng　聲
　　　lìhng　靈　　ting　聽　　chīng　清
　　　jing　證　　sing　性　　chìhng　情
　　　mìhng　明　　gīng　驚　　jihng　靜
　　　yìhng　盈　　yihng　認　　bihng　病
　　　dihng　訂　　chìhng　程　　hīng　輕

—*Chanyuan zhongsheng* 禪院鐘聲,
Cheng Kam Cheong 鄭錦昌, LS: 905 (pre-1980)

(50)　jihng　靜　　tìhng　停　　ying　應
　　　chīng　清　　dihng　定　　tìhng　停
　　　mihng　命　　ping　拼　　mìhng　鳴
　　　yìhng　形　　sīng　星

—*You shei gongming* 有誰共鳴,
Leslie Cheung (1987)

5.3.4. It is common knowledge that Cantonese words with *-ing* are often pronounced with *-eng* instead in colloquial speech. In fact, *-eng* has gained such a prevalence in recent years that some words, once pronounced with *-ing*, appear only in *-eng*. In singing, however, as the lyrics are mostly literary in style, the *-ing* version is preferred, as exemplified in the previous section. While 病 keeps its bookish reading as *bing* in example (49), it is always *beng* in speech. On the other hand, songs produced in the 1960s, a period known for its propensity for incorporating colloquialism into song lyrics, show a frequent use of *-eng*.

(51) geng 鏡   chēng 青   méng 名
      kèhng 擎   téng 艇   déng 頂
      tēng 廳   géng 頸   dēng 釘
      léng 嶺   hēng 輕   kēng 惊
      jēng 精   sēng 腥   béng 餅
      deng 掟   jeng 正

—*Zhuiqiu sanbu qu* 追求三部曲,
Sam Hui, LS: 931 (pre-1980)

Despite the fact that I do not have the recording on tape, it was one of those songs that I grew up with around the 1960s. These rhyme words are all *-eng*'s in singing. And, in addition, many of the words appear in expressions that only exist in colloquial Cantonese and are therefore incompatible with an *-ing* reading.

5.3.5. The largest rhyme category in Cantonese songs is a hybrid class that includes two major members: *-eung* and *-ong*. Together, they constitute almost 10% of the entire song corpus. Phonetically, the two finals are drastically different in pronunciation: the latter contains a much more open [ɔ], more to the back, than the vowel [œ] in the former final. However, the following figures of distribution unequivocally argue for treating *-eung* and *-ong* as one *yunbu*.

Exclusive use of *-eung*:	7 songs	8.5%
Exclusive use of *-ong*:	4 songs	14.9%
Combined use of *-eung* and *-ong*:	36 songs	76.6%
	47 songs	100%

Examples are:

<u>Exclusive use of *-eung*</u>

(52) sèuhng 常   séung 想   jeung 漲
      yēung 央   seuhng 上   cheung 暢
      chèuhng 長   sēung 相   heung 向
      chēung 窗   jeuhng 象   yéung 樣

—*Houchuang* 後窗,
Tat Ming Pair 達明一派 (1987), lyrics by Keith Chan 陳少琪

Exclusive use of -*ong*

(53)　fóng　訪　　fóng　晃　　tong　趟
　　　 gwōng　光　　móhng　惘　　mohng　望
　　　 kwòhng　狂　　móhng　網　　pòhng　傍
　　　 fong　放　　kong　抗

—*Ningwang* 凝望,
Danny Chan 陳百強 (1986), lyrics by Cheng Kwok Kong

Mixed use of -*eung* and -*ong*

(54)　leuhng　亮　　hēung　鄉　　mohng　望
　　　 seuhng　上　　yèuhng　洋　　lohng　浪
　　　 mòhng　忘　　chèuhng　腸　　gwōng　光
　　　 sēung　霜

—*Tianya guke* 天涯孤客,
Adam Cheng, LS: 895 (pre-1980)

(55)　lohng　浪　　dohng　盪　　sēung　霜
　　　 mohng　望　　fōng　芳　　sēung　傷
　　　 gwōng　光　　hēung　鄉　　yèuhng　陽
　　　 leuhng　亮　　séung　想　　yèuhng　揚

—*Ta de gesheng* 她的歌聲,
George Lam (1980)

As in speech, the distinction between -*eung* and -*ong* is all clearly preserved in the taped singing. Yet, the phonetic disparity does not seem to deter writers from freely combining them into one single rhyme scheme. The mixed use, again, poses a challenge to the basic rhyming principle, a principle that requires rhyme words to share the same final or, by extension, the same vowel in songs. Could there be a reason for this obvious violation, or could there be another condition that prescribes or allows for this irregular practice of cross rhyming? Our data shows no clear answer.

The song corpus also provides cases of -*ong* rhyming with -*on*, both sharing the same vowel -*o*-. As noted above, the distinction between -*n* and -*ng* is, in general, negligible in song rhyming. The following is an example of the interaction between -*on* and -*ong*.

(56) fōng 慌   dohng 蕩   tōng 劏
    mohng 望   gōn 肝   lohng 浪
    gwōng 光   wóng 柱   hon 看
    johng 撞   bóng 綁   lòhng 狼
    song 喪   ngohng 戇 dong 當
    hón 悍

—*Guima dajia le* 鬼馬大家樂,
Sam Hui, LS: 933 (pre-1980)

While -*on* rhymes with -*ong*, which also rhymes with -*eung*, does -*on* likewise interact with -*eung*? It does, but primarily through the mediation of -*ong*. In fact, there are only a few songs in which -*on*, in the absence of -*ong*, rhymes with -*eung*. The following is an example of this triangular association.

(57) chēung 槍   chéung 腸   jeung 帳
    hēung 鄉   jeuhng 象   wóhng 往
    yéung 樣   gōng 崗   hon 看
    sēung 相   jēung 張

—*Xiangchang, wenzhang, jiguanqiang* 香腸、蚊帳、機關槍,
Kenny Chung 鍾鎮濤 (1986), lyrics by Andrew Lam

The intermediary function of -*ong* is best illustrated by the sequence of "*yeung . . . gong . . . hon*" in the above example, a pattern that places -*ong* in a pivotal position between -*eung* and -*on*. In other words, the rhyming goes from *eung-ong* to *ong-on*, the first pair sharing the same -*ng* ending, the second the same vowel -*o*-. Hence, -*ong* provides phonetic links at both ends to the words before and after it. There are more examples of this nature in the corpus, essentially following the same pattern in mixing the three finals in rhyming.

5.3.6. The most stable *yunmu* in Cantonese, as in all Chinese dialects, is -*ung*. It is also one of the most often used rhyme categories in Cantonese songs. There are a total of 30 songs with -*ung*, including a membership of 73 different words. With the exception of a few cases where -*ung* interacts with its *rusheng* counterpart -*uk*, its activities are primarily restricted within the group.

(58) gūng 公 yùhng 蓉 gūng 工
múhng 懵 hùhng 雄 dūng 東
túhng 筒 gūng 功 hùhng 紅
tūng 通 sūng 鬆 lùhng 龍
hūng 兇 yùhng 容 hūng 胸
júng 粽 gung 貢 lùhng 籠
chūng 沖 hùhng 熊 fūng 風
tùhng 同 jūng 中 lūng 窿
gūng 攻 chūng 聰

—*Da que yingxiong zhuan* 打雀英雄傳,
Sam Hui, LS: 926 (pre-1980)

(59) nùhng 濃 fūng 風 fùhng 逢
jūng 中 muhng 夢 hūng 空
hùhng 紅 mùhng 濛 nuhng 弄
chùhng 重

—*Xiangsi fengyu zhong* 相思風雨中,
Jacky Cheung and Karen Tong (1992), lyrics by Jian Ning 簡寧

5.3.7. The last nasal final in the Cantonese rhyming system is *-un*, a rather small category with only 15 members. The data show no interactions between *-un* and *-ung*. Although both are transcribed with *-u-*, the two nasal finals are quite dissimilar in vocalic quality. Phonetically, the vowel in *-un* is [u] and that in *-ung* is [ʊ], a distinction that readily explains why they follow different paths in rhyming.

(60) fún 款 buhn 半 huhn 換
pùhn 盆 fūn 歡 múhn 滿
mùhn 門 gún 管 gūn 觀
pun 判 buhn 拌

—*Menli menwai* 門裡門外,
Johnny Yip (1982), lyrics by Cheng Kwok Kong

5.4. *Rusheng yun*

Checked syllables are characterized by their consonantal endings in Chinese: *-p*, *-t*, and *-k*. They are short and abrupt in pronunciation, a phonetic feature that makes them less agreeable to melodious singing. Perhaps, for this reason, they are not often chosen as end words in songs. The data show

14 songs, i.e., 3% of the total collection, with *rusheng* finals, and many of them contain only one stanza or a few lines with checked finals. For example, in the following song, *-ik* appears in a short stanza of four lines:

(61) sēungsām geiyīk 傷心記憶
 muhngléuih ngaatbīk 夢裡壓逼
 bāt séung keuhngyán 不想強忍
 gyunyihm líuh gūjihk 倦厭了孤寂
 —*Buji lianren* 不羈戀人,
 Priscilla Chan 陳慧嫻 (1988), lyrics by Jian Ning

Again, the next song contains one stanza of four lines rhyming in *-aak*.

(62) baahk 白 hāak 克 waahk 劃
 chāak 測
 —*Ai miliu* 愛彌留,
 Tat Ming Pair (1990), lyrics by Chow Yiu Fai 周耀輝

The final *-uk* is an exception, with three songs, relatively long, written exclusively with this rhyme. One of the examples is:

(63) hūk 哭   duhk 獨   chūk 束
 sūk 縮   juhk 逐   fūk 福
 jūk 捉   juhk 續   guhk 局
 jūk 觸   fuhk 服   chūk 促
 —*Shei ming langzi xin* 誰明浪子心,
 Dave Wang (1989), lyrics by Calvin Poon 潘源良

In a 1991 song, *-ok* appears in 9 words that dictate the rhyme scheme of 23 lines:

(64) gok 覺   pok 撲   fok 霍
 mohk 寞   hok 殼   jok 作
 bok 縛   lohk 落   ngohk 愕
 —*Hello, Ganjue* 哈囉感覺,
 Sandy Lam (1991), lyrics by Thomas Chow

In all other cases with *rusheng yun*, cross rhyming is a common phenomenon.

Mixed use of -*it*, -*yut*, and -*ip*

(65) syut 説   gip 溜   git 結
      gip 劫   biht 別   jit 節
      jyut 絕   tyut 脫

—*Wujin qingjie* 無盡情結,
Alan Tam (1992), lyrics by Jolland Chan

Mixed use of -*it*, -*yut*, and -*ik*

(66) giht 傑   miht 滅   dihk 敵
      liht 烈   yuht 月

—*Shujian enchou lu* 書劍恩仇錄,
LS: 915 (pre-1980)

Mixed use of -*aat* and -*aak*

(67) saat 殺   chaak 賊

—*Huanghou dadao* 皇后大道,
Tat Ming Pair (1990), lyrics by Chow Yiu Fai

Mixed use of -*at* and -*ak*

(68) yaht 日   mahk 脈   sāt 失
      maht 物

—*Huajia* 畫家,
George Lam (1980)

A close look at these examples of cross rhyming shows that, in spite of the differences in consonantal endings, the vowels of the rhyme words are either identical or similar in every case. Example (66) seems to be a counter-example. However, the vowels in -*it* [it] and -*yut* [yt] share the same high, front features, and this shared quality, as described above, allows them to rhyme in open syllables (-*i* : -*yu*) as well as in nasal finals (-*in* : -*yun*). In addition, the the cross rhyming of the short [ɪ] in 敵 *dihk* with the longer longer [i] in 傑 *giht*, 滅 *miht*, and 烈 *liht* seems to contradict what we have observed in section 5.3.3, namely that these two vowels do not interact in -*im/-in* and -*ing*. The only explanation we can offer here is that as checked and short syllables, such differences might not be as distinct in singing, and hence negligible.

6. The above comparative study between the rhyming practice and the actual speech habits in contemporary Cantonese songs has unequivoably shown that the two systems are not necessarily accurate or reliable reflections of each other. In contrast to the 53 finals in modern Cantonese, the tabulations from our sample of contemporary songs yield the following 24 rhyme groups.

(1)	-a	(13)	-am, -an, -ang
(2)	-e	(14)	-im, -in, -yun
(3)	-o	(15)	-ing
(4)	-i, -yu, -ei, -eui	(16)	-eng
(5)	-u	(17)	-on, -ong, -eung
(6)	-aai	(18)	-un
(7)	-ai	(19)	-ung
(8)	-oi	(20)	-ip, it, -ik, -yut
(9)	-au	(21)	-uk
(10)	-iu	(22)	-ok
(11)	-ou	(23)	-aat, -aak
(12)	-aam, -aan, -aang	(24)	-at, ak

Or, as listed in the following table:

a	aam, aan, aang	aat, aak
aai	am, an, ang	at, ak
ai		
au		
e		
o	eng	
oi	on, ong, eung	ok
ou		
i, yu, ei, eui	im, in, yun	ip, it, it, yut
iu	ing	
u	un	
	ung	uk

Aside from the missing finals as listed in section 5.1, the reconstructed system exhibits behaviors that are not observed in the actual language. In many cases, rhyming is based upon vocalic identity, i.e., sharing the same vowel, rather than the exact correspondence in the way a *yunmu* is made up of. Furthermore, rhyming happens among finals that are phonetically quite dissimilar. The observations raise a serious question regarding our belief that phonetic identity is the essential and only requirement in rhyming. Could there be other factors involved, factors that would allow rhyming to take place on a non-phonetic basis? If so, what are such factors? Our study of the Cantonese practice provides ample examples that contradict that principle, and we may now take advantage of these "deviations" to reconsider the notion of rhyming and reassess our past practice to rely on rhyming as a means to get to know the sound system of the past.

6.1. The concept of phonetic identity as a working principle for rhyming has undergone different modes of interpretations throughout the long history of Chinese poetics. Identity in sound has always been partial since rhyming does not involve the initial consonants. In other words, of the three components that make up a Chinese syllable, the final and the tone are the only players in the rhyming game. For many centuries, their roles seemed equally important. Not without exceptions, distinctions in tone as well in the finals were strictly observed in early compositions. In medieval China, the dichotomy between level and oblique tones (*ping/ze* 平仄) was enforced not only in rhyming but also in metrical device.[13] Since then, however, tonal requirements were gradually loosened over time. In *ci* 詞 (poetry), the *shang* 上 and *qu* 去 words interacted freely in rhyming. The *qu* 曲 genre further relaxed its rhyming strictness by allowing the *ping* 平 words to participate. Subsequently, all songs enjoy free associations among the three tones.[14] It is generally understood that words with the same final unit form an independent rhyme category inclusive of members of all tonal contours. The *rusheng*, distinctly marked by stop endings, was never included in this general trend of tonal loosening; they have always formed their own separate groups. While suprasegmentally identity has finally been removed as a requirement in rhyming, segmental similarity seems to remain

---

[13] For a detailed discussion of the *ping/ze* dichotomy and its relevance to Chinese poetics, see Ting (1975b).

[14] See Wang (1958) for a description of how traditional rhyme groups have been coalesced in the writing of poems.

an inviolable condition, a condition that underlies the phonological practice of *xilian*. Our Cantonese data, however, illustrate that segmental similarity alone is insufficient to account for many of the rhyming phenomena otherwise inexplicable under the traditional approach.

6.2. Essentially, there are three types of rhyming as observed in our corpus of Cantonese songs.

(1) Syllabic rhyming: Rhyming that adheres to the traditional requirement of segemental identity in *yunmu*. A large percentage of rhyming Cantonese songs falls under this category.

(2) Vocalic rhyming: Rhyming that requires vocalic identity only. The scope of phonetic identification has narrowed from the entire final to the main vowel. Even when their syllabic endings are different or when they belong to various syllabic types, rhyming is possible so long as the words share the same vocalic nucleus. Examples from the Cantonese corpus indicate interactions among three different types of nasal finals. There are also a few cases in which rhyming cuts across the boundaries among open syllables, nasal syllables, and checked syllables.

(3) Historical rhyming: Rhyming that is based upon a historical practice, no longer phonetically accountable in the present-day language. For example, by any stretch of the imagination, phonetic affinity is the least possible or convincing factor responsible for the interaction between *-ong* and *-eung*, or for the cross rhyming between *-i* and *-eui*. Neither pair can be characterized as vocalically grouped for rhyming purposes. Historically, however, rhyming associations between *-ong* and *-eung* and those between *-i* and *-eui* date back to the Song dynasty when the *ci* poetics allowed certain convenient flexibility in rhyming. To what extent these rhyming maneuvers were phonetically motivated remains to be explored. Nonetheless, the maneuvers became standardized in subsequent forms of versification, a tradition which Cantonese songs follow even today. Consequently, choice of rhyme words may be simply by convention and does not require phonetic justification. Unaware of this convention, one might commit an embarrassing blunder by claiming linguistic fusion while the versatility of cross rhyming exists only on paper.

Rhyming in Cantonese songs is a phenomenon that can no longer be adequately explained in traditional terms. The traditional principle of phonetic identity is either too restrictive or simply irrelevant when applied to the multifarious rhyming behaviors in the language. Words rhyme because of shared vowels or for historical reasons. In some compositions, we witness all three types of rhyming at work simultaneously. For example, the following are two songs each containing five or six different rhyming finals.

(69) pòhng 旁　　hòhng 行　　lohng 浪
　　 mohng 望　　gōn 乾　　mohng 望
　　 yèuhng 陽　　chèuhng 長　　seuhng 上
　　 hōi 開　　yeuhng 樣　　sēung 傷
　　 pòhng 旁　　hohng 行　　lohng 浪
　　 seuhng 上　　mohng 望　　ngoi 愛
　　 leuhng 亮　　sōng 桑　　chong 愴
　　 ngóh 我　　sōng 桑　　chong 愴
　　 mòhng 忘　　pòhng 旁　　hòhng 行
　　 lohng 浪　　mohng 望　　gōn 乾
　　 mohng 望　　sēung 傷　　chong 愴
　　 ngóh 我

—*Hei'an de kongjian* 黑暗的空間, Dave Wang (1989), lyrics by Poon Wai Yuen

(70) só 鎖　　bok 膞　　lohk 落
　　 gok 覺　　mohk 漠　　sok 索
　　 sēung 霜　　gon 幹　　yeuhng 樣
　　 johng 狀　　jeuhng 象

—*Feixiang jingjie* 飛翔境界, Jenny Tseng (1986), lyrics by Calvin Poon

The first song has 34 rhyming words: 2 with *-o*, 2 with *-oi*, 2 with *-on*, 20 with *-ong*, and 8 with *-eung*. The second has 11 rhyming words: 1 with *-o*, 1 with *-on*, 1 with *-ong*, 5 with *-ok*, and 3 with *-eung*. In either case, even though the historical rhyming between *-ong* and *-eung* dominates, the vocalic rhyming among *-o*, *-oi*, *-on*, *-ong*, and *-ok* asserts its presence through harmony and resonance. The combination represents a compromise between two systems, a product of both linguistic reality and literary convention. Rhyming in Cantonese songs can be hybrid in nature. Its indiscriminate use can be deceptive in what it tells about the actual language. To continue subscribing to the traditional concept of phonetic identity, there is no alternative but to consider cross rhyming as indicative of various phonological fusions. Few of them represent such actual happenings in the living language.

6.3. Admittedly, to a great extent the rhyming system in our corpus adheres to what we already know about the sounds in Cantonese. The finals in speech are mostly preserved in songs; and, in some cases, the corpus seems to have even captured new developments in the language. For example, as reported at the beginning of this study, some speakers, especially those of the younger generation, tend to pronounce -*ang* as -*an*, a merging that may have explained the cross rhyming between -*ang* and -*an* in Cantonese songs. Develarization has been gaining force in recent years, so much so that it affects not only -*ang* and -*aang*, but also -*eung* [œŋ], thereby possibly adding a new phoneme to the Cantonese vowel system. Unfortunately, this study detects no use of -*eun* [œn] as a rhyme and is therefore unable to confirm the interaction between -*eun* and -*eung*. Nonetheless, in regard to the cross rhyming between -*an* and -*ang* in Cantonese songs, does the phenomenon betray a timely reflection of and a conscientious response to the linguistic innovation? Research into earlier materials proves otherwise. In a collection of Cantonese folk songs published in the early 19th century, mixed rhyming among -*am*, -*an*, and -*ang* was already in operation. In other words, the merger in rhyming predates the actual change in language by more than 160 years. What the folk songs exhibit was, indeed, not so much a linguistic change as it was an early example of rhyming relaxation.

Given this discrepancy between what poetry shows in rhyming and what a language actually owns, I wonder to what extent we can continue to invest our faith in an approach to study an ancient phonological system simply on the basis of rhyming. If the rhyming data of a certain time period demonstrate merger of three nasal finals, could one argue in good faith that the language on which these data were based had indeed lost the three-way distinction? Without evidence from other sources, the claim could be dangerously deceptive, as has been shown in Cantonese.

The same caution should be applied to the use of *xilian* as an approach to reconstructing a sound system of the past. Unlike traditional poetry whose rhyming patterns are clearly prescribed by convention, folk songs are independent, unrestrained, or even sporadic in their use of rhymes. The rhyming schemes vary from one song to another: some choose to use the same rhyme every line throughout the entire composition, some opt for every other line, and some change rhymes every few lines. There are no fixed patterns of rhyming, perhaps for the purpose to enliven a song or to add to its musicality; but the versatile format could cause difficulty in identifying and tracing words to be grouped together by *xilian*. How does one decide which word rhymes with which, and in which line? Phonetic identity is certainly a useful clue. However, as it has been shown that such identity could be reduced to partial affinity in folk song rhyming, how much compromise are we allowed in our efforts to sort out the rhyming words, to establish a rhyming pattern, and to reconstruct a rhyming category? In a song entitled *Xi feng* (LS: 884 [pre-1980]), there are 31 lines, 28 of which rhyme in -*a*. The other three lines end with *yuhk* 肉, *yuhk* 肉, and *faat* 髮. It is obvious that *yuhk* cannot be part of the rhyming scheme. The status of *faat* is ambiguous. Structurally, *faat* belongs to a different syllable type from that of -*a*. Yet, on the other hand, by virtue of its vocalic nucleus, *faat* could belong to the same rhyme group with all the -*a* words. The decision, one way or the other, would be arbitrary. A similar difficulty is found in another song which contains a short stanza with the following end words:

(71) gok 角   lohk 落   gok 覺
      wāan 灣   ngóh 我   wō 渦

—*Chang jie de yijiao* 長街的一角,
Sandy Lam (1986), lyrics by Siu Mei 小美

Excluding *waan*, which is phonetically incompatible with the other words, the sequence can be divided into two groups, the first three with -*ok* and the last two with -*o*. Do they represent two separate rhyme units, or do they form one rhyme sequence with -*o* as the dominating vocal feature? Either treatment would be just as valid. However, by the same token, would it be possible to describe -*ung* and -*ou* in the following song as variants of the same rhyme? After all, the two finals are acoustically quite similar in vocalic resonance.

(72) jūng 中   jung 蹤   duhng 動
      jūng 中   duhng 洞   dúng 懂
      dung 凍   mòuh 無   sou   掃
      tóu   土   lòuh 顧   dōu   刀
      dou   到   sou   訴   jūng 中
      hùhng 紅

—*Xuerou lai dang wushi dao* 血肉來擋武士刀, Johnny Yip (1982), lyrics by Richard Lam

In short, the concept of phonetic affinity is at times quite arbitrary and needs to be handled with discretion when applied to *xilian* tabulation.

7. The language of a Cantonese song often mediates between the literary tradition and the real sounds and words in speech. The inheritance of a literary tradition loom distinctly not only in the use of old rhyming patterns, but also in regard to choice of diction. As noted above, most of the compositions produced over the last ten years or so are highly polished in style. Some lyrics incorporate expressions that exist only in the written language, expressions that would make it difficult to comprehend in singing. They may even create problems for singers, who are not necessarily trained or steeped in the classical language. In one case, a singer mistook the classical character 捋 *lyuht* as 採 *choi*, an embarrassing error of mistaken identity that was recorded in the album. On the other hand, it is also a common practice to intersperse the literary lyrics with regional words and slangs, colloquialisms that are often intelligible only to the natives. Such a stylistic mixture may result in alternative pronunciations of certain words, thereby qualifying them for rhyming in different schemes.[15] One example is 死, the colloquial pronunciation of which is *séi* and the literary reading is *sí*. The following are examples of its dual status in two different rhymes.

---

[15] Dave Wang, *Jiangbuchu de tongku* 講不出的痛苦, lyrics by Albert Leung 林夕 (1990). The word 捋 *lyuht* rhymes in the song with 血 *hyut*, 缺 *kyut,* and 脫 *tyut.*

(73) hei 氣　　　　séi 死　　　　deih 地

—Chuzou 出走,
Danny Summer 夏韶聲 (1991), lyrics by Albert Leung

(74) jí 止　　　jí 子　　　sī 絲
　　 cí 此　　　sí 死　　　yìh 疑
　　 jí 紙　　　chíh 持　　sī 詩
　　 yi 意

—Juedou 決鬥,
Alan Tam (1992), lyrics by Jolland Chan

Although cross rhyming is possible between *-i* and *-ei*, the difference in pronunciation is clearly conditioned by the lyrical choice.

Interactions between Cantonese and Mandarin accounts for some otherwise inexplicable rhyming arrangements. For example, in the following Cantonese song, the expression *muihmuih* 妹妹 rhymes with the words of the *-ei* family simply because the singer switches to Mandarin when he sings *meimei*.

(75) pèih 皮　　　ei 四　　　　 néih 你
　　 mèih 眉　　 bei 臂　　　　pèih 皮
　　 bei 痺　　　say　　　　　 muih (mei) 妹
　　 mēi 尾　　　wait　　　　　hei 戲
　　 kèih 期　　　hei 氣

—Wo de meimei 我的妹妹,
Sam Hui (1986), lyrics by Richard Lam

This song also exhibits another case of rhyming across the language boundary, namely, the inclusion of the English words "say" and "wait." Both carry the diphthong /-ei/ and, hence, the singing goes harmoniously well with all the *-ei* forms in Cantonese and Mandarin.

Bilingual rhyming between Cantonese and English is a common and provocative feature in Hong Kong songs especially in the post-1980 era. Under the reign of the British for more than a hundred years, the Hong Kong language is known for its paradoxical mix of Chinese and English, a hybrid style of speech often referred to as "Chinglish." In all levels of Cantonese discourse, English elements are often found present in one form or another. Hybrid rhyming is both a product and a reflection of this linguistic multiplicity. The following are more examples:

(76) *How will I know?*
　　 Ngoh sām jūng tīm fàahnnóuh.　我心中添煩惱
　　 How will I know?
　　 Ngóh yih gāpgāp tóugou.　　　我已急急禱告
　　　　　　　　　　　　　　　　—*Xinyuan* 心願,
　　　　　　Danny Chan (1986), lyrics by Chen Jiaguo 陳嘉國

(77)　saai　　曬　　　baaih　敗　　　faai　　快
　　　gāai　　街　　　taai　　態　　　waaih　壞
　　　gwaai　怪　　　*high*
　　　daih　　娣　　　láih　　禮　　　fāi　　輝
　　　wai　　慧　　　ngáih　蟻　　　daih　　蒂
　　　tái　　　體　　　daih　　遞　　　gai　　髻
　　　tonight
　　　　　　　　　　　　　　　　—*Tiaowu jie* 跳舞街,
　　　　　　　Priscilla Chan (1986), lyrics by Andrew Lam

In the first example, Cantonese words with *-ou* rhyme with "know." The same rhyme scheme is used in another song where words such as *dou* 到, *lóuh* 老, *nóuh* 惱, *pou* 鋪, *douh* 蹈, *bouh* 步, *louh* 路, *nouh* 怒, and *chōu* 操 all rhyme with "cappuccinos" and "cappuccino" (*One Cappuccino*, Karen Tong [1992], lyrics by Feng Zheng 馮正). The *-s* ending in the first occurrence of "cappuccinos" does not interrupt the rhyme scheme with /-ou/. In fact, as also illustrated in the second example where "tonight" rhymes with *-ai* words, consonantal endings seem to have little impact on the rhyming choice. The next three examples display hybrid rhyming that is conditioned by vocalic quality regardless of syllabic endings.

(78)　*one*　　　　　　bān　　檳　　　yàhn　　人
　　　nàhng　能　　　jahng　贈　　　sām　　心
　　　ngam　　暗　　　gāng　　更　　　hahm　　憾
　　　hàhng　行　　　sām　　深
　　　　　　　　　　　　　　　　—*Ai ni tai shen* 愛你太深,
　　　　　　　　Alam Tam (1983), lyrics by Richard Lam

(79)　gaai　　街　　　maaih　賣　　　wàaih　懷
　　　paai　　派　　　hàaih　鞋　　　*mind*
　　　sunshine
　　　　　　　　　　　　　　　—*Bu zhuangshi de shijie* 不裝飾的世界,
　　　　　　　　Jenny Tseng (1986), lyrics by Richard Lam

(80) fōng   方   gwōng 光   hon   看
      góng   講   fong   放   fōng   芳
      ngóh   我   dō   多   gwo   過
      huó   火   joh   助   doh   惰
      more

—*Ye qingqing* 夜傾情,
Sammi Cheng 鄭秀文 (1992), lyrics by Sandy Cheung Mei Yin 張美賢

In this next example, the song composed in the rhyme of *-ok* concludes with the English phrase: "Oh, My God!"

(81) mohk   寞   hok   殼   lohk   落
      gok   覺   bohk   薄   hohk   學
      pok   撲   bohk   雹   tok   托
      God

—*Jimo sanshi* 寂寞三十
Lowell Lo 盧冠廷 (1986), lyrics by Lou Wing Keng 盧永強

In British pronunciation, "god" carries an *-o-* vowel that is similar in quality to that in the final *-ok*. Since consonantal endings are unimportant, "god" forms a perfect hybrid scheme with the Cantonese forms. However, when listening to the tape, I realized that the singer was rendering the English word with an American accent, namely, that "god" was pronounced with a more open [a]. The difference would have justifiably disqualified it from the rhyming scheme. I do not know which version of "god" the writer had in mind when he composed the lyrics. However, by its positioning at the end of the song, the British -o- would seem a more likely choice so as to bring the rhymed verse to a full conclusion. If this was indeed what the writer wished to achieve, the divergence between the intended reading and the actual performance reveals another interesting, albeit troubling, issue in rhyming in songs. What one sees in writing is not always what one hears in singing. If the lyricist and the singer differ in speech habits, the latter may dismiss or modify the linguistic distinctions that the former possesses, or he/she may introduce phonological features that are not in the lyricist's language. When cross rhyming is detected between *-ong* and *-on* in songs, it is claimed that such a phenomenon is the result of reduced phonetic identity in rhyming and that, in no way it betrays anything happening in the real language. Even if the recorded singing proves that the two finals are strictly kept apart, how can we be sure that the merger is not real for the writer? After all, such a change has been observed in the speech of at least some contemporary speakers. The line between a convention, poetically licensed, and an actual sound change in language is indeed difficult to draw.

When dealing with the present corpus of Cantonese songs, I was able to check rhyming patterns with native informants. I was able to refer to the actual phonological system of modern-day Cantonese when analyzing and explaining unusual rhyming behaviors. Such privileges, however, are not always readily available to those who direct their investigations to an ancient language. Rhymed writings are useful sources of information, but only when utilized with care and discretion. I have shown through this study of Cantonese songs some of the inadequacies of the traditional *xilian* approach in diachronic investigation. More importantly, I hope that by documenting the differences between the two systems now, it will prevent any attempt in the future to construe rhyming anomalies as indications of new changes in the current sound system.

References

Bauer, Robert S. 1979. "Alveolarization in Cantonese: A Case of Lexical Diffusion." *Journal of Chinese Linguistics*, 7.1: 132–141.

Dong Tonghe 董同龢. 1968. *Hanyu yinyunxue yanjiu* 漢語音韻學研究. Taiwan: Guangwen Books.

Handel, Zev J. 1992. "Notes on Consonantal Cluster Endings in Archaic Chinese." MA thesis, Department of East Asian Languages, University of California, Berkeley.

Li, Paul Jen-kuei 李壬癸. 1986. "Rhyming and Phonemic Contrast in Southern Min." *The Bulletin of the Institute of History and Philology*, 57.3: 439–461.

Luo Changpei 羅常培, and Zhou Zumo 周祖謨. 1958. *Han Wei Jin Nanbeichao yunbu yanbian yanjiu* 漢魏晉南北朝韻部演變研究. Beijing: Kexue chubanshe 科學出版社.

Ting Pang-hsin 丁邦新. 1975a. *Chinese Phonolgy of the Wei-Chin Period: Reconstruction of the Finals as Reflected in Poetry* 魏晉音韻研究. Taiwan: Institute of History and Philology, Academia Sinica.

———. 1975b. "A New Interpretation of the Even and Oblique Tones." *The Bulletin of the Institute of History and Philology*, 47.1: 1–15.

Wang Li 王力. 1958. *Hanyu shilüxue* 漢語詩律學. Shanghai: Xinhua Books.

This article originally appeared in *The Journal of Chinese Linguistics*, 24.1 (1996): 1–54.

Completing the Completive: Reconstructing Early Cantonese Grammar

285 唨 1.去唨。 2.食唨, 3.熄唨, 4.開唨。 5.曬唨
Chóh 唨, 7.寶唨。 8.叫唨。 9.伴唨, 10.攞唨.
今朝去唨(咯)。 12.我哋食唨飯(咯)。 13.佢
唨燈(咯)。 14.叫唨挺唔曾呢? 15.火船開唨㗎
16.我叫佢曬唨衣服咯。 17.使唨咁多*銀都唔得
18.昨日寶唨七百銀。 19.頭先我伴唨*銀佢去攞
咯)。 20.攞啊鐵釘㬹嚟未呀?

86 嘵 1.㗎嘵。 2.過嘵。 3.買嘵。 4.寫嘵。 5.洗嘵,
Hiu 閂嘵。 7.用嘵。 8.釘嘵。 9.㨁嘵。 10.番嘵,
隻艇㗎嘵咯。 12.日子過嘵咯、 13.你買嘵糖菓唔
呢? 14.你寫嘵幾多字呢? 15.洗嘵地唔曾呀? 1
閂嘵門至好去瞓呀。 17.我用嘵你幾塊板牐
釘嘵兩部書咯、 19.我㨁嘵幾十嚿磚嚟你咯。 18.
幾日佢番嘵嚟(咯)。 20

Abstract: Corresponding to the perfective *liuh* 了 in Mandarin, Cantonese has its distinct verbal suffix *jo* 咗 to mark completion of an action. In early Cantonese, however, there were two markers, *hiu* 曉 and *jo* 咗, often interchangeable in use as evidenced in colloquial writings prepared by missionaries and language pedagogues in the 19th and early 20th centuries. This article conducts a statistical study of six titles compiled between 1841 and 1947, and compare their relative prevalence in use throughout the years. It also looks into the use of changed tone to mark the perfective, a morphophonemic process that may in part account for the eventual disappearance of *hiu* in the 1930s. The article concludes with a discussion of the origins of the two suffixes, each following its own path of historical derivation.

Keywords: perfective; early Cantonese; *hiu* 曉; *jo* 咗; *liuh* 了; changed tone

1. Introduction

While dialectology has always been an important area of investigation in Chinese linguistics, diachronic inquiry has thus far focused primarily on the use of dialectal materials to reconstruct ancient sound systems. Studies of dialectal grammar with a historical perspective have not been particularly productive, a situation that is due not so much to lack of interest as to shortage of data. For centuries, the classical language was the base for all major forms of writing, a tradition that supplies little record of the grammatical evolution in the spoken language. Granted that there was an emerging trend for composing in the vernacular since the Tang dynasty (618–907), the majority of such works were written in Mandarin of one form or another.

The earliest extant work in Cantonese is a collection of folksongs that dates to the early 19th century.[1] The songs, however, were written mostly in a composite style of mixing the vernacular with classical, and the lyrics do not have much to reveal about the underlying grammatical operations of the spoken language. In fact, it was not until the middle of the 20th century that a large quantity of Cantonese writings began to appear, especially in newspapers that catered to a native readership in Hong Kong. Interest in Cantonese grammar as a linguistic discipline began in the 1960s and studies since then have been essentially restricted to synchronic analyses of the contemporary language.[2]

1.1. Linguistic Study of Cantonese

Long before it became the object of academic scrutiny, Cantonese had been the focus of pedagogical attention. When the Manchu government opened Canton to the West for trading in the early 1800s, and especially

---

[1] Entitled *Yuht-au* (*Yue'ou* 粵謳), the collection includes close to a hundred love songs composed by Jiu Jiyung (Zhao Ziyong 招子庸) in 1828. See Peter Morris's introduction to his 1992 translation, *Cantonese Love Songs: An English Translation of Jiu Ji-yung's Cantonese Songs of the Early 19th Century* (Hong Kong: Hong Kong University Press).

[2] See Cheng (1993) for a list of works on the Cantonese language published since 1900.

after Hong Kong was ceded to the British in 1842, there was a growing demand for Cantonese language instruction to meet the urgent needs of Western officials, businessmen, and missionaries who came to Canton and Hong Kong to pursue their activities. To interact with the locals, they had to learn how to converse in their local language. One of the first textbooks, compiled in 1841, was *Chinese Chrestomathy in the Canton Dialect*. In almost seven hundred pages, this language manual covered a wide range of linguistic and cultural topics written mostly in colloquial Cantonese. A series of other primers followed suit in subsequent years, making a conscientious effort to update the language and to introduce subject matters more relevant to the time. *How to Speak Cantonese: Fifty Conversations in Cantonese Colloquial* went through four printings from 1889 to 1912, each edition carefully revised by the author, J. Dyer Ball. Even as late as the 1970s, pedagogical endeavor continued with new materials prepared for latecomers in foreign service, business sectors, and churches of various Christian denominations. In addition, as Canton and Hong Kong grew in economic prosperity, many traveling merchants came from neighboring cities and provinces to make a living. As a result, special texts were written in the 1930s to teach Cantonese to dialect speakers. In 1947, Y. R. Chao published his *Cantonese Primer*, which marked the beginning of textbook compilation for American college students learning Cantonese. All in all, the pool of teaching materials has been vast in number and varied in both pragmatic concerns and pedagogical devices. Taken together, they provide a most valuable source of colloquial data documenting the changes that the language underwent over a span of a hundred and fifty years. Linguistic significance aside, it is also interesting to muse upon the contents of the texts: who is being represented and what is being addressed in the dialogues. While in the 1841 *Chinese Chrestomathy* the Chinese were often represented as figures of low social standing, such as coolies and peddlers, submissive to their foreign masters, in the Yale textbooks of the 1960s they were portrayed as successful professionals equal in status to their American friends. A careful comparison of various pedagogical series will indeed allow us to reconstruct a socio-political landscape that unfolds from the colonial past to the capitalist present.

Admittedly, the use of pedagogical materials for linguistic analysis has its shortcomings. As teaching materials in general are prescriptive by design and tend to use simple or simplified sentences, especially in beginning chapters, the paradigms do not always represent or reflect the complex operations of the actual language. In fact, a cursory look at some of the elementary texts prepared either then or now makes one wonder if a native ever speaks in such a strangely curt and paradigmatic fashion. On the other hand, as Cantonese textbooks are primarily written in romanization of one kind or another, the transcriptions preserve the colloquial flavor otherwise impossible to achieve in the regular writing system. Many dialectal expressions lack appropriate character representations, and certain morphological changes are characterized by tonal modification. By virtue of its phonetic make-up, a romanized text is more readily equipped to record and reflect these features than a character version. In this regard, the Cantonese pedagogical materials are richly informative.[3]

1.2. Sources Used for This Study

In her article entitled "The Lexicon in Syntactic Change: Lexical Diffusion in Chinese Syntax," Yue-Hashimoto utilizes pedagogical materials to reconstruct patterns of lexical diffusion in the emergence of the V-neg-V question form in Cantonese (1993b: 232–239), a project that readily attests to the usefulness of this corpus of data hitherto little known to most linguists. The present study continues the linguistic inquiry by focusing on one particular grammatical topic, namely the completive or perfective aspect. The sources examined are described below, in chronological order according to dates of publication. From here on, they will be referred to by the abbreviations given in parentheses. All Chinese names and titles

---

[3] For example, Lam (1987) refers to works by Ball and others in his investigation of the phonological changes in Macau Cantonese during the last hundred years.

are romanized according to Cantonese pronunciation following the Yale system; Mandarin readings are given in parentheses.

1841 (CC)

Bridgman, E. C. *Chinese Chrestomathy in the Canton Dialect*. 693 pages. Seventeen chapters, each covering a specific cultural topic such as kindred relations, government affairs, and protocols in the commercial world. The dialogues are mostly in the colloquial language, but are at times quite formal in style. The book also includes long passages from the classics as part of the cultural education. The pronunciations as reflected in the romanization are slightly different from those in the present. For example, 你 is *ni* and 去 is *hü*. The book includes a useful 89-page vocabulary index.

1888 (PB)

Stedman, T. L., and K. P. Lee 李攀龍. *A Chinese and English Phrase Book in the Canton Dialect*. 186 pages. Forty-one lessons on selected subjects of everyday use. Originally conceived as a project for "furnishing to the Chinese, residing in (the US), the means of acquiring an elementary knowledge of English," the book bears the Chinese title 英語不求人 *Yingyuh bat kauh yahn* (*Yingyu bu qiu ren*), highlighting its purpose of providing self-taught English. However, the authors made it also serviceable to English speakers who "desired to acquire some knowledge of Chinese." Hence, each text is given in both languages, on opposing pages, and the pronunciation of each word in English is indicated in Chinese, and that of Chinese in Roman characters.

1908 (CME)

Ball, J. Dyer. *The Cantonese Made Easy Vocabulary*. 3rd edition. Preface to the 1st edition not dated. Preface to the 2nd edition: 1892. 294 pages. Alphabetically arranged according to English entries, the dictionary provides equivalent words and phrases in Cantonese, in both characters and romanization. Explanatory notes contain useful information on word usages with plentiful illustrations.

1912 (HSC)

Ball, J. Dyer. *How to Speak Cantonese: Fifty Conversations in Cantonese Colloquial.* 4th edition. 1st edition preface: 1889. 2nd edition: 1902. 3rd edition: 1904. 229 pages. The author intends the conversations to be lifelike in language and engaging in subject matter. Each text is given in both characters and romanization, accompanied by a literal translation and a free rendition. The revised edition makes a particular effort to correctly mark all variant tones.

1927 (BC)

Wisner, O. F. *Beginning Cantonese (Rewritten)*, Part One. Incomplete. 280 pages. A dictionary of common Cantonese usages, BC lists 975 words, each of which is appended with many illustrations. The words are given in characters and English spelling. Sample sentences, however, are written in characters only. Changed tones are indicated by diacritical marks. The dictionary includes a 14-page introduction on sounds and grammar.

1930s (FL)

Taahm Gwaikeuhng (Tan Jiqiang) 譚季強. *Fanleuih tunghahng Gwongjauwah jinaahm* (*Fenlei tongxing Guangzhouhua zhinan*) 分類通行廣州話指南 (A classified guide to the Cantonese language). 55 pages. A reference to the 1932 Japanese occupation of Manchuria dates the work tentatively to the 1930s. The language guide includes a variety of colloquial conversations and short stories of general interest. It also includes a Cantonese syllabary at the end. The author, Taahm Gwaikeuhng of the Punyuh (Panyu 番禺) district in the Pearl River Delta, prepared the manual for speakers of other dialects anxious to learn standard Cantonese, the lingua franca of the city of Canton.

1935 (ZY)

Louh Jifohng (Lu Zifang) 盧子防. *Jyuyam Gwongjauyuh* (*Zhuyin Guangzhouyu*) 注音廣州語 (Cantonese with phonetic notations). 87 pages. Postface at Canton in 1935. Catering to speakers of the Min dialect, the textbook provides dialogues, stories, and short essays, all written in colloquial Cantonese. It also includes lists of common dialectal words and expressions. Cantonese pronunciation is marked with the national phonetic letters system 注音符號.

1941 (FYC)

O'Melia, Thomas A., M. M. *First Year Cantonese*. 2nd edition. 306 pages. 1st edition preface dated 1938. A Catholic priest teaching in Hong Kong, O'Melia compiled the reader for use by Cantonese-speaking missionaries, emphasizing both the colloquial aspect of the language and the religious concerns of the church. In forty-two lessons, the manual teaches different grammatical topics and provides extensive drills for each pattern.

1947 (CP)

Chao, Y. R. 趙元任. *Cantonese Primer*. 242 pages. A textbook that grew out of a summer Cantonese course Chao taught at Harvard in 1942, *Cantonese Primer* provided the first systematic analysis of Cantonese, a base on which he later produced *Mandarin Primer* (1948). Using his own transcription that builds tones into the spelling, Chao writes twenty-four lessons of amusing stories and engaging conversations. Not always graded in terms of language difficulty, the lessons are richly annotated with grammatical explanations.

The above materials cover a period of more than a hundred years with a concentration on the first three decades of the 20th century. For the 19th century, I have only two titles: Bridgman's CC of 1841, and Stedman and Lee's PB of 1888. However, the two books by Ball, CME (1908) and HSC (1912), both came out in their first editions in 1892 and 1889 respectively, and may therefore be considered as representing the language in transition between the two centuries. If their early editions ever become available, it would be interesting and important to examine how the differences therein inform the grammatical modification of the language. I did not include any materials from beyond the 1950s, primarily because I grew up speaking the dialect in the post-war period.

2. The Perfective Aspect

Much has been written on the perfective or completive aspect in standard Cantonese (e.g., Cheung 1972: 142–156; Gao 1980: 43–60; Yue-Hashimoto 1993a: 69–87; Matthews and Yip 1994: 204–205). The marker is a post-verbal *jo* 咗, which disappears in a negative sentence with the negative marker *mh* 唔 changing to *meih* 未. The transformation is a pattern that finds its parallel to the use of *le* 了 in Mandarin. In the early pedagogical materials as listed above, there are two perfective markers, *jo* and *hiu*, the latter of which seems to have become obsolete after the 1930s. The following are examples of both markers and some observations of their general behaviors.[4]

2.1. The Perfective *Jo*

(1) 打阻一點未呀？ (CME: 248)
Da**jo** yatdim meih a?
Has it struck one o'clock?

(2) 嚟咗……唔曾嚟。 (CME: 37)
Laih**jo** ... Mhchahng laih.
Has come ... Has not come.

(3) 講咗唔使再講，你一直講落去喇。 (HSC: 120)
Gong**jo** mhsai joi gong, neih yatjihk gonglohkheui la.
After saying it, there is no need for repeating. Go straight on.

(4) 我昨晚聯咗兩條褲咯。 (BC: 178)
Ngoh johkmaahm lyuhn**jo** leuhngtiuh fu lok.
I sewed two pairs of pants last night.

(5) 一幅畫好地地，俾佢撕爛左。 (FL: 30)
Yatfuk wa houdeihdeih, bei keuih silaahn**jo**.
It's such a good picture and he tore it up.

---

[4] As the pedagogical materials utilize a variety of romanization systems, an effort is made in this article to standardize all transcriptions by following the Yale system. If the original spelling represents a different pronunciation of any significance, the difference will be retained in the Yale transcription. Please note that tones are not included in the spelling.

(6) 佢既仔去咗花旗好耐，冇信嚟，佢心掛掛咯。 (ZY: 39)
Keuih ge jai heui**jo** Fakeih hou noih, mouh seun laih, keuih samgwagwa lok.
It's been long since his son went to the States and he still hasn't written. He is worried.

(7) 佢整壞咗我嘅顯微鏡。我而家睇唔得見啲嘢。 (FYC: 289)
Keuih jingwaaih**jo** ngoh ge hinmeihgeng. Ngoh yihga taimhdakgin di yeh.
He has tampered with my microscope and put it out of order. Now I cannot see the things.

(8) 你嘅中文重未曾學得識⋯⋯到你學識咗個陣時呀⋯⋯ (CP: 126)
Neih ge Jungmahn juhng meihchahng hohk-dak-sik . . . douh neih hohksik**jo** gojahnsih ah . . .
You have not yet thoroughly learned your Chinese . . . by the time you have learned it . . .

The first striking feature about the occurrences of *jo* in these early materials is its lack of consistent graphic representation. It is written variously in different materials as 咗, 阻, 咀, 左, and 咗, variations that sometimes even appear in the same text and on the same page. With the exception of 咀, the characters are all pronounced as *jo*, a homophony that accounts for their interchangeability. Homophony is of course one of the underlying principles for creating dialectal or colloquial characters, a process that is often signified by the inclusion of a mouth radical (口) on the left side of the new graphs. On the other hand, 咀 is normally pronounced as *jeui* and is here an apparent case of borrowing on the basis of graphic similarity to 咗. The relation or derivation clearly indicates that 咗 was an earlier representation than 咀. The characters 阻, 咗, and 咀 all appeared in pre-1930 materials, and 咀 was restricted to the 1908 CME text. *Beginning Cantonese* of 1927 displayed the earliest and infrequent use of 左, but the predominant form was 咗. Beyond the 1930s, however, the former gradually gained prominence, and since the 1970s the modified form 咗 has become the sole representation.

Despite graphic dissimilarity, the grammatical use of *jo* in pre-1950 writings displays no difference from its current behaviors. The marker is placed immediately after the verb it qualifies; it precedes the object, but comes behind a verb-complement unit as in (5) and (7). Its corresponding negative is *mhchahng* 唔曾 + V or *meih(chahng)* 未曾 + V, without *jo*, as in examples (2) and (8). The interrogative is formed with V + *jo* followed by its negative, as in example (1). In the grammatical notes of the 1941 *First Year Cantonese*, it was noted that *jo* was a "mere sign of the past" (p. 262), a grammatical characterization that has been subsequently revised. For example, Chao in his 1947 *Cantonese Primer* describes *jo* as expressing either completion or past time (p. 40). Example (8), cited from CP, demonstrates the use of *jo* as an aspectual marker rather than an indicator of tense.

2.2. The Perfective *Hiu*

(9) 我嘅鏢壞咻，同我整好佢。 (PB: 159)
Ngoh ge biu waaih**heu**, tuhng ngoh jing hou keuih.
My watch is out of order, please repair it for me.

(10) 出世就盲曉眼。 (CME: 18)
cheut sai jauh maahng**hiu** ngaahn.
to be blind from birth.

(11) 我叫人做乜嘢，佢就要做咯，唔係我即刻辭曉佢咯。 (HSC: 138)
Ngoh giu yahn jouh matyeh, keuih jauh yiu jouh lok. Mhhaih, ngoh jikhak chih**hiu** keuih lok.
If I tell anyone to do anything, he does it; if not, I dismiss him at once.

(12) 我打爛曉個花樽呀。 (BC: 180)
Ngoh dalaahn**hiu** go fajeun a.
I have broken the vase.

(13) 淋曉花未啊？……未淋。 (BC: 113)
Lahm**hiu** fa meih a? ... Meih lahm.
Have you watered the flowers? ... I haven't.

(14) 你收曉工銀唔曾呢？ (BC: 103)
Neih sau**hiu** gungngahn mhchahng ni?
Have you received the payment for the work?

(15) 一連落曉幾日雨，總唔出得街。 (FL: 6)
Yatlihn lohk**hiu** geiyaht yuh, juhng mhcheutdakgaai.
It's been raining continuously for a few days, and we still can't go out.

(16) 多煩你話聲過佢知，我去嘵澳門之後，啲信件就未再寄嚟　　(ZY: 46)
呢處咯。
Dofaahn neih wah seng keuih ji, ngoh heui**hiu** Oumuhn jihouh, di seungin jauh meih joih gei laih nisyu lok.
Please tell him not to send any mail here after I have moved to Macau.

Hiu exhibits exactly the same behavioral patterns as *jo* does, occupying a post-verbal position, appearing after a verb-complement unit as in example (12), and forming its negative and interrogative with *meih(chahng)* or *mhchahng* as in examples (13) and (14). Its function to mark completion of an action is clear from examples (11) and (16). The two markers are in fact sometimes used interchangeably in the same text as the following examples illustrate:

(17) 你淋嘵呢啲花未呢？我今朝淋阻咯。　　(HSC: 96)
Neih lahm**hiu** nidi fa meih ni? Ngoh gamjiu lahm**jo** lok.
Have you watered these flowers? I watered them this morning.

(18) 揼嘵個啲字紙落火爐喇⋯⋯個的有用嘅物件就揼咽佢喇。　　(BC: 140)
Wing**hiu** godi jihji lohk folouh la. . . . Godi mouhyuhng ge mahtgin jauh wing**jo** keuih la.
Throw the scratch paper into the burner. . . . Throw out those things that are of no use.

(19) 鎮邦街燒咗一櫥，連阜安街棉安街都燒嘵好多。　　(FL: 11)
Janbonggaai siu**jo** yatgyuht, lihn Fauhongaai Mihnongaai dou siu**hiu** hou do.
A section of Janbong Street was burnt down, and even Fauhon Street and Mihnon Street suffered much loss in the fire.

Unlike *jo* whose character representation has been modified time and again, *hiu* has been regularly written as a dialectal character marked with the mouth radical. In the 1888 *Phrase Book in the Canton Dialect*, however, the perfective marker is rendered as 咻 in character and as *heu* in pronunciation. See example (9). Though limited to only one text, the discrepancies are important to our speculation on the origin of the marker. The character is made up of two components: 口, the dialectal indicator, and 休. The primary meaning of 休 is "to stop or cease," a reading that readily qualifies the word to take on the grammatical notion of perfection. Extension from a verbal usage to marking an aspect is a process of grammaticalization not uncommon in language, and the Mandarin *le* 了 is a prominent example. The use of 休 to mark completion has been documented in the literature.[5]

However, in order to claim 休 as the origin of *hiu*, we have to account for the phonological relationship between the two forms or to argue that one form was derived from the other. The modern pronunciation for 休 is *yau*, which is hardly close to *hiu* or *heu*. In fact, the lack of phonetic similarity makes one wonder why the graph 休 was included in the dialectal character if not for a semantic reason. However, in many of the dialects around the Pearl River Delta, and especially in the area known as the Four Districts (Seiyap [Siyi] 四邑), the word 休 carries a distinctive *h*-initial. For example,

Toihsaan (Taishan 台山)	*hiu*33
Hoipihng (Kaiping 開平)	*heu*33
Yanpihng (Enping 恩平)	*hei*33
Sanwuih (Xinhui 新會)	*haeu*33[6]

Historically, in fact, 休 began with an *h*-. If our suspicion is correct, then what we witness in the use of *hiu* in standard Cantonese represents either a borrowing from the neighboring dialects or a linguistic process that has preserved the ancient pronunciation in a particular lexical item. Given the great segmental similarity, the hypothesis of linguistic borrowing is highly attractive except for one point. Tonally, the Cantonese *hiu* and the Seiyap equivalents are different. Even though they all belong to the *yinping* 陰平 category, the former is high-falling in value and the latter forms are all mid-level. If the Cantonese speaker were to borrow *hiu*33 from their Toihsaan (Taishan) neighbors to mark the perfective, it is not likely that they would consciously or conscientiously adjust the tonal value so as to match the tonal category. Besides, the mid-level tone 33 already exists in Cantonese. Had our texts displayed a mid-level *hiu*, the inter-dialectal borrowing would have been evident. However, precisely

---

[5] The use of 休 in the vernacular language is often compared to that of 罷, meaning "to stop." See Kosaka (1992), pp. 443–444.

[6] See Zhan and Cheung (1987), p. 167.

because of the identity in tonal category but not in tonal value, it is apparent that Cantonese and the Seiyap dialects share the same 休 both in pronunciation and in writing. Historically, while the regular 休 and other members of the same ancient *h*-initial class have shed the initial consonant in Cantonese, the perfective marker alone retains the fricative feature. The adding of the mouth radical to the character highlights that modification in pronunciation, a pattern which we also observe among other dialectal characters in early Cantonese materials. (One example is the new character 噲 *wuih*, which is kept distinct from the regular 會 *wuih*, for the meaning "to know how to.") However, because of the mismatch between the regular reading *yau* for 休 and the colloquial pronunciation *hiu* of 咻, which the natives must have found unsatisfactory, a new character was subsequently constructed: 嘵, a coinage evidently modeled after 曉, which is indeed pronounced as *hiu*,[7] sharing the same syllabic make-up.

2.3. Relationship between *Hiu* and *Jo*

The frequent interchange in use between *hiu* and *jo* as observed in the previous section was a synchronic phenomenon restricted to the period between the 1900s and the 1940s. According to our data, *hiu* was the only marker used before the 1900s, and *jo* has eventually become the sole representative since the 1940s. Historically, therefore, a displacement process was at work. The statistics in Table 1 pertain to the use of both markers in our corpus of six titles. Because the works vary in size and nature, their uses of the perfective differ drastically in frequency count. Hence, the actual numbers of occurrences are not necessarily as revealing as the contrast in percentage between *hiu* and *jo*.

The statistics of appearance clearly describe a case of competition between two linguistic items over a rather brief period of sixty years. If our data is representative of the actual historical development, *jo* did not come into the Cantonese aspectual system until the turn of the century; but, once introduced, it gained increasing momentum in the following thirty

---

[7] The coinage is, of course, to be distinguished from the character 嘵, also pronounced as *hiu*, meaning "querulous; a cry." The word appears in certain literary expressions only.

years. It competed rigorously with *hiu*, which had been the dominant form until then.

	Verb + *hiu*	Verb + *jo*
PB 1888	5 (100%)	0 (0%)
CME 1908	21 (68%)	10 (32%)
HSC 1912	8 (29%)	20 (71%)
BC 1927	152 (80%)	38 (20%)
FL 1930s	23 (49%)	24 (51%)
ZY 1935	6 (9%)	62 (91%)

Table 1

In *Beginning Cantonese*, a 1927 handbook of contemporary Cantonese usage, both *hiu* and *jo* were listed as separate entries, each containing twenty sample sentences or phrases; however, in the rest of the book where illustrations were given to show the actual use of the verbs, *hiu* was chosen as the primary perfective marker. The 1930s was a critical period when *jo* accelerated in usage, at first sharing prevalence with *hiu*, but ultimately replacing it. There was not even one single occurrence of *hiu* in the 1941 publication of *First Year Cantonese*. Neither was there any mention of it in Y. R. Chao's 1947 *Cantonese Primer*, a book that contains the first comprehensive account of Cantonese grammar ever written. HSC of 1912 seems to pose an anomaly as it displays a ratio (29% : 71%) that reverses what we observe in the works both before (68% : 32% in CME) and after it (80% : 20% in BC). The deviation may be due to a variety of factors, including the particularly infrequent use of the perfective in HSC, but we will return to this puzzling contradiction in the next section for another plausible explanation.

2.4. Tonal Modification

Besides the use of a verbal suffix, Cantonese may also modify the tone of a verb to mark the perfective aspect. In other words, instead of saying V + *jo*, one may cast the verb itself in a special tonal mode and forego the suffix. There are two modified tone patterns, both applied to single syllable verbs only. For a verb whose original tone is either high-falling or high-level, the modified tone is high-level, i.e., 55; for a verb with any other tone, the modified form is invariably a high-rising 35.

V [+H] → V [55]
V [-H] → V [35]

In either case, the pronunciation is slightly extended beyond the normal length. Though no longer a prevalent phenomenon among the younger generations, the practice has been reported in the literature and may still be observed among speakers in their forties or above (see Cheung 1972: 144–145). It has been the belief among linguists that the modified syllable with a high-rising tone is a phonetic fusion of the verb and the following marker *jo*. While the verb keeps its segmental form, it assumes the tonal representation of *jo*, which is originally high-rising in contour:

V + *jo* [35] → V [35]

The slight lengthening in pronunciation indicates the preempting of a following syllable. The hypothesis is theoretically provocative and empirically plausible in that it represents a morphophonemic process which is not uncommon in Cantonese. However, it fails to take into consideration the high tone syllables which maintain a high-level 55 contour rather than the high-rising 35 manifestation after the fusion. The discrepancy prompts us to look elsewhere for a better explanation. The historical inquiry of materials from the last hundred years may readily offer another possibility. Could *hiu* be the catalyst responsible for the changed tone?

The romanized materials in our data, namely CME (1908), HSC (1912), and BC (1927), contain a fairly large number of cases with changed tone marking for the perfective. The following are some examples to illustrate the contrast between a verb with its regular tone and a verb with changed tone. The latter is marked with an asterisk after the syllable.

(20a) 嚟未？ (CME: 37)
Lai* (35) meih?
Has he come?

(20b) 唔曾嚟。
Mhchahng**laih**(53).
He has not come.

(20c) 嚟咯。
Lai*(35) lok.
I have come.

(21a) 喏，咕哩，食飯喇嗎？ (HSC: 84)
Nah, gulei, **sik***(35) faahn la ma?
Now, coolies, have you had your dinner?

(21b) 食囉，唔該吖。
Sik*(35) lo, mhgoi a.
Yes, we have, thank you.

(21c) 好囉。食飽飯未呢？要去好遠路呀。
Hou lo. **Sihk**baau meih ni? Yiu heui hou yuhn louh a.
That is well. Have you had a hearty meal? I want to go a long way.

In both cases, the changed tone is high-rising and its function, as can be inferred from the original translations, is obvious. In HSC, the changed tone is specifically defined as a "sign of past time" (p. 7). The following is an example of the changed tone in high-level.

(22) 窗門開呢，就俾呢張紙過裡頭啲人睇。佢就交信出嚟俾你。一交信過你快趣的翻上嚟至得。 (HSC: 101)
Cheungmun hoi ni, jauh bei nijeung ji gwo leuihtauh godi yahn tai. Keuih jauh **gaau**(53) seun cheut laih bei neih. Yat **gaau***(55) seun gwo neih, neih faaicheuidi faanseuhnglaih jidak.
When the windows are opened you show this paper to the people inside, and they will hand you the letters. As soon as they are handed to you, you must come up quickly.

(23a) 洗衣服佬擰衫翻嚟唔曾呢？ (HSC: 159)
Saiyifuhklou ning saam faanlaih mhchahng ni?
Has the washerman brought the clothes in yet?

(23b) 交咯。
Gaau*(55) lok.
He has.

Completing the Completive | 91

Example (22) provides a good context to demonstrate the semantic difference between *gaau* (to hand) and *gaau** (to [have] be[en] handed). The author again clarifies the use of the changed tone by remarking: "The variant upper even tone shows the past tense" (p. 159). Grammatically misleading as it may be since the variant tone in (22) signifies completion rather than past action, the remark does explicitly note the phenomenon of changed tone and its pertinent morphophonemic function.

Unlike the phenomenon in the later stage of development where the verb and its suffix are necessarily fused into one syllable, the early materials exhibit cases in which the suffix is kept together with the changed tone verb. To wit,

(24a) 冇曉 (CME: 14)
mouh(13) **hiu**
is not (i.e., dead)

(24b) 冇曉咯 (CME: 84)
mou*(35) **hiu** lok
gone (gone out of existence)

(25a) 大曉 (CME: 17)
daaih(22) **hiu**
got big

(25b) 大曉 (CME: 88)
daai*(35) **hiu**
grown up

(26a) 去曉 (CME: 84)
heui(33) **hiu**
gone

(26b) 去曉 (HSC: 7)
heui*(35) **hiu**
gone

(26c) 去咯 (BC: 11)
heui*(35) lok
gone

(27a) 唉吔，有一隻檯腳鬆曉略，唔做得咯。 (HSC: 187)
Aiya, yauh yatjek toigeuk sung*(55) **hiu** lok. Mhjoukdak lo.
Oh, one of the feet is loose. That will not do.

(27b) 一隻腳鬆咩？唉吔，係咯。
Yatjek geuk sung(53) me? Aiya, haih lok.
One of the legs is loose, is it? Dear me, so it is.

(28) 有一日，我行街，喺路邊執倒一對刀，係賊佬嘅。佢怕差捉佢，噉就抷曉嘅。 (HSC: 95)
Yauh yat yaht ngoh haahng gaai, hai louhbin japdou yatdeui dou, haih chaahklou ge. Keuih pa chaai juk keuih, gam jauh wing*(55) **hiu** ge.
I picked up a pair of daggers at the side of the road one day when I was out for a walk. They had been thrown away by thieves, who were afraid of being arrested.

Examples (24) to (26) are cases with a high-rising changed tone, and examples (27) to (28) with a high-level changed tone. Even though the number of occurrences is small, the fact that the perfective suffix is retained together with the changed tone in these early materials indicate that this is probably an intermediary stage in the development of a fused form. In other words, the aspectual morphophonemic process may be charted as follows:

Stage 1: V + suffix
Stage 2: V* + suffix
Stage 3: V*

While the data display an abundance of examples of both stage 1 and stage 3, cases of stage 2 number only 5 in our total corpus. The scarcity could be due to the fact that some pedagogical materials are prepared exclusively in Chinese characters, thereby leaving no trace of any change in tone height or contour. In any case, what stage 2 represents is a case of linguistic redundancy, and its quick exit is phonologically both justifiable and practical.

Between the two aspect markers, only *hiu* is found to appear in stage 2. Although *jo* is emerging as a competitive candidate for the perfective function, there is no example where it accompanies a changed tone verb. It seems, therefore, if the stages above represent a natural process of development resulting in the fusion of two syllables, *hiu* is the only marker that displays a gradual reduction from a full form to a tonal shading on the preceding syllable. As a matter of fact, *hiu* provides a better explanation for the results of changed tone.

As marked everywhere in our romanized materials, *hiu* is a high tone syllable, either high-level or high-falling in contour. When the morphophonemic process begins with changing the tone of the verb, it identifies the high tone of the following *hiu* as the end point of the new tone contour. If the original verb is high-falling in tone, the changed tone is from high to high, hence a high-level tone. If the original verb contains a non-high tone, the result glides upward from non-high towards the targeted high, yielding a high-rising contour.

V [+H] + hiu [+H] → V 55 ˥
V [-H] + hiu [+H] → V 35 ˥

Example (27) is an illustration of the change from *sung*53 to *sung**55. Although we do not have an example of *wing*53 contrasting with *wing**55 in (28), the special diacritic marking in the text clearly indicates that this is a case of changed tone.[8] Examples (24) to (26) are cases of high-rising as a result of tonal fusion. Example (24) shows an original low-rising changing to high-rising, an adjustment in height for distinction.[9] The data

---

[8] Changed tones are marked differently in the text, e.g., ₀*sung* vs. *sung**. A high-rising changed tone is marked with an asterisk at the end of the syllable, and a high-level with a little circle at the lower left corner.

[9] The morphophonemic process as described here finds its parallel in another case of tonal modification in Cantonese. An adjective may be reduplicated in the following pattern for intensification:

    Adjective + *yat*(5) + Adjective

The intermediary *yat*(5) is written as " 一 " in character. An alternate pattern is to change the tone of the first adjective to high-rising or high-level, depending on the original lone height of the syllable, and drop the following *yat*(5):

    Adjective* + Adjective

As in the case of the perfective, the modification is to achieve the pitch height of *yat*(5), which is a high tone syllabic. The only difference is that while the modification process from V + *hiu* to V* + *hiu* and ultimately to V* is documented in the early pedagogical data, there is no extant materials to demonstrate the immediate stage in the adjective case.

reveal no information about the behavior of verbs with the original high-rising tone.

Recall the discussion in the previous section concerning the hypothesis of fusion in creating a changed tone verb. As noted, the inadequacy of describing the process as taking the tone feature of *jo*35 and superimposing it on the preceding verb is that it fails to include high tone verbs which move from high-falling to high level. If we take *hiu*55 as the catalyst effecting a changed tone, it satisfactorily accounts for the behaviors of verbs of both tonal categories. In fact, the morphophonemic process explains why *hiu* eventually disappears from the language. As *hiu* has been tonally incorporated into the preceding verb, its presence becomes redundant and therefore readily dispensable.

If we accept *hiu* as the form responsible for the changed tone, creating a new verbal unit that eventually and swiftly drops the suffix, we should then count all cases of changed tone verbs in our materials as derivatives from the V + *hiu* pattern. Accordingly, the statistics provided in Table 1 need to be revised. In Table 2, the total percentage figure in the third column of each row represents a combination of the percentages of both V + *hiu* and V* patterns.

	Verb + *hiu*	Verb*	Total	Verb + *jo*
PB 1888	5 (100%)	0	100%	0 (0%)
CME 1908	21 (55%)	7 (19%)	74%	10 (26%)
HSC 1912	8 (16%)	22 (44%)	60%	20 (40%)
BC 1927	152 (77%)	7 (4%)	81%	38 (19%)
FL 1930s	23 (49%)	0	49%	24 (51%)
ZY 1935	6 (9%)	0	9%	62 (91%)

Table 2

In section 2.3, when examining the distribution of the two markers, we noted the apparent contradiction in Table 1 between CME and BC on the one hand and HSC on the other. HSC exhibits a more frequent use of *jo*, a preference that was not characteristic of that time period. The new statistics as shown in Table 2 correct that bias. With V + *hiu* and V* combined, the ratio is consistent in that the use of *hiu* is larger than that of *jo*. Like the other titles in that early period, HSC shows a larger percentage in the use of *hiu* than that of *jo*: 44% vs. 40%, a preference consistent with the practice in pre-1930s. Chronologically, the use of the perfective in early Cantonese may be summarized as in Table 3.

	Verb-*hiu*	Verb*	Verb-*jo*
pre-1900	×		
1900–1930	×	×	×
1930–1940	×		×
1940–1970		×	×
post-1970			×

Table 3

The apparent inconsistency in the table pertains to the absence of the changed tone in the 1930–1940 period. As noted earlier, materials available from that period are in characters only, making it impossible to know if a changed tone was involved. However, judging by the fact that the phenomenon was still common, though decreasingly so, from the 1940s to the 1960s, it is safe to assume that the trend continued throughout the first half of the 20th century. Table 4 is a modification of Table 3, reflecting this practice until the 1970s. By that time, the use of the changed tone was considered a remnant feature of the past and only people over a certain age observed the practice.

	Verb-*hiu*	Verb*	Verb-*jo*
pre-1900	×		
1900–1930	×	×	×
1930–1940	×	×	×
1940–1970		×	×
post-1970			×

Table 4

2.5. The Use of *Liuh*

Our list of pedagogical materials begins with *Cantonese Chrestomathy* of 1841, a book to which we have not referred in our discussion thus far. The exclusion is simply because there are no examples of *hiu*, *jo*, or the changed tone in that text of close to 700 pages.[10] In the following dialogue where a perfective marker is generally expected, CC uses a simple verb.

(29a) 換過個兩張被單。拈開兩張污漕嘅，揀過兩張乾淨嘅嚟。 (CC: 158)
Wuhngwo go leuhngjeung pihdaan. Nim hoi leuhngjeung wujou ge, pigwo leuhngjeung gonjihng ge laih.
Change that pair of sheets, take away the dirty ones and put on a clean pair.

(29b) 我已經換咯。
Ngoh yihging wuhn lok.
I have already changed them.

As the translation indicates, the answer in (29b) stresses that the action has been performed. Such a completive reading, however, is not linguistically marked and may only be inferred from the context.

The absence of the perfective marker in CC may, however, be accounted for with different explanations. The first possibility is that CC fails to capture the actual linguistic reality of that time. Although the author, E. C. Bridgman, claims in his introduction that the Chinese is written in the local dialect, specifically "the dialect spoken by all the inhabitants of this metropolis (i.e., Canton) and by great numbers in adjacent cities and villages" (p. i), even a cursory look at the lessons reveals that the writing betrays an occasional mixture in style of the colloquial and the literary. It may have been Bridgman's personal preference not to include *hiu*, *jo*, or the use of changed tone in his work; or, the omission may have been simply an oversight. However, the text does not shy away from employing other aspectual markers such as the experiential *gwo* 過, the tentative *hah* 吓, and the habitual *hoi* 開. In fact, at times the writing is chattily colloquial especially in its use of intonational particles such as *bo* 噃, *me* 咩, *lok* 咯, *je* 啫, *ni* 呢, etc. In this regard, the sole exclusion of the colloquial perfective seems too strange to be either intentional or inadvertent on the part of the author.

---

[10] Each lesson in *Cantonese Chrestomathy* includes a Chinese character text, a romanized rendition and an English translation. The three sections are printed in three separate columns on each page, and explanatory notes are given at the bottom. The romanized text gives no indication of variation in pronunciation of any sort.

Another possibility is that the changed tone rule might have applied. The verb in (29b), 換, was not *wuhn* but rather *wun* with the high-rising contour, a tonal modification which the textual transcription chose to ignore. However, in view of the lack of such explicit marking in romanization and also on account of the absence of *hiu* in the entire CC text, the suggestion of a morphophonemic mechanism at work seems at best an attractive speculation.[11]

Still a third possible interpretation of this puzzling lack is that neither *hiu* nor *jo* actually existed in the language at the middle of the 19th century. Their emergence was a relatively late phenomenon, and *hiu* survived for only a few decades before it was replaced by *jo*. However, as the perfective is a ubiquitous element in all modern Chinese dialects (Yue-Hashimoto 1993a: 69), the assumption that Cantonese never had one historically until this century seems at best dubious.

The northern counterpart to *hiu* or *jo* is 了, *liao* in Mandarin pronunciation and *liuh* in Cantonese, a form that has been active in the language since the Tang Dynasty (Cheung 1977). Except in writing, *liuh* never appears in modern Cantonese. In CC, however, there are a fair number of cases where *liuh* is used precisely in the capacity of a perfective marker. For example,

(30) 家君去了好耐。 (CC: 79)
Gagwan heui**liuh** hou noih.
My father has been gone a long time.

(31) 汗衫洗了唔曾？ (CC: 149)
Hohnsaam sai**liuh** mhchahng?
Has the shirt been washed or not?

(32) 依你咁話，不如關了門唔做生意咯。 (CC: 243)
Yi nih gam wah, batyuh gwaan**liuh** muhn, mhjouh saangyi lok.
According to what you say, my best plan would be to shut my doors, and wholly desist from business.

---

[11] Transcription errors do exist in CC as Bridgman acknowledges in his preface: "Many of the errors in the orthography of Chinese words, and in their tones and aspirates, are attributable to the withdrawal of native assistants engaged to aid in compiling the work."

Was *liuh* an early grammatical form that predated both *hiu* and *jo*? In fact, *liuh* is defined in CC as "denot[ing] that the act has already been complete" (p. 49). Nonetheless, to claim *liuh* as a native aspectual marker seems counterintuitive to Cantonese speakers. Could the use then be construed as a direct borrowing from the written language, which is essentially based upon the northern language in both grammar and diction? The choice of the highly formal term *gagwan* (my father) in example (30) seems to relegate the sentence to a speech register quite different from the vernacular. However, colloquial elements are observed in all three sentences such as *hou noih* in (30), *mhchang* in (31), and *gam* in (32). As mentioned above, the language of CC is characterized by a hybrid writing style. Could Bridgman be simply using a standard form in the written language to represent a colloquial Cantonese form for which there was no proper graphic representation? The practice is indeed not unfamiliar to those who write in the colloquial language.[12] In other words, the word *liuh* could appear in the CC text not as a grammatical borrowing from the standard northern language, but rather as a graphic loan to render a colloquial perfective marker. If that is the case, which colloquial marker could it be representing? *Hiu* or *jo*? Or both?

The use of *liuh* is also found in PB, a book compiled a few decades after CC. Written in 1888, PB offers an ample supply of *liuh*, all serving the function of marking the perfective. For example,

(33a) 你一向做乜嚟呢？ (PB: 113)
Nih yatheung jouh mat laih ni?
What have you been doing before?

(33b) 我做了三年廚，兩年企檯。
Ngoh jouh**liuh** saamnihn chyuh, leuhngnihn kitoih.
I was a cook for three years and a waiter for two.

---

[12] Another example to illustrate this process of graphic borrowing is the use of 鼻吼 in CC, p. 52, for the colloquial word *pilung*, meaning "a nostril." Though phonetically different, the traditional character 孔 is chosen as the loan for the colloquial *lung* simply because both forms share the same semantic reading of "a hole, an aperture." And, the mouth radical is added to mark its colloquial usage.

(33c) 俾封薦信我睇吓。
Bi fung jinseun ngoh tai hah.
Let me see your references.

Again, the above exchange of conversation is highly colloquial in style, and the content pertains to everyday life. Unless *liuh* represented a grammatical form already active in the Cantonese language, it would seem pragmatically infeasible and undesirable to interrupt the flow of the conversation with an unnecessary bookish term. Between the two colloquial forms, *jo* was probably the marker that *liuh* was chosen to stand for in the PB language. The reason is apparent. As noted before, *hiu* is already present in the text, distinctly rendered as 唹 in graph and as *heu* in spelling. The following sentences further contrast *liuh* and *heu*, which are identical in function and evidently interchangeable in use.

(34a) 你來了呢個國有幾耐呢？ (PB: 161)
Ni loih**liuh** nigo gwok yauh ginoih ni?
How long have you been in this country?

(34b) 來嘵五年，幾中意。
Loih**heu** nghnihn, gi jungyi.
I have been here five years, and I like it pretty well.

Nonetheless, insofar as our data are concerned, *liuh* and *hiu/heu* are two separate graphic markers serving the same grammatical function. In fact, by comparison, *liuh* was a much more prevalent form than *hiu* at the end of the 19th century. If *liuh* was in effect, as argued, a graphic representation of the colloquial *jo* and since the first occurrence of *hiu* did not appear until PB, then chronologically *jo* is antecedent to *hiu* predating it by at least half a century.

2.6. Development of the Perfective

Table 5, a revision of Table 4, summarizes the development of the perfective system in the Cantonese language since 1841. In the historical materials I have observed, there have been a total of three formal markers: *liuh*, *hiu*, and *jo*. While *liuh* may be a mere graphic alternate to *jo*, phonologically *hiu* may result in a changed tone. It is evident that the various means of marking have competed in the process, old members being replaced by newcomers. However, because of the limited scope of data, it is not clear if patterns of lexical diffusion can be reconstructed for the changes.[13] For example, even though motion verbs such as *laih* 嚟 and *heui* 去 are involved in all forms of marking in the texts, it is difficult to tell whether the presence is merely due to the high frequency of occurrence of the verbs or if indeed they are susceptible, or resistant, to new changes. Other verbs, but not always the same ones, are also similarly marked at every stage. However, regarding the use of a changed tone, a process that is no longer active in the present-day Cantonese, I am aware of residual cases such as *sik35* faahn la* 食飯喇 (have eaten) or *heui35* meih* 去未 (have gone?). These individual items have lexically preserved the phenomenon of morphophonemics even though they also readily participate in the contemporary process of marking with *jo*.[14]

	Verb-*liuh*	Verb-*hiu*	*Verb	Verb-*jo*
pre-1850	×			
1850–1900	×	×		
1900–1930		×	×	×
1930–1940		×	×	×
1940–1970			×	×
post-1970				×

Table 5

2.7. The Origin of *Jo*

Aside from its eventual disappearance in the language, *hiu* is also unusual in that it contains a velar initial, a phonological feature that may invite investigation of a different nature. Cantonese is known to have a rich

---

[13] See, for example, the discussion in Yue-Hashimoto (1993b) concerning the phenomenon of lexical diffusion vis-à-vis the behavior of the interrogative in early Cantonese.

[14] The best example of a changed tone form preserved in a lexical item is the idiomatic expression *chong*(35) gwai* 撞鬼 (to have run into a ghost, to be in bad luck). The regular form *chohngjo gwai* 撞咗鬼 is never used.

aspectual system and most of its aspect markers are characterized with a velar initial. For example, *gan* 緊 for the progressive, *gwo* 過 for the experiential, *hoi* 開 for the habitual, *gwo* 過 for the compensative, *hah* 吓 for the tentative, and *ha* 吓 for the change. *Hiu* snugly fits into the system, a system that would automatically reject *liuh* as a native member. Likewise, *jo* 咗 is foreign to this morphological grouping. However, it should be noted that the durative *jyuh* 住 and the habitual/adversative *chan* 親 are other aspect markers in Cantonese that carry dental obstruent initials.

In several of his articles, Mei Tsu-lin (1979; 1988; 1994) argues that the aspect marker *zi* 仔 in the Wu dialect represents both the durative and the perfective, and that it is historically derived from *zhu* 著. 著 belongs to the *yu* 魚 rhyme in the *Qieyun* 切韻 system, which contains an -*o* vowel. Even though certain words of the 魚 rhyme are now rendered with the high front round vowel *yu* [ü] in Cantonese, some other members retain a more open *o* [ɔ]. Examples are *cho* 初, *joh* 助, *so* 梳, etc., all of which are members of the historical 莊-initial series. In other words, the same ancient final 魚 rhyme has given rise to two different modern finals, -*yu* and -*o*, and the distinction is phonologically conditioned. If we follow Mei's argument and make a similar claim for Cantonese, we can consider 著 to be the origin of both the durative *jyuh* and the perfective *jo* in the modern language. But unlike the situation in the Wu dialect where only one form suffices, the two aspectual readings are phonologically distinguished in Cantonese: while the durative has evolved from -*o* to -*yu*, the perfective has retained the original -*o*. Historical retention of phonological features in grammatical forms is of course not an unusual phenomenon in language evolution. Almost as if by coincidence, *hiu*, the other perfective, is also an anomaly in that it was exempted from the phonological change yielding all historical *hiu* words to *yau* in modern Cantonese. There is, however, one problem in this hypothesis that remains to be resolved. Tonally, 著 and *jo* are a mismatch. While the former is historically a word of the *qusheng* 去聲 category, low-level in modern Cantonese, the latter is a word that carries a high-rising tonal contour, characteristic of the *yinshang* 陰上 category. The irregularity could be argued as a result of tonal modification, a common phenomenon in Cantonese where a large number of words, regardless of tonal origins, assume a high-rising contour in colloquial speech. If the argument stands, the derivation of *jo*, therefore, represents two different stages of evolution: the preservation of the ancient vowel and the manifestation of a modern changed tone.

Granted that the above effort to reconstruct the origin of *jo* is highly speculative and therefore not necessarily conclusive, the implications are nonetheless provocative and far-reaching. In essence, the hypothesis argues for two aspectual systems in Cantonese, one of the velar series and one of the dental series. While the two systems each operate on their own specific aspects, they coalesce in one single category: the perfective. The result is a competition between *hiu* and *jo*, a phenomenon that has been documented in the historical materials as we have witnessed. Mei (1994) argues that the *zi* marker in the Wu dialect was a historical feature of the lower Yangzi region of the 10th century. Would our speculation on *jo* being derived from the same origin as *zi* point to a general dialectal grouping, including Wu, Yue, and Min, that readily set itself apart from the language north of the Yangzi River? Nonetheless, in spite of that general areal grouping, Cantonese seems to have developed its own indigenous system of the velar series, covering a wide range of aspects. If so, *hiu* or its changed tone form would have been in the language for a much longer time than our materials indicate. Table 5 could be accordingly revised to Table 6, with only two markers, *hiu* and *jo*, both existing in the language from prior to the 1850s. The former was eventually preserved in a morphophonemic form: the changed tone version, which though absent in our data during the period of 1930–1940, must have been active until the 1970s. If the dental series was a language feature characteristic of the lower Yangzi region, could the velar series be indicative of another areal grouping, say of the southern region or even of non-Chinese origin? The issue is complex and awaits further investigation of both synchronic and diachronic dimensions.

	Verb-*hiu*	*Verb	Verb-*jo*
pre-1850	×	×	×
1850–1900	×	×	×
1900–1930	×	×	×
1930–1940	×	×	×
1940–1970		×	×
post-1970			×

Table 6

3. Conclusion

As in all lines of diachronic investigation, shortage of materials is one of the greatest problems that a linguist faces in studying the past of a language. Although historically Cantonese lacked a written tradition which would provide information regarding changes in both grammar and diction, it is blessed by an ample and almost continuous supply of pedagogical materials from the 19th century onward. The materials, including textbooks and dictionaries prepared for both speakers of English and other Chinese dialects, record colloquial Cantonese as it was spoken then. A cursory look at the pages brings joy when one identifies certain words or expressions that are now obsolete or still in use; a methodical examination tells how the language has changed in less than two hundred years, changes that are observed in grammar and word usages, as well as in character writing.

In addition, as these lessons were prepared in romanization, they represent important materials from which to learn about the phonological development over the past century, a knowledge otherwise unavailable in traditional writings. For example, the romanization informs the language of its tone sandhi phenomenon and the contexts in which it happened. Because of their contents ranging from missionary activities in China to Chinese immigrants living in the US, from bargaining in a marketplace to attending a high court, the materials invite academic research of all sorts. They are, however, especially promising in terms of their linguistic relevance. Possible topics for investigation include tone sandhi, distinction between literary and colloquial readings, loan words from English, dialectal expressions, the double object construction, the potential complement, aspects, the interrogative, and many more.

Initial efforts have been made to collect materials and to examine some of the linguistic phenomena therein contained. The work, however, is still at its initial stage. Materials are extremely difficult to gather. For example, for the present study, I have had access to only a small number of titles. It has been recorded that a Dr. Robert Morrison published a Cantonese dictionary in 1829 (Bridgman 1841: i), which if available would have pushed my study further back by another two decades. Many of the titles I used are later editions, some being revisions of versions twenty years before. Had I been able to study the earlier editions and compare the revisions, I might have even more to comment on *hiu* and *jo*, a topic that I have examined in some detail in this article. The grammatical form *hiu* has disappeared from contemporary usage. Neither was it found in other Cantonese materials such as the folksongs of the early 19th century or the *chantefable* entitled *Fajingei* (*Huajianji*) 花箋記 of the 18th century. If not for the conscientious efforts of the early pedagogues, its presence in the language would have never been known. I am thankful to our predecessors, and I am hopeful that I will eventually come across more of their materials. My analysis presented here is tentative and I look forward to future revisions.

References

Ball, J. Dyer. 1908. *The Cantonese Made Easy Vocabulary*. 3rd edition. Hong Kong: Kelly and Walsh.

———. 1912. *How to Speak Cantonese: Fifty Conversations in Cantonese Colloquial*. 4th edition. Hong Kong; Shanghai; Singapore; Yokohama: Kelly and Walsh.

Bridgman, Elijah C. 1841. *Chinese Chrestomathy in the Canton Dialect*. Macao: S. Wells Williams.

Cao Guangshun 曹廣順. 1995. *Xiandai Hanyu zhuci* 現代漢語助詞 (Particles in pre-modern Chinese). Beijing: Yuwen chubanshe 語文出版社.

Chao, Yuen Ren. 1947. *Cantonese Primer*. Cambridge, MA: Harvard University Press.

———. 1968. *A Grammar of Spoken Chinese*. Berkeley, CA: University of California Press.

Cheng, Ting Au 鄭定歐. 1993. *A Selected Bibliography of Cantonese Chinese Linguistics (1900–1993)*. Hong Kong: Educational and Cultural Press.

Cheung Hung-nin Samuel 張洪年. 1972. *Xianggang Yueyu yufa de yanjiu* 香港粵語語法的研究 (Studies on Cantonese grammar as spoken in Hong Kong). Hong Kong: The Chinese University of Hong Kong.

———. 1977. "Perfective Particles in the Dunhuang *Bianwen*." *Journal of Chinese Linguistics*, 5.1: 55–74.

Gao Huanian 高華年. 1980. *Guangzhou fangyan yanjiu* 廣州方言研究 (A study of the Canton dialect). Hong Kong: The Commercial Press.

Kosaka, Jun'ichi 香坂順一. 1992. *Shuihu cihui yanjiu* 水滸詞彙研究 (A study of words in *Shuihu*). Translation. Beijing: Wenjin chubanshe 文津出版社.

Lam Paakchuhng (Lin Bosong) 林柏松. 1987. *Jin bainian lai Aomenhua de fazhan bianhua* 近百年來澳門話的發展變化 (Changes in the Macau language in the last one hundred years). Unpublished conference paper.

Louh Jifohng (Lu Zifang) 盧子防. 1935. *Jyuyam Gwongjauyuh* (*Zhuyin Guangzhouyu*) 注音廣州語 (Cantonese with phonetic notations). Swatow: Lingnan gongsi 嶺南公司.

Matthews, Stephen, and Virginia Yip. 1994. *Cantonese: A Comprehensive Grammar*. London: Routledge.

Mei Tsu-lin 梅祖麟. 1979. "The Etymology of the Aspect Marker *tsi* in the Wu Dialect." *Journal of Chinese Linguistics*, 7.1: 1–14.

———. 1988. "Hanyu fangyanli xuci 'zhe' zi sanzhong yongfa de laiyuan" 漢語方言裡虛詞「著」字三種用法的來源 (The function word *zhe* in Chinese dialects: The origin of its three different usages). *Zhongguo yuyan xuebao* 中國語言學報, 3: 193–216.

———. 1994. "Wuyu 'chi zai fan' de duandai wenti" 吳語「吃仔飯」的斷代問題 (*Chi tsi fan*: Dating in the Wu language). Conference paper presented at the University of California, Berkeley.

O'Melia, Thomas A., M. M. 1941. *First Year Cantonese*. 2nd edition. Hong Kong: Maryknoll House.

Stedman, Thomas L., and K. P. Lee. 1888. *A Chinese and English Phrase Book in the Canton Dialect*. New York: William R. Jenkins.

Taahm Gwaikeuhng (Tan Jiqiang) 譚季強. n.d. *Fanleuih tunghahng Gwongjauwah jinaahm* (*Fenlei tongxing Guangzhouhua zhinan*) 分類通行廣州話指南 (A classified guide to the Cantonese language). No place of publication.

Wisner, O. F. 1927. *Beginning Cantonese (Rewritten)*, Part One. No place of publication. Incomplete.

Yue-Hashimoto, Anne. 1993a. *Comparative Chinese Dialectal Grammar*. Paris: Ecole des Hautes Etudes en Sciences Sociales.

———. 1993b. "The Lexicon in Syntactic Change: Lexical Diffusion in Chinese Syntax." *Journal of Chinese Linguistics*, 21.2: 213–253.

Zhan Bohui 詹伯慧, and Cheung Yat-shing 張日昇. 1987. *A Survey of Dialects in the Pearl River Delta, Vol. 1: Comparative Morpheme-Syllabary* 珠江三角洲方言字音對照. Hong Kong: New Century Publishing House.

This article originally appeared in *Studies on the History of Chinese Syntax*, *Journal of Chinese Linguistics*, Monograph series number 10 (1997), pp. 133–165.

The Interrogative Construction: (Re-)constructing Early Cantonese Grammar

1. Who are you?
2. He is my father.
3. Have you a mother?
4. When did you marry?
5. More than ten years ago.
6. Have you any children?
7. I have several daughters, but no sons.
8. How old is the eldest?
9. She is between ten and twenty.
10. Is she married?
11. How many brothers have you?
12. One elder brother, one younger.
13. Have you any sisters?
14. I have one elder sister and one younger.
15. Are you married?
16. Not yet.
17. I am uncertain when I shall marry.
18. My wife is in the house.
19. I think you will get married next year.
20. Why is your child crying?
21. He is hungry.
22. Give him something to eat.
23. Call the nurse to carry him.
24. Take him out

Abstract: While there are different types of questions in Chinese, each exhibiting its own pattern of historical development over the centuries, the *yes/no* question demonstrates a unique path of formation that involves the juxtaposition of a positive verb phrase and its negative counterpart. This article focuses on the *yes/no* question in Cantonese and illustrates the processes of syntactic and phonological deletions responsible for producing acceptable forms at different historical stages in time. More specifically, it traces the development of the construction, as observed in materials from 1828 to the second half of the 20th century, that has undergone a fundamental change in the direction of deletion. It also argues that, as a consequence of this change in direction, the revised pattern of truncation gives rise to a new form of interrogation, commonly referred to as the *ma*-question.

Keywords: early Cantonese interrogative; *yes/no* question; deletion; disyllabic words; the *ma*-question

1. Introduction

As in all lines of diachronic investigation, shortage of materials is one of the greatest problems that a linguist faces in studying the past of a language. Cantonese is particularly challenging in this regard, as it lacks the support of a literary tradition that would otherwise inform us of changes in the use of grammar and diction. Even to this day, Cantonese is considered primarily a form of colloquialism, inappropriate as a medium for proper writing. However, as a spoken language, Cantonese has gained increasing importance on the international stage since the 1800s when Westerners first came to the Pearl River Delta for various political, religious, and business endeavors. To assist the newcomers with their linguistic needs in communicating with the locals, concerted efforts were launched into compiling language textbooks and dictionaries of Cantonese. The efforts continued to grow in the 20th century, yielding works that were targeted even at other dialect speakers. Despite their differences in both pedagogical concerns and approaches, the instructional materials nonetheless document various stages of development that Cantonese underwent in the last two centuries. The pool of materials in fact constitutes a wealthy supply of raw data for a meaningful enquiry into the history of the Cantonese language. The purpose of this analysis is to use a number of these titles as a means to approach and reconstruct early Cantonese grammar. Specifically, we will investigate the formation of the interrogative construction by focusing on its behaviors in twelve sets of language teaching materials compiled between 1828 and 1963. The list of the texts consulted is provided in the Appendix.

2. The Interrogative Construction

There are essentially four types of question in Chinese: (1) the interrogative pronoun question, (2) the disjunctive question, (3) the particle question, and (4) the *yes/no* question. The following are examples from Mandarin to illustrate the differences. While the interrogative pronoun question contains a specific interrogative pronoun soliciting pertinent information, the disjunctive question poses a choice between two or more options. The particle question is formed primarily by placing an interrogative particle at the end of the sentence, whereas the *yes/no* question is constructed by juxtaposing the positive and the negative counterparts of the verb phrase.[1]

The interrogative pronoun question
(1) 你是誰？
Ni shi shei?
"Who are you?"

The disjunctive question
(2) 你是張三還是李四？
Ni shi Zhang San haishi Li Si?
"Are you Zhang San or Li Si?"

The particle question
(3) 你是張三嗎？
Ni shi Zhang San ma?
"Are you Zhang San?"

The *yes/no* question
(4) 你是不是張三？
Ni shi bushi Zhang San?
"Are you Zhang San?"

Of the four types, this study identifies the last one as the focus for our historical investigation. While the other three types of questions exhibit some changes in Cantonese over the last two hundred years, the differences are primarily in the choice of interrogative markers.[2] The *yes/no* question, on the other hand, displays drastic modification of the word order in

---

[1] Mandarin examples are transcribed in *pinyin*, and Cantonese according to modern Cantonese pronunciation using the Yale system. Exceptions are made for the particle *ne*, which was *ni* until the 1940s. Translations are cited from the original; but for the following texts which do not provide English equivalents, the renditions are mine: Wisner (1927), Leih (1932), Taahm (1930), and Heui (1930s). Please note that tones are not marked in the transcription.

[2] For example, the marker for the disjunctive question is *dinghaih* 定係 or *juhnghaih* 重係 in modern Cantonese; its equivalent in early Cantonese was *bihhih* or *beihhaih* 嘅係.

which the question is phrased. In the following pages, I shall trace the development as observed in materials from 1828 to the second half of the 20th century and show that the construction has undergone a fundamental change in the direction of deletion.

A *yes/no* question is posed to solicit a *yes* or *no* answer. It is a neutral question without any presupposition or preconceived answer on the part of the speaker. In contemporary Cantonese, a *yes/no* question may appear in either one of the following two patterns. Each pattern is illustrated with different types of verbal constituents.[3]

<u>The VP-*ma* question</u>
(5) 你去嗎？
     Neih heui ma?
     "Are you going?"

(6) 你去外國嗎？
     Neih heui ngoihgwok ma?
     "Are you going abroad?"

<u>The *A-not-A* question</u>
(7) 你去唔去呀？
     Neih heui mh-heui a?
     "Are you going (or not)?"

(8) 你去唔去外國呀？
     Neih heui mh-heui ngoihgwok a?
     "Are you going abroad (or not)?"

(9) 你想唔想去外國呀？
     Neih seung mh-seung heui ngoihgwok a?
     "Do you want to go abroad?"

(10) 你知唔知佢想去外國呀？
     Neih ji mh-ji keuih seung heui ngoihgwok a?
     "Do you know that she wants to go abroad?"

(11) 你希唔希望去外國呀？
     Neih hei mh-heimohng heui ngoihgwok a?
     "Do you wish to go abroad?"

---

[3] For further discussion on the question type, see Cheung (1972), Gao (1980), and Matthews and Yip (1994).

Structurally, the *ma*-question in (5) and (6) is a particle question, marking a *yes/no* enquiry with a sentence-final *ma* 嗎. Historically, however, this question type may be viewed as a reduction from a true *A-not-A* question, as will be discussed in Section 8. An *A-not-A* question, on the other hand, is formed by juxtaposing the positive and the negative versions of a verb phrase, as in examples (7) to (11), with an optional particle *a* 呀 at the end. In Cantonese, the general negative marker is *mh* 唔.

Pattern A illustrates this basic structural scheme and Pattern B shows object deletion from the first verb phrase, as exemplified by sentence (8).

Pattern A: [V+O] + *mh*-[V+O]
Pattern B: [V]　　+ *mh*-[V+O]

The process of backward deletion, represented by Pattern B, is also observed in questions with auxiliary verbs or verbs taking sentential objects, as in sentences (9) and (10). In sentence (11), deletion affects even a disyllabic verb (XY) by blocking out the second syllable (Y) in the first verb *heimohng* 希望. In sum, the *A-not-A* question in modern Cantonese may be characterized by the following pattern, with V standing for the truncated version of the original positive verb phrase:

V+*mh*-VP

All versions of the *yes/no* question in modern Cantonese find antecedents in earlier texts. There are, however, other interrogative patterns in our historical materials which render the picture far more complex than what the current language exhibits. Aside form the *ma*-form and the *V+mh-VP* pattern, we find a larger number of examples phrased in paradigms that are no longer productive or that do not even exist in the speech of the 1990s and the early millennium. Some of the differences pertain to word order and some have to do with choice of markers. Table 1 lists all the *yes/no* question types that appear in the twelve sets of Cantonese teaching materials of the last two hundred years. The table gives both the actual number of occurences for each pattern in every text and the percentage it yields in terms of all *yes/no* questions in that entire text. As in all statistical studies, contrasts in percentage are generally more meaningful and revealing than actual differences in number.

	VP+*mh*-VP		VP-*mh*		VP-*mh-chahng*		VP+*mh*-V		V+*mh*-VP		VP-*ma*		Total
	No.	%	No.	%	No.	%	No.	%	No.	%	No.	%	No.
(1)	12	40	0	0	6	20	10	33	0	0	2	7	30
(2)	15	22.4	11	16.4	13	19.4	27	40.3	0	0	1	1.5	67
(3)	0	0	12	13.8	3	3.5	2	2.3	0	0	70	80.5	87
(4)	5	9.3	0	0	9	16.7	36	66.7	0	0	4	7.4	54
(5)	19	21.2	3	3.3	20	22.2	27	30	0	0	21	23.3	90
(6)	84	13.2	156	24.4	174	27.3	218	34.2	5	0.8	1	0.2	638
(7)	17	24.7	11	15.9	11	15.9	25	36.2	0	0	5	7.3	69
(8)	2	10	6	30	5	25	5	25	0	0	2	10	20
(9)	10	12.8	9	11.5	7	9.0	16	20.5	6	7.7	30	38.5	78
(10)	48	37.5	8	6.3	20	15.6	36	28.1	15	11.7	1	0.8	128
(11)	18	18.9	7	7.4	3	3.2	9	9.5	45	47.3	13	13.7	95
(12)	25	21.6	0	0	9	7.8	23	19.8	43	37.1	16	13.8	116
Total	255	17.3	223	15.2	280	19.0	434	29.5	114	7.8	166	11.3	1,472

Note: The texts referred to are as follows: (1) Morrison (1828); (2) Bridgman (1841); (3) Stedman and Lee (1888); (4) Ball (1907); (5) Ball (1912); (6) Wisner (1927); (7) Leih (1932); (8) Taahm (1930s); (9) Heui (1930s); (10) O'Melia (1941); (11) Chao (1947); (12) Chan (1951).

Table 1. Frequency of six *A-not-A* interrogatives in twelve texts

We should note that there are certain gaps in the table and some strangely large or small figures for occurences which are inconsistent with the overall patterns of distribution. For example, Ball's 1907 text shows no occurrence of the pattern VP-*mh*. The omission, however, should be viewed as nothing more than accidental since the pattern is present not only in an earlier text, Stedman and Lee (1888), but also in a subsequent 1912 manual compiled by Ball. Or, to take the ues of *ma* as another example, we should not be overly alarmed by its sudden prominence (80%) in the 1888 text by Stedman and Lee. The excessive use, as compared with a mere 1.5% in Bridgman (1841) and a slightly larger 7.4% in Ball (1907), is probably due to factors such as style and content and does not necessarily carry any grammatical significance. In fact, except in this one text, the use of *ma* has always remained a subsidiary *yes/no* pattern in the history of Cantonese interrogatives. Statistical figures may represent idiosyncratic preferences of individual writers or texts, and their function as a diachronic gauge should be assessed with caution and in context only.

3. VP+*mh*-VP

Though never a dominant pattern in our historical data, the basic construction of a Cantonese *A-not-A* question, that is, VP followed by *mh*-VP, has steadily held its ground over the last two centuries. The percentage of occurrences varies from 40% in Morrison's 1828 dictionary to 21.6% in Chan's 1951 textbook. One of the lowest rates is 9.3% in Ball (1907), and yet, in a work by the same author, Ball (1912), there is a stable 21.2%. The pattern actually includes two variations: juxtaposition of two simple verbs and combination of two full verb phrases. While the former is still active in contemporary Cantonese, the latter, as noted above, requires reduction of identical constituents from the first verb phrase.

The following are a few examples to illustrate the simple sequencing of a verb and its negative counterpart.

V+*mh*-V

(12) 啱唔啱？
Ngaam mh-ngaam?
"Is it correct?" (Morrison 1828)[4]

(13) 個啲荷囒羽緞賣嘅咯的，重有啲羽緞仔，你愛唔愛呢？
Godi Hohlaan yuhdyun maaihsaai lok, juhng yauh di yuhdyunjai, neih *oi mh-oi* ni?
"Of those Dutch camlets, I have sold all I had, but I have still some English imitations of Dutch, would you like them or not?"
(Bridgman 1841: 243)

(14) 好唔好吖？我嘅至好。
Hou mh-hou a? Ngoh ge ji hou.
"Is it good? Mine are the best." (Ball 1907: 20)

(15) 若有人稱先生做鬼，先生願唔願呢？
Yeuhk yauh yahn ching sinshaang jouh gwai, sinshaang *yuhn mh-yuhn* ni?
"If anyone were to style you a devil, would you be pleased?"
(Ball 1912: 168)

---

[4] Morrison (1828) has no pagination.

(16) 有人話的野人唔食鹽就生得一身好長毛㗎。你信唔信呢？
Yauh yahn wah di yehyahn mh sihk yihm jauh saangdak yatsan hou cheuhng mouh woh. Neih *seun mh-seun* ni?
"It's been said that savages don't eat salt and therefore grow a bodyful of long hair. Do you believe it?" (Wisner 1927: 130)

(17) 原來你尋日去逛市場。你今日重去唔去呀？
Yuhnloih neih chahmyaht heui gwaahng sihcheuhng. Neih gamyaht juhng *heui mh-heui* a?
"So, you went to the market yesterday. Are you going again?"
(Heui 1930s: 63)

(18) 你俾你部書佢，俾唔俾呢？
Neih bei neih bouh syu keuih, *bei mh-bei* ni?
"Are you giving him/her your book or not?" (O'Melia 1941: 62)

(19) 我去街番嚟做，得唔得？
Ngoh heui gaai faanlaih jouh, *dak mh-dak*?
"I go out, come back, (and then) do it, would that be all right?"
(Chan 1951: 30)

The majority of the V+*mh*-V examples are formed with monosyllabic verbs, as shown above, and they consist of verbs of various types including common action verbs and adjectives. There are also many questions with the possessive/existential *yauh* 有 and the copula *haih* 係 as in examples (20) and (21). In the former case, the negative form of *yauh* yields *mouh* 冇.[5] In the case of the copula, *haih mh-haih* often functions as a tag question asking for confirmation, as in (22). In fact, a large number of the V+*mh*-V questions in Ball (1912) and O'Melia (1941) are in the form of a confirmatory *haih mh-haih*.

(20) 有人思疑，有冇呢？
Yauh yahn siyih, *yauh mouh* ni?
"Someone is suspicious, aren't they?" (Bridgman 1841: 18)

(21) 佢係唔係？
Keuih *haih mh-haih*?
"Is s/he or is s/he not?" (Wisner 1927: 2)

---

[5] O'Melia (1941) mentions an occasional use of *mh yauh* (p. 31). In Morrison (1828), there is one example of *mouh yauh* (not have–have).

(22) 鴉片煙呢，係有好多入口，係唔係呢？
Ngapinyin ni, haih yauh hou do yahphau, *haih mh-haih* ni?
"And what about opium: there is a great deal of it imported, is there not?" (Ball 1912: 200)

My data also include a few examples of disyllabic verbs, which are preserved as full units in the VP+*mh*-VP pattern.

(23) 你歡喜唔歡喜？
Neih *funhei mh-funhei*?
"Do you like to have it?" (Morrison 1828)

(24) 你話古怪唔古怪呢？
Neihwah *gugwaai mh-gugwaai* ni?
"Would you say this is strange?" (Leih 1932: 32a)

(25) 你明白唔明白呢？我都唔多明白。
Ni *mihngbaahk mh-mihngbaahk* ni? Ngoh dou mh do mihngbaahk.
"Do you understand it? I am still not too clear on it." (O'Melia 1941: 70)

(26) 佢嘅人清楚唔清楚呢？
Keuih ge yahn *chingcho mh-chingcho* ne?
"Is his mind clear?" (Chao 1947b: 76)

The last text, Chao (1947b), also provides a case in which the first disyllabic verb in the *A-not-A* question undergoes partial reduction:

(27) 佢個人清唔清楚呢？
Keuih go yahn *ching mh-chingcho* ne?
"Is his mind clear?" (Chao 1947b: 29)

The contrast between (26) and (27) clearly shows that the mechanism of backward deletion on disyllabic verbs (XY *mh*-XY → X *mh*-XY) was already at work in the 1940s, an operation that has now become standard in the Cantonese language.

Besides simple verbs with one or more syllables, there is a small number of full verb phrases that appear in the VP+*mh*-VP pattern. While some are in the form of Verb + Object, others appear in a special V-*dak* (V-得) pattern, marking an affirmative potential reading, namely, "can + V" as shown in examples (31) to (34). In either case, the verb phrase is kept in full in both segments of the *A-not-A* question.

VP+*mh*-VP

(28) 女事頭喺處唔喺處呢？
Neuih sihtauh <u>hai syu mh-hai syu</u> ni?
"Is your mistress at home?" (Ball 1907: 10)

(29) 係野唔係野？
<u>Haih yeh mh-haih yeh</u>?
"Is it a thing?" (Wisner 1927: 2)

(30) 嗰啲先生喺處唔喺處呢？去嗮咯。
Godi sinsaang <u>hai syu mh-hai syu</u> ni? Heui saai lohk.
"Are the teachers in? They have all gone." (O'Melia 1941: 263)

(31) 你估我學得唔學得呢？
Neih gu ngoh <u>hohk-dak mh-hohk-dak</u> ni?
"Do you suppose I am able to learn?" (Bridgman 1841: 2)

(32) 晚頭瞓得唔瞓得呢？
Maahntau <u>fan-dak mh-fan-dak</u> ni?
"Are you able to sleep at night?" (Ball 1907: 24)

(33) 你擰嚟個啲野，食得唔食得呀？
Neih ninglaih godi yeh <u>sihk-dak mh-sihk-dak</u> a?
"Are the things that you have brought edible?" (Wisner 1927: 33)

(34) 你坐喺嗰處咁遠，睇得見唔睇得見呢？
Neih choh hai gosyu gam yuhn, <u>tai-dak-gin mh-tai-dak-gin</u> ni?
"Sitting there so far away, can you see?" (O'Melia 1941: 289)

As described earlier, modern Cantonese requires deletion of some of the identical constituents in an *A-not-A* sequence. To most modern speakers, the above sentences with full VPs in both segments sound strangely cumbersome if not totally unacceptable. As a matter of fact, juxtaposition of two full verb phrases has never been a favored practice. Of the 255 cases of VP+*mh*-VP in these materials, there are only eleven cases (fewer than 5%) of such combinations. O'Melia (1941) was the last book to have recorded the usage, but even in that text, an alternative is offered:

(35) 你做得唔做得呢？
Neih <u>jouh-dak mh-jouh-dak</u> ni?
"Can you do it?" (O'Melia 1941: 107)

(36) 你做唔做得呢？
Neih *jouh mh-jouh-dak* ni?
"Can you do it?" (Ibid.)

Two forms are listed side by side: the full form VP+*mh*-VP and the shortened version V+*mh*-VP.[6] Though initially given as an option, the short form is soon found to replace the full version in all subsequent materials in my data. Elimination of repeated constituents is a common linguistic phenomenon in all languages, but the direction in which deletion operates varies. Example (36) represents one form of deletion, but, as will be discussed in the next few sections, most of the examples in the early Cantonese materials demonstrate a different preference.

4. VP+*mh*-V

When an *A-not-A* question gives both the positive and the negative verb phrases, deletion may operate in either direction to remove one of the identical constituents. Hence, if the VP is made up of a verb and its object, the resultant forms are as follows:

	[V+O]	+	*mh*-[V+O]	=	VP	+	*mh*-VP
Backward deletion:	[V]	+	*mh*-[V+O]	=	V	+	*mh*-VP
Forward deletion:	[V+O]	+	*mh*-[V]	=	VP	+	*mh*-V

I have noted that, in modern Cantonese, deletion operates in a backward direction on *A-not-A* questions. The historical data, however, display a very different pattern, with a gradual change over time from forward deletion to backward deletion. In fact, backward deletion did not become active in the language until the 1940s.[7] Texts of the 19th century and those of the early 20th century adopt forward deletion exclusively. As the

---

[6] In addition, the text gives "*Neih jouh-dak mh?*" as another possible question form. The question involves a further reduction, a pattern which is to be examined in section 6.

[7] Yue-Hashimoto (1993) reports two cases of V+*mh*-VP in a 1912 text entitled *A Cantonese Phonetic Reader*, by Jones and Woo. I have not seen this text myself and, therefore, have not included it in the present study.

figures in Table 2 illustrate, *Beginning Cantonese* of 1927 was the first text to record emergence of the V+*mh*-VP pattern, and it was not until the 1960s that backward deletion gained eventual and complete dominance in the formation of an *A-not-A question*. The percentages given in Table 1 have been recalculated for *A-not-A* questions so as to contrast the rates of occurrence between the two deletion patterns. For comparison, I have added figures from a 1963 text, entitled *Speak Cantonese*, which shows no examples of VP+*mh*-V.

	VP+*mh*-V		V+*mh*-VP		Total
	No.	%	No.	%	
(1)	10	100%	0	0%	10
(2)	27	100%	0	0%	27
(3)	2	100%	0	0%	2
(4)	36	100%	0	0%	36
(5)	27	100%	0	0%	27
(6)	228	98%	5	2%	233
(7)	25	100%	0	0%	25
(8)	5	100%	0	0%	5
(9)	16	73%	6	27%	22
(10)	36	71%	15	29%	51
(11)	9	17%	45	83%	54
(12)	23	35%	43	65%	66
(13)	0	0%	76	100%	76
Total	444		190		634

Note: The texts referred to are as follows: (1) Morrison (1828); (2) Bridgman (1841); (3) Stedman and Lee (1888); (4) Ball (1907); (5) Ball (1912); (6) Wisner (1927); (7) Leih (1932); (8) Taahm (1930s); (9) Heui (1930s); (10) O'Melia (1941); (11) Chao (1947); (12) Chan (1951); (13) Huang and Kok (1963).

Table 2. Forward deletion and backward deletion in Cantonese *yes/no* questions

The following are examples of VP+*mh*-V in the early texts.

(37) 你識字唔識字呀？
Neih *sik* jih *mh-sik* jih a?
"Do you know characters?" (i.e., Can you read?)   (Morrison 1828)

(38) 重要的乜野添唔要呀？
Juhng *yiu* di matyeh tim *mh-yiu* a?
"Do you want something else?"   (Bridgman 1841: 171)

(39) 呢間係打得律風館唔係呀？
Nigaan *haih* da dakleuhtfung gun *mh-haih* a?
"Is this a public telephone station?"   (Stedman and Lee 1888: 47)

(40) 你中意喺呢處唔中意呢？
Neih *jungyi* hai nisyu *mh-jungyi* ni?
"Do you like being here?"   (Ball 1907: 12)

(41) 我晚晚要你點過嚟，睇吓齊嚡唔齊？
Ngoh maahnmaaahn yiu neih dimgwosaai, taihah *chaih* saai *mh-chaih*?
"I want you to count them over every night and see if there are any wanting."   (Ball 1912: 162)

(42) 你見佢揸針聯野唔見呀？
Neih *gin* keuih ja jam lyuhn yeh *mh-gin* a?
"Have you seen him/her sew things with a needle?"   (Wisner 1927: 178)

(43) 使講價唔使呢？要呀。
Sai gong ga *mh-sai* ni? Yiu a.
"Do I have to bargain? You need to."   (Leih 1932: 5a)

(44) 噉樣行為，係要求解放獨立嘅唔係呢？
Gamyeung hahngwaih, *haih* yiukauh gaaifong duhklaahp ge *mh haih* ni?
"Is this the kind of behavior that could make a demand for liberation and independence?"   (Taahm 1930s: 25)

(45) 張大哥，你起咗身好耐囉。今日番學唔番呀？
Jeung daaihgo, neih heijo san hou noih loh. Gamyaht *faan* hohk *mh-faan* a?
"Brother Jeung, you've been up for a while. Are you going to school today?"   (Heui 1930s: 70)

(46) 你信天主唔信呢？
Neih *seun* Tinjyu *mh-seun* ni?
"Do you believe in God?"   (O'Melia 1941: 89)

(47) 黃姑娘嘅聲音好似好熟敢，唔知有喺邊度見過冇呢？
Wong guneuhng ge singyim houchih housuhk gam, mhji *yauh* hai bindouh gingwo *mouh* ne?
"Your voice seems very familiar, Miss Wong. I wonder whether we have met somewhere."   (Chao 1947b: 43)

(48) 你七點鐘喺屋企唔喺呢？
Neih chatdim jung *hai* ngukkei *mh-hai* ne?
"Will you be home at seven o'clock?"   (Chan 1951: 78)

The above examples show different types of verbs all ready to participate in the forward deletion pattern of VP+*mh*-V. There are various examples of verbs, including *haih* 係 (be), *hai* 喺 (be at), and *yauh* 有 (have), auxiliaries, and adjectives. In addition, there are also cases of complex verb phrases, such as (41) with a complement and (42) with a sentential object.

Disyllabic verbs are always kept as independent and indivisible units in forward deletion in the texts.

(49) 講論鴉片煙，唐人點話呢？中意人哋食唔中意呢？
Gongleuhn ngapinyin, Tohngyahn dim wah ni? *Jungyi* yahndeih sihk *mh-jungyi* ni?
"What do the Chinese say about the opium; do they approve of people taking it?" (Ball 1912: 200)

(50) 你歡喜行街唔歡喜呢？
Neih *funhei* haahnggaai *mh-funhei* ni?
"Would you like to take a walk?" (O'Melia 1941: 165)

Even though the data include only a few examples of disyllabic verbs, none shows a split in the form of XY *mh*-X. We have noted that in the category of VP+*mh*-VP there was an early appearance of XY-*mh*-X in Chao (1947), namely, example (27) *ching mh-chingcho* (clear or not), a case in which backward deletion affects even the internal structure of a lexical unit. Such violation is never observed in forward deletion, at least not among true disyllabic words. Disyllabic compounds, on the other hand, are not exempt from the process. The following are a few examples showing omission of a constituent from the second VP.

(51) 好食唔好吖？
Hou sihk mh-hou a?
"Is it good to eat?" (Bridgman 1841: 178)

(52) 你估中國歌仔好聽唔好呢？
Neih gu Junggwok gojai *hou teng mh-hou* ni?
"Do you think that Chinese songs are pleasant to hear?" (Wisner 1927: 167)

(53) 放暑假，你去飯唔去呢？
Fong syuga, neih *heuigwai mh-heui* ni?
"Are you going to go back during the summer vacation?" (Wisner 1927: 196)

(54) 就係而家要睇，你易攞唔易㗎？
Jauh haih yihga yiu tai, neih *yi lo mh-yi* ga?
"I need to look at it now. Is it easy to get?" (Heui 1930s: 72)

Heuigwai 去皈 in (53) is a verb-complement compound "go-return"; the compounds in the other three sentences are cases of adverbial modification. Regardless of structure, the XY compound is processed as if it were a VO sequence. In some of the earlier materials, even an Adjective-Noun compound could be split, as shown in examples (55) to (57).

(55) 個處好屋舍唔好呀？
Gochyu *hou ngukse mh-hou* a?
"Are houses there good?" (Morrison 1828)

(56) 你好手勢割野唔好呀？
Neih *hou sausai* got yeh *mh-hou* a?
"Are you, Sir, a good carver?" (Bridgman 1841: 176)

(57) 好野唔好呢？
Hou yeh mh-hou ni?
"Is it good stuff?" (Wisner 1927: 8)

The nouns in (55) and (56) are each disyllabic in phonological composition, which makes the division and deletion sound all the stranger to a modern ear.

Another unusual case is the following example that contains a verb ambigious in status. *Hiudak* 曉得 (to know) is a semantic or lexical unit which by definition should not allow internal division. Structurally, however, it is cast in the potential mode and is therefore by status a compound word susceptible to forward deletion.

(58) 你曉得整酸果唔曉呢？
Neih *hiudak* jing syungwo *mh-hiu* ni?
"Do you know how to make pickles?" (Leih 1932: 12a)

It is reported elsewhere that the dissection of *hiudak* in a VP+*mh*-V pattern takes place as early as in 1877, more than half a century before Leih (1932).[8]

---

[8] The example appeared in an 1877 text entitled *Saanyuh seisahp jeung* 散語四十章 (Forty chapters of random prose). See Yue-Hashimoto (1993), p. 234. Also, Zhang Min (1990) cites a similar example, but in Mandarin, from a 1914 novel.

Our record of forward deletion begins with Morrison's 1828 text. With one-third of all *yes/no questions* in Morrison (1828) cast in VP+*mh*-V (see Table 1), it is evident that the process had already firmly established itself in the language by the early 19th century. In the following decades, the operation appears to have gained such momentum that it would strike any combination in precisely the same manner as it would split up a Verb-Object sequence. The only exception is when the XY sequence constitutes a true two-syllable lexical unit. In the following section, however, we shall show how disyllabic words are subject to a new development in the deletion process.

5. V+*mh*-VP

In the 1920s, the *A-not-A* question begins to reverse its direction of deletion affecting the affirmative instead of the negative segment in the VP series. Between the two patterns of VP+*mh*-V and V+*mh*-VP, the figures in Table 2 above clearly demonstrate a trend of moving from forward deletion to backward deletion. While the figures for forward deletion rapidly decline after the 1930s and early 1940s, the percentage for backward deletion grew from less than 30% in the same period to over 50% in the late 1940s and the 1950s. By the 1960s, the pattern completely took over as the dominant form of deletion in an *A-not-A* question.[9] The following are examples of both forms appearing in the same texts:

(59)　你識寫字唔識呢？
　　　Neih *sik* se jih *mh-sik* ni?
　　　"Do you know how to write?"　　　　　　　(Wisner 1927: 20)

(60)　你識唔識寫字呢？
　　　Neih *sik mh-sik* se jih ni?
　　　"Do you know how to write?"　　　　　　　(Ibid.)

---

[9]　The form VP+*mh*-V still occasionally appear in present-day language, perhaps only as a remnant feature of old Cantonese.

(61) 你嚌係想叫我同你告假唔係呀？
Neih laih *haih* seung giu ngoh tuhng neih gou ga *mh-haih* a?
"Is it true that you have come here because you want me to ask for leave for you?" (Heui 1930s: 70)

(62) 你係唔係想我同你一齊去番學呀？
Neih *haih mh-haih* seung ngoh tuhng neih yatchaih heui faan hohk a?
"Is it true that you want me to go to school together with you?" (Ibid.)

(63) 你識呢個人唔識呢？
Neih *sik* nigo yahn *mh-sik* ni?
"Do you know this man?" (O'Melia 1941: 149)

(64) 你識唔識佢呢？
Neih *sik mh-sik* keuih ni?
"Do you know him?" (Ibid.)

(65) 你有鉛筆冇呀？
Neih *yauh* yuhnbat *mouh* a?
"Do you have a pencil?" (Chao 1947: 53)

(66) 你有冇鉛筆呀？
Neih *yauh mouh* yuhnbat a?
"Do you have a pencil?" (Ibid.)

(67) 你要錢唔要呢？
Neih *yiu* chin *mh-yiu* ne?
"Do you want money?" (Chan 1951: 30)

(68) 使唔使錢呢？
Sai mh-sai chin ne?
"Does it cost money?" (Chan 1951: 37)

Other examples of V+*mh*-VP in the early stage of development include:

(69) 你知唔知佢去呢？
Neih *ji mh-ji* keuih heui ni?
"Do you know if he is going?" (Wisner 1927: 28)

(70) 使唔使我去呀？
Sai mh-sai ngoh heui a?
"Do I need to go?" (Wisner 1927: 41)

(71) 我帶得五十個銀錢去，你估我咁多野夠唔夠納稅呢？
Ngoh daaihdak nghsahpgo ngahnchihn heui, neih gu ngoh gam do yeh *gau mh-gau* naahp seui ni?
"I have taken along only fifty dollars. Do you think it will be enough to pay for the duties for all my things?" (Heui 1930s: 127)

(72) 我同埋你去上課喇，不過而家鐘點怕唔怕太遲？
Ngoh tuhngmaaih neih heui seuhng fo laak. Batgwo yihga jungdim *pa mh-pa* taai chih?
"I will go to school together with you. But, time-wise, does it matter that it's too late now?" (Heui 1930s: 63)

When the V+*mh*-VP pattern first emerged in the language, there was a distinction in participation between two types of verbs: the verb *yauh* 有 versus all the other verbs. In Cantonese, *yauh* is a full verb meaning "to have" and "there is"; but it may also serve to mark a past action. Using the statistics in Table 1, I further break down the pertinent figures according to various uses of *yauh*. The results in Table 3 clearly indicate that *yauh* was much slower than other verbs in joining the new pattern of backward deletion. For example, while Heui (1930s) offers not even one example of *yauh* in backward deletion, the same text already shows an even distribution between forward and backward deletions for all other verbs.

	VP+*mh*-V	V+*mh*-VP	*yauh* X *mouh*	*yauh mouh* X
(1)	100	0	100	0
(2)	96	4	99	1
(3)	50	50	100	0
(4)	60	40	86	14
(5)	0	100	60	40
(6)	21	79	48	52
(7)	0	100	0	100

Note: The texts referred to are as follows: (1) Ball (1912); (2) Wisner (1927); (3) Heui (1930s); (4) O'Melia (1941); (5) Chao (1947); (6) Chan (1951); (7) Huang and Kok (1963).

Table 3. Comparison of *yauh* and other verbs in the forward and backward deletions

The growth rate for *yauh* in the new pattern is consistently behind that for all other verbs. By the time *yauh* reached a 50% rate of participation in 1951, the new pattern had already become standard practice for other verbs from the late 1940s. In fact, a further examination of the data reveals that of all the *yauh* occurrences in backward deletion, the first ones affected were the possessive or existential *yauh* taking a nominal object. For example, O'Melia (1941) records three cases of *yauh* in backward deletion, and all three are possessive in usage. In Chao (1947), there are six cases, five marking possession. Only one sentence shows *yauh* followed by a verb phrase, casting it in a past time frame. As a tense-marking device, *yauh* was not fully engaged in the V+*mh*-VP pattern until the 1950s.[10] This is shown in Table 4.

yauh mouh	(1)	(2)	(3)	(4)	Total
Possessive/existential *yauh* *yauh mouh* NP	3	5	14	12	34
Past-time *yauh* *yauh mouh* VP	0	1	14	22	37
Total	3	6	28	34	71

Note: The texts referred to are as follows: (1) O'Melia (1941); (2) Chao (1947); (3) Chan (1951); (4) Huang and Kok (1963).

Table 4. Backward deletion for possessive *yauh* and past-time *yauh*

Table 5 further illustrates the different rates at which the two *yauh*'s took part in the development from forward to backward deletion.

	(1)	(2)	(3)	(4)	Total
Possessive/existential *yauh*					
yauh NP *mouh*	12 (80%)	5 (50%)	6 (30%)	0 (0%)	
yauh mouh NP	3 (20%)	5 (50%)	14 (70%)	12 (100%)	
	15	10	20	12	57
Past-time *yauh*					
yauh VP *mouh*	6 (100%)	4 (80%)	10 (42%)	0 (0%)	
yauh mouh VP	0 (0%)	1 (20%)	14 (58%)	22 (100%)	
	6	5	24	22	57
Total					114

Note: The texts referred to are as follows: (1) O'Melia (1941); (2) Chao (1947); (3) Chan (1951); (4) Huang and Kok (1963).

Table 5. Forward deletion and backward deletion for the two types of *yauh*

---

10 In his discussion of Cantonese grammar, Chao notes the use of *yauh mouh* VP as a form of the *A-not-A* question (Chao 1947), p. 40. In the twenty-four lessons in the textbook, he gives a total of six *yauh mouh* questions each containing a VP. However, only one of them is phrased in the form of *yauh mouh* VP, and the other five are all in *yauh* VP *mouh*.

Now, let us examine some examples of both forms of *yauh* occurring in the backward deletion pattern:

yauh mouh NP
(73) 你<u>有冇</u>佢嘅衫呢？
 Neih *yauh mouh* keuih ge saam ne?
 "Do you have his clothes?" (O'Melia 1941: 28)

(74) 唔知河口處嘅戰事<u>有冇</u>新嘅發展呢？
 Mhji hohhousyu ge jinsih *yauh mouh* san ge faatjin ne?
 "I wonder whether there is any new development in the fighting around River Junction?" (Chao 1947b: 43)

yauh mouh VP
(75) <u>有冇</u>讀古文呢？
 Yauh mouh duhk gumahn ne?
 "Did you read ancient essays?" (Chao 1947b: 46)

(76) 你<u>有冇</u>做過呢的功夫？
 Neih *yauh mouh* jouhgwo nidi gongfu?
 "Have you ever done this kind of work?" (Chan 1951: 92)

In Wisner's 1927 text there is, however, one example of *yauh mouh* VP, a case of backward deletion which seems to contradict my claim above that the operation did not take place until the 1950s.

(77) 你<u>有無</u>講大話呢？
 Neih *yauh mouh* gong daaihwah ni?
 "Did you tell a lie?" (Wisner 1927: 274)

This sentence is in fact the only case in all the pre-1930 texts that shows a *yauh mouh* combination followed by a VP, a usage that predates the next occurrence in my data by twenty years. The usage, however, appears a little suspicious as genuinely colloquial. In none of the three 1930 texts do we find the use of *yauh* in a backward deletion pattern, an inconsistent gap that calls the validity of sentence (77) into question. Besides, the character chosen for the negative is 無 *mouh* and not 冇 *mouh*, the former being the classical form for "not have" in the standard language, i.e., Mandarin. In the same section in Wisner (1927) where sentence (77) appears, a distinction is made between *mouh* 無 and *mouh* 冇 as representing two different styles of speech.[11] It should be noted that, while 無 and 冇 carry different tones, the former being low-falling and the latter low-rising, Wisner gives no romanization, hence no indication of actual pronunciation. In any case, even if the sentence does reflect a colloquial usage, its presence indicates that as a tense marker *yauh* had already taken on the V+*mh*-VP pattern in the standard language. And, it is most likely due to the influence of language contact and borrowing that Cantonese eventually switched from the backward deletion *yauh* VP *mouh* to the forward pattern of *yauh mouh* VP. For more discussion of this point, please refer to section 9.

6. VP-*mh*

While it is a common and preferred practice in Cantonese, both present and past, to delete some of the identical constituents from either VP in an *A-not-A* question, early Cantonese could carry the practice to the extreme by eliminating the entire VP from the second segment. Only the negative marker *mh* is retained at the end, signalling interrogation. The *yes/no* question therefore appears in the form of VP-*mh*. Examples are:

(78) 漁人能隨處捕魚唔呢？
Yuhyahn nahng cheuihchyu bouh yuh *mh* ni?
"Are fishermen allowed to take fish in whatever places they please?"
(Bridgman 1841: 347)

(79) 要的耶穌生日嘅貼唔呢？
Yiu di Yehsou shaangyaht ge tip *mh* ni?
"Don't you want some Christmas cards?" (Stedman and Lee 1888: 159)

---

[11] For example, in the following sentence, *mouh* 無 contrasts with *mouh* 冇 in terms of stylistic usage:
天父係無所不在，冇一笪地方佢唔在嘅。
Tinfu haih *mouh*-so-bat-joih, *mouh* yatdaat dihfong keuih mh-joih ge.
"Our father is omnipresent, there is not a place where He is not present."
(Wisner 1927: 276)

(80) 你見我嘅頂針唔呢？我係同埋個對鉸剪擠落鏡妝台處嘅。
Neih gin ngoh ge dingjam *mh* ni? Ngoh haih tuhngmaaih godeui gaaujin jailohk gengjongtoih syu ge.
"Have you seen my thimble? I put it on the dressing table with the pair of scissors." (Ball 1907: 126)

(81) 佢想從良唔呢？
Keuih seung chuhng leuhng *mh* ni?
"Does she want to get out (of prostitution) by getting married?" (Wisner 1927: 278)

(82) 你食牛油唔呢？我唔食牛油，食牛肉啫。
Neih sihk ngauhyauh *mh* ni? Ngoh mhsih ngauhyauh, sihk ngauhyuhk jek.
"Do you eat butter? I don't eat butter. I eat beef only." (Leih 1932: 6)

(83) 你曉講省城話唔呀？我會講國語，未學過廣州話。
Neih hiu gong saangsehng wa *mh* a? Ngoh wuih gong Gwokyuh, meih hohkgwo Gwongjauwa.
"Do you know how to speak the city language? I speak Mandarin, and I have not studied Cantonese." (Taahm 1930s: 6)

(84) 喂，醫生喺處唔呀？
Wai, yisang hai syu *mh* a?
"Hello, is the doctor in?" (Heui 1930s: 163)

(85) 你知嗰個人係邊個唔呢？
Neih ji gogo yahn haih bingo *mh* ni?
"Do you know who that person is?" (O'Melia 1941: 150)

(86) 呢個西人講唐話講得好唔呢？
Nigo saiyahn gong Tohngwa gongdak hou *mh* ne?
"Does this westerner speak Chinese well?" (Chao 1947: 60)

In most cases, the question appears with a final particle, either *ni/ne* 呢 or *a* 呀. There are, however, occasional occurrences without a particle, such as the following sentence:

(87) 游街用鞭杆唔？
Yau gaai yong bingon *mh*?
"Do you use a cane when you go in the streets?" (Bridgman 1841: 152)

As shown in Table 6, the percentage for the use of VP-*mh* fluctuates from text to text. The numbers are adapted from Table 1. The pattern is apparently absent in the earliest materials (Morrison 1828) and it has again disappeared completely from the language after the 1950s. During the one hundred and ten years in between (1841–1951), the development seems unstable or even confusing. For example, the use appears to first gain acceptance during the second half of the 19th century, peaking in the 1920s and 1930s with an average of 21% of occurrences in four texts: Wisner (1927), Leih (1932), Taahm (1930s), and Heui (1930s). However, the two titles by Dyer Ball—*Cantonese Made Easy* (1907) and *How to Speak Cantonese* (1912)—show little activity in the period in between. In short, the textbooks of the early 20th century seem more receptive to the pattern, while its use began to decline in the 1940s. VP-*mh* is practically unheard among speakers of this generation.

	VP+*mh*
(1)	0%
(2)	16%
(3)	14%
(4)	0%
(5)	3%
(6)	24%
(7)	16%
(8)	30%
(9)	12%
(10)	6%
(11)	7%
(12)	0%
(13)	0%

Note: The texts referred to are as follows: (1) Morrison (1828); (2) Bridgman (1841); (3) Stedman and Lee (1888); (4) Ball (1907); (5) Ball (1912); (6) Wisner (1927); (7) Leih (1932); (8) Taahm (1930s); (9) Heui (1930s); (10) O'Melia (1941); (11) Chao (1947); (12) Chan (1951); (13) Huang and Kok (1963).

Table 6. Frequency of VP-*mh* questions

It should be noted that up until the 1940s, VP-*mh* remained the primary form to use for a question that contains a potential *dak* 得 expression.

(88) 朝頭早熱頭晒得入房<u>唔</u>呀？
Jiutauhjou yihttau saai-dak-yahp fong <u>mh</u> a?
"Can the morning sun shine into the room?" (Bridgman 1841: 156)

(89) 你估呢件案，我告得補銀<u>唔</u>呢？
Neih gu nigihn ngohn, nghoh gou-dak bou ngahn <u>mh</u> ni?
"Do you think I shall be able to recover damages in this case?"
(Stedman and Lee 1888: 135)

(90) 一日要煮三餐嘅嘛，你做得㗎<u>唔</u>呀？
Yahtyaht yiu jyu saamchaan ge bo, neih jouh-dak-laih <u>mh</u> a?
"You need to cook three meals a day. Are you able to do it?"
(Wisner 1927: 127)

(91) 你信得呢個人過<u>唔</u>呢？
Neih seun-dak nigo yahn gwo <u>mh</u> ni?
"Can you trust this person?" (Leih 1930s: 10b)

(92) 多煩你順便同我買的野番嚟，做得<u>唔</u>呢？
Dofaahn neih seuhnbihn tuhng ngoh maaih di yeh faanlaih, jouh-dak <u>mh</u> ni?
"Could I bother you to bring back something for me? Can that be done?"
(Taahm 1930s: 5)

(93) 請你想吓，可以調得番轉頭<u>唔</u>呢？
Cheng neih seunghah, hoyih diuh-dak faanjyuhn tauh <u>mh</u> ni?
"Please think about it. Can the situation be turned around?"
(Heui 1930s: 244)

(94) 你嚟得我處<u>唔</u>呢？
Neih laih-dak ngoh syu <u>mh</u> ni?
"Can you come to my place?" (O'Melia 1941: 107)

(95) 書唔開嘅時候，裡面嘅字睇得見<u>唔</u>呢？
Syu mhhoi ge shihhauh, leuihmihn ge jih tai-dak-gin <u>mh</u> ne?
"When a book is not opened, can you read the words inside?"
(Chao 1947: 59)

The data from twelve textbooks and dictionaries include a total of 78 *yes/no* questions with the potential complement marker *dak*, and 60 of them, a prominent 77%, are posed with the pattern of VP-*mh*. If I break down the figures by titles as in Table 7, we see that VP-*mh* is consistently the preferred form for potential questions until the 1940s when backward deletion began to take root in the language. The striking contrast in frequency count in Wisner's 1927 text for VP+*mh*-VP versus VP-*mh* (2:41) bespeaks the almost exclusive dominance of the latter pattern over potential questions.

	V-*dak*-X *mh*-V-*dak*-X	V-*dak*-X *mh*	V+*mh*-V-*dak* X	V-*dak*-X-*ma*	Total
(1)	3	2	0	0	5
(2)	0	1	0	0	1
(3)	1	0	0	0	1
(4)	0	0	0	1	1
(5)	2	41	0	0	43
(6)	0	4	0	0	4
(7)	0	1	0	0	1
(8)	0	5	0	0	5
(9)	4	3	2	0	9
(10)	0	2	5	0	7
(11)	0	1	0	0	1
Total	10	60	7	1	78

Note: The texts referred to are as follows: (1) Bridgman (1841); (2) Stedman and Lee (1888); (3) Ball (1907); (4) Ball (1912); (5) Wisner (1927); (6) Leih (1932); (7) Taahm (1930s); (8) Heui (1930s); (9) O'Melia (1941); (10) Chao (1947); (11) Chan (1951).

Table 7. Frequency of the potential complement in four *yes/no* question types

7. VP+*mh-chahng*

In our data spanning close to two hundred years, the one pattern that has maintained prevalence throughout the history of Cantonese *yes/no* questions is the construction VP+*mh-chahng*. The construction is essentially marked by a sentence final cluster: the negative marker *mh* 唔 in combination with the adverb *chahng* 曾 meaning "already" or "yet." The cluster may also appear in the form of *meih-chahng* 未曾 or even simply *meih* 未. The following are some examples to illustrate its use.

(96) 你打定主意未曾呢？
Neih dadihng jyuyi *meih-chahng* ni?
"Have you made up your mind?" (Morrison 1828)

(97) 你有炊定的多時唔曾呀？
Neih yauh hongdihng di dosih *mh-chahng* a?
"Have you prepared any toast?" (Bridgman 1841: 174)

(98) 你喺人家屋做過廚唔曾？
Neih hai yahnga nguk jouhgwo chyu *mh-chahng*?
"Have you ever done cooking in a private family?"
(Stedman and Lee 1888: 109)

(99) 你娶老婆未曾呢？
Neih cheui louhpoh *meih-chahng* ni?
"Are you married?" (Ball 1907: 14)

(100) 喉吔，你食過老鼠未呀？
Aihyah, neih sihkgwo louhsyu *meih* a?
"Dear me! Have you eaten rats?" (Ball 1912: 74)

(101) 講啱價錢未曾呀？
Gongngaam gachihn *meih-chahng* a?
"Have you settled on a price?" (Wisner 1927: 70)

(102) 你收曉工錢唔曾呢？
Neih sauhiu gungchihn *mh-chahng* ni?
"Have you received your pay for work?" (Leih 1932: 11b)

(103) 杭州西湖至好風景，通世界至聞名嘅咯。你去過未呢？
Hohngjau Saiwu jihou fengging, tung saigaai ji mahnmihng ge lok. Neih heui-gwo *meih* ni?
"West Lake at Hangzhou has the most beautiful scenery, well-known all over the world. Have you been there?" (Taahm 1930s: 12)

(104) 我已經食咗咯。你食咗未呀？
Ngoh yihging sihkjo lok. Neih sihkjo *meih* a?
"I have aleady eaten. Have you?" (Heui 1930s: 62)

(105) 你去過香港唔曾？
Neih heuigwo Heunggong *mh-chahng*?
"Have you been to Hong Kong yet?" (O'Melia 1941: 262)

(106) 而家行咗一半路未呀？
Yihga haahngjo yatbuhn louh *meih* a?
"Have we walked halfway yet?" (Chao 1947b: 37)

(107) 你結咗婚未呀？
Neih gitjo fan *meih* a?
"Are you married?" (Chan 1951: 228)

This pattern is generally employed for questions regarding completed actions; the verb itself often carries a perfective -*jo* 咗 or -*hiu* 曉, an experiential -*gwo* 過, or some kind of result complement. The aspectual reading is highlighted by the presence of -*chahng* 曾, a marker that appears in the interrogative question as well as in the negative answer. For example:

(108) 你計數唔曾呀？唔曾計清楚咯。
Neih gaisou <u>*mh-chahng*</u> a? <u>*Mh-chahng*</u> gai chingcho lok.
"Have you made up your accounts? I have not made them up completely yet." (Ball 1907: 22)

(109) 你娶老婆未曾呢？未曾/唔曾娶咯。
Neih cheuih louhpoh <u>*meih-chahng*</u> ni? <u>*Meih-chahng / Mh-chahng*</u> cheui lohk.
"Are you married? Not yet." (Ball 1907: 14)

(110) 水退未呀？未曾水退呀。
Seui tui <u>*meih*</u> a? <u>*Meih-chahng*</u> seui tui a.
"Has the water receded? The water hasn't receded." (Wisner 1927: 257)

(111) 你上過山頂唔曾呢？未。
Neih seuhnggwo saandeng <u>*mh-chahng*</u> ni? <u>*Meih*</u>.
"Have you been to the peak? Not yet!" (Ball 1912: 50)

Since *chahng* is clearly part of the negative component, it is only reasonable to analyze a VP+*mh-chahng* question as a reduction from the full form VP+*mh-chahng*-VP. The forward deletion, when carried out in full force, removes the entire VP from the negative segment, leaving behind only the negative marker and the aspectual adverb. It is important that *chahng* is retained so as to distinguish this type of question from a regular VP-*mh* enquiry. For example, the following two questions are identical in structure; and it is the presence of *chahng* in example (113) that signals a different aspectual interpretation.

VP-<u>*mh*</u>
(112) 你食牛油唔呢？
Neih sihk ngauhyauh <u>*mh*</u> ni?
"Do you eat butter?" (Leih 1932: 6a)

<u>VP-*mh-chahng*</u>
(113)　你食飯唔曾呢？
　　　　Neih sihkfaahn *mh-chahng* ni?
　　　　"Have you eaten (your meal)?"　　　　　　　　(Leih 1932: 9a)

It is interesting to note that of the 223 examples of VP-*mh* in the materials, none contains the use of the perfective *-jo* or *-hiu*, or the experiential *-gwo*. In other words, all completed actions or experiential verbs are found with the pattern of VP+*mh-chahng*. The only exception is that when *yauh* is used to mark a past action, it may occur with either *mh* or *mh-chahng*, as in the following two *yes/no* questions. The reason for this seeming anomaly is simply that, as *yauh* functions essentially as a tense indicator, its presence automatically sets the scenario in the past.

(114)　你有見嗰個人唔呢？
　　　　Neih *yauh* gin gogo yahn *mh* ni?
　　　　"Have you seen that man?"　　　　　　　　　(Wisner 1927: 4)

(115)　有定嘅日子唔曾呀？
　　　　Yauh dihngjo yahtji *mh-chahng* a?
　　　　"Has the date been decided upon?"　　　　　(Heui 1930s: 103)

The final cluster in a *VP+mh-chahng* question may appear as *mh-chahng* or *meih-chahng*, or it may be shortened to *meih*. The three forms are identical in use, as evidenced by the following sentences all taken from the same 1927 text by Wisner.

(116)　你見過啲生物唔曾呢？
　　　　Neih gingwo godi sangmaht *mh-chahng* ni?
　　　　"Have you ever seen those beings?"　　　　　(Wisner 1927: 31)

(117)　你見過水牛未曾呢？
　　　　Neih gingwo seuingauh *meih-chahng* ni?
　　　　"Have you ever seen a buffalo?"　　　　　　 (Wisner 1927: 36)

(118)　你見過怪物未呢？
　　　　Neih gingwo gwaaimaht *meih* ni?
　　　　"Have you ever seen a strange animal?"　　　 (Wisner 1927: 279)

In terms of occurrence, the three forms are interchangeable from early on in the 19th century. But *mh-chahng* is the dominant form throughout all periods until the early 1940s. Since then, *meih* has taken over as the standard word in phrasing questions of this type. The process of replacement is evident from Table 8, which shows the distribution of all three markers in the twelve texts.

	VP-*mh-chahng*	VP-*meih-chahng*	VP-*meih*	Total
(1)	4	6	0	10
(2)	6	1	6	13
(3)	3	0	0	3
(4)	6	3	1	10
(5)	12	0	8	20
(6)	20	6	148	174
(7)	1	0	4	5
(8)	11	0	0	11
(9)	1	2	3	6
(10)	2	0	18	20
(11)	0	0	3	3
Total	66	18	191	275

Note: The texts referred to are as follows: (1) Morrison (1828); (2) Bridgman (1841); (3) Stedman and Lee (1888); (4) Ball (1907); (5) Ball (1912); (6) Wisner (1927); (7) Leih (1932); (8) Taahm (1930s); (9) Heui (1930s); (10) O'Melia (1941); (11) Chao (1947).

Table 8. Three types of aspectual *yes/no* questions in Cantonese

8. The *ma* Question

Finally, there is the *ma* pattern which has been in the language since at least the early 19th century. Its use, again, fluctuates among various texts and across periods. The figures given in Table 9, extracted from Table 1, include both the actual number of occurrences and the percentage of use in the respective titles, compared with other structures.

	No.	%
(1)	2	7
(2)	1	1.5
(3)	70	80.5
(4)	4	7.4
(5)	21	23.3
(6)	1	0.2
(7)	2	10
(8)	5	7.3
(9)	30	38.5
(10)	1	0.8
(11)	13	13.7
(12)	16	13.8
Total	166	n/a

Note: The texts referred to are as follows: (1) Morrison (1828); (2) Bridgman (1841); (3) Stedman and Lee (1888); (4) Ball (1907); (5) Ball (1912); (6) Wisner (1927); (7) Leih (1932); (8) Taahm (1930s); (9) Heui (1930s); (10) O'Melia (1941); (11) Chao (1947); (12) Chan (1951).

Table 9. Frequency of *ma* questions within each text

The *ma* question is the most prominent interrogative form in Stedman and Lee (1888), comprising more than 80% of the total number of questions in the text. Within forty years, however, the number dips to a low 0.16% in Wisner (1927) with only one occurrence out of 637 *yes/no* questions. Despite its seemingly unstable rate of occurrence, the pattern has never disappeared from the language. In recent years, however, VP-*ma* is no longer a favored form of the *yes/no* question, especially among younger speakers. Between the two options of a *ma* question and an *A-not-A* form, the latter is always the preferred choice.

The following are examples of the VP-*ma* question in our data.

(119)   你撞鶴神嗎？
        Neih johng hohk sahn <u>ma</u>?
        "Have you rushed against the crane god, eh?"   (Morrison 1828)

(120)   你開一間鋪賣各樣布匹，係嗎？
        Neih hoi yatgaan pou maaih gokyeuhng boupat, haih <u>ma</u>?
        "You have opened a shop for the sale of different kinds of cloth. Have you not?"   (Bridgman 1841: 245)

(121) 要五十箇仙車腳。你想先俾銀嗎？
Yiu nghsahpgo sin chekeuk. Neih seung sin bei ngahn *ma*?
"The ride costs 50 cents. Do you want to pay first?"
(Stedman and Lee 1888: 43)

(122) 佢冷親咩？佢咳嗎？
Keuih laahngchan me? Keuih kat *ma*?
"Has he got cold? Does he cough?" (Ball 1907: 24)

(123) 我見坐街邊嗰個補衣服婆戴個銀戒指，係嫁個陣戴嘅嗎？
Ngoh gin choh gaaibin gogo bou yifuhk poh daai go ngahn gaaiji, haih ga gojahnsih daai ge *ma*?
"I see the seamstress at the street corner has a silver ring on. Is that a marriage ring?" (Ball 1912: 64)

(124) 醫生喺處嗎？
Yisang hai syu *ma*?
"Is the doctor in?" (Wisner 1927: 227)

(125) 醫得好嗎？
Yi dak hou *ma*?
"Is this curable?" (Leih 1932: 23b)

(126) 府上各位都平安吖嗎？
Fuseuhng gokwaih dou pihng'on a *ma*?
"Is everyone in your family safe and sound?" (Taahm 1930s: 4)

(127) 呢幾日真係熱到了不得，你處涼嗎？
Ni geiyaht jan haih yiht dou liuhbatdak. Neihsyu leuhng *ma*?
"It's been incredibly hot these last few days. Is it cool at your place?"
(Heui 1930s: 89)

(128) 你去嗎？
Neih heui *ma*?
"Are you going?" (O'Melia 1941: 2)

(129) 你話現在有好多軍用品運到咧，係嗎？
Neih wah yihnjoih yauh hou do gwanyuhngbahn wahndoujo, haih *ma*?
"You said that a lot of military supplies had now arrived, didn't you?"
(Chao 1947b: 43)

(130) 你聽日得閒嗎？
Neih tingyaht dakhaahn *ma*?
"Are you available tomorrow?" (Chan 1951: 72)

In his *First Year Cantonese,* O'Melia observes that "*mh a* often contracts to *ma*" (1941: 32). Although in his entire book of 42 lessons O'Melia includes only one example of *ma*, the observation he makes about its formation is both astute and original. The one example he gives for *ma*, namely (128), can indeed be understood to have derived from the following VP-*mh* question:

(131) 你去唔呀？
Neih heui *mh a*?
"Are you going?"

As noted above, it is a general practice for a VP-*mh* question to conclude with a particle, either *ni/ne* or *a*.[12] When the particle *a* is positioned immediately after the negative *mh*, the fusion between a syllabic nasal and an immediate following vowel is not only possible but also highly desirable in terms of easy pronunciation.[13] The data include a total of 223 VP-*mh* questions, and only 27 questions appear with *a*. The low percentage, slightly larger than 10%, tells us not so much about the incompatibility between the pattern and the particle as about the morphological process accounting for the presence of *ma* or, for that matter, the lack of *mh a*. In fact, it may be argued that *ma* derives its mid-level tone from the particle *a* in the process of change from *mh* + *a* → *ma*.[14]

---

[12] In Taiwanese, the negative marker is also a syllabic *m* 唔. Unlike Cantonese, however, this Southern Min language does not use particles in its questions. Hence, its VP-*neg* question often appears in the form of VP *a m*? The pre-negative *a* is a marker of disjunction: "or." See Li (1986).

[13] Taahm (1930s) provides another case of phonological fusion in a VP-*mh* question:

坐船嗰陣，會辛苦唔㗎？
Choh syuhn gojahn, wuih sanfu *mh ga*?
"Will it be rough during the boat ride?" (Taahm 1930s: 3)

The form *ga* is a combination of two particles, the emphatic *ge* and an interrogative *a*.

[14] In contemporary Cantonese, the expression *haih mh-haih* (is or is not, yes or no) is often rendered in casual speech as *haih maih*, where the negative segment *mh-haih* is contracted into one phonological unit with a tonal pitch identical to that of the second unit *haih*. Phonological fusion is a common phenomenon in many Sinitic languages. H. Chappell notes, in a personal communication, that fusion "seems possible for many particles and coverbs in Taiwanese" and may be used for semantic reconstruction. One such example is the combination of the pretransitive marker *kah* and the third person singular pronoun *i* 伊 to give rise to *ka* 甲.

kah (low falling) + *i* (high level) → *ka* (high level)

Stedman and Lee (1888) contains seventy cases of VP-*ma* but none with VP-*mh*, a phenomenon that can be explained in terms of Stedman and Lee's own preference for the contracted form *ma*. On the other hand, Morrison (1828) shows no incidence of VP-*mh*; yet, because of the presence of VP-*ma* in the text, we can safely claim the pattern to be already in existence, but only in a contracted form. Even though the pattern VP-*mh* eventually disappears from the language (see Table 6), the exit pace is much faster for VP-*mh a* than for VP-*mh ni*. While the latter is still active in the late 1940s, the former had already become obsolete by the early 1940s. Nonetheless, the fused form *ma* has survived. Even long after the VP-*mh* pattern has ceased to exist in the language, VP-*ma* remains a vestige of this once very productive mechanism (see Table 9).[15]

9. Conclusion

My discussion thus far has identified six types of *yes/no* questions in Cantonese, each with its own pattern and pace of development over the last two hundred years. Structurally, however, they can be described as all evolving from the same basic formula of juxtaposing the positive and negative verb phrases.

(1) VP+*mh*-VP or V+*mh*-V
(2) VP+*mh*-VP → VP+*mh*
(3) VP+*mh*-VP+*a* → VP+*mh*+*a* → VP-*ma*
(4) VP+*mh*-VP → VP+*mh*-V
(5) VP+*mh*-*chahng* VP → VP+*mh*-*chahng*
(6) VP+*mh*-VP → V+*mh*-VP

If Type (1) is taken to be the prototype of the *yes/no* interrogative, the other five types are derived from it through different processes of deletion. Types (2) through (5) involve forward deletion in removing certain

---

[15] For a further discussion on the derivation of *ma* from *mh a*, see Yue-Hashimoto (1993). Yue-Hashimoto argues that, since *ma* can only appear in an affirmative question, it is reasonable to assume that the form already contains a negative *mh*, thereby excluding another *mh* from occurring before the verb.

identical constituents from the second VP; in Type (6) the deletion is conducted in a backward direction, affecting the first VP instead. The data show that backward deletion was a rather late phenomenon in the language, taking full effect primarily in the period between the 1930s and 1940s. Forward deletion, on the other hand, was an early phenomenon; its various patterns of omission are observed in language materials even as early as the first half of the 19th century. Although the operation experienced a gradual decline beginning in the 1940s, its force has been lexically preserved in *meih* and *ma* question forms which are still in use today. Table 10 highlights some of the important developments in the history of Cantonese *yes/no* interrogation.

	VP+*mh*-VP	VP+*mh*	VP-*ma*	VP+*mh*-V	VP+*mh*-*chahng*	V+*mh*-VP
1800–1850	+	+	+	+	+	—
1850–1900	+	+	+	+	+	—
1900–1930	+	+	+	+	+	—
1930–1950	xy *mh* xy → x *mh* xy, VP+*mh*-VP disappearing	declining	+	xy *mh* x disappeared	*meih* replacing *mh-chahng*	emerging active in 1940s *yauh mouh* NP
1950–1960	—	—	+	—	+ (*meih*)	+ *yauh mouh* NP

Table 10. History of Cantonese *yes/no* interrogatives

Aside from the emergence of the V+*mh*-VP pattern, the twenty-year period between 1930 and 1950 also witnessed a great many other changes. In fact, most of these new developments are related to or even triggered by the operation of backward deletion. In a VO+*mh*-VO sequence, for example, the new rule in the 1930s removed the first object and introduced a new sequence of V+*mh*-VO. By analogy, a disyllabic verb XY was subject to the same principle of omission, giving rise to the paradigm of X-*mh*-XY. The new format of backward deletion competed with the century-old practice of forward deletion, gradually substituting VP+*mh*-V with V+*mh*-VP, and ultimately putting an end to patterns such as VP+*mh*-VP and VP-*mh*. Even the final cluster *mh-chahng*, marker of an aspectual question in forward deletion, was permanently replaced by *meih*, a new façade that could no longer betray the force of Cantonese interrogatives, a transition through which Cantonese has joined other Chinese dialects in forming a *yes/no* question with a universal pattern of V+*mh*-VP.

It has been pointed out that the pattern V+NEG-VP is native to the south (Zhu 1990) and that it was due to language contact with Southwestern Mandarin that the Mandarin dialects of the north began to switch to backward deletion in the early 1900s.[16] The 1930s and 1940s were a period when China was beset by various political turmoils, resulting in many waves of southward migration. For example, the composition of the population in Hong Kong underwent drastic changes in terms of regional representation in the 1940s. Speakers of various dialectal origins gathered and interacted. Could it be that such regular and massive contacts during this particular period activated changes in the Cantonese language itself?

To reach any conclusion, we need first to learn more about the host language and the languages with which it has been in contact. When Zhu (1985) first proposed a typological distinction between VP-NEG-V and V-NEG-VP patterns, he claimed the former type occurs primarily in Northern Mandarin, and the latter in southern Chinese dialects, including Cantonese. Our data have more than adequately shown that Cantonese, contrary to his characterization, was historically a VP-NEG-V language. Evidently, Zhu did not have access to the kind of materials investigated in this study, materials that would have allowed him to gain an intimate and perhaps different look into the past of the language.

If we are now to suggest that, on a par with its northern counterparts, Cantonese acquired its V-NEG-VP pattern from Southwestern Mandarin, how much supporting evidence do we really have beyond surface observation of contemporary Southwestern Mandarin? That Cantonese experienced a radical transformation in its interrogative formation for *yes/no* questions during the 1930s and 1940s is an undeniable fact. As to how to account for such a phenomenon, we will have to await further research into the past, both within Cantonese and also across other Sinitic languages.

---

[16] See Yue-Hashimoto (1993), who quotes from Zhang (1990).

In recent years, the issue of *yes/no* questions has attracted increasing attention in the field of Chinese dialectology. Yue-Hashimoto has written extensively on the phenomenon in Cantonese (see 1992; 1993). On the basis of her study of six language textbooks compiled between 1877 and 1938, she claims in the 1993 study that the VP-NEG form was native to the Yue dialects and that the VP-NEG-VP pattern was later introduced through language contact. Furthermore, VP-NEG-V entered the language before V-NEG-VP, and its entrance followed a basic pattern of lexical diffusion, first affecting common words such as the copula *haih*, the existential/possessive *yauh*, and the optatives. My findings differ from hers in several regards.

As our materials do not always overlap in titles or periods, our observations are bound to be dissimilar. Yue-Hashimoto cites the dominant use of VP-NEG in an 1877 work as supporting evidence for claiming the nativity of the pattern, a pattern that gradually declines in the five subsequent writings. I do not have this 1877 title at my disposal, but my figures from 1828 to 1947 (see Table 1) display a rather different picture. V-*mh* never appears to be a ruling pattern at any stage in the last two hundred years. In fact, it was conspicuously absent in our earliest title of 1828.

Yue-Hashimoto notices the overwhelming appearances of certain common verbs in the initial stage of introducing VP-NEG-VP into the language. In fact, she notes that in the 1877 work, there are only two verbs, other than *yauh* and the auxiliaries, that took part in the VP-NEG-VP pattern. Granted that there is in my data a large number of questions phrased in the form of *haih-mh-haih* (Is it correct?) or *hou mh hou* (Is it fine?), a usage that is actually quite common in the language at all times, my materials also show a variety of verbs and adjectives in these VP-NEG-VP question frames, even in the early 19th century. Examples are *ngaam* 啱 (correct), *yiu* 要 (desire), *funhei* 歡喜 (like) (all in Morrison 1828); and *housihk* 好食 (delicious), *ngoi* 愛 (want), *maaih* 買 (buy), *hohk* 學 (study), and *se* 寫 (write) (all in Bridgman 1841).

If Yue-Hashimoto is correct in assuming that VP+*mh*-Y came into Cantonese through language contact, my data would have to push that stage back probably by at least half a century. Since Morrison's 1828 text already includes general action verbs such as *yam chah* 飲茶 (drink tea), *sih jih* 識字 (read characters), and also adjectival phrases such as *hou ngukse* 好屋舍 (good accommodation), the VP+*mh*-V mechanism would have had to be introduced much earlier if it was to take effect on these verbs by 1828. Furthermore, it seems that, with the exception of V+*mh*-VP, all *A-not-A* patterns were active in the language, side by side, from the early 19th century. We see a gradual disappearance of certain patterns such as VP-*mh* in the 1940s but we do not witness a gradual appearance and expansion of VP+*mh*-VP or of VP+*mh*-V as the language entered the 20th century. In fact, for lack of such material support, it seems dubious to argue for one form to be native and the others to be borrowed.

On the basis of my findings, it is equally valid to suggest all forms (except for, perhaps, V+*mh*-VP) to be native to Cantonese, with reductions applying uniformly in the forward direction. Structurally, instead of categorizing VP+*mh-chahng* as a VP-NEG pattern, it would be more consistent and logical to characterize VP+*mh-chahng* as a derivation of an *A-not-A* question, with *chahng* standing as a remnant feature, as I argued above, of the deleted negative VP. Yue-Hashimoto bases her study on Cantonese *yes/no* questions on a much larger investigation of other dialects, including different varieties of the Yue language. In contrast, my work is focused on twelve sets of Cantonese learning materials compiled over the last two hundred years. It is a longitudinal and microscopic examination and the findings it yields speak more of internal development than of external influence. So, until further evidence presents itself, it is only safe to conclude that in generating *yes/no* questions, Cantonese operated primarily on forward deletion until the mid-20th century.

It should be noted that during the course of reversal from forward to backward deletion, the change seemed to affect different syntactic patterns at different times. Compared with other verbs, *yauh* was much slower in joining the process, which could be construed to be a case of lexical diffusion. However, the data clearly betray a distinction between two patterns of *yauh*, namely, *yauh mouh* NP predated *yauh mouh* VP by almost a decade. In other words, the change appeared to be syntactically selective rather than lexically diffusive. To cite another example, the potential *dak* construction displayed a special preference for the VP-*mh* question, a choice that lasted until the 1940s. We must study these phenomena more closely before attempting any explanation; nonetheless, we should be aware of the dimension in which the syntactic change was carried out in Cantonese, both across the lexicon and interacting with other components of the grammar.

As recorded in the language teaching materials of the last two centuries, Cantonese has undergone many changes in the use of both grammar and the lexicon. If it were not for the efforts of these pedagogues, a great many changes would have occurred and disappeared from the language, unnoticed and never recorded. Misinterpretation and misconception often arise because of an inadequate supply of first-hand materials. We are blessed with a copious stock of pedagogical writings on Cantonese which, under proper scrutiny, could enable us to gain a better and further look into the evolution of the language. My data supplement Yue-Hashimoto's. As we avail ourselves of even more materials in the years to come, our knowledge of the past will for sure grow in both scope and depth.

References

Chao, Yuen Ren. 1947. *Cantonese Primer*. Cambridge, MA: Harvard University Press.
———. 1968. *A Grammar of Spoken Chinese*. Berkeley, CA: University of California Press.
Cheung Hung-nin Samuel 張洪年. 1972. *Xianggang Yueyu yufa de yanjiu* 香港粵語語法的研究 (Studies on Cantonese grammar as spoken in Hong Kong). Hong Kong: The Chinese University of Hong Kong.
Gao Huanian 高華年. 1980. *Guangzhou fangyan yanjiu* 廣州方言研究 (A study of the Canton dialect). Hong Kong: The Commercial Press.
Li Ying-che. 1986. "Historical Significance of Certain Distinct Grammatical Features in Taiwanese." In *Contributions to Sino-Tibetan Studies, Cornell Linguistic Contributions*, ed. John McCoy and Timothy Light, 5: 393–415. Leiden: E. J. Brill.
Matthews, Stephen, and Virginia Yip. 1994. *Cantonese: A Comprehensive Grammar*. London: Routledge.
Yue-Hashimoto, Anne 余靄芹. 1992. "Neutral Questions in the Kaiping Dialect of Guangdong" 廣東開平方言中的中性問句. *Zhongguo Yuwen* 中國語文, 4: 279–286.
———. 1993. "The Lexicon in Syntactic Change: Lexical Diffusion in Chinese Syntax." *Journal of Chinese Linguistics*, 21.2: 213–253.
Zhang Min 張敏. 1990. *A Typological Study of Yes-No Questions in Chinese Dialects: A Diachronic Perspective* 探討漢語方言反覆問句的類型分布. PhD dissertation, Peking University.
Zhu Dexi 朱德熙. 1985. "Two Kinds of Yes-No Questions in Chinese Dialects" 漢語方言裡的兩種反複問句. *Zhongguo Yuwen* 中國語文, 184: 10–20.
———. 1990. "Dialectal Distribution of V-neg-VO and VO-neg-V Interrogative Sentence Patterns." *Journal of Chinese Linguistics*, 18.2: 209–230.

This article originally appeared in *Chinese Grammar: Synchronic and Diachronic Perspectives*, ed. Hilary Chappell (Oxford University Press, 2001), pp. 191–231.

Appendix: Sources of Data on the Cantonese Interrogative

The following is a list of works from which I have collected my data on the Cantonese interrogative. The works are arranged chronologically according to date of publication. As elsewhere in the article, all Chinese words are romanized according to Cantonese pronunciation following the Yale system; Mandarin readings are given, whenever necessary, in parentheses. I do not include any materials from beyond the 1950s, primarily because I grew up in Hong Kong speaking Cantonese in the post-war period. At times, however, I have consulted *Speak Cantonese* by Huang and Kok.[17]

(1) Morrison, Robert. 1828. *A Vocabulary of the Cantonese Dialect*. Macau: East India Company's Press. 3 parts, no pagination.

(2) Bridgman, E. C. 1841. *Chinese Chrestomathy in the Canton Dialect*. Macao: S. Wells Williams. 693 pages.

(3) Stedman, T. L., and K. P. Lee. 1888. *A Chinese and English Phrase Book in the Canton Dialect*. New York: William R. Jenkins. 186 pages.

(4) Ball, J. Dyer. 1907. *Cantonese Made Easy*. 3rd edition. Hong Kong: Kelly and Walsh. 186 pages.[18]

(5) Ball, J. Dyer. 1912. *How to Speak Cantonese: Fifty Conversations in Cantonese Colloquial*. 4th edition. Hong Kong: Kelly and Walsh. 229 pages.[19]

(6) Wisner, O. E. 1927. *Beginning Cantonese (Rewritten)*, Part One. Incomplete. No place of publication. 280 pages.

(7) Leih Yatmahn (Li Yimin) 李一民. 1932. *Yuhtyuh chyuhnsyu (Yueyu quanshu)* 粵語全書 (A complete Cantonese reader). Shanghai: Shanghai yanmouhguhk 上海印務局. 80 pages.

---

[17] For this investigation, I have used only the last five lessons of their book, *Speak Cantonese*, Book 1 (1963).

[18] *Cantonese Made Easy* went through four printings. The preface to the first edition bears the date of 1883. The second edition was published in 1888, the third edition in 1907, and the fourth edition in 1924. There is a *Vocabulary*, the third edition of which is dated 1908.

[19] The preface to the first edition of *How to Speak Cantonese* is dated 1889. The second edition came out in 1902, and the third edition in 1904.

(8) Taahm Gwaikeuhng (Tan Jiqiang) 譚季強. 1930s. *Fanleuih tunghahng Gwongjauhwah jinaahm* (*Fenlei tongxing Guangzhouhua zhinan*) 分類通行廣州話指南 (A classified guide to the Cantonese language). No date or place of publication. 55 pages.[20]

(9) Heui Syuthohng (Xu Xuehang) 許雪航. 1930s. *Sanpin Gwongdung saangsihng baahkwah* (*Xinbian Guangdong shengcheng baihua*) 新編廣東省城白話 (Newly edited vernacular of the Guangdong provincial capital). Bangkok: Mahnfa jyuhjih gungsi 文化鑄字公司. 247 pages.[21]

(10) O'Melia, Thomas A., M. M. 1941. *First Year Cantonese*. 2nd edition. Hong Kong: Maryknoll House. 306 pages.

(11) Chao, Y. R. 1947a. *Cantonese Primer*. Cambridge, MA: Harvard University Press. 242 pages.

(12) Chao, Y. R. 1947b. *Character Text for Cantonese Primer*. Cambridge, MA: Harvard University Press. 112 pages.

(13) Chan, Yeung Kwong. 1951. *Everybody's Cantonese*. 3rd edition. Hong Kong: The Man Sang Press. 285 pages.

(14) Huang, Parker Po-fei, and Gerard P. Kok. 1963. *Speak Cantonese*, Book 1. New Haven, CO: Yale University, Far Eastern Publications.

---

[20] There is no date of publication. A reference to the 1932 Japanese occupation of Manchuria dates the work tentatively to the 1930s.

[21] The book includes no date of publication. The contents in general give the impression that it was a composition of the 1930s. Furthermore, there seems a great deal of overlapping in content with Taahm's work, approximately dated in the 1930s.

The Pretransitive in Cantonese

2.2.3.4. 前及物式結構

及物動詞都是帶一個普通的賓語，表示受事，但是中文裏賓語提前，成爲前及物式的結構 (pretransitive construction) 洗咗啲衫：將啲衫洗咗 sáijó dì sāam: jèung dì

（洗了衣服：把衣服洗了）

Abstract: The pretransitive construction is a grammatical process that transposes the Object from an S-V-O sequence to a pre-verbal position, with the Object explicitly marked by a coverb such as *ba* 把 in Mandarin or *jeung* 將 in Cantonese. While the construction is a dialect-universal feature in Chinese, the conditions required for its use and the semantic readings it generates vary among dialects. The present article conducts a detailed analysis of its behaviors in Cantonese and examines the factors that condition the use and non-use of the pattern. In particular, it compares the use of *jeung* in contemporary Cantonese with its counterpart in Mandarin, noting in particular the differences between the two dialects in the kind of verbs they are compatible with, the syntactic patterns they are restricted to, and the pragmatic readings they generate through the operation.

Keywords: *jeung* in Cantonese; *ba* in Mandarin; disposal; Verb-Object construction; topicalization

1. Introduction

The pretransitive construction, or the *ba*-sentence as it is commonly referred to in Mandarin, is a language-specific but dialect-universal feature in Chinese grammar. Structurally, the construction may be described as a process by means of which a regular S-V-O sequence is changed to that of S-O-V, with the preposed object explicitly marked by a coverb such as 把 *ba* in Mandarin. Although the permutation of sentential constituents is a phenomenon quite common in all languages, the syntactic, semantic, and pragmatic conditions involved in the Chinese pretransitive construction are so complex that linguists have often claimed that "no similar construction has been found in any other language in the world."[1] In fact, the unique complexity of this construction constitutes one of the most discussed and debated topics in Chinese linguistics. During the last few decades, our understanding of the construction has undergone successive stages of revision and refinement as more data have been included for examination and newer theories have been adopted as referential frameworks.[2] Yet, in spite of the growing interest in the topic, observations and discussions of the pretransitive have been primarily confined to its behavior in Mandarin. While most dialectal studies record and report sentences similar to those of *ba* in Mandarin, none has made a systematic attempt to examine the construction in any detail. In *Hanyu fangyan gaiyao* 漢語方言概要 (Yuan 1961), the first comprehensive survey of Chinese dialects, only sketchy notes and a handful of examples are given to describe the use of the pretransitive in each of its eight major dialect groupings. Aside from noting the obvious fact that different dialects may employ different pretransitive markers, dialectologists in general seem to find little difference in behavior between the pretransitive in Mandarin and its counterparts in other dialects. Indeed, it appears that the conditions ascribed to the use of *ba* in Mandarin are universally applicable across all dialects.

---

[1] Tsao (1987), p. 2.

[2] For a critical review of the various studies conducted during the last few decades on the use of the pretransitive construction in Chinese, see Cheung (1973) and Sanders (1986).

In their respective grammatical treatises on standard Cantonese, Cheung (1972) and Gao (1980) essentially follow the same Mandarin rules in their characterizations of the pretransitive in the southern dialect,[3] where the marker is 將 *jiang*, or *jeung*[4] in Cantonese pronunciation, a morpheme that was historically used in free variation with *ba* in the early vernacular language.[5] However, as Rao accurately notes in his 1981 *Cantonese Dictionary*,[6] the preference for use of the pretransitive construction varies drastically between Mandarin and Cantonese. For example, while both dialects admit the regular and pretransitive arrangements as grammatical sentences as illustrated in the following table, the preferred choice in Cantonese is quite the contrary to that in Mandarin.[7]

(1)	**Non-pretransitive**	**Pretransitive**
Mandarin	Xi ganjing zhe xie yifu. 洗乾淨這些衣服。 Wash-clean-these-clothes.	Ba zhe xie yifu xi ganjing. (*Preferred*) 把這些衣服洗乾淨。
Cantonese	Sai gonjehng di saam. (*Preferred*) 洗乾淨啲衫。 Wash-clean-the-clothes.	Jeung di saam sai gonjehng. 將啲衫洗乾淨。

"Wash the clothes!"

As we shall see in the following pages, the dissimilarity in selection is but one of the many differences between the two dialects in their use of the pretransitive. To characterize the construction as an active syntactic mechanism common to all Chinese dialects may not be an inaccurate representation of the role its plays in the language; yet, to generalize its behavior across the vast topography of China simply on the basis of what we know about it in Mandarin is certainly an oversimplification.

---

[3] Both works devote very little attention to the construction in Cantonese. Cheung (1972), pp. 86–87; and Gao (1980), p. 226.

[4] This article follows the Yale system of Cantonese romanization. Tones are not included in the transcription, for both Cantonese and Mandarin.

[5] For a general discussion on the early use of *ba* and *jiang*, see Wang (1955), pp. 172–174.

[6] Rao (1981), p. 260.

[7] Wang Li (1955) claims that the disposal use of *jeung* is absent in both Cantonese and the Hakka dialect. See pp. 174–175.

Our understanding, to date, of the idiosyncractic behaviors of the pretransitive in dialects other than Mandarin remains regretably partial and vague, a limitation that is all the more severe with reference to the southern dialects whose distinctions from Mandarin, in both phonology and grammar, are generally much more prominent than what we find among the northern dialects. It is the purpose of this study to provide a comprehensive examination of the use of the pretransitive in standard Cantonese, to describe and account for the factors that condition the use and non-use of the pattern, and to offer examples, cross-referenced with those in Mandarin, highlighting the dialectal differences that may help us to better understand the operation of the construction in the language in general.

2. Data

The major sources of data for this study include the following:

(a) Four hours of recording from TV and radio programs made in Hong Kong during the early 1990s.

(b) Interviews and articles written in colloquial Cantonese as published in various issues of Hong Kong weekly magazines. The texts examined are about 108,000 characters in length.

The data were submitted to two rounds of screening. In the first round, I identified and collected all the sentences that involved the use of *jeung*. In the second round, I orally translated the texts into Mandarin, jotting down the cases where the pretransitive was not used in Cantonese but would be required or preferred in Mandarin.

I have also occasionally drawn samples from newspapers and personal conversations with friends and relatives. Some of the examples are from my own speech. Regardless of sources, I have double checked the acceptability or unacceptability of all my examples with a native speaker, who was born in Canton and was educated in Hong Kong through college.

3. General Description of the Pretransitive Construction in Chinese

As aforementioned, the pretransitive construction may be structurally described as the placement of the object before the transitive Verb in a sentence, hence the term "the pretransitive." In this regard, the construction may be characterized as follows:

(2)   Subject   + Pretransitive +   Object   + Verb Phrase
        Noun Phrase   Marker   Noun Phrase

Much of the discussion on the topic in the last few decades has focused upon the relationship between the Verb and the Object, and also the kinds of nouns and verbs that can partake in this process. In summary, it is agreed that: (1) the Object (O), or the pretransitive Noun Phrase (NP), has to be definite or generic in reference; and (2) the Verb Phrase (VP) has to represent a disposal action that directly or indirectly affects the entity referred to in the pretransitive NP. To represent the disposal nature of the action, the VP generally contains an element such as a complement or an aspect suffix to highlight resultative effect. The idea of disposal was first introduced by Wang Li (1955) who described the pretransitive as *chuzhishi* 處置式, an execution form.[8] This characterization was later rejected by grammarians such as Y. R. Chao (1968), who did not consider such a semantic labeling appropriate or broad enough to encompass all kinds of pretransitive sentences, including those of the following type in which the pretransitive object is evidently the agent rather than the patient of the verb.[9]

(3)   Ba ge zei pao le.
        把個賊跑了。
        "The thief ran away."

---

[8] Wang (1955), pp. 164–171. He uses the label "execution form" to render the Chinese term *chuzhishi*.

[9] Chao (1968), p. 345.

(4) <u>Ba</u> wo mang de shou mang jiao luan.
把我忙得手忙腳亂。
"It kept me so busy that my hands and feet were all confused."

However, beginning with Li and Thompson (1981), the concept of disposal has returned to the grammatical scene, this time in a slightly revised role.[10] Disposal is now viewed not as "how to dispose of the pretransitive object" but rather as "what happens to it." In this new guise, the construction becomes more of a pragmatic or discoursal device rather than a syntactic necessity. The pretransitive NP represents the focus of information and is hence treated as the topic of the sentence in both Tsao (1987) and Hsueh (1989).[11] The verbal portion functions primarily as comment on the topic, a fluid discoursal relationship that does not have to be defined in terms of action and agent/patient. To borrow Hsueh's definition, we can sum up the pretransitive construction in the following manner:[12]

Syntactic structure: A *ba* B + C
Semantic implication: In connection to A, B turns out to be what C describes.

In our following investigation of the pretransitive in Cantonese, we will study the various linguistic conditions that necessitate the employment of the construction and we will examine its use as a means of topicalization. We will consider the *jeung*-construction as serving essentially two separate functions in the language: on the one hand, it is a form of pragmatic device marking the focus in an utterance; on the other hand, the mechanism is also at times syntactically or lexically required in order to produce a grammatical sentence. This bipartite treatment may not be deemed satisfactory as there lacks a unifying force that would

---

[10] Li and Thompson (1981) devote an entire chapter to the discussion of the *ba*-construction. On the notion of disposal, see pp. 466–480.

[11] There is a difference between Tsao and Hsueh is their treatments of the *ba* NP as a topic. According to Tsao (1987), the initial NP in a sentence is a regular topic and the *ba* NP is a secondary topic. Hsueh (1989), however, considers the *ba* NP the main topic of the sentence; syntactically, it is the subject of the following predicate. For his arguments, see pp. 107–109.

[12] Hsueh (1989), p. 111.

place all variations under the same interpretative mode. However, as our examples will illustrate, the *jeung*-construction wears two different hats, the distinction between which may not be as readily discernable in other dialects as in Cantonese. Another characteristic feature of the Cantonese pretransitive is its restrictive nature in terms of the notion of disposal. To highlight the contrast in use between Cantonese and Mandarin, all pertinent examples will be given in both dialects.

4. The Disposal Nature of the Pretransitive

In spite of the controversy it raises in terms of its application to Mandarin, the original definition of the pretransitive by Wang Li as a form of disposal is more than adequate to characterize the *jeung*-construction in Cantonese. In his words, "The disposal form states how a person is handled, manipulated, or dealt with; how something is disposed of; or how an affair is conducted."[13] Of all the Cantonese examples we have collected, the majority displays a disposal relationship among the three major sentential elements: the subject NP, the action VP, and the pretransitive NP. The subject is always the agent or actor of the action, which generates a direct result on the entity as represented by the pretransitive object. As in the case of Mandarin, the resultative aspect of the action is generally indicated by some kind of a grammatical element such as the perfective marker, a complement of various types, a second object, or an adverbial. For example,

(5) C. Keuih yihging *jeung* daahp lau maaihjo ge laahk. (V-Aspect)
佢已經將沓樓賣咗嘅喇。

M. Ta yijing *ba* fangzi mai le.
他已經把房子賣了。
"He has already sold the flat."

---

[13] Translation by Li (1974), pp. 200–201.

The Pretransitive in Cantonese | 159

(6) C. Keuih saisailihk *jeung* douh muhn saanmaaih. (V-Directional)
    佢細細力將度門閂埋。

   M. Ta qingqingde *ba* men guanshang.
      他輕輕地把門關上。
      "He closed the door lightly."

(7) C. Mhgoi neih *jeung* di yeh toih yahplaih a. (V-Directional)
    唔該你將啲嘢抬入嚟呀。

   M. Mafan ni *ba* dongxi taijinlai.
      麻煩你把東西抬進來。
      "Please carry the things in."

(8) C. Cheng neih *jeung* ni di yeh gaau bei keuih. (V-Indirect Object)
    請你將呢啲嘢交俾佢。

   M. Qing ni *ba* zhexie dongxi jiao gei ta.
      請你把這些東西交給他。
      "Please give these things to him."

(9) C. Ngoh mouh *jeung* go taaipuhn heung jo nihng a. (Adverb-V)
    我冇將個呔盤向左擰啊。

   M. Wo mei *ba* lunpan xiang zuo ning a.
      我沒把輪盤向左擰啊。
      "I didn't turn the steering wheel to the left."

(10) C. Keuih a-bah *jeung* keuih da dou mhhahng dak gam jaih. (V-Complement)
     佢阿爸將佢打到唔行得咁滯。

   M. Ta baba *ba* ta da de cha yidianr zou bu dong lu.
      他爸爸把他打得差一點兒走不動路。
      "His dad hit him so hard that he almost couldn't walk."

(11) C. *Jeung* ga che tan hauh di. (V-Complement)
     將架車退後啲。

   M. *Ba* che wang hou tui yidianr.
      把車望後退一點兒。
      "Back up the car a little bit."

(12) C. Mat neih juhng meih *jeung* di faahn <u>sihk saai</u> ah? (V-Complement)
乜你重未將哋飯食晒呀？

M. Zenme ni hai mei *ba* fan <u>chi wan</u>?
怎麼你還沒把飯吃完？
"How come that you still haven't finished eating your meal?"

The above sentences, by no means exhaustive of the kinds of VPs the pretransitive construction requires, invariably show a disposal reading of the relationship between the agent subjects and the patient objects. The actions direct their impacts onto the pretransitive NP. Hence, in the last example, the resultative state of *sihk saai* (finish eating the entire quantity) clearly refers to the object *faahn* (rice or meal). However, if we compare example (12) with the following pair, we detect a violation of this general principle of disposal since the resultative state of "being full" in example (13) refers to the eater and not to the food. For this reason, the sentence is not good in Cantonese.

(13) C. *Mat neih juhng meih *jeung* di faahn sihk baau a?
乜你重未將哋飯食飽呀？

M. Zenme ni hai mei *ba* fan chi bao?
怎麼你還沒把飯吃飽？
"How come that you still haven't had enough?"

Yet, in contrast to the strict observation of the disposal requirement in Cantonese, Mandarin accepts the corresponding form as a well-formed sentence.[14] In fact, as exemplified by the following sentences, Mandarin exhibits a much higher degree of tolerance than Cantonese for the transgressive or versatile use of the pretransitive construction.

---

[14] The behavior of *chi fan* in example (13) is not necessarily representative of other Mandarin verbs in this regard. For example, it is not possible to say *ba yifu xi de hen lei* 把衣服洗得很累 (to feel exhausted from washing clothes). However, from the examples to be cited later, it is evident that the semantic requirement of a disposal reading is not to be taken literally to account for the great variety of situations in which the pretransitive construction is used in Mandarin.

(14) M. Wo *ba* ta hen tou le.
我把他恨透了。

C. *Ngoh *jeung* keuih hahn tau la.
我將佢恨透喇。
"I hate his guts."

(15) M. Ni *ba* wo ji huai le.
你把我急壞了。

C. *Neih *jeung* ngoh gap waih la.
你將我急壞喇。
"You got me worried sick."

(16) M. Ta *ba* ge erzi bing si le.
他把個兒子病死了。

C. *Keuih *jeung* go jai behng seijo.
佢將個仔病死咗。
"He lost his son through death."

(17) M. Ta *ba* wo ku de xin dou fan le.
他把我哭得心都煩了。

C. *Keuih *jeung* ngoh haam dou sam dou faahn saai.
佢將我喊到心都煩晒。
"He cried so much that he got on my nerves."

(18) M. Zhe ge gushi *ba* wo xiao de duzi dou teng le.
這個故事把我笑得肚子都疼了。

C. *Ni go gujai *jeung* ngoh siu dou touh dou tung maai.
呢個故仔將我笑到肚都痛埋。
"This story made me laugh so mush that my belly ached."

In example (14), *hen tou* (to bear extreme hatred) stands for the emotional state of *wo* (I), the impact being more on the subject NP rather than on the pretransitive NP. In (15) and (16), the verbal phrases are both status descriptions of the pretransitive NPs; but in neither case is the subject NP directly responsible for the outcome. The verb *ku* (to cry) in (17) does not have the pretransitive object *wo* as its goal of action. The grammatical subject in (18), *zhe ge gushi* (this story), is clearly not the actor of the verb *xiao* (to laugh). In short, none of the sentences is a true case of disposal, which explains why the pretransitive is not applicable in Cantonese. Yet, all of them may appear in the *ba*-paradigm in Mandarin. In this regard, the two dialects vary drastically in their readiness to relax and extend the semantic reading of disposal to include a wide variety of behaviors, some of which, such as (18), may be readily characterized as a stylistic device to achieve a special effect in vivid narration.[15]

To take another look at this device of vivid narration, let us compare the following sets of examples:

(19) C. a. Ngoh se ni go bougou se dou tauhtauh sih douh.
我寫呢個報告寫到頭頭是道。

b. Ngoh *jeung* ni go bougou se dou tauhtauh sih douh.
我將呢個報告寫到頭頭是道。

c. *Ni go bougou se dou ngoh tauhtauh sih douh.
呢個報告寫到我頭頭是道。

d. *Ni go bougou *jeung* ngoh se dou tauhtauh sih douh.
呢個報告將我寫到頭頭是道。

M. a. Wo xie zhe ge baogaob xie de toutou shi dao.
我寫這個報告寫得頭頭是道。

b. Wo *ba* zhe ge baogao xie de toutou shi dao.
我把這個報告寫得頭頭是道。

c. *Zhe ge baogao xie de wo toutou shi dao.
這個報告寫得我頭頭是道。

d. *Zhe ge baogao *ba* wo xie de toutou shi dao.
這個報告把我寫得頭頭是道。

"I wrote the report in such a manner that the arguments are both clear and logical."

---

[15] In justifying the notion of disposal as characteristic of the use of *ba* in Mandarin, Li and Thompson (1981) argue that disposal may be inferred to or understood in an implicit way. They claim a nondisposal verb like *ai* 愛 (to love) may take on a disposal reading when an hyperbolic expression like *yao si* (want to die) is added to the verb as in the sentence: *Ta ba xiao mao ai de yao si* 他把小貓愛得要死 (He loves the kitten so much that he wants to die). They suggest that "such intense love must have some effect on the small cat," an implied case of disposal which "is sufficient to warrant the use of the *ba* construction" (pp. 468–469). However, as *yao si* refers to the person who loves and not the object of the passion, the hyperbolic disposal seems to be directed more to the Subject than to the *ba* Object. This is but one of the many cases that have yet to be resolved in the framework of disposal. In Cantonese, *jeung* is never used in this manner.

(20) C. a. Ngoh se ni go bougou se dou sehng maahn mouh fan.
我寫呢個報告寫到成晚冇瞓。

b. *Ngoh *jeung* ni go bougou se dou sehng maahn mouh fan.
我將呢個報告寫到成晚冇瞓。

c. Ni go bougou dou ngoh sehng maahn mouh fan.
呢個報告寫到我成晚冇瞓。

d. *Ni go bougou *jeung* ngoh se dou sehng maahn mouh fan.
呢個報告將我寫到成晚冇瞓。

M. a. Wo xie zhe ge baogao xie de yi ye me shui.
我寫這個報告寫得一夜沒睡。

b. ? Wo *ba* zhe ge baogao xie de yi ye mei shui.
我把這個報告寫得一夜沒睡。

c. Zhe ge baogao xie de wo yi ye mei shui
這個報告寫得我一夜沒睡。

d. Zhe ge baogao *ba* wo xie de yi ye mei shui.
這個報告把我寫得一夜沒睡。

"Writing the report kept me up the whole night."

In the first set, the complement expression refers to the quality of the report which the agent achieves through his writing effort. The event represents a bona fide case of execution; hence, the pretransitive permutation is permissable in both Cantonese and Mandarin, as shown in examples (19b). Sentences (19c) and (19d), on the other hand, are incorrect because only the agent and not the patient may occupy the regular subject position. The situation is, however, quite different in the second set. As a stylistic device, both dialects allow a modification of the regular word order. As the agent and the patient swap positions in the sentence as in (20c), the telling of the event becomes more dramatic in result. There is only one condition attached to this stylistic modification, namely, the complement expression ("to be up the whole night") has to refer back to the agent ("I") and not to the patient ("report"), a stipulation that both Mandarin and Cantonese observe as shown in the ungrammaticality of (19c). But beyond this step the two dialects part company. Only Mandarin, and not Cantonese, may apply the pretransitive construction to the secondary or derived object, the agent writer. Hence, (20d) is acceptable in one dialect but not in the other one. If we examine the above sentences in pairs, it is evident that the pretransitive construction in Mandarin may readily apply to any sentence with an object, regardless of its derivational relationship with the verb. In Cantonese, however, the operation discriminates against a derived object, as evidenced by (20d). This difference in object identification and selection explains why none of the following Mandarin sentences are acceptable in Cantonese.[16]

(21) M. Zhe duan lu *ba* Xiao Li pao de shang qi bu jie xia qi.
這段路把小李跑得上氣不接下氣。

C. *Ni dyuhn louh *jeung* A-Leih jau dou seuhng hei mhjip hah hei.
呢段路將阿李走到上氣唔接下氣。
"Little Li was out of breath through running this route."

(22) M. Zhe ping maotaijiu *ba* ta he de lan-zui-ru-ni.
這瓶茅台酒把他喝得爛醉如泥。

C. *Ni jeun maauhtoihjau *jeung* keuih yam dou laahn-jeui-yuh-naih.
呢樽茅台酒將佢飲到爛醉如泥。
"He became completely drunk after a bottle of *maotai*."

(23) M. Zhe ban xuesheng *ba* Wang laoshi jiao de xin-hui-yi-leng.
這班學生把王老師教得心灰意冷。

C. *Ni baan hohksaang *jeung* Wohng saang gaau dou sam-fui-yi-laahng.
呢班學生將王生教到心灰意冷。
"Teacher Wang became depressed from teaching this class of students."

(24) M. Kan, *ba* ta lei de ...
看，把他累得……

C. *Tai, *jeung* keuih guih dou ...
睇，將佢癐到……
"Look, how exhausted he is!"

To some linguists, the pretransitive form in the above sentences may seem causative in function.[17] Hence, sentence (21), for example, is derived from (21a) and (21b).

(21a) Zhe dan lu a, shi Xiao Li pao de shang qi bu jie xia qi.
這段路呀，使小李跑得上氣不接下氣。

---

[16] The following sentences (21) to (24) are all taken from Hsueh (1989).

[17] For this causative reading of the pretransitive form, see Chao (1968), p. 345; and Tsao (1987), pp. 38–41.

(21b) Zhe duan lu pao de Xiao Li a, shang qi bu jie xia qi.
       這段路跑得小李呀，上氣不接下氣。

As Xiao Li sits in the object position in (21b), it is readily qualified for the pretransitive operation. Such qualification for the causative usage of the pretransitive is, however, nonexistent in Cantonese.

5. The Pretransitive as a Linguistic Necessity

5.1. Insofar as there is a regular S-V-O sentence corresponding to the pretransitive form in the language, the pretransitive construction seems to be an optional mechanism in Chinese, an operation perhaps more preferable in one dialect than the other. As shown in the examples (1) and (25), Mandarin and Cantonese differ in their choice for the pretransitive. Deviation from the habitual pattern of selection may sometimes yield a strange, but not necessarily unacceptable, sentence.

(25) C. a. Keuihdeih nahmjyuh duhk hou syu jauh syunsou ge laak.
            佢哋諗住讀好書就算數嘅喇。
     b. ? Keuihdeih nahmjyuh *jeung* syu duk hou jauh syunsou ge laak.
            佢哋諗住將書讀好就算數嘅喇。

     M. a. ? Tamen xiang nian hao shu jiu suan le.
            他們想念好書就算了。
        b. Tamen xiang *ba* shu nian hao jiu suan le.
            他們想把書念好就算了。
            "They think their job will be done when they finish their schooling."

Both dialects, however, have a large of number of sentences where the use of the pretransitive is a necessity and not an option. In a 1948 article, Lü made the first attempt to discuss the various syntactic conditions under which the pretransitive construction had to be employed.[18] He examined a wide variety of early vernacular texts and offered a list of seven conditions to characterize its obligatory use. Interested readers may refer to the article

---

[18] Lü (1948) lists a total of 13 conditions to account for the obligatory and optional uses of the pretransitive construction. His examples are drawn from a variety of vernacular writings mostly of the Ming/Qing era, from the 14th to the 19th centuries.

and also reviews of it by Wang (1959) and Sanders (1986). In general, Lü claims that "this construction is used in most cases when there is a postverbal element other than the ordinary object, that cannot be easily separated from the verb" (p. 212). In modern Mandarin, for example, the *ba*-construction is required to produce the following sentences:

(26) Ta like *ba* na feng jinji de xin song gei shouxinren.
他立刻把那封緊急的信送給收信人。

*Ta like song na feng jinji de xin gei shouxinren.
他立刻送那封緊急的信給收信人。
"He immediately delivered the urgent letter to the receiver."

(27) Qu *ba* damen shangle suo.
去把大門上了鎖。

*Qu shangle suo damen.
去上了鎖大門。
"Go lock the main door."

(28) Ta *ba* qian la zai jiali le.
他把錢落在家裡了。

*Ta la qian zai jiali le.
他落錢在家裡了。
"He left his money at home."

(29) Ta xiang *ba* xin mai de bu zuo cheng mian'ao.
他想把新買的布做成棉襖。

*Ta xiang zuo xin mai de bu cheng mian'ao.
他想做新買的布成棉襖。
"He wanted to use the new cloth to make a padded jacket."

(30) Tamen *ba* ta kan zuo ziji de nü'er.
他們把她看作自己的女兒。

*Tamen kan ta zuo ziji de nü'er.
他們看她作自己的女兒。
"They treated her like their own daughter."

Without going into much detail, it is evident that all of the above cases involve two NP's in the predicate, an object NP and another NP of some sort: an indirect object, a retained object, a locative, etc. It seems that, as a general rule of thumb, when there are two NPs in a predicate, it is considered too clustered a grouping of information for clear communication.[19] Thus, it becomes necessary or highly desirable to evict one of them, usually the one whose reference has been established in the discourse, from the immediate domain of the verb so as to reserve room for the main message. In the above examples, since the message concerns primarily the location, relocation, or some kind of a transformation of a certain item, that item, which is the direct object NP, is targeted for the pretransitive movement. Similar reasoning may be applied to the preferred, albeit optional, use of the pretransitive with the directional complement in Mandarin.

(31) *Ba* ta qing lai.
把他請來。
"Invite him over."

(32) *Qu ba* tamen zhao huilai.
去把他們找回來。
"Go find them and bring them back."

(33) *Ba* zhe ge na chu waibian qu.
把這個拿出外邊去。
"Take this outside."

In fact, it has been reported that the most common situation where the pretransitive is used is when the sentence contains a directional expression.[20]

Compared with Mandarin, the Cantonese dialect is less restrictive with its syntactic rules on the operation of the pretransitive. In the following

---

[19] Also to be avoided is the grouping of Object and Complement in the same postverbal slot. Either the Object is to be lifted out of the confines, or the Verb will be repeated to provide each component its own verbal domain.

[20] According to a study based upon colloquial essays, stories, and speeches, 40% of the collected *ba*-sentences end with a directional suffix and another 28% contain a directional phrase. Figures are quoted in Li and Thompson (1981), p. 490. A half-hour TV program which I listened to have a total of seven *ba*-sentences, all of which were related to the directional complement. This prominent use of *ba* in directional sentences poses actually an important question in terms of language pedagogy. Even on the basis of these preliminary findings, it is obvious that a good textbook should introduce the *ba*-construction before the directional complement, thereby equipping the students with the necessary linguistic skill to produce proper sentences. The 1980 Beijing text entitled *Practical Chinese Reader* does not follow this order of presentation and, as a consequence, it teaches sentences such as:

Ni na hui na feng xin lai le ma?
你拿回那封信來了嗎？
"Have you gotten and returned with that letter?"

set of sentences where *ba* is almost always required in Mandarin, the southern dialect prefers the non-*jeung* pattern.

(34) M. Qing ni ti wo *ba* zhe bun shu huan gei tushuguan.
請你替我把這本書還給圖書館。

C. Mhgoi neih bong ngoh waahn faan ni bun syu bei touhsyugun la.
唔該你幫我還翻呢本書俾圖書館喇。
"Please return this book to the library for me."

(35) M. Zhongguo ren *guan* mama de mama jiao shenme?[21]
中國人管媽媽的媽媽叫什麼？

C. Junggwok yahn ngaai mahma ge mahma jouh matyeh a?
中國人嗌媽媽嘅媽媽做乜嘢呀？
"What do the Chinese call their mother's mother?"

(36) M. Ni ba wo de maozi fang zai nar le?
你把我的帽子放在哪兒了？

C. Neih jaijo ngoh deng mouh hai bin syu a?
你擠咗我頂帽喺邊處呀？
"Where did you put my hat?"

(37) M. Bie *ba* zhi reng zai cesuo li.
別把紙扔在廁所裡。

C. Mhhou dam di ji hai chiso syu.
唔好抌吔紙喺廁所處。
"Don't throw the paper into the toilet."

(38) M. Zanshi *ba* che ting zai menkou.
暫時把車停在門口。

C. Jaamsih ting ga che heung muhnhau douh.
暫時停架車响門口度。
"Park your car in front the gate for the time being."

(39) M. Ta *ba* yao yong de dongxi dou ban xia lou lai le.
他把要用的東西都搬下樓來了。

---

[21] *Guan* 管 is one of the pretransitive variants, but its use is limited to only one verb, *jiao* 叫 (to call [by some name]). See Chao (1968), p. 343.

C. Keuih bun saai yiu yuhng ge yeh lohklaih louhhah laak.
佢搬晒要用嘅嘢落嚟樓下喇。
"He has moved to downstairs all the items he needs to use."

While there is the same need to avoid crowding the verb domain with crucial information, Cantonese prefers the serial verb construction over that of the pretransitive, thereby finding for each NP its own verbal niche. It is perhaps because of this prevalence in structural choice that the pretransitive construction is sometimes described as foreign to Cantonese or a borrowing from the northern dialects.[22] There are, however, some situations where the *jeung*-construction is compulsory in Cantonese. The following is a discussion of the conditions in which the pretransitive has to be utilized.

5.2. When the complement component in the predicate is a verbal expression that contains its own NP, the standard practice is to adopt the serial verb sequence: V1+O1+V2+O2. However, when the complement verb (V2) is by nature a bound form and has to be attached to the main verb (V1) to form a free unit, the object of the main verb (O1) has to be transposed out of the domain by means of the pretransitive movement: *jeung*+O1+V1–V2+O2. For example, contrast the following two sentences:

(40) C. Tuhng ngoh yihk ni geui jouh Yingman.
同我譯呢句做英文。
Tuhng ngoh *jeung* ni geui yihk jouh Yingman.
同我將呢句譯做英文。

M. Ti wo ba zhe ju fan cheng Yingwen.
替我把這句翻成英文。
"Please translate this sentence into English for me."

(41) C. Tuhng ngoh *jeung* ni geui yihksihng Yingman.
同我將呢句譯成英文。
*Tuhng ngoh yihk ni geui sihng Yingman.
同我譯呢句成英文。

M. Ti wo *ba* zhe ju fan cheng Yingwen.
替我把這句翻成英文。
Please translate this sentence into English for me." (Same as [40])

---

[22] See Norman (1988), p. 221.

While both *jouh* and *sihng* carry the same function of marking the medium into which the sentence is translated, the former is a free morpheme and the latter is bound. The free status of *jouh* allows it to appear in two different word orders as illustrated in (40). On the other hand, the bound form *sihng* in (41) is attached to the main verb *yihk*, blocking out the original space for the object *geui*. As a result, the pretransitive is the only possible path to follow, transposing *geui* to a preverbal slot. This obligatory use of *jeung* pertains essentially to one complement verb *sihng*. The following is a few more examples to illustrate its use.[23]

---

[23] On the use of Verb-*sihng*, it should be noted that in the following three sentences where the non-pretransitive is used, the objects are placed differently. If the verb is monosyllabic, *sihng* has to be attached to the verb to form one functioning unit, with the object coming afterwards. If, on the other hand, the verb is a two-syllable form, *sihng* may appear either before or after the object. In the former case, it becomes part of the verb; in the latter, it forms alliance with *gam*, a pro-adverbial meaning "in this manner."

    (i)   Mat ha sihng neih gam a? (How have they bullied you?!)
             乜蝦成你咁呀？
    (ii)   Mat jitmoh sihng neih gam a? (How have they tortured you?!)
             乜折磨成你咁呀？
    (iii) Mat jitmoh neih sihng gam a?
             乜折磨你成咁呀？

In the following pair of examples (iv) and (v), however, semantic ambiuguity arises as the postverbal objects may be the objects of the verbs or objects in the complements. Hence, there are two possible readings: "to make you up in such a way," or "to make someone else up like you."

    (iv) Mat fa sihng neih gam a? (They've made you up like this!)
             乜化成你咁呀？
    (v)   Mat fajong sihng neih gam a?
             乜化裝成你咁呀？

Sentence (vi) can have only one meaning, so do sentences (vii) and (viii) which are phrased in the *jeung* pattern.

    (vi) Mat fajong neih sihng gam a? (They've made you up like this!)
             乜化裝你成咁呀？
    (vii) Mat *jeung* neih fa sihng gam a?
             乜將你化成咁呀？
    (viii) Mat *jeung* neih fa jong sihng gam a?
             乜將你化裝成咁呀？

(42) C. *Jeung* go daahngou chit*sihng* saam fahn.
將個蛋糕切成三份。
"Cut the cake into three pieces."

(43) C. *Jeung* Tin'onmuhn sihgin se*sihng* yat go kekbun.
將天安門事件寫成一個劇本。
"Turn the Tiananmen incident into a play."

(44) C. *Jeung* neih dabaahn*sihng* yat go baakyepo.
將你打扮成一個伯爺婆。
"Dress you up like an old lady."

(45) C. *Jeung* neih di tauhfaat jin*sihng* go pungtauh.
將你哋頭髮剪成個崩頭。
"Turn your hair into the punk style."

5.3. When a verb takes both a direct object (DO) and an indirect object (IO) in a sentence, the order in which they appear in Cantonese is the exact opposite of that in Mandarin. Hence,

(46) M. Gei wo (IO) qian (DO).
給我錢。
C. Bei chin (DO) ngoh (IO).
俾錢我。
"Give me money."

If the DO is definite in reference, the preferred ordering in Mandarin is in the *ba*-pattern. Cantonese, on the other hand, still opts for the non-pretransitive.

(47) M. *Ba* na xie qian gei wo.
把那些錢給我。
C. Bei go di chin ngoh.
俾嗰啲錢我。

This selection pattern holds true in general when the DO is a nonhuman noun. However, if both the DO and IO are human terms, the situation in Cantonese becomes quite complicated, as indicated in the following table.

(48)

Direct O	Indirect O	Pretransitive	Non-pretransitive
Noun	Noun	Yes	No
	Proper Noun	Yes	Yes
	Pronoun	Yes	Yes
Proper Noun	Noun	Yes	No
	Proper Noun	Yes	No
	Pronoun	Yes	Yes
Pronoun	Noun	Yes	No
	Proper Noun	Yes	No
	Pronoun	Yes	No

There seems to be two principles at work. First, if both the DO and IO belong to the same grammatical category, e.g., both are nouns, proper nouns, or pronouns, then the pretransitive form is strongly preferred. The juxtaposition of two objects of the same type next to each other in the same post-*bei* slot may easily create confusion as to *who* is giving *whom*. Examples are:

(49) C. *Jeung* ni go guhaak bei go go fogei. $(DO_N - IO_N)$
將呢個顧客俾嗰個伙記。
? Bei ni go guhaak go go fogei.
俾呢個顧客嗰個伙記。

M. *Ba* zhe ge guke gei na ge huoji.
把這個顧客給那個伙記。
"Give this client to that clerk."

(50) C. *Jeung* Baahk siuje bei Chahn taai. $(DO_{PpN} - IO_{PpN})$
將白小姐俾陳太。
? Bei Baahk siuje Chlhn taai.
俾白小姐陳太。

M. *Ba* Bai xiaojie gei Chan taaitaai.
把白小姐給陳太太。
"Give Ms. Bai to Mrs. Chan."

(51) C. *Jeung* keuih bei neih. $(DO_{Pn} - IO_{Pn})$
將佢俾你。
*Bei keuih neih.
俾佢你。

M. *Ba* ta gei ni.
把他給你。
"Give her to you."

The second underlying principle is that there is a selection criterion based upon the specificness of the NP. Generally speaking, a noun is less specific than a proper noun, which in turn is less specific than a deitic pronoun. A personal noun stands for a general class of people while a pronoun represents a specific member in a set. Even though a noun may be qualified by a definite demonstrative, the reference of, say, *that student* may not be particular enough for an immediate identification. A proper noun such as *Mr. Wang* is, on the other hand, more specific than a noun but not as specific as a pronoun. There may be more than one Mr. Wang in a room but there can be no more than one *you* at one time. If we adopt a scale from 1 to 3 to indicate the specificness of a noun phrase, with 3 marking the highest degree of specificity, we may modify the above table in (48) by showing the association between the two NPs in this regard:

(52)

Direct O		Indirect O		Pretransitive	Non-pretransitive
	=	Noun	1	Yes	No
Noun 1	<	Proper Noun	2	Yes	Yes
	<	Pronoun	3	Yes	Yes
	>	Noun	1	Yes	No
Proper Noun 2	=	Proper Noun	2	Yes	No
	<	Pronoun	3	Yes	Yes
	>	Noun	1	Yes	No
Pronoun 3	>	Proper Noun	2	Yes	No
	=	Pronoun	3	Yes	No

Now, with regard to the double object construction in Chinese, the general reading of the two objects is that the IO is more specific in reference than the DO. For example, if the DO is in the interrogative form, hence non-specific in reference, the general order in Cantonese is for IO to follow DO, a direction from nonspecific to specific.

(53)　C.　Ngoh yinggoi bei bin bun syu neih a?
　　　　　我應該俾邊本書你呀？
　　　　　"Which book should I give you?"

On the other hand, if the IO is interrogative, the regular order of IO followed by DO will turn to the direction from specific to nonspecific in the predicate, a reversal that Cantonese does not readily endorse. As a result, the specific DO needs to be transferred out of the VP either through topicalization or the pretransitive.

(54) C. ? Ngoh yinggoi bei bun syu bin go a?
我應該俾本書邊個呀？
Bun syu ngoh yinggoi bei bin go a?
本書我應該俾邊個呀？
Ngoh yinggoi *jeung* bun syu bei bin go a?
我應該將本書俾邊個呀？
"Who should I give this book to?"

If we examine the ratings of the NP's in (52) in light of this directional reading from less specific to more specific, we see that whenever the principle is violated, the regular sequence of DO + IO is barred. When the DO rating is higher than that of IO, the direction is from more specific to less specific, a course that calls for the use of the pretransitive. Otherwise, when the DO is less specific than the IO, the pretransitive is an optional choice, with perhaps a slight difference in emphasis. In the case where there is an equation in rating between the two NPs, they are identical in grammatical status. And, in accordance with the first principle, the pretransitive is obligatory. The following are further examples to demonstrate the complexity of the double object construction.[24]

(55) C. Bei ni go hohksaang Chahn taai.   ($DO_N < IO_{PpN}$)
俾呢個學生陳太。
Jeung ni go hohksaang bei Chahn taai.
將呢個學生俾陳太。

M. *Ba* zhe ge xuesheng gei Chen taitai.
把這個學生給陳太太。
"Give this student to Mrs. Chan."

---

[24] Of course, the dative can be marked by another *bei* 俾. For example, *Bei syu ngoh* 俾書我 — *Bei syu bei ngoh* 俾書俾我 ("Give me the book"). Yet, when both objects are pronouns, even the use of the second *bei* would not improve the acceptability of the string *bei neih bei ngoh* ("Give you to me").

(56) C. *Bei Chahn taai ni go hohksaang.　　　　　(DO$_{PpN}$ > IO$_N$)
俾陳太呢個學生。
Jeung Chahn taai bei ni go hohksaang.
將陳太俾呢個學生。

M. *Ba* Chen taitai gei zhe ge xuesheng.
把陳太太給這個學生。
"Give Mrs. Chen to this student."

(57) C. *Bei keuih go go louhbaan.　　　　　(DO$_{Pn}$ > IO$_N$)
俾佢嗰個老板。
Jeung keuih bei go go louhbaan.
將佢俾嗰個老板。

M. *Ba* ta gei na ge laoban.
把他給那個老板。
"Give him to that boss."

(58) C. Bei Baahk xiuje ngohdeih la.　　　　　(DO$_{PnN}$ < IO$_{Pn}$)
俾白小姐我哋啦。
Jeung Baahk xiuje bei ngohdeih la.
將白小姐俾我哋啦。

M. *Ba* Bai xiaojie gei women ba.
把白小姐給我們吧！
"Why don't you give Miss Bai to us?"

(59) C. *Bin go wah bei ngohdeih Chahn saang ga?　　　　　(DO$_{Pn}$ > IO$_{PpN}$)
邊個話俾我哋陳生㗎？
Bin go wah *jeung* ngohdeih bei Chahn saang ga?
邊個話將我哋俾陳生㗎？

M. Shei shuo *ba* women gei Chen xiansheng de?
誰說把我們給陳先生的？
"Who said that we'd be given to Mr. Chan?"

(60) C. Bin go wah bei Chahn saang ngohdeih ga?　　　　　(DO$_{PnN}$ < IO$_{Pn}$)
邊個話俾陳生我哋㗎？
Bin go wah *jeung* Chahn saan bei ngohdei ga?
邊個話將陳生俾我哋㗎？

M. Shei shuo *ba* Chen xiangsheng gei women?
誰説把陳先生給我們？
"Who said that Mr. Chen would be given to us?"

In Cantonese, *bei* 俾 (to give) is the ubiquitous marker of the double object construction. In some cases, when another verb is added to the sentence more descriptive of the actual manner of the giving action, the structure changes into a serial verb construction, e.g., *bei* → *sung bei* 送俾 (to give as a present). Each verb in the predicate can take on its own object, the DO following the action verb and the IO following *bei*. The complexity regarding specificness becomes irrelevant to the arrangement of the two objects. The pretransitive is always an optional choice. A few examples of the V-*bei* type are:

(61) C. Ngoh gaau go mui bei neih la.   (DO < IO)
我交個妹俾你喇。
Ngoh *jeung* go mui gaau bei neih la.
我將個妹交俾你喇。

M. Wo *ba* meimei jiao gei ni la.
我把妹妹交給你了。
"I'm turning over my sister to you."

(62) C. Gaangngaang sak keuih bei ngoh.   (DO = IO)
監硬塞佢俾我。
Gaangngaang *jeung* keuih sak bei ngoh.
監硬將佢塞俾我。

M. Ying *ba* ta sai gei wo.
硬把他塞給我。
"(Someone) stuck him to me against my will."

(63) C. Batyuh je Chan seuh bei go baan la.   (DO > IO)
不如借陳sir俾嗰班啦。
Batyuh *jeung* Chan seuh je bei go baan la.
不如將陳sir借俾嗰班啦。

M. Buru *ba* Chen laoshi jie gei na ban ba.
不如把陳老師借給那班吧！
"Why don't we loan Mr. Chen to that class?"

5.4. When the main verb of the sentence is in itself a Verb-Object in combination, leaving no room for an additional NP to follow it, the proper disposal object has to appear in the pretransitive position. For example,

(64) C. *Jeung* douh muhn yauh huhngsik.
將度門油紅色。
*Yauh douh muhn huhngsik.
油度門紅色。

M. *Ba* men qi(cheng) hongse.
把門漆（成）紅色。
"Paint the door red."

Huhngsik (red color) is the nominal in the verbal unit that takes precedence over *muhn* in occupying the post-verbal position. However, in the following sentence of the same reading where the color term *huhng* is now an adjective rather than a noun, the post-verbal nominal position become available. Hence, the pretransitive is no longer compulsory. In fact, between the following two sequences, the non-pretransitive form seems more preferable.

(65) C. Yauh huhng douh muhn.
油紅度門。
Jeung douh muhn yauh huhng.
將度門油紅。

M. *Ba* men qi hong.
把門漆紅。

Some more examples of the V-O compound type are:

(66) C. Neih *jeung* di *jyuyuhk chitjo pin* meih?
你將啲豬肉切咗片未呀？
"Have you sliced the pork?"

(67) C. Mhhou dang yahndeih *jeung* ngoh *dihng yihng*.
唔好等人哋將我定型。
"Don't let others fix my image."

(68) C. *Jeung* neih *baahn haai*.
將你扮蟹。
"Turn you into a crab: Tie you up."

(69) C. Mhgeidak *jeung* douh muhn *seuhng so*.
唔記得將度門上鎖。
"I forgot to lock the door."

(70) C. Sihsih *jeung* ga che *da laahp* wuih hou di ga.
時時將架車打蠟會好啲架。
"It'd be better if you wax the car often."

5.5. When the message of a sentence stresses the all-inclusiveness of the action, covering the entirety of the disposed object, the *jeung*-construction is very often used. In some cases, it is even required in order to produce an acceptable sentence. For example, in the following sentences, the use of the adverbial *hahmbaahnglaahng* and *chyuhnbouh*, both meaning "all," automatically calls for the operation of the pretransitive.

(71) C. Keuih tai cho saai di taihmuhk.
佢睇錯晒啲題目。
"He read all the questions wrong."

(72) C. Keuih *jeung* di taihmuhk *hahmbaahnglaahng* tai cho saai.
佢將啲題目冚唪唥睇錯晒。
*Keuih *hahmbaahnglaahng* tai cho saai di taihmuhk.
佢冚唪唥睇錯晒啲題目。
"He read all the questions wrong."

(73) C. Ngoh yihging *jeung* diyeh *chyuhnbouh* ning jau la.
我已經將啲嘢全部擰走喇。
*Ngoh yihging *chyuhnbouh* ning jau di yeh la.
我已經全部擰走啲嘢喇。
"I have already moved away everything."

This situation in Cantonese is similar to the use of *dou* or *quan*, both meaning "all" in Mandarin. As noted in other studies, these inclusive adverbs refer only to the scope or quantity of the noun standing before the verb and never to that of the one after it. Therefore, if it is the object that is being focused, the pretransitive construction may apply to move the Object-NP to a preverbal position.[25] Sentences in (74) are examples from Mandarin to illustrate this characteristic behavior of the scope adverbs.

(74a) M. Ta *ba* timu dou kan cuo le.
他把題目都看錯了。

---

[25] Lü (1955), pp. 142–143.

(74b) M. Ta *ba* timu quan kan cuo le.
 他把題目全看錯了。
 "He read all the questions wrong."

Again, like Mandarin, Cantonese may employ the interrogative word to indicate the all-inclusiveness of an action. Examples are:

(75) C. Keuih *jeung* mat chin dou yuhng saai.
 佢將乜錢都用晒。
 *Keuih dou yuhng saai mat chin.
 佢都用晒乜錢。

 M. Ta *ba* shenme qian dou yong wan le.
 他把什麼錢都用完了。
 "He used up all the money."

(76) C. Keuih *jeung* matyeh yahn dou dakjeuih saai.[26]
 佢將乜嘢人都得罪晒。
 *Keuih dou dakjeuih saai matyeh yahn.
 佢都得罪晒乜嘢人。

 M. Ta *ba* shenme ren dou dezui le.
 他把什麼人都得罪了。
 "He has offended everyone."

Another form that falls under this general category of scope is the verbal complement *muhn* (full). For example,

(77) C. Keuih *jeung* buhng cheuhng gwa muhn saai wa.
 佢將埲牆掛滿晒畫。
 "He has hung pictures all over the wall."

---

[26] This inclusive use of an interrogative in a pretransitive construction is limited to *matyeh* (what) and its associations. Other interrogative words do not seem able to participate in this operation. For example, compare (76) with the following sentence (i), and also (ii) with (iii).
 (i) *Keuih *jeung* bingo yahn dou dakjeui saai.
  佢將邊個人都得罪晒。
  "He has offended everyone."
 (ii) Keuih *jeung* matyeh dehngfong dou dasou dak gongonjehngjehng.
  佢將乜嘢地方都打掃得乾乾淨淨。
 (iii) *Keuih *jeung* bindouh dehngfdng dou dasou dak gongonjehngjehng.
  佢將邊度地方都打掃得乾乾淨淨。
  "He has made every place spotlessly clean."

One thing to notice about (77) is that there is another object in the sentence, *wa* (pictures), which is the true object of the verb *gwa* (to hang). Semantically, *buhng cheuhng* (the wall) is more like the place where the pictures are hung. However, as convincingly argued in Teng (1975), *cheuhng* here is not a true locative for the simple reason that for a noun to serve in this capacity, it needs to take on a locative marker, *syu* in Cantonese, as in the following sentence.[27]

(78) C. Keuih *jeung* di wa gwa muhn saai hai buhng cheuhng syu.
佢將啲畫掛滿晒喺埲牆處。
"He has hung all the pictures on the wall."

In other words, the nominal *buhng cheuhng* (the wall) in (77) identifies not so much the location where the pictures are hung but rather the location which the agent decorates with pictures. It is the object of a disposal action which in itself contains a verb and an object. As for the scope of the action verb, it is evidently the preverbal *cheuhng* (the wall) and not the postverbal *wa* (the pictures) that the complement *muhn* refers to. It should be noted that if the notion of all-inclusiveness is absent in the sentence, as in the following cases, the use of the pretransitive would be incorrect. Their counterparts in Mandarin are, however, acceptable.[28]

(79) C. *Keuih *jeung* buhng cheuhng gwajo hou do wa.
佢將埲牆掛咗好多畫。

M. Ta *ba* qiang gua le hen duo huar.
他把牆掛了很多畫兒。
"He hung a lot of pictures on the wall."

---

[27] Teng (1975), pp. 90–93.

[28] I do not know how to explain this dialectal difference. Semantically, *cheuhng* (the wall) may serve as the disposal object as in sentence (77), and grammatically there is the formal absence of the locative marker. Yet, unlike the situation in Mandarin, sentence (80) is not acceptable in the southern dialect. For more discussion on the Mandarin version, see Wang Huan (1959), pp. 12–13; and Li and Thompson (1981), pp. 470–472.

(80) C. *Keuih *jeung* go fajeun chaapjo yat jah fa.
佢將個花樽插咗一拃花。

M. Ta *ba* huaping chale yi ba huar.
他把花瓶插了一把花兒。
"He placed a bunch of flowers in the vase."

The notion of all inclusiveness applies to the following cases where the pretransitive seems optional. Yet, to some native speakers, the use of the *jeung*-construction seems more dramatic in telling the encompassing nature or totalling effect of the action. *Sehng*-measure marks the entirety of the following noun.

(81) C. Keuih yat sau pouh hei ngoh sehng go yahn.
佢一手抱起我成個人。
Keuih yat sau *jeung* ngoh sehng go yahn pouh hei.
佢一手將我成個人抱起。
"He lifted me up completely in one grab."

(82) C. ? Mat johng waaih saai sehng ga che ga?
乜撞壞晒成架車㗎?
Mat *jeung* sehng ga che johng waaih saai ga?
乜將成架車撞壞晒㗎?
"How come that you have crashed the entire car?"

One may have noticed the presence of the morpheme *saai* 晒 in most of the above examples of all-inclusiveness. *Saai* is a verbal suffix that appears after a verb or a verb-complement unit, marking again completeness in reference to the relevent noun. Yet, despite this semantic reading, its sole presence does not require the use of the pretransitive. In the following pair of examples, the first one in fact sounds more natural to a native ear.

(83) C. Sihk saai di faahn la.
食晒啲飯啦。
Jeung di faahn sihk saai la.
將啲飯食晒啦。
"Finish the rice."

5.6. The last group of disposal verbs we will examine in relation to the necessary use of the pretransitive construction comprises individual words and expressions with idiomatic readings or usages. Some of them are literary forms, whose colloquial counterparts fare just as well in a non-pretransitive pattern. Others appear in morphological patterns that generally do not require the pretransitive. Their idiosyncratic needs have, therefore, to be individually recorded in a dictionary.

(84) C. Neih bahba *jeung* heimohng *geitok* hai neih san seuhng.
你爸爸將希望寄託喺你身上。
*Neih bahba *geitok* heimohng hai neih san seuhng.
你爸爸寄託希望喺你身上。
"Your father places his hope on you."

cf. Neih bahba *jai* saai di heimohng hai neih san seuhng.
你爸爸擠晒啲希望喺你身上。

(85) C. Yiu *jeung* samleihhohk *poupinfa*, samleihhohkga bunsan sin yiu jeungngaak kwahnjong samleih.
要將心理學普遍化，心理學家本身先要掌握群眾心理。
*Yiu *poupinfa* samleihhohk . . .
要普遍化心理學……
"To promote the study of psychology, psychologists have first to gain a firm understanding of the mind of the people."

cf. Yiu *teuigwohng* samleihhohk, . . .
要推廣心理學……

(86) C. Ni go sehwuih sihsih wuih *jeung* di yahn *seungyihpfa*.
呢個社會時時會將啲人商業化。
*Ni go sehwuih sihsih wuih *seungyihpfa* di yahn.
呢個社會時時會商業化啲人。
"This society often commercializes the masses."

cf. Ni go sehwuih sihsih wuih *gaauwaaih* yahn.
呢個社會時時會教壞人。
"This society has a corrupting influence on people."

(87) C. Ngoh hou seung *jeung* di gongfu *chyuhn lohkheui*.
我好想將啲功夫傳落去。
*Ngoh hou seung *chyuhn* di gongfu *lohkheui*.
我好想傳啲功夫落去。
"I really would want to pass down my *kungfu* skills."

cf. ... *chyuhn* di gongfu bei houhyahn.
　　……傳啲功夫俾後人。
"... pass the *kungfu* to the future generations."

cf. Yauh seuhngbihn *chyhhn* di yeh *lohkheui*.
　　由上邊傳啲嘢落去。
"Pass this down from upstairs."

(88) C. Gitgwo keuihdeih *jeung* ni gihn sih *gwaijeui* yu bin go a?
　　結果佢哋將件事歸罪於邊個呀？
　　*Gitgwo keuihdeih *gwaijeui* ni gihn sih yu bin go a?
　　結果佢哋歸罪呢事於邊個呀？
　　"So, finally who did they blame this on?"

cf. Gitgwo keuihdeih *laaih* saai gihn sih hai bin go douh a?
　　結果佢哋賴晒件事喺邊個度呀？

(89) C. Jeuigahn keuih jyunjo di haumeih, *jeung* keuih ge sanyihng *yauhchihng* yat di, jeuk faan di kwahn.
　　最近佢轉咗啲口味，將佢嘅身型柔情一啲，著翻啲裙。
　　"She has recently changed her taste, feminizing her appearance by wearing skirts."

The verbs in (85) and (86) both carry the suffix *fa*, which Chao describes as a modern and somewhat foreign suffix corresponding in function to that of "-ize" English.[29] The use of *chyhhn lohkheui* in (87) is a metaphorical extension of the directional complement in a temporal sense. The expression *gwaijeui yu* in (88) is a derivative from the classical language, as indicated by its old locative posposition *yu*. In the last example, the word *yauhchihng* is originally a noun meaning "tender feelings"; its use as a verb to mean "to feminize" is highly unconventional, probably the spontaneous product of a whimsical writer who likes to play on words.

6. The *Jeung*-Construction as a Form of Topicalization

6.1. Linguists have long been puzzled by the flexibility of the pretransitive construction. Aside from specific cases where its presence is required by

---

[29] Chao (1968), pp. 225–226.

certain linguistic conditions, some of which have been discussed above, there are many situations in which the use of the pretransitive seems entirely optional. Speakers may also vary in their speech habits and preferences. But, is the use of the pretransitive truly a matter of arbitrary choice, dependent on the whims of the speaker at the time? Wang Huan in her 1959 article strongly argues for a contextual examination to capture not only the grammatical factors but also the discoursal scenarios that explain the variation in use.[30] As noted by linguists later, the regular V-O sequence and the pretransitive form are in reality answers to completely different questions.[31] For example,

(90) M. Wo maile na liang che le.
我賣了那輛車了。
"I sold that car."

(91) M. Wo *ba* na liang che mai le.
我把那輛車賣了。
"I sold that car."

In spite of the same English rendition, the first sentence reports an event as an answer to "What did you do?," whereas the second answers the question: "What have you done with that car?" *Che* (car) is part of the message to be conveyed in (90); whereas in (91), *che* is the center of the utterance and a comment is made about its transaction. The two sentences are therefore quite different in terms of the messages they are intended to deliver. The pretransitive highlights *che* as the topic on the discoursal level, even though structually it may be described as the object of the verb *mai* (sell). In other words, even when there are no apparent grammatical needs, the pretransitive construction may still be triggered for discoursal reasons. To advance a post-verbal NP in a sentence is to assign it a new topical role as deemed necessary from the context.

Contrary to Mandarin, Cantonese would use the same S-V-O sentence as answers in both scenarios as outlined above.

---

[30] Wang Huan (1959), pp. 12–13.

[31] A number of linguists have utilized the question-answer format to uncover the discoursal difference between the two forms. See Thompson (1973), pp. 215–216; Li and Thompson (1981), p. 483; and Tsao (1987), p. 22.

(92) C. Ngoh maaihjo ga che la.
     我賣咗架車喇。
     "I sold the car."

It is true that the *jeung*-construction may be employed to topicalize the object as in (93), but a more common form of topicalization for a case like this would be simply to place *che* at the very front of the sentence as in (94).

(93) C. Ngoh *jeung* ga che maaihjo la.
     我將架車賣咗喇。

(94) C. Ga che, ngoh maaihjo la.
     架車，我賣咗喇。

Based on the Cantonese data that we have studied and rendered into Mandarin, it is quite evident that the pretransitive is not as productive a topicalization device in the southern dialect. The following are a few more examples to show this dialectal difference:

(95) C. Mahfaahn neih *fax* go di yiuching seun bei ngoh taitai.
     麻煩你 fax 嗰啲邀請信俾我睇睇。

    M. Qing ni *ba* na xie yaoqing xin *fax* gei wo kankan.
     請你把那些邀請信 fax 給我看看。
     "Please fax those invitation letters to me for a look."

(96) C. Lauh go jai hai ngukkei, mhhaih gei hou gwa.
     留個仔喺屋企，唔係幾好啩！

    M. *Ba* xiaohar liu zai jiali, bu tai hao ba.
     把小孩兒留在家裡，不太好吧！
     "It isn't too good to leave the kids at home, is it?"

(97) C. Mihngmihng jidou gihn sih ganyiu la, dimgaai juhng jouh dak gihn sih gam lasai ge?
     明明知道件事緊要啦，點解重做得件事咁捼西嘅？

    M. Mingming zhidao shiqing yaojin, zenme hui *ba* shiqing zuo de zeme mahu?
     明明知道事情要緊，怎麼會把事情做得這麼馬虎？
     "You obviously knew about the importance of this task. How could you have done such a lousy job?"

(98) C. Go neui dim? Mhhou mahn laak! Keuih louhdauh ning keuih cheutheui dong yeh maaih, neih wah chaam mhchaaam a!
個女點？唔好問喇！佢老竇擰佢出去當嘢賣，你話慘唔慘呀？

M. Nüer zenme yang? Bie wen le! Ta baba *ba* na chuqu dang huowu mai, ni shuo kelian bu kelian?
女兒怎麼樣？別問了！她爸爸把她拿出去當貨物賣，你說可憐不可憐？
"What happened to the girl? Her father took her out and traded her like a piece of commodity. Isn't that pathetic?"

(99) C. Fongsam la, ngoh mhwuih dongjo neih haih sauhyahn ge.
放心喇！我唔會當咗你係仇人嘅。

M. Fangxin ba. Wo bu hui *ba* ni dang zuo chouren de.
放心吧！我不會把你當作仇人的。
"Don't worry, I won't regard you as my enemy."

The contrast in choice clearly testifies that, by comparison, Cantonese is rather dilatory in its readiness to adopt the pretransitive for the topical function. However, that all the above sentences can be rephrased with a *jeung*-pattern also indicates that the mechanism is readily available should the speaker chooses to opt for it. Our data, in fact, supply us with ample evidence pointing to such a discoursal versatility. Yet, despite the S-V-O sequence in sentence (92), it is necessary to use the *jeung*-construction to phrase the pertinent question: "What did you do with the car?" or "How did you dispose of your car?"

(100) C. Neih *jeung* ga che dim la?
你將架車點啦？
M. Ni *ba* che zenme le?
你把車怎麼了？

Like *zenme* (how) in Mandarin, *dim* is a pro-verb,[32] whose identity is derived from that of an interrogative adverb in combination with an unknown verb: *dim*+Verb (how to Verb?). Because of this dual status, *dim* may occupy the position regularly reserved for a verb in a sentence; but it may not take on an Object as a regular verb can. So, where would an

---

[32] For the behavior of the pro-verb *zenme* in Mandarin, see Chao (1968), pp. 349, 660–662.

Object appear in a pro-verb question? The pretransitive construction is called on to resolve the dilemma. In this capacity, the pretransitive may indeed be characterized as a grammatical necessity. But, insofar as the pretransitive is used to introduce the grammatical object as the discoursal focus of the conversation, its topical function is both vital and clear. If we compare the following two *dim*-questions, it is just as evident that the pretransitive is not only topical in function but also disposal in meaning.

(101) C. Neih *jeung* ga che dim a?
你將架車點呀？
"What did you do with the car?"

(102) C. Ga che dim a?
架車點呀？
"What about the car?"

While (102) may connote the meaning of "What did you do with it?," in which case *che* has been turned into the primary topic of the sentence occupying the subject position in the sequence,[33] it may also be intended as a question to elicit an answer such as: "The car is great!" The disposal reading is, however, unequivocally delivered in the pretransitive form in (101).

6.2. The topical function of the pretransitive is most evident in a scenario where its presence is necessary to focus the attention on the object under discussion. For example, the difference between the following two forms is not immediately discernable unless placed in their respective contexts.

(103a) C. Yauh Saamfaahnsih ja ga che faan laih . . .
由三藩市揸架車翻嚟……

(103b) C. *Jeung* ga che yauh Saamfaahnsih ja faan laih . . .
將架車由三藩市揸翻嚟……
"To drive (the car) back from San Francisco . . ."

The scenario is essentially about a car trip back from San Francisco. If the emphasis is on its impact on the driver, stressing physical exhaustion, the non-pretransitive form is used as in (104).

---

[33] For more discussion on the primary and secondary topics and the interaction between the two, see Tsao (1987).

(104) C. Yauh Saamfaahnsih ja ga che faanlaih, pa wuih hou guih gwa.
由三藩市揸架車翻嚟，怕會好攰啩！
"To drive (the car) back from San Francisco? I'm afraid that it will be exhausting."

On the other hand, if it is the condition of the car that is of concern here, the *jeung*-form would be used to bring *che* to the foreground, as in (105).

(105) C. *Jeung* ga che yauh Saamfaahnsih ja faanlaih, pa mhdak gwa.
將架車由三藩市揸翻嚟，怕唔得啩。
"To drive the car back from San Francisco? I don't think it (i.e., the car) is going to make it."

To rephrase (105) in the following manner by foregoing the *jeung*-pattern would be confusing as to what exactly is the factor that would cause apprehension: the condition of the car, the health condition of the driver, the road condition, the weather situation, the time factor, or what?

(106) C. Yauh Saamfaahnsih ja ga che faanlaih, pa mhdak gwa.
由三藩市揸架車翻嚟，怕唔得啩。

6.3. The pretransitive construction is often used when the disposed object serves as the topic of a series of comments. Structurally, the pretransitive NP is the grammatical object of each of the ensuing verbs, as the following sentences illustrate:

(107) C. Keuih yatgo yahn *jeung* luhkgo jaineuih *chou daaih$_1$, yeungyuhk sihng yahn$_2$,* jan haih mhgaandaan.
佢一個人將六個仔女湊大，養育成人，真係唔簡單。

M. Ta yige ren *ba* liuge ernü dai da, yangyu cheng ren, shizai bu jiandan.
他一個人把六個兒女帶大，養育成人，實在不簡單。
"It's truly not an easy job for him to bring up six children, taking good care of them until they become grownups."

(108) C. *Jeung* tiuh laailin *chaakjo lohklaih$_1$, jin dyun siusiu$_2$, joih deng faan seuhngheui$_3$.*
將條拉鏈拆咗落嚟，剪短少少，再釘翻上去。

M. *Ba* lalian chai xialai, jian duan yidianr, zai ding shangqu.
把拉鏈拆下來，剪短一點，再釘上去。
"Take off the zipper, cut it a bit shorter, and sew it back on."

(109) C. *Jeung* di ngkuhyuhk *hai seuihauh chungchung₁, chit sihng bohk pin₂, joih yuhng siusiu yihm lala₃,* yihnhou sinji *lohk wohk heui chaau₄.*
將啲牛肉喺水喉冲冲，切成薄片，再用少少鹽㪐㪐，然後先至落鑊去炒。

M. *Ba* niurou zai shuilongtou dixia xi yi xi, qie cheng bao pian, zai yong yan yanyan, ranhou zai fang dao guoli qu chao.
把牛肉在水龍頭底下洗一洗，切成薄片，再用鹽醃醃，然後再放到鍋裡去炒。
"Wash the beef under running water, slice into thin pieces, marinate with a little salt, and then stir fry in the wok."

In a setup with a series of comments, a disposal object that would not normally appear in the pretransitive with certain verbal expressions is often ready to temporarily disregard the restriction. For example, unlike its northern counterpart, Cantonese does not accept the following type of sentences where the pretransitive NP share a part-whole relation with the direct object of the verb, or where the direct object is the so-called retained object of the pretransitive NP.[34]

(110) C. *Keuih jeung* pihnggwo sihkjo saam go.
佢將蘋果食咗三個。

M. Ta *ba* pingguo chi le san ge.
他把蘋果吃了三個。
"He ate three of the apples."

(111) C. *Go chaahklou jeung* keuih bong hai leuhng jek sau.
個賊佬將佢綁起兩隻手。

M. Na ge zei ba ta bang qi liang zhi shou.
那個賊把他綁起兩隻手。
"The thief tied up his hands."

In the first sentence, the three apples are part of a bigger quantity; and, in the second, the hands belong to the victim that has been robbed. To phrase these in idiomatic Cantonese, one would have to say:

(112) C. Keuih sihkjo saam go pihnggwo.
佢食咗三個蘋果。

---

[34] Both topics on the part-whole relation and the retained object have been closely studied in many works. Particularly, see Lü (1955), pp. 133–135; and Li and Thompson (1981), pp. 470–572.

(113a)　C.　Go chaahklou bong hei keuih leuhng jek sau.
　　　　　　個賊佬綁起佢兩隻手。

(113b)　C.　Go chaahkloi *jeung* keuih leuhng jek sau bong hei.
　　　　　　個賊佬將佢兩隻手綁起。

However, when expanded into longer utterances, both (110) and (111) are found acceptable in the following sentences.

(114)　C.　Keuih *jeung* pihnggwo sihkjo saamgo, dam jo seigo, juhng lauhfaan yatgo bei neih.
　　　　　佢將蘋果食咗三個，扻咗四個，重留翻一個俾你。

　　　　M.　Ta *ba* pinguo chile sange, rengle sige, hai gei ni liu le yige.
　　　　　　他把蘋果吃了三個，扔了四個，還給你留了一個。
　　　　　　"He ate three of the apples, threw away four, and saved one for you."

(115)　C.　Go chaahklou jeung keuih *bong hei leuhng jek sau, bong hei leuhng jek geuk, sakjo sehng go yahn yahp mahbaudoih syu.*
　　　　　個賊佬將佢綁起兩隻手，綁起兩隻腳，塞咗成個人入麻包袋處。

　　　　M.　Na ge zei *ba* ta bangqi liangzhi shou, bangqi liangzhi jiao, *ba* ta zhengge ren seidao mabao koudaili.
　　　　　　那個賊把他綁起兩隻手，綁起兩隻腳，把他整個塞到麻包口袋裡去。
　　　　　　"The thief tied up his hands and legs, and put him in a sack."

The oddity of the initial VP in each of the sentences disappears as it is succeeded by other verbal expressions, all commenting on the same pretransitive object. When followed by a series of comments, the discoursal role of the disposal NP as topic becomes increasingly prominent, thereby allowing the temporary suspension of its syntactic association with the verbs in the ensuing comments. What one may initially reject on the basis of grammatical rules may no longer appear objectionable in a discoursal context. The following are more examples of this nature.

(116a)　C.　**Jeung* jek chaang mok peih.
　　　　　　將隻橙剝皮。

　　　　M.　*Ba* juzi bao pi.
　　　　　　把橘子剝皮。
　　　　　　"Peel the orange."

(116b) C. *Jeung* jek chaang mok peih, mit hoi gei kaai.
將隻橙剝皮，搣開幾楷。

M. *Ba juzi* bao pi, fen kai jibanr.
把橘子剝皮，分開幾瓣。
"Peel the orange and separate it into sections."

(117a) C. **Jeung* tiuh fu wuhn yattiuh laailin.
將條褲換一條拉鏈。

M. *Ba* kuzi huan yitiao lalian.
把褲子換一條拉鏈。
"Change the zipper of the pants."

(117b) C. *Jeung* tiuh fu wuhnjo laailin sinji jeuk la.
將條褲換咗拉鏈先至著啦。

M. *Ba* kuzi huanle lalian zai chuan ba.
把褲子換了拉鏈再穿吧。
"Change the zipper of the pants before putting them on."

(118a) C. **Jeung* neih ge dihnsih bei yatga ngoh.
將你嘅電視俾一架我。

M. *Ba* ni de dianshi gei wo yitai.
把你的電視給我一台。
"Give me one of your TV sets."

(118b) C. *Jeung* neih ge dihnsih bei yaga ngoh, bei yatga ngoh muihmui. Neih wah dim a?
將你嘅電視俾一架我，俾一架我妹妹。你話點呀？

M. *Ba* ni de dianshiji gei wo yitai, zai gei wo meimei yitai. Ni shuo hao ma?
把你的電視機給我一台，再給我妹妹一台。你說好嗎？
"Give me one of your TV sets and give another one to my sister. How about that?"

(119a) C. **Jeung* go fajeun chaapjo yat jah fa.
將個花樽插咗一拃花。

M. *Ba* huaping chale yiba huar.
把花瓶插了一把花兒。
"He placed a bunch of flowers in the vase."

(119b) C. Keuih *jeung* go fajeun chaapjo di fa, baai hai go haakteng syu, janhaih gei houtai ga.
佢將個花樽插咗啲花，擺喺個客廳處，真係幾好睇㗎。

M. Ta *ba* huaping chale yixie huar, fang zai keting li, zhenshi ting haokan de.
他把花瓶插了一些花兒，放在客廳裡，真是挺好看的。
"He placed some flowers in the vase and put it in the living room. It really looked pretty."

While the above sentences illustrate how the pretransitive form may extend its operation beyond the scope of one sentence, serving as the head of a succession of verbal comments, the following examples show a juxtapostion of several pretransitive expressions, with only the first one being explicitly marked by *jeung*. The disposed objects are different, but the repeated markers may be deleted in the surface form.

(120) C. Cheng *jeung* yuhtwai sungchih, geiyuhk sau gan.
請將穴位鬆弛，肌肉收緊。

M. Qing *ba* xuewei songchi, jirou shou jin.
請把穴位鬆弛，肌肉收緊。
"Relax your acupoints and tighten your muscles, please."

(121) C. Yanwaih mhseung chouhjyuh yahndeih, soyih *jeung* go dihnwa mangjo, danggwong gaau ngam, dihnsih nauh saiseng di.
因為唔想嘈住人哋，所以將個電話搣咗，燈光較暗，電視扭細聲啲。

M. Yinwei bu xiang darao bieren, suoyi *ba* dianhua ba diao, diandeng ning an, dianshi kai xiaosheng yidianr.
因為不想打擾別人，所以把電話拔掉，電燈擰暗，電視開小聲點兒。
"As he didn't want to disturb others, he unplugged the phone, dimmed the light, and turned down the volume of the TV."

6.4. We have thus far provided many examples from our data to demonstrate that, as a process of topicalization, the pretransitive construction moves the object from a post-verbal to a preverbal position. Unlike the situation in Mandarin, the pretransitive NP is almost always the direct object of the verb in the predicate. The movement process could have followed two different routes. It may have simply lifted the object out of its regular post-verbal position and placed it preverbally, or it may have first copied the object to the preverbal position and deleted the postverbal version afterwards. In either case, the pretransitive marker may have been in the deep structure as marker of the accusative or it may have been created through the topicalization process.[35] Compared with the first scenario of direct transposition, the second hypothesis seems not only cumbersome in that it requires two steps of copying and deletion, it also finds little support from Mandarin where the post verbal slot is always left empty after the movement of the object. Our studies of the Cantonese material, however, may seem to supply us with evidence that copying may indeed be the first step to take in this particular process of topicalization.

In each of the following examples, we find not only a transposed object unequivocally marked by *jeung*, but also a pronoun that occupies the postverbal object position.

(122) C. Ngoh seung *jeung* po syu chaamjo *keuih*.
我想將棵樹斬咗佢。

M. Wo xiang *ba* shu kanle.
我想把樹砍了。
"I want to chop down the tree."

(123) C. Chinkeih mhhou *jeung* di tauhfaat yihm hak *keuih*.
千祈唔好將啲頭髮染黑佢。

M. Qianwan bie *ba* toufa ren hei.
千萬別把頭髮染黑。
"Be sure not to dye your hair black."

(124) C. Neih yauh mouh *jeung* di syu jai faan hou *keuih* a?
你有冇將啲書擠翻好佢呀？

M. Ni *ba* shu ge hui yuanchu le ma?
你把書擱回原處了嗎？
"Have you put the books back properly?"

---

[35] For example, Li (1971) considers *ba* to be the accusative case marker, which is normally deleted on the surface unless it occupies the pretransitive position.

(125) C. Mahfaahn neih bong ngoh *jeung* fung seun dada *keuih*.
麻煩你幫我將封信打打佢。

M. Laojia nin gei wo *ba* zhe feng xin da yi da.
勞駕您給我把這封信打一打。
"May I ask you to type this letter for me?"

(126) C. Ngoh gei sih yauh *jeung* go loupoh leihjo *keuih* a?
我幾時有將個老婆離咗佢呀？

M. Wo shenme shihou *ba* ge taitai gei li le?
我什麼時候把個太太給離了？
"When did I divorce my wife?"

(127) C. *Jeung* keuih jaathei *keuih*!
將佢紮起佢。

M. *Ba* ta bang qilai.
把他綁起來。
"Tie him up."

The use of a postverbal *keuih* in a pretransitive sentence is quite a common phenomenon in Cantonese, although Mandarin speakers in general do not accept this "tagged-on" object, which they consider redundant and therefore not necessary.[36] The redundancy may indeed be viewed as a case of copying, by means of which a postverbal object is copied to the pretransitive position for discoursal reasons. As a result, there are two identical NPs in the sentence, the second of which becomes either pronominalized, or deleted, or first pronominalized and then deleted. The following diagram schematizes this process:

(128) S + V + O —— Topicalization ——→ S + *jeung*-Object + V + Object
                            ↓
           —— Pronominalization ——→ S + *jeung*-Object + V + *keuih*
                            ↓
           —————— Deletion ——————→ S + *jeung*-Object + V

---

[36] Some speakers seem to accept the following sentence: *Ni ba cha hele ta* 你把茶喝了他. However, even for them, the redundant *ta* may appear only in a command and not in other types of sentences. This use also seems to be acceptable in the Wu dialects.

The same scheme may be proposed for Mandarin, the only difference being that the last step of deletion is compulsory in Mandarin but optional in Cantonese. Under certain conditions, however, the deletion of *keuih* is also obligatory in Cantonese. As noted at the beginning of this discussion, the VP in a pretransitive sentence has to contain, in addition to the verb itself, an extra element that may be a suffix, a complement, another object, or an adverb. With the exception of the adverb, all the elements that may appear in the VP do so postverbally. As the direct object NP is also by nature a postverbal element, the sequence in the VP may be in two different orders as represented below. X stands for that extra element in the VP.

(129) (i)   V + X + Object
       (ii) V + Object + X

If (129) is submitted to the process described in (128), there are two different results in word order if the last step of deletion is skipped:

(130) (i)   S + *jeung*-Object + V + X + *keuih*
       (ii) S + *jeung*-Object + V + *keuih* + X

Sentences (122) to (127) are examples of the first type of arrangement. The second type, namely with *keuih* sitting before X, is however not acceptable in Cantonese, thereby making the deletion a compulsory step. As illustrated in the following sentences, it is also not possible to reverse the order between *keuih* and the X element in (130ii), even though by doing so it would produce an order identical to (130i). Only those that are derived directly from (130i) are acceptable in the language.

(131a) C. diu di yeh lohklaih   → *jeung di yeh diu *keuih* lohklaih
            吊啲嘢落嚟   將啲嘢吊佢落嚟
                                    → *jeung di yeh diu lohklaih *keuih*
                                       將啲嘢吊落嚟佢
                                    → *jeung* di yeh diu lohklaih
                                       將啲嘢吊落嚟
                                       "lower the things down with a rope"

(131b) C. jai dai di yeh   → *jeung* di yeh jai dai *keuih*
            擠低啲嘢   將啲嘢擠低佢
                                       "put down the things"

(132a) C. waahn faan bun syu bei touhsyugun
            還翻本書俾圖書館   → *jeung bun syu waahn faan keuih bei
                                      touhsyugun
                                      將本書還翻佢俾圖書館
                                   → *jeung bun syu waahn faan bei
                                      touhsyugun keuih
                                      將本書還翻俾圖書館佢
                                   → jeung bun syu waahn faan bei
                                      touhsyugun
                                      將本書還翻俾圖書館
                                      "return the book to the library"

(132b) C. waahn faan bun syu   → jeung bun syu waahn faan keuih
            還翻本書   將本書還翻佢
                                      "return the book"

(133a) C. jip gou go jauh   → jeung go jauh jip gou keuih
            摺高個袖   將個袖摺高佢
                                      "roll up the sleeve"

(133b) C. jip gou di go jauh   → jeung go jauh jip gou di keuih
            摺高啲個袖   將個袖摺高啲佢
                                      "roll up the sleeve a bit more"

(133c) C. jip gou go jauh saam chyun → *jeung go jauh jip gou keuih
            摺高個袖三寸   saam chyun
                                          將個袖摺高佢三寸
                                       → ?jeung go jauh jip gou saam
                                          chyun keuih
                                          將個袖摺高三寸佢
                                          "roll up the sleeve by 3 inches"

(134a) C. dajo go jai yat chaan   → *jeung go jai dajo keuih yat chaan
            打咗個仔一餐   將個仔打咗佢一餐
                                      → *jeung go jai dajo yat chaan keuih
                                          將個仔打咗一餐佢
                                      → jeung go jai dajo yat chaan
                                          將個仔打咗一餐
                                          "beat up the son"

(134b) C. da sei jek man   → jeung jek man da sei keuih
            打死隻蚊   將隻蚊打死佢
                                      "kill the mosquito"

(135a)   C.   yauh douh muhn huhngsik → *jeung douh muhn yauh huhngsik keuih
油度門紅色
將度門油紅色佢
→ jeung douh muhn yauh huhngsik
將度門油紅色
"paint the door red"

(135b)   C.   yauh huhng douh muhn → jeung douh muhn yauh huhng keuih
油紅度門
將度門油紅佢
"paint the door red"

There are other restrictions and problems regarding this use of *keuih*, which makes the above argument on its derivation from a retained and, therefore, redundant object somewhat speculative, awaiting further investigation. For example, regardless of the number of the object NP, singular or plural, the final pronoun is always in the third person singular, *keuih*.

(136)   C.   Nau dak jai, *jeung* baan fogei chaau saai *keuih*.
嬲得滯，將班伙記炒晒佢。
*Nau dak jai, *jeung* baan fogei chaau saai keuihdeih.
嬲得滯，將班伙記炒晒佢哋。

M.   Tai qi le, *ba* huoji quan dou kaichu le.
太氣了，把伙記全都開除了。
"In a fury, he fired his assistants."

Also, unlike sentence (127) where both the pretransitive object and the retained object can be in the third person pronoun, the following cases with pretransitive objects in the first or second person pronouns are not allowed to follow suit.

(137)   C.   *Ngoh geisih yauh *jeung* neih wan maaih *neih* a?
我幾時有將你搵埋你呀？
Ngoh geisih yauh *jeung* neih wan maaih a?
我幾時有將你搵埋呀？

M.   Wo shenme shihou *ba* ni guan qilai le?
我什麼時候把你關起來了？
"When did I lock you up?"

(138)　C.　*Gam yuhngyih jauh *jeung* ngoh gaau dihm *ngoh*?
　　　　　　咁容易就將我攪掂我？
　　　　　　Gam yuhngyih jauh *jeung* ngoh gaau dihm?
　　　　　　咁容易就將我攪掂？

　　　　M.　Zeme rongyi jiu *ba* wo bai ping?
　　　　　　這麼容易就把我擺平？
　　　　　　"You can take care of me so easily?"

It is apparent from the above data that the pronoun *keuih* appears only at the end of the pretransitive sentence. However, in some non-pretransitive sentences such as the following, this sentence-final pronoun is also conspicuously present. The disposal verb is now followed by both the object and its pronominalized version.

(139)　C.　Jaamjo po syu *keuih*.
　　　　　　斬咗棵樹佢。

　　　　M.　*Ba* shu kanle.
　　　　　　把樹砍了。
　　　　　　"Take down the tree."

(140)　C.　Fong cheuhng jek jauh *keuih*.
　　　　　　放長隻袖佢。

　　　　M.　*Ba* xiuzi fang chang.
　　　　　　把袖子放長。
　　　　　　"Make the sleeve longer."

(141)　C.　Keuih hou seung dihn lyun di tauhfaat *keuih*.
　　　　　　佢好想電孿啲頭髮佢。

　　　　M.　Ta hen xiang *ba* taufa tang de hen juan.
　　　　　　他很想把頭髮燙得很捲。
　　　　　　"He wants to have his hair permed in a really curly fashion."

(142)　C.　Keuih yihging japfaan gonjehng gaan fong *keuih* la.
　　　　　　佢已經執翻乾淨間房佢喇。

　　　　M.　Ta yijing *ba* fangjian shoushi ganjing le.
　　　　　　他已經把房間收拾乾淨了。
　　　　　　"He has already cleaned up the room."

Our speculation on this object redundancy phenomenon is that when a pretransitive form is converted back to its regular V-O sequence, the pronominalized form is kept as a remnant feature of the pretransitivization. As the following diagram shows, in spite of the seeming resemblance between stages (i) and (iv), the latter is a secondary S-V-O sequence, three steps removed from the primary form.

(143) (i) Subject + Verb - X + Object
↓
(ii) Subject + *jeung*-Object + Verb - X + Object
↓
(iii) Subject + *jeung*-Object + Verb - X + *keuih*
↓
(iv) Subject + Verb - X + Object + *keuih*

One way to prove the relationship between the product in (iv) and the pretransitive operation is that the same kind of restrictions that apply to the pronominalization in step (iii) are found in step (iv) as well. Corresponding to the set of starred items in (131)–(135), the following sentences where the object comes before the X element in the verb phrase exhibit similar constraints in the non-pretransitive form.[37]

(144a) C. diu di yeh lohklaih → *diu di yeh *keuih* lohklaih
吊啲嘢落嚟　　　吊啲嘢佢落嚟
→ *diu di yeh lohklaih *keuih*
吊啲嘢落嚟佢
"lower the things down with a rope"

(144b) C. jai dai di yeh → jai dai di yeh *keuih*
擠低啲嘢　　　擠低啲嘢佢
"put down the things"

---

[37] A very interesting case to note here is the curse expression *Seijo keuih* 死咗佢 (Drop dead!). As the intransitive verb does not take on an object in any case, the presence of the final *keuih* is truly intriguing.

(145a) C. waahn faan bun syu bei toushyugun
還翻本書俾圖書館
→ *waahn faan bun syu *keuih* bei tousyugun
還翻本書佢俾圖書館
→ *waahn faan bun syu bei tousyugun *keuih*
還翻本書俾圖書館佢
"return the book to the library"

(145b) C. waahn faan bun syu
還翻本書
→ waahn faan bun syu *keuih*
還翻本書佢
"return the book"

(146a) C. jip gou go jauh
摺高個袖
→ jip gou go jauh *keuih*
摺高個袖佢
"roll up the sleeve"

(146b) C. jip gou di go jauh
摺高啲個袖
→ jip gou go di jauh *keuih*
摺高啲個袖佢
"roll up the sleeve a bit more"

(146c) C. jip gou go jauh saam chyun
摺高個袖三寸
→ *jip gou go jauh *keuih* saam chyun
摺高個袖佢三寸
→ *jip gou go jauh saam chyun *keuih*
摺高個袖三寸佢
"roll up the sleeve by three inches"

(147a) C. dajo ge jai yat chaan
打咗個仔一餐
→ *dajo ge jai *keuih* yat chaan
打咗個仔佢一餐
→ *dajo ge jai yat chaan *keuih*
打咗個仔一餐佢
"beat up the son"

(147b) C. da sei jek man
打死隻蚊
→ da sei jek man *keuih*
打死隻蚊佢
"kill the mosiquito"

(148a) C. yauh douh muhn huhngsik
油度門紅色
→ *yauh douh muhn *keuih* huhngsik
油度門佢紅色
→ *yauh douh muhn huhngsik *keuih*
油度門紅色佢
"paint the door red"

(148b) C. yauh huhng douh muhn
油紅度門
→ yauh huhng douh muhn *keuih*
油紅度門佢
"paint the door red"

The striking similarity in behavior between the two types of *keuih*-final sentences strongly suggests that they are derivationally related. In both cases, *keuih* behaves like a grammatical marker of a transformational process that pretransitivizes a sentence for discoursal purposes.[38]

7. The Pretransitive Noun Phrase

7.1. As emphatically characterized in all the studies on the pretransitive construction, a preverbal object has to be either "definite" or "generic" in reference.[39] When an object is indefinite, it generally cannot occur in a pretransitive sentence. The following sentences demonstrate the same reference restriction in Cantonese.

    (149)   C.   Keuih *jeung ni gihn sih* tai dak taai gaandaan la.
                        佢將呢件事睇得太簡單喇。

                M.   Ta *ba* zhe shi kan de tai jiandan le.
                        他把這事看得太簡單了。
                        "He has oversimplified this matter."

    (150)   C.   *Keuih jeung yat gihn sih tai dak taai gaandaan la.
                        佢將一件事睇得太簡單喇。

                M.   *Ta *ba* yi jian shi kan de tai jiandan le.
                        他把一件事看得太簡單了。
                        "He has oversimplified a matter."

---

[38] There are, however, some examples that display a more rigid use of this final *keuih* in the non-pretransitive sentence. A long object NP may appear with the final pronoun in a pretransitive form but rejects it in the non-*jeung* form. Examples are:

  (i) (a) C. *Jeung* ngoh gong ge yeh se dai *keuih*.
                  將我講嘅嘢寫低佢。
      (b) C. *Se dai ngoh gong ge yeh *keuih*.
                  寫低我講嘅嘢佢。
                "Write down what I said."
  (ii) (a) C. Mat neih seung *jeung* ngoh sung bei neih go po syu chaamjo *keuih* a?
                  乜你想將我送俾你嗰喬樹斬咗佢呀？
      (b) C. *Mat neih seung chaamjo ngoh sung bei neih go po syu *keuih* a?
                  乜你想斬咗我送俾你嗰喬樹佢呀？
                "What! You want to cut down the tree that I gave you as a present?"

[39] For more on this topic, see Li and Thompson (1981), pp. 465–466.

As in Mandarin, the noun phrase *ni gihn sih* in (149) consists of three elements: the demonstrative, the measure word, and the noun, and it is the presence of the demonstrative *ni* 呢 (this) that establishes the definiteness of the noun referent. *Ni* is a definite demonstrative and it is also deictic in reference. Its counterpart for "that" is *go* 嗰, corresponding to *na* 那 in Mandarin. However, unlike Mandarin which does not have any means to mark neutral reference like what "the" does in English, Cantonese resorts to the measure word, also known as the classifier, for this function. As discussed elsewhere, a Measure-Noun (M-N) combination in Cantonese may indicate definite but non-deictic in reference.[40] Hence, *Bun syu hou houtai* means "The book is interesting." The measure word *di* 啲 stands for plural reference, as in *di syu* (the books). With this understanding of the referential function in an M-N unit, we may now see why the pretransitive NP in most of the examples cited above are in the pattern of M-N. The following is another sentence to show this difference between the two dialects.

(151) C. *Jeung go* sauyamgei hoi daaihseng di.
將個收音機開大聲啲。

M. *Ba ge shouyinji kai dasheng yidianr.
把個收音機開大聲一點兒。
"Turn up the radio a little bit."

When used postverbally, a M-N unit may stand for either definite or indefinite reference, the latter being a short form of *yat*-M-N (a Noun). Therefore, the following sentence can have two readings.

(152) C. Bei go jai ngoh.
俾個仔我。
(a) Give me the son. *Or,*
(b) Give me one of the sons.

In a pretransitive position, however, there is only one possible interpretation.[41]

---

[40] For a detailed discussion on the use of M-N as a definite indicator, see Cheung (1989).

[41] A Measure-Noun combination may appear as a *ba* object in Mandarin as a short form for *yi*-M-N. For example, *Ta ba ge haizi si le* 他把個孩子死了 (He lost his child through death). See Tsao (1987), pp. 30–32; and Hsueh (1989), pp. 108–109. Sentences of this type do not appear in Cantonese.

(153) C. *Jeung* go jai bei ngoh.
將個仔俾我。
Give me the son.

7.2. Relating to this issue of reference is the fact that while most cases of the pretransitive contain preverbal M-N unit, there are some where the measure word is omitted. In general, there is a difference in meaning between the two forms as illustrated below.

(154) C. Mhhou *jeung* yeh jai hai syu.
唔好將嘢擠喺處。
"Don't put things here."

(155) C. Mhhou *jeung* di yeh jai hai syu.
唔好將啲嘢擠喺處。

M. Bie ba dongxi fang zai zher.
別把東西放在這兒。
"Don't put the things here."

In contrast, the non-pretransitive form corresponding to the *jeung*-sentence always contains the measure word. As commonly known, a Verb-Object combination without an intervening measure word often connotes a general action, and the non-modified object does not necessarily carry any particular reference. A classic example is *sihk faahn* (to eat), literally meaning "eat-rice." Hence, in the following two sentences, the first one without the measure serves more like a general reminder whereas the second sentence with the M-N unit refers to specific unwelcomed objects.

(156) C. Mhhou jai yeh hai syu.
唔好擠嘢喺處.
"Don't put things here."

(157) C. Mhhou jai di yeh hai syu.
唔好擠啲嘢喺處。
"Don't put *the* things here."

That distinction remains in the pretransitive pair, (154) and (155). The former is for sure less specific as to what it points to, but its reference is clearly something that both the speaker and addressee are aware of.

7.3. In summary, the following table describes the referential characteristics of a nominal unit in reference to the pretransitive construction.

(158)

	Non-pretransitive V-NP	Pretransitive *jeung*-NP-V
[M-N]$_{NP}$	+ Definite - Definite	+ Definite
[N]$_N$	- Definite	+ Definite

8. Other Remarks

This article has discussed with ample illustrations the general characteristic features of the pretransitive in Cantonese, some of which are conspicuously absent in Mandarin. On the one hand, the Cantonese version is more restrictive in that it only applies to disposal verbs, disallowing all the extended usages of the pattern that characterize the *ba*-construction as one of the most versatile structures in Mandarin. On the other hand, however, there are fewer syntactic conditions that require its use in Cantonese. Even when there is a choice, the dialect opts for the post-verbal arrangement rather than the pretransitive. As a pragmatic device, the pretransitive is often used to highlight the topic in a conversation, a discoursal operation that may sometimes override the grammatical regulations. Pretransitive sentences that may otherwise sound unacceptable in isolation are found permissable in a discoursal context. The sentence-final *keuih* in both the pretransitive and non-transitive sentences poses as a possible indicator of a transformation that consists of both copying and pronominalization.

Like its Mandarin counterpart *ba, jeung* was historically a full verb meaning "to take." It appeared in the serial verb construction in texts dated from the sixth century and began to take on a disposal reading in the Tang dynasty.[42] As amply exemplified in Lü's work (1948), the use of the pretransitive in the Yuan/Ming vernacular writings already betrayed

---

[42] For some general discussion on the historical development of the *ba*-construction, see Ohta (1958), Lü (1948), Huang (1986), and an unpublished paper by Sun Chaofen (1986).

signs of its later development (e.g., the retained object in the postverbal position). However, it seems that it was not until the 18th century that the northern Chinese began to use the pretransitive for non-disposal sentences. By comparison, Cantonese is rather reserved in its grammatical development in this regard. Although its pretransitive does serve the function of marking topicalization, its use seldom extends beyond the scope of disposal. In our study, we have noted that the construction is also sometimes stylistically conditioned. It appears less in casual conversation than in formal discourse. A verb more literary in style tends to find itself more susceptible to the *jeung*-mechanism than another colloquial form with the same meaning. The following are a few examples to further illustrate this stylistic difference.

(159) C. Chinkeih mhhou jong ngoh heung Wohhahpsek.
            千祈唔好葬我响和合石。

       M. Qianwan bie *ba* wo zang zai Heheshi.
            千萬別把我葬在和合石。
            "Be sure not to bury me in Wo Hop Shek Cemetery."

(160) C. Geidak yatdihng yiu *jeung* keuih ngonjong hai yigunchung.
            記得一定要將佢安葬喺衣冠塚。

       M. Jizhu, yiding yao *ba* wo anzang zai yiguanzhong.
            記住一定要把他安葬在衣冠塚。
            "Remember, you have to bury his remains in the tomb where his personal effects are to be kept."

(161) C. Faaidi jaap dai ngoh gong ge yeh.
            快啲箚低我講嘅嘢。

       M. Kuai *ba* wo shuo de hua xie xialai.
            快把我說的話寫下來。
            "Quick, jot down the things I said."

(162) C. Mhseuiyiu *jeung* ngoh gong ge yeh geiluhk lohklaih ge.
            唔需要將我講嘅嘢記錄落嚟嘅。

       M. Bu xiyao *ba* wo shuo de hua jilu xialai.
            不需要把我說的話記錄下來。
            "There is no need to record the things I said."

As the written language in Cantonese is based essentially on Mandarin, it is conceivable that both stylistic and linguistic features of the northern language may readily find their way into the Cantonese dialect, first through writing then in speech. The present study is by no means a stylistic investigation of the pretransitive construction and makes no claim that Cantonese speakers are more ready to adopt the form when they write than when they speak. A project of this nature requires a much larger corpus, both written and spoken, than what I have gathered. Further efforts to continue the investigation, scrutinizing data of various sorts and comparing them with both historical and dialectal materials, will help us better understand the very complex behavior of the pretransitive in Cantonese.

References

Chao, Yuen Ren. 1968. *A Grammar of Spoken Chinese*. Berkeley, CA: University of California Press.

Cheung Hung-nin Samuel 張洪年. 1972. *Xianggang Yueyu yufa de yanjiu* 香港粵語語法的研究 (Studies on Cantonese grammar as spoken in Hong Kong). Hong Kong: The Chinese University of Hong Kong.

———. 1973. "A Comparative Study in Chinese Grammars: The *ba*-Construction." *Journal of Chinese Linguistics*, 1.3: 343–382.

———. 1989. "Yueyu liangci yongfa de yanjiu" 粵語量詞用法的研究. *Proceedings of the Second International Conference on Sinology*, pp. 753–774. Taipei: Academia Sinica.

Gao Huanian 高華年. 1980. *Guangzhou fangyan yanjiu* 廣州方言研究 (A study of the Canton dialect). Hong Kong: The Commercial Press.

Hsueh, Frank F. S. 1989. "The Structural Meaning of *ba* and *bei* Constructions in Mandarin Chinese: Do They Really Mean *Disposal* and *Passive*?" In *Functionalism and Chinese Grammar*, Monograph Series No. 1, ed. J. Tai and F. Hsueh. Chinese Language Teachers Association.

Huang, Shuanfan. 1986. "The History of the Disposal Construction Revisited: Evidence from Zen Dialogues in the Tang Dynasty." *Journal of Chinese Linguistics*, 14.1: 43–52.

Li, Charles, and Sandra Thompson. 1981. *Mandarin Chinese: A Functional Reference Grammar*. Berkeley; Los Angeles: University of California Press.

Li Ying-che. 1971. *An Investigation of Case in Chinese Grammar*. South Orange, NJ: Seton Hall University Press.

———. 1974. "What Does 'Disposal' Mean? Features of the Verb and Noun in Chinese." *Journal of Chinese Linguistics*, 2.2: 200–218.

Lü Shuxiang 呂叔湘. 1948. "*Ba-zi* yongfa de yanjiu" 把字用法的研究. *Hanyu yufa lunwenji* 漢語語法論文集. 1955. Beijing: Kexue chubanshe 科學出版社.

Mei Guang 梅廣. 1978. "*Ba-zi ju*" 把字句. *Wenshizhe xuebao* 文史哲學報, 27: 145–180. Taiwan: National Taiwan University.

Norman, Jerry. 1988. *Chinese*. Cambridge: Cambridge University Press.

Ohta, Tatsuo 太田辰夫. 1958. *Zhongguoyu lishi wenfa* 中國語歷史文法. Tokyo: Koonan Shoin.

———. 1987. *Zhongguoyu lishi wenfa* 中國語歷史文法. Trans. Jiang Shaoyu 蔣紹愚 and Xu Changhua 徐昌華. Beijing: Peking University.

Rao Bingcai 饒秉才, et al. 1981. *Guangzhouhua fangyan cidian* 廣州話方言詞典. Hong Kong: The Commercial Press.

Sanders, Robert. 1986. *Diversity and Frequency As a Reflection of Social Factors: The Application of Variable Rules to the Analysis of Disposal in the Beijing Speech Community*. PhD dissertation, University of California, Berkeley.

Sun, Chaofen. 1986. "A Historical Study of the Evolution of the Chinese *ba*: A Case of Analogy." Unpublished paper.

Teng, Shou-hsin. 1975. *A Semantic Study of Transitivity Relations in Chinese*. Berkeley; Los Angeles: University of California Press.

Thompson, Sandra. 1973. "Transitivity and Some Problems with *ba* Construction in Mandarin Chinese." *Journal of Chinese Linguistics*, 1.2: 208–211.

Tsao, Feng-fu. 1987. "A Topic-Comment Approach to the *ba* Construction." *Journal of Chinese Linguistics*, 15.1: 1–54.

Wang Huan 王還. 1959. *Ba-zi ju he bei-zi ju* 把字句和被字句. Shanghai: Shanghai Jiaoyu chubanshe 上海教育出版社.

Wang Li 王力. 1955. *Zhonggwo yufa lilun* 中國語法理論. Shanghai: Zhonghua shuju 中華書局.

Yuan Jiahua 袁家驊. 1960. *Hanyu fangyan gaiyao* 漢語方言概要. Beijing: Wenzi Gaige chubanshe 文字改革出版社.

Zhu Dexi 朱德熙. 1984. *Yufa jianghua* 語法講話. Beijing: The Commercial Press.

This article originally appeared in *Chinese Languages and Linguistics: Chinese Dialects,* Symposium Series of the Institute of History and Philology, Academia Sinica, Number 2 (1992), pp. 241–303.

Naming the City: Language Complexity in the Making of an 1866 Map of Hong Kong

Abstract: Place names often reveal not only the history of the localities and their inhabitants but also of the language in which they were coined. In the practice of naming villages, towns, and streets in Hong Kong, a variety of languages have been at work. While Cantonese is the primary medium responsible for names especially of modern times, other languages and dialects have their imprints in appellations from the past. This article focuses on an early map of Hong Kong and reports on findings that betray such a linguistic complexity. In particular, we will be studying an 1866 map by Fr. Simone Volonteri, an atlas that provides both Chinese characters and alphabetic transcriptions for place names in Hong Kong and its neighboring regions.

Keywords: Fr. S. Volonteri; *Map of the San-on District*; place names in Hong Kong; language of the 19th century; Cantonese; *Kejia* (Hakka) dialect

1. A place name is a linguistic label by which people refer to a location where they come upon, travel to, gather, or live. It is a spatial reference that may also serve as a signpost into the past, an account that relates the history of the place and its inhabitants. In addition, as a place name is orally transmissible, its pronunciation is often ready to inform us about the language in which it is coined. When the small fishing village at the mouth of the Pearl River came to be known as 香港 (lit. "fragrant harbor"), it was not so much the fisheries that the name tried to capture in its aromatic reading; rather, it was the incense transport the villagers were engaged in that was highlighted in the appellation.[1] When the Chinese name was introduced to the Western world, the appellation underwent an exercise of transliteration: Hong Kong. Which Western language was responsible for the rendition? English or another European language? Which Chinese dialect informed the act? Cantonese or Mandarin? With the return of the sovereignty of Hong Kong to China, will its Western name be eventually modified according to Putonghua, the official language, and transcribed as "Xianggang"? As the Chinese character writing system is not particularly phonologically informative, transliteration of place names is indeed one way that may help us to gauge at the way how they were actually pronounced at least during the period when the translingual practice was undertaken. This article will focus on one particular bilingual map of Hong Kong and its vicinity, compiled in the 19th century, making a first attempt to look at the ways in which the Chinese place names were rendered in the map and speculate on the reasons why they were spelled in that manner. It is hoped that our findings will help us better understand the language situation in 19th-century Hong Kong.

Map-making has enjoyed a long history in China. The earliest maps of Hong Kong that we have been able to assemble, however, date back to the 15th century, with a few drawn by Westerners in the 17th and 18th centuries. These maps are mostly monolingual, in either Chinese or Western labeling; and their inclusion of Hong Kong was often limited and incomplete. The first comprehensive and bilingual map of the region was

---

[1] See Fok (1998).

produced in 1866 by an Italian priest dispatched to the Roman Catholic Diocese in Hong Kong. Fr. Simeone Volonteri (1831–1904) arrived at the city, a British Colony since 1842, at the age of 29, and was busily engaged with his missionary assignments for several years. He was later transferred to northern China where he eventually became the Bishop of Henan. During his stay in Hong Kong, where he was variously known as Fr. Hua 華, Fr. He 和, and Fr. Ho,[2] Volonteri made tremendous efforts to travel far and near in the region. As aptly described in a report of 1969, "a most remarkable fruit of his four years' professional labor was undoubtedly the San On District Map 'drawn from actual observations,' a frequently consulted historical and geographical document for those interested in the area, especially of the period before the New Territories was leased to Britain in 1898."[3] First appearing in 1866, the map was hailed by many of his time as the "first and only map hitherto published,"[4] "a fairly correct map of the country" showing the coast line and the position of all villages, streams, and roads.[5] A copy of the map is attached in Appendix I. In Volonteri's own words,

> The scope of this Map embraces an area of about Forty Five miles from North to South, and of about Sixty miles from East to West—that is to say the District of Sun-on whereof Nam-tao, is the departmental town. It is within the district of Sun-on that Hongkong and its dependencies stood prior to their cession, and the whole Coast line for many miles adjacent is under the jurisdiction of the Mandarin at Nam-tao.[6]

---

[2] Volonteri was referred to as "華倫泰理神父" and "和神父" in documents compiled by Holy Spirit Study Centre 聖神研究中心 in 1983. In an article authored by Ronald Ng (1969), the priest appears as Padre Ho, "a name derived from the transliteration in the local dialect of the first syllable of his surname" (p. 141).

[3] Ng (1969).

[4] Ibid.

[5] Hayes, "The San On Map of Mgr. Volonteri," *Journal of the Hong Kong Branch of the Royal Asiatic Society*, 10 (1970): 193.

[6] Ibid., p. 195.

San-on 新安 was a district, initially established in the 16th century, that covered a wide area in south China, including both Hong Kong and Shenzhen.[7] Only the island of Hong Kong was ceded to the British when Volonteri was working on the map. He ventured out to the entire district, recording 900 settlements in over 750 square miles. According to Ng, the number of 368 villages and market towns shown in that part of San-on which became British 30 years later is fairly consistent with the official figure of 416 for 1898. It has also been noted that, while villages were in general accurately located and named, sites in western San-on were often left out unmarked on the map.[8] "Although it cannot be ascertained whether Mgr. Volonteri had received any cartographic training, either before or after he entered the priesthood, the map displays no sign of amateurism."[9] Neither do we know very much about Volonteri's linguistic background, but, given his demanding missionary assignments and achievements in the Colony and eventually in northern China, he must have been proficient in the language. Nonetheless, on all journeys in San-on, he was accompanied by a local collaborator, Don Andrea Maria Liang, who must have been the scribe in writing out the Chinese place names on the map. Unfortunately, there is not much information on this collaborator, information that would otherwise help us better appreciate the linguistic, or phonological, reality of the naming and transliteration device.

As noted earlier, the Volonteri map is a comprehensive bilingual map, the first of its kind ever compiled of the area.[10] Almost all place names are labeled in both Chinese and English. The English names are mostly transliterations of the Chinese characters. As bilingual maps continued to appear in subsequent years of the expanded colony, including Hong Kong, Kowloon, and the New Territories, it is our goal that, by comparing transliterations of various periods, we can map out changes in the Chinese

---

[7] See Shu (1819).
[8] Ng (1969), p. 144.
[9] Ibid., p. 142.
[10] The map is now preserved in the National Library of Australia.

language since the 19th century. And, for this reason, we will limit our investigation of the Volonteri map to Hong Kong, Kowloon, and the New Territories. At a later time, we hope to expand the study and examine other areas on the San-on map, tracing the linguistic features that the map betrays and also the implications of any change as shown in later Chinese maps and documents.

2. The Volonteri map records a total of 464 place names in its Hong Kong section. Twenty-eight names appear only in English, most being English names without Chinese equivalents, e.g., Quarri Bay, Cape d'Aguilla, Castle Peak, and S. John Cathedral. There are, however, a small number of names (15) given in transliteration only, e.g., Tai-kok-tsui, Yung-shu-ha, and P'ing-tsia. Their Chinese equivalents can be found in maps of the 20th century: Tai-kok-tsui 大角咀, Yung-shu-ha 榕樹下, and P'ing-tsia 坪輋. Another 16 names are in Chinese characters without accompanying spelling, e.g., 井頭, 馬灣, and 田心. In later maps, these names are spelled out as Tseng Tau, Ma Wan, and Tin Sam respectively. For our purposes, there is a total of 405 names, i.e., 87% of all names, recorded in both Chinese characters and English transliteration, which we can use as raw data for an inquiry about the phonological nature of the language in 1866. What was the language that the transliteration was based on? As few of these names ever appeared in Western spelling in documents prior to Volonteri's days, he and his colleague must have transcribed the names according to the ways in which the local inhabitants pronounced the words. If there was a discrepancy in spelling the same Chinese word in the map, the discrepancy could be the results of erroneous transcription. Or, it could reflect a faithful attempt to capture divergent pronunciations, pronunciations in more than one dialect.

It is generally agreed that the bilingual map was essentially Cantonese and English and the transcription was based upon the system given in Williams's *A Tonic Dictionary of the Canton Dialect* published in 1856, i.e., ten years before Volonteri's map appeared.[11] The Canton Dialect,

---

[11] Ng (1969), p. 146.

Williams defines, is the language "which is spoken in the greatest purity in the city of Canton itself."[12] What I will do in the following pages is to compare the spellings in the map with the Cantonese sound system as reconstructed from pedagogical materials of the late 19th century. In particular, I will be referring to the system introduced by Dyer Ball (1847–1919), a system that was essentially of the same tradition as laid down by Williams.[13] It is hoped that a careful scrutiny will help us identify whether the pronunciations given on the map were truly those of the Canton dialect, or whether they were products of a different language community.

3. At this onset, we should note two major distinctions in spelling between the map and the pedagogical materials:

(1) Word tones are not marked on the map. For example, *ma* is given for 馬 in 馬鞍山 (Ma-on-shan), 麻 in 麻竹嶺 (Ma-chuk-ling), and 媽 in 亞媽笏 (A-ma-t'at). In works by Williams and others, 馬 is given as ⁼*ma*, 麻 as ₌*ma*, and 媽 as ₌*ma*, diacritically distinguished for tones.[14]

(2) The length distinction between the long *á* and the short *a* in Williams is not always consistently maintained in the map. Hence, 林 in 林村 (Lam-ts'ün) and 藍 in 大藍寮 (Tai-lam-liu) are both spelled as *lam*, whereas they are orthographically kept apart in Williams, the former as *lam* and the latter as *lám*.

With these conditions combined, a syllable like *pak* in the map can stand for two very different forms, 白 in 白蠟 (Pak-lap) and 北 in 北萌 (Pak-long). The two words are both tonally and vocalically different in Williams' transcription: 白 is given as pák₌ and 北 as pak₌.

3.1. The omissions of these very important phonological distinctions could be construed as indicators of a different dialect then spoken in 19th-century Hong Kong. Such a scenario is of course far from possible. Both of these

---

[12] Williams (1844), *An English and Chinese Vocabulary, in the Court Dialect*, p. vii.

[13] For details of the Ball system, see Cheung (2006).

[14] For the tonal marking device in the dictionary, see Williams (1844), pp. xiii–xv. Generally speaking, the tone is marked diacritically at the corner of a character: 陰平 ₌X, 陽平 ₌X, 陰上 ⁼X, 陽上 ⁼X, 陰去 X⁼, 陽去 X₌, 陰入 X₌, 陽入 X₌.

segmental and supra-segmental distinctions were characteristic features of many Yue dialects. The omissions could, however, be attributed to a different romanization system of Cantonese, a system that was responsible for an early dictionary by Robert Morrison in 1828. Entitled *A Vocabulary of the Canton Dialect*, the dictionary made no distinction between the long and short *a*'s. Neither did it mark any of the tones. While conscientious efforts were taken by subsequent linguists and pedagogues to modify the spelling system, the dictionary remained a major source for Cantonese studies at the time. Volonteri and his colleague might have decided to follow suit in their romanization. The map was relatively small in size (85.4 × 107.3 cm), and filling in with diacritic marks could be cluttering and, thus, less preferable as a choice for the map-makers. The vowel length distinction between *i* and *í*, and that between *u* and *ú*, both non-phonemic in nature, was also eliminated in the map. Another diacritic mark, the apostrophe for consonantal aspiration, was kept but not with consistency; the same word could be spelled with an aspirated stop in one instance and without aspiration in another, e.g., 潭 rendered as *tam* in 潭仔, and as *t'am* in 北潭村.

3.2. Despite these orthographic infelicities, the map shows a high degree of correspondence in phonological representation to the Cantonese language manuals of the 19th century. Of the 405 place names, there is a total of around 300 single characters being used in the naming. The following table shows the distribution of syllables containing the long vowel *á* according to the traditional dichotomy of the initial and the final. To distinguish the long *á* from the short *a*, as reported above, we will transcribe the former with "aa." Distribution of other syllables are attached in Appendix II.

	aa	aai	aao	aam	aan	aang	aap	aat	aak
p			炮					八	柏白
p'		排							
m	麻媽馬		茅		萬	孟			
f	花								
t	打	大帶		淡擔潭	丹灘			塔	
t'					炭			撻	
n					南				
l				藍纜籃欖	欄爛			蠟	
k	家	界街	蛟滘		澗				隔
k'									
kw									
kw'									
h	下蝦廈			涵咸		坑			
ng	衙			岩巖	眼				額
ts		柴							
ts'									
s				三嶂					
ch		寨		插?[15]					
ch'									
sh	沙		筲		山				石
sz									
w					灣還環	橫			
j									
0	亞鴉丫		凹			罌			

3.3. The Volonteri system contains a total of 22 initial consonants and 44 finals:

Initials (IPA)

p	p'	m	f	
t	t'	n		l
ts	ts'		s	
ch	ch'		sh	y
k	k'	ng	h	
kw	kw'			w

---

[15] 插竹灣, a town in the Sai Kung 西貢 area, is spelled as Cham Chuk Wan in the map. The rendition of 插, regularly pronounced as *chap*, as *cham* is problematic. There is, however, a town near Sai Kung now known as 斬竹灣, where 斬 is indeed pronounced as *cham*. So, the pairing in the map is evidently a graphic error instead of an anomaly in pronunciation.

Finals (IPA)

	-i	-u	-m	-n	-ŋ	-p	-t	-k
a	ai	au	am	an	aŋ	ap	at	ak
	ɐi	ɐu	ɐm	ɐn	ɐŋ	ɐp	ɐt	ɐk
	ei							
ɛ					ɛŋ			ɛk
i		iu	im	in		ip	it	
					ɪŋ			ɪk
ɿ								
ɔ	ɔi			ɔn	ɔŋ		ɔt	ɔk
		ou	om			op		
œ					œŋ			œk
	θi			ən			ət	
u	ui			un			ut	
					ʊŋ			ʊk
y				yn			yt	
m	ŋ							

In the above table of finals, the shaded ones are in language manuals of the late 19th century but missing from the map. The gaps are probably due to the fact that these finals were not used in any of the place names. For example, *ün* [yn] and *üt* [yt] would form a natural pair with a dental coda, the former with a nasal and the latter a stop. The missing of *üt* would therefore best be construed as an accidental gap in distribution. Except for these gaps in the system, we can safely characterize the Volonteri phonology as essentially identical with that of the late 19th century, as reconstructed from other sources of that period.[16] In other words, what the map represents is basically a Cantonese system.

The following are a few examples to illustrate that resemblance in spelling, and hence pronunciation, between the map of 1866 and maps of the 21st century.[17]

---

[16] Cf. the reconstructed system of Ball's language in Cheung (2006).

[17] While there is a large number of maps produced in recent years, the spellings here follow those in *Hong Kong Guide 2009*, prepared by the Survey and Mapping Office, Lands Department, the Government of the Hong Kong Special Administrative Region.

Naming the City | 219

1866		2009	
黃家圍	Wong-ka-wai	皇家圍	Wong Ka Wai
馬鞍岡	Ma-on-kong	馬鞍岡	Ma On Kong
粉嶺	Fan-ling	粉嶺	Fan Ling
橫台山	Wang-t'oi-shan	橫台山	Wang Toi Shan
白蠟	Pak-lap	白臘	Pak Lap
筲箕灣	Shau-ki-wan	筲箕灣	Shau Kei Wan
石排灣	Shek-pai-wan	石排灣	Shek Pai Wan

3.4. The map also bears witness to some of the phonological changes that Cantonese underwent during the 19th century.[18] The following are examples to illustrate the differences in spelling place names between then and now.[19]

One such change is a vowel split responsible for the change from *i* to *ei*. Hence, we find a contrast between the use of a monothong in Volonteri's rendition of names and a diphthong in modern maps.

筲箕灣 Shau-<u>ki</u>-wan	→	筲箕灣 Shau <u>Kei</u> Wan
蓮花地 Lin-fa-<u>ti</u>	→	蓮花地 Lin Fa <u>Tei</u>
沙角尾 Sha-kok-<u>mi</u>	→	沙角尾 Sha Kok <u>Mei</u>

A similar split from *u* to *ou* can be observed in the following example. While 路 is now pronounced as *lou*, it is given as *lu* in K'un-tai-lu 群帶路 on the map.

The letter "o" is used to represent two different sounds in Volonteri's language. In language manuals prepared by Williams and Ball, the diphthong [ou] is spelled as *o*, with diacritic marking *ó* or *ò*, and is to be distinguished from a simple *o* which

---

[18] For more discussion on phonological changes in early Cantonese, see Cheung (2003).

[19] Small pictures of the 1866 map are reproduced in order to show the actual recording of the place names in the map.

stands for [ɔ]. As noted above, diacritic marking is abandoned in Volonteri's system. Hence, words with these two finals are spelled alike.

		[ɔ]	vs.			[ou]
婆	平婆尾	P'ing-p'o-mi	vs.	莆	莆心排	P'o-sam-p'ai
籮	三擔籮	Sam-tam-lo	vs.	老	老鼠嶺	Lo-shü-ling
荷	荷木墩	Ho-muk-tan	vs.	蠔	蠔涌	Ho-ch'ung

When properly studied within the context of the 19th-century transcription, the seemingly irregular use of symbols is simply a matter of convention.

4. While the evidence thus far argues in favor for Cantonese as the language underlying the cartographic project, not all names are typically Cantonese as will be shown in the following examples. The Volonteri language, in fact, demonstrates a certain mixture of Cantonese and a different dialect or dialects. We will study a few of these complications and attempt to identify the sources of the atypical appellations.

4.1. 家

土家灣 *To-ka-wan* is the designation for an area in Kowloon, traditionally known as 土瓜灣,[20] a name that is still in use today. While the different choice of characters for the second syllable may appear merely graphic, the variation also betrays an important phonological

---

[20] In the "Map of Hong Kong with British Kowloon" (1888), the place name is spelled as "Tokwawan."

modification. 瓜 [kwa] differs from 家 [ka] in its inclusion of a -w- glide, a medial that has had its regular presence in traditional Chinese phonology since ancient times. The loss of the w-glide is not something unfamiliar in Cantonese, as shown in cases such as 光 [kwɔng] pronounced as 剛 [kɔng], and 國 [kwɔk] as 角 [kɔk] in modern-day Hong Kong Cantonese.[21] The delabialization, however, is a rather late phenomenon, distinctly absent in the 19th-century Cantonese manuals. In all early documents, 瓜 carried only one reading: *kwa*. The choice of 家 [ka] for a place name otherwise written as 瓜 [kwa] would indicate that the pronunciation was based upon a dialect other than Cantonese, a dialect in which 瓜 was pronounced without the w-glide: [ka]. A quick check around the region comes up with a number of neighboring dialects where 瓜 and 家 share the same reading [ka].[22]

	家	瓜
Cantonese	ka	kwa
Volonteri	**ka**	**ka**
中山、珠海	ka	ka
開平、恩平	ka	ka
惠州、東莞	ka	ka

It is possible that the Volonteri reading was a borrowing from any of these dialects. While Zhongshan 中山, Zhuhai 珠海, Kaiping 開平, and Enping 恩平 are all members of the Yue dialect, the latter two belong to Seiyap 四邑 (*Siyi* in Mandarin), a branch that has its own phonological characteristics.[23] Huizhou 惠州 and Dongguan 東莞, on the other hand, are of the Hakka 客家 (*Kejia* in Mandarin) family, distinctly different from the Yue family. If the [ka] reading of 瓜 was a borrowing, it could have come from a neighboring Yue dialect or it could have come from a non-Yue dialect. The answer would not be readily available without a further investigation of other alternate readings.

---

[21] See Bauer (1997), pp. 19–22.

[22] Dialectal materials that we have consulted include Zhan and Cheung (1987).

[23] Ball conducted a detailed description of the Zhongshan dialect in his 1897 work entitled "The Höng Shán or Macao Dialect," *The China Review*, 22.2. An early study of the Seiyap dialect was compiled by Y. R. Chao in 1951 in his work entitled "Taishan yuliao" 台山語料, *The Bulletin of the Institute of History and Philology* 歷史語言研究所集刊, 23: 25–76.

4.2. 逕

逕 appears quite often in place names as a generic term meaning "village" or "path." In standard Cantonese, this word is pronounced as *king* [kɪŋ], with possibly a colloquial alternate *keng* [kɛŋ].[24] In the Volonteri map, it is given as *kang*, without any further indication as to whether the *a* is a long *á* or a short *a*. The following examples list in pairs the 1866 and the 2009 readings.

1866		2009	
蕉逕	Tsiu-<u>kang</u>	蕉逕	Tsiu-<u>keng</u>
赤逕	Ch'ik-<u>kang</u>	赤逕	Chek-<u>keng</u>
逕口	<u>Kang</u>-hau	逕口	<u>Keng</u>-hau
莨逕	Long-<u>kang</u>	浪逕	Long-<u>keng</u>

The *kang* reading is apparently foreign to Cantonese, and its inclusion in the Volonteri map is most likely based upon a different dialect. Other dialects in the region that provide such a pronunciation include Zhongshan, Zhuhai, Huizhou, and Dongguan.

	逕
Cantonese	king
Volonteri	**kang**
中山、珠海	keng/kɐng
開平、恩平	keng
惠州、東莞	kang

As *kang* is not marked in the map for its exact length quality, its presence could be an indication of a phonological influence from either Zhongshan and Zhuhai where the vowel could be short, or from Huizhou and Dongguan where the vowel is a long *a*. In other words, while Seiyap can be safely ruled out as the source for borrowing, the influence in this case

---

[24] Such an alternation between -*ing* and -*eng* is quite common in Cantonese, the former being a literary reading and the latter a colloquial one. Examples include 驚, 名, 靈, 請, etc.

could have come from the Hakka dialects or from one of the neighboring Cantonese dialects, namely Zhongshan and Zhuhai.

4.3. 霜 and 相

There is a small island in the north of the New Territories which Volonteri marks as 霜洲, romanized as *Song-chau*, in his map. The name has, however, disappeared in modern maps. To the south, near Saikung, there is a bay named 相思灣, which Volonteri romanizes as *Siong-sz-wan*. Historically, 霜 and 相 come from different phonological origins, a difference that is not preserved in Cantonese. Both words share the same pronunciation [sœŋ] in language materials of the 19th century, a reading that remains unchanged in modern-day Cantonese.

In other words, the different spellings for 霜 and 相 must have been based on a dialect other than Cantonese. In addition, the presence of a medial *-i-* in *siong* is an unknown feature in Cantonese. None of the materials, old or new, displays such a syllabic formation. The following table shows the pronunciations of the two words in some of the other dialects in the region.

	霜	相
Cantonese	sœng	sœng
Volonteri	**song**	**siong**
中山、珠海	sœng	sœng
新會	song	siong
惠州、東莞	song	siong

Xinhui, Huizhou, and Dongguan display the same distinction as found in the map. Of the three, while Huizhou and Dongguan are members of the Hakka family, Xinhui belongs to the Seiyap branch. As in the previous case, Hakka could be the source for the *siong* reading, but the influence could have also come from one of the Seiyap dialects.

4.4. 尾

尾, literally meaning "tail," is a common generic term, marking the back or end of a location. Its antonym, 頭 ("head" and by extension "front"), is also used as a location marker.[25] The following are a few examples of 尾 where the spelling differs between the old and new transcriptions.

1866		2009	
沙角尾	Sha-kok-mi	沙角尾	Sha-kok-mei
窩尾	Wo-mi	窩美	Wo-mei
蝦尾	Ha-mi	蝦尾	Ha-mei
平婆尾	P'ing-p'o-mi	(not found)	

Unlike its modern reading *mei*, 尾 is spelled differently as *mi* in the 1866 system, a difference that is due not so much to dialectal influence as to a historical sound change, as described in section 3.4. Around the turn of the 20th century, the final *-i* underwent a vowel split giving rise to a diphthong *-ei*. There is, however, one spelling for 尾 in the map that is strikingly unfamiliar in early Cantonese. That spelling appears only once in the name 涌尾.

1866		2009	
涌尾	Ch'ung-mui	涌尾	Chung-mei

Upon checking other dialects, here is a list of some of the pronunciations of 尾.

	尾
Cantonese	mei
Volonteri	**mui**
中山、珠海	mi
開平、恩平	ᵐbei
惠州、東莞	mi/mui

---

[25] For example, 頭 and 尾 are found as a pair in Shenzhen: 沙頭 and 沙尾.

Only Huizhou and Dongguan show a reading that is similar to the Volonteri spelling. Other Hakka dialects confirm that reading, as shown in:

東莞	mui
深圳	mui
從化	mui

If it was a dialectal borrowing, the Volonteri reading of 尾 could have only come from one source, namely Hakka.

4.5. The following chart lists the findings according to dialect groups. When there is a match between the Volonteri and the dialectal pronunciations, the match is marked with an ×.

	Volonteri	中山	四邑	客家
瓜 ka	×	×	×	×
逕 kang	×	×		×
霜 vs. 相	×		×	×
尾 mui	×			×

These four cases are admittedly random samples; but, even given such a limited corpus, the distribution seems to argue that, of all possible dialectal input, Hakka was probably the culprit behind these "irregular" readings in an otherwise Cantonese map.

5. To further confirm the influence from Hakka on the naming practice in 19th-century Cantonese, we will conduct a comparative study between the language of the 1866 map and the Hakka phonology.

5.1. *an* vs. *in*

There are two pronunciations of 新 in the map: *san* and *sin*. The former is the regular pronunciation in Cantonese.

1866		2009	
新屋仔	San-uk-tsai	新屋仔	San Uk Tsai
新圍	Sin-wai	新圍	San Wai

There are in fact a number of names with 新 in the 1866 map, but only one with the *sin* reading. That reading does not exist in Seiyap or in Zhongshan. But, it is the prevalent pronunciation in Hakka, as shown in the following table.[26] Pronunciations in Guangzhou, Zhuhai, and Xinhui are included for comparison.

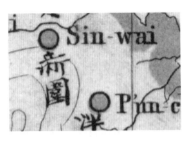

	新
Ancient Chinese 中古音	臻開三平真心
Volonteri	**san, sin**
Guangzhou 廣州	sɐn
Zhuhai 珠海	sɐi
Xinhui 新會	sæn
Huizhou 惠州	sin
Qingxi 清溪, Dongguan 東莞	sin
Shatoujiao 沙頭角	sin
Meixian 梅縣	sin
Wengyuan 翁源	sin
Liannan 連南	sin
Heyuan 河源	sin
Lai Chi Chong 荔枝莊	ʃin
Ma Tseuk Leng 麻雀嶺	ʃin
Chek Nai Ping 赤泥坪	ʃin

5.2. *ou* vs. *au*

The contrast between the two finals, *ou* and *au*, in Cantonese is a reflection of a phonological distinction in ancient Chinese. Examples from the map are 毛 [mou] and 茅 [mau]. Historically, these two words belong to different divisions of the 效攝, the former being a member of the first division 一等 word and the latter of the second division 二等. In the map, however, the two words are often spelled alike, *mau*, as shown below.

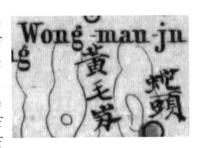

---

[26] A total of 12 varieties of Hakka dialects are included in the table. For detailed information, please see Li and Chang (1992); Chang and Zhuang (2003).

1866		2009	
黃毛坳	Wong-<u>mau</u>-jn	黃毛應	Wong <u>Mo</u> Ying[27]
茅坪	<u>Mau</u>-p'ing	茅坪	<u>Mau</u> Ping

Similar pairs include:

高洲	<u>Kau</u>-chau	vs.	交椅洲	<u>Kau</u> Yi Chau
	(*Ko* in 20th century)			(*Kau* in 20th century)
老圍	<u>Lau</u>-wai	vs.	老圍	<u>Lo</u> Wai

The first pair gives the same spelling *-au* to 高 (of the first division) and 交 (second division), thus erasing a historical distinction which has actually been kept in Cantonese.[28] The second pair illustrates an alternation between two different readings of the same character 老, *-au* and *-ou*. The coalescence and free variation between *au* and *ou* in the map must have been based on a dialect where that divisional distinction has been lost. In fact, that new pronunciation must have been *au* instead of *ou*. As the following table shows, Hakka displays that phonological characteristic.

	茅	毛	高	交	老
中古音	效二肴明	效一豪明	效一豪見	效二肴見	效一晧來
Volonteri	**mau**	**mau**	**kau**	**kau**	**lau**
廣州	mau	mou	kou	kau	lou
中山石岐	mau	mou	kou	kau	lou
新會	ᵐbau	ᵐbou	kou	kau	lau
開平	ᵐbau	ᵐbɔ	kɔ	kau	lau
惠州	<u>mau</u>	<u>mau</u>	<u>kau</u>	<u>kau</u>	<u>lau</u>
東莞清溪	<u>mau</u>	<u>mau</u>	<u>kau</u>	<u>kau</u>	<u>lau</u>
沙頭角	<u>mau</u>	<u>mau</u>	<u>kau</u>	<u>kau</u>	<u>lau</u>
梅縣		mau	kau	kau	lau
翁源		mou	kou	kau	lau
河源		<u>mau</u>	<u>kau</u>	<u>kau</u>	<u>lau</u>
荔枝莊	ᵐ<u>bau</u>	ᵐ<u>bau</u>	<u>kau</u>	<u>kau</u>	<u>lau</u>
麻雀嶺	<u>bau</u>	<u>bau</u>	<u>kau</u>	<u>kau</u>	<u>lau</u>
赤泥坪	<u>bau</u>	<u>bau</u>	<u>kau</u>	<u>kau</u>	<u>lau</u>

---

[27] Though spelled with "mo," the actual pronunciation of 毛 is [mou].

[28] For example, in Ball's *Cantonese Made Easy* (1883), 毛 is romanized as *mò* [mou] and 茅 as *máu* [mau].

5.3. *ik* vs. *ak*

The character 石 has three different readings in Volonteri's map.

		1866		2009	
(1)	shik	多石	To-<u>shik</u>	多石	To <u>Shek</u>
		紅石門	Hung-<u>shik</u>-mun	紅石門	Hung <u>Shek</u> Mun
(2)	shek	石籬背	<u>Shek</u>-li-pui	石梨貝	<u>Shek</u> Lei Pui
		石坑	Shek-hang	石坑	<u>Shek</u> Hang
(3)	shak	三茅石	Sam-mau-<u>shak</u>	三抱石	Sam Po <u>Shek</u>
		牛皮石	Ngau-pi-<u>shak</u>	牛皮沙	Ngau Pei <u>Sha</u>

石 was historically a member of the third division in 梗攝. Its modern rendering contains either *ik* [ik] or *ek* [ɛk] as its final, the former being a literary reading 文讀 and the latter a colloquial reading 白讀. Both readings were recorded in the 19th-century materials,[29] with *sek* eventually replacing *sik* as the only pronunciation in modern Cantonese. *Shak* appears to be a suspicious candidate as such a syllable simply does not exist in Cantonese syllabary. 牛皮沙's ending *sha* is an interesting example in that the modern reading has retained the vowel *a* in 石 by dropping its *-k* ending: *shak* → *sha*.

Another case in the map that shows a similar variation between *ik* and *ak* is 赤, appearing in the following place names. The modern reading is invariably *chek*.

1866		2009	
赤逕	Ch'<u>ik</u>-kang	赤徑	<u>Chek</u> Keng
赤柱	<u>Chak</u>-chü	赤柱	<u>Chek</u> Chue

When we turn to Hakka, as shown in the following table, *shak* and *chak* are the regular readings in the dialects.

---

[29] 石 is transcribed as Bridgman's *shik* in *Chinese Chrestomathy* (1841) and *shek* in Ball's *Cantonese Made Easy* (1883) respectively.

中古音	石 梗三昔禪	赤 梗三昔昌
Volonteri	**shak**	**chak**
廣州	sɛk	ts'ɛk
中山石岐	siak	ts'ik
新會	siak	ts'ik
惠州	siak	ts'iak
東莞清溪	sak	ts'ak
沙頭角	sak	ts'ak
梅縣	sak	ts'ak
翁源	sak	ts'ak
河源	sak	ts'ak
荔枝莊	ʃak	tʃak
麻雀嶺	ʃak	tʃak
赤泥坪	ʃak	tʃak

5.4. A medial -i-

As noted in section 4.3, a typical syllable in Cantonese does not allow the presence of a medial -i- sitting between the initial consonant and the vocal nucleus. While 相, *siong*, cited above, might seem to be an exception, it has been shown to display resemblance to its corresponding forms in Hakka. There are, in fact, quite a few other words that exhibit a similar syllabic make-up.

	1866			2009	
驚 king	黃驚凹	Wong-kiang-au	黃豔仔	Wong King Tsai
夾 kip	禾鸚夾	Wo-li-kiap	和宜合	Wo Yi Hop
坪 p'ing	坪山	P'iang-shan	屏山	Ping Shan
斜 ts'ɛ	上禾斜	Sheung-wo-tsia	上禾峯	SheungWo Che

Again, if we compare these readings with the Hakka dialects, we see a clear correspondence.[30]

---

[30] It should be noted that, in this section where we find a medial -i-, we detect a similarity with Sheyu 畲語 where 峯 is pronounced as *tsia*. Does this similarity point to a possible Sheyu layer responsible for the naming practice? That would await a further attempt to look into any possible interaction with or borrowing from an aboriginal language.

	驚	夾	平	斜（畧）
中古音	梗三庚見	咸二洽見	梗三庚並	假三麻邪
Volonteri	**kiang**	**kiap**	**piang**	**tsia**
廣州	kɪŋ/kɛŋ	kap	p'ɪŋ/p'ɛŋ	ts'ɛ
中山石岐	kɪŋ/kiaŋ	kap	p'ɪŋ/p'iaŋ	ts'e
新會	kɪŋ/kiaŋ	kap	p'ɪŋ	ts'ia
惠州	kiaŋ	kap	p'əŋ	ts'ia
東莞清溪	kiaŋ	k'iap	p'in/p'iaŋ	ts'ia
沙頭角	kin/kiaŋ	k'iap	p'in/p'iaŋ	sia
梅縣	kiaŋ		p'in/p'iaŋ	sia
翁源	kiaŋ		p'in/p'iaŋ	ts'ia
河源	kiaŋ		p'in	ts'ia
荔枝莊	kiaŋ	kap	p'iaŋ/p'in	tʃ'ia
麻雀嶺	kiaŋ	kap	p'iaŋ/p'in	tʃ'ia
赤泥坪	kiaŋ	kap	p'iaŋ/p'in	tʃ'ia

5.5. The following table is a summary of correspondence between the 1866 readings and their contemporary pronunciations in different dialects near Hong Kong. The non-shaded cells marking such correspondence are mostly found within the solid square between Huizhou and Chek Nai Ping, all within the domain of the Hakka language.

	1	2	3	4	5	6	7	8	9	10
	瓜	徑	石	霜	相	尾	新	毛	驚	平
Volonteri	ka	kang	shak	song	siong	mui	sin	mau	kiang	piang
廣州	kua	kɪŋ	sɛk	sœŋ	sœŋ	mei	sɐn	mou	kɪŋ/kɛŋ	p'ɪŋ/p'ɛŋ
中山石岐	kua	kɪŋ	siak	sœŋ	sœŋ	mi	sɐn	mou	kiaŋ	piaŋ
新會	kua	kɪŋ	siak	sɔŋ	siɔŋ	ᵐbei	sæn	ᵐbou	kiaŋ	p'ɪŋ
惠州	ka	kaŋ	siak	sɔŋ	siɔŋ	mi	sin	mau	kiaŋ	p'əŋ
東莞清溪	ka	kaŋ	sak	sɔŋ	siɔŋ	mui	sin	mau	kiaŋ	p'iaŋ
沙頭角	ka	kin	sak	sɔŋ	siɔŋ	mui	sin	mau	kiaŋ	p'iaŋ
梅縣	kua	kin	sak	sɔŋ	siɔŋ	mi	sin	mau	kiaŋ	p'iaŋ
翁源	ka	kin	sak	sɔŋ	siɔŋ	mui	sin	mou	kiaŋ	p'iaŋ
荔枝莊	ka	kaŋ	ʃak	ʃɔŋ	ʃiɔŋ	ᵐbui	ʃin	ᵐbau	kiaŋ	p'iaŋ
麻雀嶺	ka	kaŋ	ʃak	ʃɔŋ	ʃiɔŋ	bui	ʃin	bau	kiaŋ	p'iaŋ
赤泥坪	ka	kaŋ	ʃak	ʃɔŋ	ʃiɔŋ	bui	ʃin	bau	kiaŋ	p'iaŋ

The examples, ten in total, are clear evidence to argue that, while Volonteri romanized place names primarily according to Cantonese, efforts were made to incorporate pronunciations from other dialects as well. As a result, the same word might be spelled differently in different place names, producing spellings that appear to represent a sound system other than what we know of the Cantonese language. And, as argued, the most likely candidate that informs such a non-Cantonese spelling is Hakka, with characteristic sound features readily incorporated into the naming device.

6. Aside from the internal evidence that prompts us to speculate that Hakka was linguistically responsible for these non-Cantonese spellings in the 1866 map, we gain additional support from demographic statistics of the period. When we look at the distribution of these possible Hakka place names, we see clustering of these spellings in certain areas in the territory. The attached map illustrates the spread of place names that contain the above ten Hakka features. The numbers in the map refer to the non-Cantonese sound features listed above.

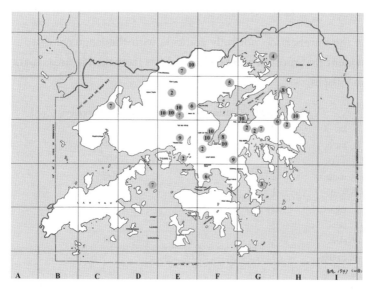

In 1898, Stewart Lockhart produced a report[31] for the colonial Hong Kong, a report in which he characterized the population status of certain

---

[31] Entitled "A Report on the Extension of the Colony of Hong Kong," the document was prepared by James Haldane Steward Lockhart in 1898. Lockhart (1858–1937) was a British colonial official stationed in Hong Kong in the late 19th century, where he was Registrar General and Colonial Secretary of Hong Kong. Lockhart Road on the Hong Kong Island was named after him.

villages and towns by labeling them as areas of Cantonese or Hakka settlements.[32]

The following table lists the number of villages provided by the report vis-à-vis the pronunciation of the place names. For example, 逕, one of the examples cited above, appears as *kang* in six place names, five of which are of the Hakka area, marked as H in the report; only one is of the Cantonese region, marked as P for *pun-ti* 本地 (local). Hence, the percentage contrast is 83% Hakka vs. 17% Cantonese.

赤逕	kang	H	
蕉逕	kang	H	
逕口	kang		P
萌逕	kang	H	
茜逕	kang	H	
狗爬逕	kang	H	

While the numbers do not fully coincide with the language distribution, it is evident that most of the Hakka readings happened in areas marked as Hakka villages.

	Total	Cantonese villages	Hakka villages
瓜 ka	2	50%	
逕 kang	6	17%	83%
石 shak	2		50%
毛 mau	1		100%
高 kau	1		
鰲 ngau	2	50%	50%
老 lau	1		
新 sin	1		100%
坪 piang	1	100%	
驚 kiang	1		100%
輋/斜 tsia	9	33%	67%
夾 kiap	1		100%
相 siong	1	100%	
尾 mui	1		100%

---

[32] Aside from Cantonese and Hakka, the report also identifies Tanka 蜑家 as another group of settlers in Hong Kong.

The most telling example is, perhaps, the striking contrast between *Sin-wai* and *San-wai*, two different spellings for the same place name in Chinese characters 新圍, as reported in section 5.1. The two villages are separated by quite a distance, and, according to the report, Sin-wai is a Hakka village and San-wai a Cantonese village. Because of the difference in population make-up, the two villages apparently spoke distinct dialects, which accounts for the difference in pronouncing an otherwise identical place name.

7.   As a conclusion, we can safely argue that there was a Hakka population in 19th-century Hong Kong, whose language played a part in the naming practice as recorded in the 1866 map project. The existence of a Hakka language layer in Hong Kong is of course not a surprising finding to scholars in the field. Efforts have been made to identify special generic nomenclatures, such as 屋, 坑, 下, 窩, 嶺, and 洋 in Hong Kong place names, as those of the Hakka origin.[33] Many of these old generic terms are found in the 1866 map. Their presence, in character forms, however, does not readily or necessarily tell us that Hakka was still an active medium for communication or for the naming practice. They might have simply been preserved as fossilized forms from the past. When names were transcribed in accordance with the actual pronunciation, the transliteration tells a different story. A conscientious missionary and scholar who made extensive visits to various regions in the San-on district, Volonteri must have consulted the locals when he recorded the place names in spelling. Variations in spelling therefore betray a complex linguistic reality where more than one dialect, namely Cantonese, was spoken. This article concludes that Hakka was one such dialect that contributed to the complexity. Other candidates might include the Min dialect or even aboriginal languages in the region.[34] Further analysis of the map and other documents of similar nature will continue to help us better understand the linguistic heterogeneity that underlies the naming practice in a region

---

[33]   For example, see Lau (2001).

[34]   An example of the Min influence is the name 深水埗 romanized as *Tsam Choy Poo* in the map entitled "Peninsula of Kowloon" (1866), a clear indication of a Min pronunciation. The characters would have been spelled as *Sham Shui Po* according to Cantonese.

where speakers of various dialects had gathered to make their living in a land at the southern tip of the Chinese atlas.

References

Ball, J. Dyer. 1883. *Cantonese Made Easy*. 1st edition. Hong Kong: The China Mail Office.
———. 1888. *Cantonese Made Easy*. 2nd edition. Hong Kong: The China Mail Office.
———. 1897. "The Höng Shán or Macao Dialect." *China Review*, 22.2: 501–531.
———. 1907. *Cantonese Made Easy*. 3rd edition. Singapore: Kelly and Walsh.
———. 1924. *Cantonese Made Easy*. 4th edition. Hong Kong: Kelly and Walsh.
Bauer, Robert S., and Paul K. Benedict. 1997. *Modern Cantonese Phonology*. Berlin; New York: Mouton de Gruyter.
Bridgman, Elijah C. 1841. *Chinese Chrestomathy in the Canton Dialect*. Macao: S. Wells Williams.
Chang Song-hing 張雙慶, and Zhuang Chusheng 莊初升, eds. 2003. *Xianggang Xinjie fangyan* 香港新界方言. Hong Kong: The Commercial Press.
Chao Yuen Ren 趙元任. 1951. "Taishan yuliao" 台山語料. *The Bulletin of the Institute of History and Philology* 歷史語言研究所集刊, 23: 25–76.
Cheung, Hung-nin Samuel 張洪年. 2003. "21 shiji de Xianggang Yueyu: Yi ge xin yuyin xitong de xingcheng" 21世紀的香港粵語：一個新語音系統的形成. In *Di 8 jie guoji Yue fangyan yantaohui lunwenji* 第八屆國際粵方言討會論文集, ed. Zhang Bohui 詹伯慧, pp. 129–152. Beijing: China Social Sciences Press 中國社會科學出版社.
———. 2006. "One Language, Two Systems: A Phonological Study of Two Cantonese Language Manuals of 1888." *Bulletin of Chinese Linguistics*, 1.1: 171–200.
Fok Kai Cheong 霍啟昌. 1998. "19 shiji zhongye yiqian de Xianggang" 十九世紀中葉以前的香港. In *Xianggang shi xinbian* 香港史新編, ed. Wang Gungwu 王賡武, pp. 37–58. Hong Kong: Joint Publishing.
Hayes, James. 1970. "The San On Map of Mgr. Volonteri." *Journal of the Hong Kong Branch of the Royal Asiatic Society*, 10.

Holy Spirit Study Centre 聖神研究中心. 1983 (June 24). "Xianggang tianzhujiao lishi ziliao (15): Ditu—Fuyin chuanbo meijie zhiyi" 香港天主教歷史資料（十五）：地圖——福音傳播媒介之一, *Kung Kao Po* 公教報.

Hong Kong Guide 2009. Hong Kong: Survey and Mapping Office, Lands Department, the Government of the Hong Kong Special Administrative Region.

Lau Chun-fat 劉鎮發. 2001. "Xianggang de Ke fangyan diming" 香港的客方言地名. *Xianggang Ke Yue fangyan bijiao yanjiu* 香港客粵方言比較研究. Guangzhou: Jinan University Press.

Li Rulong 李如龍, and Chang Song-hing 張雙慶, eds. 1992. *Ke Gan fangyan diaocha baogao* 客贛方言調查報告. Xiamen: Xiamen University Press.

Lockhart, Stewart. 1898. "Extracts from a Report by Mr. Stewart Lockhart on the Extension of the Colony of Hong Kong." Document No. 9/99. Hong Kong Government.

"Map of Hong Kong with British Kowloon." 1888. Hong Kong Government.

Ng, Ronald C. Y. 1969. "The San On Map of Mgr. Volonteri." *Journal of the Hong Kong Branch of the Royal Asiatic Society*, 9.

"Peninsula of Kowloon." 1866. Hong Kong Government.

Shu Maoguan 舒懋官. 1819. *Jiaqing Xin'an xianzhi* 嘉慶新安縣志.

Volonteri, Simeone. 1866. "Map of the San-On District (Kwangtung Province)," drawn from actual observations made by an Italian Missionary of the Propaganda in the course of his professional labors during a period of four years.

Williams, Samuel Wells. 1844. *An English and Chinese Vocabulary, in the Court Dialect*. Macao: S. Wells Williams.

———. 1856. *A Tonic Dictionary of the Chinese Language in the Canton Dialect*. Canton: Office of the Chinese Repository.

Zhan Bohui 詹伯慧, and Cheung Yat-shing 張日昇. 1987. *A Survey of Dialects in the Pearl River Delta, Vol. 1: Comparative Morpheme-Syllabary* 珠江三角洲方言字音對照. Hong Kong: New Century Publishing House.

This article originally appeared in 梅祖麟教授八秩壽慶學術論文集, ed. Hong Bo 洪波, Wu Fuxiang 吳福祥, and Sun Chaofen 孫朝奮 (Beijing: Capital Normal University Press, 2015), pp. 77–111. A Chinese version of the article, with some modifications, appeared in my 一切從語言開始 (It All Begins with Language) (Hong Kong: The Chinese University Press, 2017), pp. 49–103.

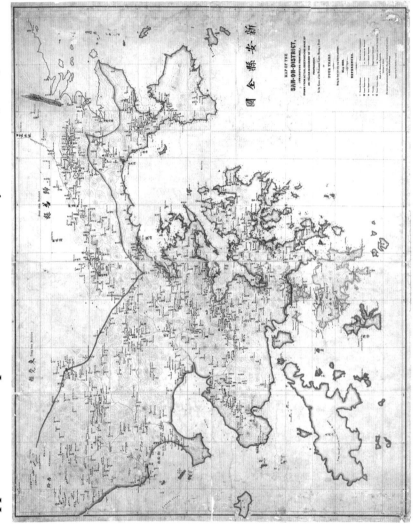

Appendix I: The Map of the San-on District by Volonteri (1866)

Appendix II: The Phonological System in Volonteri (1866)

(1) Vowel /aa/

	aa	aai	aao	aam	aan	aang	aap	aat	aak
p			炮					八	柏白
ph		排							
m	麻馬媽		茅		萬	孟			
f	花								
t	打	大帶		淡擔潭	丹灘		塔		
th					炭			撻	
n				南					
l				藍籃纜欖	欄爛		蠟		
k	家	界街	蛟滘		澗				隔
kh									
kw									
kwh									
h	下蝦廈			涵咸		坑			
ng	衙			岩巖	眼				額
ts		柴							
tsh									
s				三嵾					
ch		寨		插?					
chh									
sh	沙		筲		山				石
sz									
w					灣還環	橫			
j									
0	亞鴉丫		凹			罌			

(2) Vowel /a/

	a	ai	au	am	an	ang	ap	at	ak
p									北
ph									
m		米							
f								笏	
t					埕				
th			頭簌			藤		笏	
n		坭							
l		荔	樓	林					
k		雞	狗九	金錦		逕		吉	
kh									
kw		龜			軍			骨	
kwh		葵							
h			口						
ng			牛						
ts		仔						七	
tsh									
s		茜西		心	新				
ch			洲						
chh									
sh				深			十		
sz									
w		圍							
j			游油魷	音					
0									

(3) Vowel /e/

	e	ei	eng	ek
p				
ph				
m				
f				
t				
th				
n				
l				
k				
kh				
kw				
kwh				
h				
ng				
ts				
tsh				
s				
ch				
chh				
sh	社蛇			石
sz				
w				
j				
0				

(4) Vowel /eu/

	eu	eui	eun	eung	eut	euk
p						
ph						
m						
f						
t						
th						
n						
l						
k						
kh						
kw						
kwh						
h				香鄉響		
ng						
ts				將		
tsh						
s						
ch				樟長帳張		
chh						
sh				上		
sz						
w						
j				洋羊		
0						

(5) Vowel /i/

	i	iu	im	in	ing	ip	it	ik
p	皮			邊				壁
ph					坪平			
m	尾	廟		面				
f								
t	地	吊			汀			
th				田			鐵	
n		尿 gn-						
l	鯉籬狸	寮		蓮	領嶺			瀝
k	箕	叫			頸			
kh	歧	橋						
kw								
kwh								
h								
ng								
ts		椒蕉			井			
tsh				前	青清			
s		小		仙				
ch	枝			尖				
chh								赤
sh	屎				城			石
sz								
w								
j			鹽					
0	衣	陶			燕岇			

(6) Vowel /o/

	o	oi	o, ou	om	on	ong	op	ot	ok
p			埔寶布						薄塱
ph	婆		莆甫						
m			帽			芒			
f	火					放房			
t	多	台袋臺				璫			
th			土肚			塘堂			
n			腦						
l	籮螺	老蘆				蓢浪朗			落
k			高		乾	港岡崗			角
kh									
kw									
kwh									
h	荷	海	蠔	蚵	寒		合		鶴
ng						昂			
ts	左								
tsh			草						
s			塑簑						
ch									
chh									
sh									
sz									
w	窩禾					黃王凰			
j									
0	澳			暗庵	鞍				

(7) Vowel /u/

	u	ui	un	ung	ut	uk
p		背	泮			
ph						
m		梅	門			木
f	扶	灰		風鳳		
t				洞東		凸
th				桐		
n						
l	路	雷		龍籠壟		鹿
k	鼓牯		官觀管	公		谷鵠
kh						
kw						
kwh						
h				紅		
ng						
ts	灶	嘴				
tsh						
s						
ch				鐘中鍾		竹
chh				涌		
sh		水				
sz						
w						
j				榕		
0	烏芋		宛			屋

(8) Vowel /ü/

	ü	ün	üt
p			
ph			
m			
f			
t			
th			
n			
l			
k			
kh			
kw			
kwh			
h	圩墟		
ng			
ts			
tsh		村	
s			
ch	著	磚	
chh	川		
sh	樹鼠	船	
sz			
w			
j			
0	魚庚	園圓	

(9) Vowel Zero

	0
p	
ph	
m	
f	
t	
th	
n	
l	
k	
kh	
kw	
kwh	
h	
ng	梧 ng
ts	子 tsz
tsh	
s	思祖 sz
ch	
chh	
sh	
sz	
w	
j	
0	

Terms of Address in Cantonese

76. Paternal grandfather's sister's husband.	公公		Chéung¹ ‚kung.
77. Paternal grandfather's sister's husband.	姑公		‚Kú ‚kung.
78. Paternal grandfather's sister.	姑婆		‚Kú ‚p'ó.
79. Wife's father.	岳丈		Ngók, chéung¹.
80. Wife's father.	外父		Ngoi¹ fú'.
81. Wife's mother.	岳母		Ngók, ‘mó.
82. Wife's mother.	外母		Ngoi¹ ‘mó.
83. Wife's elder brother.	大舅		Tái² ‘k'au.
84. Wife's elder brother.	內兄		Noi¹ ‚hing.
85. Wife's younger brother.	細舅		Sai¹ ‘k'au.
86. Wife's younger brother.	內弟		Noi¹ tai².
87. Wife's brother's wife.	妗娘		‘K'am ‚néung.
88. Wife's elder sister.	大姨		Tái² ‚í ‚néung.
89. Wife's elder sister's husband.	襟兄		‚K'ám ‚hing.
90. Wife's younger sister.	細姨		Sai¹ ‚í ‚néung.
91. Wife's younger sister's husband.	襟弟		‚K'am tai².
92. Wife's nephew.	內姪		Noi¹ chat,.
93. Wife's nephew's wife.	內――婦		Noi¹ chat, ‘fú.
94. Wife's niece.	內――女		Noi¹ chat, ‘nu.
95. Wife's niece's husband.	內――婿		Noi¹ chat, sai'.
96. Elder male cousins of different surname.	表兄		‘Píu ‚hing.
97. Wives of these elder cousins.	表嫂		‘Píu ‘só.
98. Younger male cousins different surname.	表弟		
99. Wives of these younger cousins.			

Abstract: This article aims at studying the use of address terms in the Cantonese language as spoken in Hong Kong. It focuses primarily on the kinship system, examining both vocatives and designatives, and provides an analysis of the various linguistic mechanisms that are at work, including phonological variations, morphological changes, semantic shifts, and sociolinguistic borrowings. In addition, some general remarks are made with regard to social terms, which are chiefly an extension in use of the familial forms. A collection of address terms is appended at the end of the article for reference.

Keywords: Hong Kong Cantonese; kinship terms; social terms of address; vocative; designative; teknonymy

1. Introduction

Language is essentially a communicative system by means of which people speak and interact with each other in various social contexts. In the daily exchange of information with other members of the same speech community, a speaker, say a man, needs to make regular mentions of the person he addresses and of the person(s) he refers to. References can, of course, be made expediently in terms of deictic identification; hence, the use of pronouns in three persons. However, relationship words are also utilized as terms of address in discourse, i.e., instead of addressing, say, the hearer as "you," the speaker opts for a term that specifies the addressee's relation to him (e.g., "mother"). The choice of a relationship term over a personal pronoun is especially preferred when the deictic context may prove unclear as to which member of a group is actually being referred to, say, as "her." By naming "her" with a specific relationship term, the speaker is making a direct identification that is both explicit and unequivocal. The relationship term is an overt marking of the status of the person, who is either addressed or mentioned, with reference to the speaker. There may be more than one appellation used in a linguistic system to describe such a status (e.g., "mother" vs. "mommy"), and the selection of an appropriate form is often conditioned by a host of social and psychological factors such as formality and intimacy. On the other hand, different personal relationships may be designated by the same addressing term (e.g., the use of "uncle" to refer to both maternal and paternal relations), a linguistic phenomenon that may be reflective of a family structure that is lineal in nature and does not distinguish the collateral lines from each other. Since the end of the 19th century, concerted efforts have been made in the fields of anthropology and sociology to collect kinship terms from various parts of the world, examining their grouping patterns and exploring their implications with regard to family systems, marriage practices, and concepts of lineage and inheritance.[1] It is firmly believed that kinship plays

---

[1] With the publication of his *System of Consanguinity and Affinity of the Human Family* in 1871, Lewis H. Morgan laid the foundation for scientific investigation into kinship terminologies. Numerous studies have been made since then in both data description and interpretation. The earliest examination of the Chinese relationship system was also made by Morgan in his book, which gave nearly two hundred terms.

an important role both in regulating the behavior of individuals and in the formation of social groups and conventions. Linguists have also made similar studies of kin names for language comparison and classification.

As noted by Chen and Shryock, "China offers a unique field for the study of relationship terms."[2] Ever since ancient times, kinship has been the core concept of a Chinese social structure; society is viewed, in general, as an extension of a basic family organization, an outgrowth of a clan in which each member bears a certain relationship to the other, a social tie that in turn defines and dictates his rights and obligations in the community. There is a vast literature that records the use and development of kin terms throughout history, a meticulous and continuous tradition of documentation unparalleled by any other cultures in the world. Anthropologists have made good use of Chinese sources in their investigation of kinship systems. Notably, in 1937 H. Y. Feng conducted a thorough historical examination of some three hundred terms, explaining the structural principles underlying the composition of the terminologies and describing in detail the various factors (such as exogamy, cross-cousin marriage, teknonymy, etc.) that affect the operation of the system.[3] Y. R. Chao was the first scholar to look at the Chinese address system from a linguistic point of view; in his 1956 article, he offered a comprehensive analysis of the grammatical functions and the sociolinguistic conditions for the use of a variety of addressing terms, including kinship nomenclature as well as pronouns, proper names, and titles.[4] During the past few decades, dialectal surveys in China invariably include studies of kinship terms, but the data are chiefly collections of basic kin terminologies that are to be used either for lexical information or for comparison with Standard Mandarin. Little observations, however, have been made on the phonological patterning of these terms, let alone their semantic shift

---

[2] T. S. Chen and J. K. Shryock, "Chinese Relationship Terms," *American Anthropologist*, 34 (1932): 623–664.

[3] Han-yi Feng, "The Chinese Kinship System," *Harvard Journal of Asiatic Studies*, 2.2 (1937): 141–275.

[4] Y. R. Chao, "Chinese Terms of Address," *Language*, 32.1 (1956): 217–241. The article was later included in his 1976 collection, entitled *Aspects of Chinese Sociolinguistics*, pp. 309–342.

in coverage or their behaviors in a pragmatic context. This article aims at providing a preliminary investigation into the use of relationship terms in modern Standard Cantonese as spoken in Hong Kong. It will begin with a study of kin words and attempt at some generalizations pertinent to their phonological and semantic characteristics. In addition, the article will also discuss the use of social terms, which are chiefly an extension in the usage of the familial forms; a few are, however, loans from English. A list of relationship terms, by no means exhaustive, is appended at the end of the article. Wherever necessary, a distinction is made between designatives and vocatives, the former being terms of reference and the latter terms of direct address. All information is based primarily on the writer's knowledge of the language and his interviews with six native speakers ranging in age from 19 to 70.[5]

2. Kinship Terms

This article limits its description of the kinship system to essentially five generations, those of the ego (0), the parents (+1), the children (-1), the grandparents (+2), and the grandchildren (-2), the last two being further restricted to the lineal line only. The reasons for such restrictions along both vertical and horizontal planes of a family tree is quite obvious. Because of the disintegration of an extended family structure since the early 20th century, and also because of the current trends towards marrying late, few Chinese, especially of the younger generation, have collateral great grandparents or collateral grandchildren. As a result, the chances for engaging a member of the second generation of either ascending or descending order in a conversation are extremely rare. If there is ever such a need for referring to, say, a great grand uncle, the status of the person will be simply paraphrased as "the uncle of the grandfather."

---

[5] Informants are: F. Cheung (19), X. N. Wu (32), C. S. Chak (36), H. Y. Lee (39), J. F. Lok (65), and M. L. Cheng (70). They are all immigrants from Hong Kong or Canton.

2.1. Terminological Composition

To identify a relation by describing the association in overt terms such as "someone is X's Y's Z" is of course one way of forming a kinship denomination. In contrast with this analytic means, a synthetic term may be used for classification. For example, *di* 弟 (ego's younger brother) in Mandarin is a synthetic term embodying two referential features, namely sibling and age. *Difu* 弟婦 (lit. *di*'s woman), on the other hand, is an analytic name for ego's younger brother's wife, the spousal feature being explicitly marked by the word *fu*. Though composite by derivation, the term *difu* is a lexical unit and is to be distinguished from a phrasal description: *didi de taitai* 弟弟的太太 (lit. *di*'s wife), a paraphrase in the vernacular language. Most of the Cantonese kin terms are analytic compounds although members of the nucleus family are all referred to by synthetic names. The following are some of the synthetic relational terms in Cantonese.[6] The ones marked with an asterisk are bound forms, which cannot function as free and independent words.

*bā	爸	:	ego's father
mā	媽	:	ego's mother
*gō	哥	:	ego's elder brother
*daih	弟	:	ego's younger brother
*jé	姐	:	ego's elder sister
múi	妹	:	ego's younger sister
*sóu	嫂	:	ego's elder brother's wife
*yèh	爺	:	ego's father's father
*màh	嫲	:	ego's father's mother
*gūng	公	:	ego's mother's father
*pòh	婆	:	ego's mother's mother
*baak	伯	:	ego's father's older brother
*sūk	叔	:	ego's father's younger brother
*sám	嬸	:	ego's father's younger brother's wife
*gū	姑	:	ego's father's sister
*káuh	舅	:	ego's mother's brother
*yìh	姨	:	ego's mother's sister
jái	仔	:	ego's son

---

[6] Cantonese words are romanized according to the Yale system. A low tone is invariably marked with an "h" after the vowel in the syllable. Please note that romanization for Mandarin pronunciation is not marked for tones.

néui	女	:	ego's daughter
sānpóuh	新抱	:	ego's son's wife
néuihsai	女婿	:	ego's daughter's husband
ját	侄	:	ego's brother's son
yìhsāng	姨甥	:	ego's sister's son
syūn	孫	:	ego's son's son

Bound forms may acquire free status through affixation or *a-* 阿, e.g., *a-sūk* 阿叔 (uncle, ego's father's younger brother), *a-go* 阿哥 (ego's older brother), etc., or by means of mechanisms to be described later in the following pages.

A compound kin term, on the other hand, can be analyzed as a relational form in combination with one or more markers of the following types of correlatives. It should be noted, however, that the correlative terms themselves may in turn be composites of different features.[7] In some cases, a relational term may serve as a correlative marker.

Collateral
bíu	表	:	marker of descent of father's sister, mother's brother, and mother's sister
tòhng	堂	:	marker of descent of father's brother
ngoih	外	:	marker of non-sib relative, namely mother's parent and daughter's child

Generational
gūng	公	:	marker of the second ascending generation: male
pòh	婆	:	marker of the second ascending generation: female
fuh	父	:	marker of the first ascending generation: male sibling of the parent
mā	媽	:	marker of the first ascending generation: female sibling of the parent

Spousal
| jeuhng | 丈 | : | marker of husband of ego's relative of the first ascending generation |
| nèuhng | 娘 | : | marker of wife of ego's relative of the first ascending generation |

---

[7] The synthetic term *sám* 嬸, according to one theory, was etymologically a phonetic fusion of *sūk* 叔 (father's younger brother) and *móuh* 母 (generation marker) or of *saimóuh* 世母 (*sai* meaning "generation"). The term is, therefore, a reduction of an analytic compound. See discussion in Feng (1937), p. 201.

móuh	母	:	marker of wife of ego's relative of the first ascending generation
fū	夫	:	marker of husband of ego's relative of the same generation
fúh	婦	:	marker of wife of ego's relative of the same generation
sānpóuh	新抱	:	marker of wife of ego's relative of the descending generation
sai	婿	:	marker of husband of ego's relative of the descending generation

Gender
néui	女	:	marker of female gender

Ranking
daaih	大	:	eldest
yih	二	:	second
sàam	三	:	third
…			
sai	細	:	youngest

The placement of the correlatives in a compound kin term generally observes the following set order.[8]

	Ranking	Collateral	Relation	Spouse	Generation	Gender	
f f 6th b$_y$	luhk		sūk		gūng		六叔公
m 2nd b w	yih		káuh	móuh			二舅母
f f si h			gū	jeuhng	gūng		姑丈公
f si s$_o$ m b/si s$_o$	daaih	bíu	gō				大表哥
f b s$_y$ w		tòhng		daih		fúh	堂弟婦
si d			yìhsāng			néuih	姨甥女
b s w		ngoih	jaht	(sān)póuh			侄(新)抱
d s			syūn				外孫

---

[8] Abbreviated features include:

e = ego	b = brother	o = older
f = father	si = sister	y = younger
m = mother	h = husband	>= older than
p = parent	w = wife	<= younger than
s = son	d = daughter	number = ranking

For example, "f f 6th b$_y$ w" stands for father's father's sixth younger brother's wife.

There are, however, two generational markers that usually appear before a relational term, thereby violating the above arrangement format. They are: (1) *jóu* 祖 which appears before *fuh* 父 (father) and *móuh* 母 (mother); and (2) *taai* 太 which appears before *gūng* 公 (grandfather) and *pòh* 婆 (grandmother). Both terms raise the member concerned by one generation.

The choice of a particular correlative form for a kin term is often decided by convention. For example, both *nèuhng* 娘 and *móuh* 母 are spousal markers for a relative in the first ascending generation. The former appears only with *baak* 伯 as in *baaknèuhng* 伯娘 (wife of father's older brother) and the latter with *káuh* 舅 as in *káuhmóuh* 舅母 (wife of mother's brother). The form *baakmōu* 伯母 (with a changed tone) is sometimes used, but probably of the Toishan dialect origin. It should be noted that *káuhmóuh* 舅母 is pronounced as *káhmmóuh* in speech as a result of backward assimilation. By analogy, *káuhpòh* 舅婆 (f m b w) is pronounced as *káhmpòh*.

2.2. Tone Change in Kin Terminology

2.2.1. Cantonese is well-known for its use of tone change to transform a bound form into a free word. Via this morphological process, some of the bound relational terms become free forms in speech. However, as soon as they appear in compounds, they revert back to their bound status. Examples are:

Changed tone		Original tone	
néui (d)	女	néuihsai (d h)	女婿
ját (f b s)	侄	jahtnéuih (f b d)	侄女
múi (si$_y$)	妹	muihfū (si$_y$ h)	妹夫

The bound form for younger brother is *daih* 弟 as in the compound *daihfúh* 弟婦 (b$_y$ w), but one of the colloquial words used for "younger brother" is *a-dí* 阿弟, which involves not only the prefixation of *a-* but also changes in tone as well as in vowel. *Fuh* 父, a word meaning "father," is used as a generation marker in two uncle terms, namely *baakfuh* 伯父 (f b$_o$) and *káuhfú* 舅父 (m b); in the former, the marker carries the original tone, in the latter a changed tone.

2.2.2. Quite a few bound relational forms in Cantonese appear in duplication in speech. The duplication generally entails a tone change on one or both of the syllables. The change can occur in one of the following two patterns:

(1)	X↓ X˥[9]	:	bàhbā	(f)		爸爸
			màhmā	(m)		媽媽
			gòhgō	(b_o)		哥哥
			jèhjē	(si_o)		姐姐
(2)	X↓ X˦	:	dìhdí	(b_y)		弟弟
			mùihmúi	(si_y)		妹妹
			pòhpó	(m m)		婆婆
			yèhyé	(f f)		爺爺
			nàaihnáai	(h m)		奶奶
			jàihjái	(s)		仔仔
			nèuihnéui	(d)		女女

As each sandhi pattern involves a limited but separate set of terms, the distinction between "↓ ˥" and "↓ ˦" may be construed as a phonological reflection of some kind of a difference between the two groups of names. But as to what exactly conditions such groupings, it remains to be answered. One observation is that the first group consists of only four persons, all of whom are the closest members to a young child in a nucleus family. Those in the second group are usually people who are a bit more remote in relation to a child or whom a child gets to know a bit later in life. *Pòhpó* 婆婆 (m m) and *yèhyé* 爺爺 (f f) are two generations removed from ego, one generation higher than the parents; *nàaihnáai* 奶奶 (h m) is a relation connected through marriage; and *jàihjái* 仔仔 (s) and *nèuihnéui* 女女 are what comes usually after marriage. *Dìhdí* 弟弟 (b_y) and *mùihmúi* 妹妹 (si_y) seem to pose a problem since they should be just as close to ego as *gòhgō* 哥哥 (b_o) and *jèhjē* 姐姐 (si_o). However, precisely because of the old/young distinction in relation to ego, the elder siblings are the ones ego comes in

---

[9] In the Yale system of romanization, tones are marked diacritically. Hence, *ā* is a level tone, *á* is a rising tone, and *à* is a falling tone. A low tone is marked with an *h* after the vowel. Values of the tones can also be graphically marked as follows:

high-level˥ high-rising˦ high-falling˧
mid-level ˧
low-level ˨ low-rising ˩ low-falling ˩

contact with much earlier than their younger counterparts. In other words, the members in the first category represent the first acquaintances of ego, whereas his later acquaintances are marked by a different tonal pattern. To this second category, one may also add the term for wife, *taaitáai* 太太 (w), a duplicative form which, though its first syllable remains tonally intact, is marked by the distinctive high-rising ending.

2.3. The Young/Old Distinction

The differentiation of age is an important principle underlying the system of Chinese kin denomination. The age factor is fully represented in ego's own generation, hence *gòhgō* (b$_o$) vs. *dìhdí* (b$_y$), and *jèhjē* (si$_o$) vs. *mùihmúi* (si$_y$). It also accounts for the separation between two kinds of paternal uncles on the basis of age, namely *baak* 伯 (f b$_o$) and *sūk* 叔 (f b$_y$), a distinction that is universal in China. However, while most Chinese dialects restrict this distinction to the male siblings in the ascending generations, Cantonese makes a similar discrimination between the elder and younger sisters of both parents.

```
f si₀ gūmā     姑媽   vs.   f si_y gūjē    姑姐
m si₀ yìhmā   姨媽   vs.   m si_y a-yī   阿姨
```

Please note that the literal meanings of *mā* and *jē* in the *gū*- compounds are "mother" and "sister" respectively. In other words, the primary difference between *mā* and *jē* is that of generation. But as a difference in generation is usually accompanied by an age difference, the Cantonese identify the former with the latter, referring to an older paternal aunt as *gūmā* (aunt-mother) and a younger paternal aunt as *gūjē* (aunt-sister). Juniority in generational status has, therefore, been borrowed to mark juniority in age. The differentiation between an older maternal aunt and a younger one follows, however, a slightly different route. While *mā* in *yìhmā* is used in a similar manner to designate seniority, juniority is, on the other hand, indicated by a tone change on the relation term, raising its pitch from low-falling (˩) to high-level (˥). The word is further prefixed by *a-*, hence *a-yī*. In northern Chinese, a kin term containing the word *ma* generally refers to a married woman. For example, *yima* 姨媽 in Mandarin is the married sister of one's mother and *a-yi* 阿姨 is the unmarried one, regardless of the ranking order among the siblings. Likewise, *guma* 姑媽 refers to the married sister of ego's father and *gugu* 姑姑 his unmarried sister. In Cantonese, an older aunt, whether married or not, is always referred to as *gūmā* or *yìhmā*. *Mā* is, therefore, also a marker of age in Cantonese, but only an indicator of marital status in most of the other Chinese dialects. The following table illustrates such a difference in this operation.

	Cantonese	**Other dialects**
阿姨	m si$_y$	m si$_{unmarried}$
姨媽	m si$_o$	m si$_{married}$

There is some sort of asymmetry between the male and the female kin members with regard to the operation of the age distinction, a phenomenon that may be explained in terms of male domination in the family system.

(1) While, in Cantonese, both paternal aunts and maternal aunts demonstrate an age marking in denomination, only the paternal uncles display such a difference, as noted above. The maternal uncles are uniformly referred to as *káuhfú* 舅父.

	Older brother	**Younger brother**
father's	baakfuh 伯父	a-sūk 阿叔
mother's	káuhfú 舅父	

(2) The distinction between paternal uncles is operative in the ascending generations, but not maintained among "aunts" above the parent generation.

	Father				**Mother**			
	Brother		Sister		Brother		Sister	
	old	young	old	young	old	young	old	young
+1 gen.	baakfuh 伯父	a-sūk 阿叔	gūma 姑媽	gūjiē 姑姐	káuhfú 舅父	yìhmā 姨媽	a-yī 阿姨
+2 gen.	baakgūng 伯公	sūkgūng 叔公	gūpòh 姑婆		káuhgūng 舅公		yìhpòh 姨婆	

(3) Among the spousal terms, only wives of the paternal uncles and great uncles display an age distinction in naming; none of the other spouses reflect this usage.

	Father		Father		Mother		Mother	
	b's w	b's w	si's h	si's h	b's w	b's w	si's h	si's h
	old	young	old	young	old	young	old	young
+1 gen.	baaknèuhng 伯娘	a-sám 阿嬸	gūjéung 姑丈		káhmmóuh 舅母		yìhjéung 姨丈	
+2 gen.	baakpòh 伯婆	sūkpòh 叔婆	gūjeuhnggung 姑丈公		káhmpòh 舅婆		yìhjeunggung 姨丈公	

In a patrilineal family structure, where older brothers enjoy certain priority in rights and privileges over the younger brothers, it is important that the age distinction be reflected in kin denominations; wives of the brothers share this distinction in their appellations. This terminological differentiation for both sexes extends two or three generations above ego. Understandably, the age factor plays a much less important role in the female sibling classification. Usually, the ego only needs to distinguish an elder sister from a younger one of his generation. In this regard, Cantonese is exceptional among Chinese dialects in that it extends the separation to the first ascending generation as well. When the sisters are married out of the sib family, their husbands are named with the same term *fū* 夫 attached to the proper sibling reference, i.e., *jéfū* 姐夫 (si$_o$ h) and *muihfū* 妹夫 (si$_y$ h). Their involvements in sib affairs are, however, generally little and indirect; their age distinction means even less to the second generation in the sib family. Hence, there is no special need to keep apart in distinguishing an elder aunt's husband from that of a younger aunt. As for *káuhfu* 舅父 and *káhmmóuh* 舅母, the lack of a young/old distinction among the maternal uncles and aunts is a further indication of male authority in a clan structure. A woman, regardless of her age, is always inferior to her brothers in status. Hence, a nephew identifies maternal uncles as one category *sans* sub-division by age. The age factor is not operative at all among the descending generations.

2.4. Vocative vs. Designative

On a pragmatic basis, the system of kinship terminology can be divided into two major categories, the vocatives and the designatives. A designative is the term by which one refers to a person and a vocative is the term by which one calls a person. The dichotomy is often described as that between terms of reference and terms of address, the latter of which can also be used in a broad sense, as it is done in this article, to include both categories. The Chinese terms used to characterize the difference are *miancheng* 面稱 or *duicheng* 對稱 (face-to-face address) for the vocative, and *beicheng* 背稱 (behind-back address) or *yincheng* 引稱 (introduction address) for the designative.

With the exception of the nucleus family, kin relations are generally called by the same names as they are referred to. This is especially true for members of the ascending generations: the eldest brother of father is always *daaih baakfuh* 大伯父 or *daaihbaak* 大伯 in both designative and vocative contexts. As for those who are junior in generational status, age, or sibling ranking with reference to ego, they are more often called by their real names than by their relational designations. For example, ego introduces the husband of his younger sister as *muihfū* 妹夫 or wife of his brother's son as *jahtpóuh* 侄抱, but he would normally address them by their given names. Vocative forms are often prefixed with *a-* 阿, e.g.,

(a) 阿姑媽啊，你幾時嚟探我呀？
A-gūmā àh, néih géisìh lèih taam ngóh a?
Auntie (f s$_o$), when are you coming to visit me?

(b) 阿仔，你要乖乖地讀書至好呀。
A-jái, néih yiu guāaiguāaidéi duhksyū ji hóu a.
Son, you'd better be studying hard.

(c) 阿駱太啊，真係唔該你喇。
A-Lohk-táai a, jān haih mhgōi néih lahk.
I really have to thank you, Mrs. Lok.

The last sentence demonstrates the use of *a-* with a titled name.

2.4.1. Parents: The formal designatives for parents are *fuhchān* 父親 (f) and *móuhchān* 母親 (m), which are rarely used except in a very formal style of speech. The general terms are *bàhbā* 爸爸 and *màhmā* 媽媽, the obvious products of universal sound association. The vernacular forms are *lóuhdauh* 老竇 and *lóuhmóuh* 老母 respectively. Both general and vernacular pairs can be used as vocatives. In addition, *bàhbā* 爸爸 can be shortened as *a-bàh* 阿爸 or, sometimes, as *a-bā*. He can also be called as *dēdìh* 爹哋 or *a-dē* 阿爹, another case of child language association that connects a dental sound with the male parent. By comparison, the forms available for mother are all built around a nasal bilabial. *Màhmā* 媽媽 can be pronounced with a high tone on both syllables (*māmā*) or it can be shortened to *a-mā* 阿媽 or modified as *māmìh* 媽咪. There are two vernacular parental forms, *lóuhtàuhjí* 老頭子 (f) and *lóuhmājí* 老媽子 (m), which some speakers would consider vulgar and never use as vocatives. Others, however, use them on occasion to express an extra shade of endearment, and in this context *lóuhmājí* may be further shortened to *mājí*. It is a common rhetorical device to utilize terms of vulgarity, obscenity, or even animosity to address a beloved one; the negative epithets serve as emphatic indication of one's affection. A son can fondly address his mother as *lóuhmóuh* or *lóuhmājí*, but a daughter-in-law would prefer calling terms like *màhmā* and *a-mā*, which are more neutral in emotive connotation. The general terms are also the ones used in referring to the addressee's parents. Special honorific forms such as *lihngjūn* 令尊 (your father) and *lihngtóng* 令堂 (your mother), which are derivatives from the literary language, are almost obsolete in modern speech. *Baakyē* 伯爺 is occasionally used for "your father," mostly by older people.

2.4.2. Siblings: The common sibling designatives are *gòhgō* 哥哥 or *daaihlóu* 大佬 for older brother, *sailóu* 細佬 for younger brother, *gājē* 家姐 for older sister, and *saimúi* 細妹 or *mùihmúi* 妹妹 for younger sister. They all can be used as vocatives, even though the junior siblings are usually called by their names. The distancing between ego and in-law siblings is again seen in the refrain from addressing one's elder brother-in-law with the vernacular term *daaihlóu* 大佬. An alternative term to *gājē* (si$_o$) is *jèhjē* 姐姐. The former was originally a depreciatory term, with *gā* 家 (lit. "my house") serving as a marker for reference to one's own relatives; its function can still be seen in some semi-classical forms such as *gāhīng* 家兄

(my brother), *gāfu* 家父 (my father), and *gāmóuh* 家母 (my mother). *Gājē*, however, has shed, through lexicalization, the depreciation reading and can now be used to refer to someone else's sister. For example,

Ngóh séung wánmàaih néih gājē yātchàih heui tái hei.
我想搵埋你家姐一齊去睇戲。
I want to go see a movie together with your sister.

Another term for calling one's own older sister is *gāgā* 家家, apparently a product of the child's language, duplicating the first syllable of the regular term *gājē*. However, when an ordinal number is prefixed to the syllable *gā*, as in *sāam-gā* 三家 (the third elder sister), the combination is quite common even among the elderly when they speak of their own siblings.

2.4.3. Parents-in-law: A woman refers to her husband's parents as *gāgūng* 家公 (h f) and *gāpó* 家婆 (h m), but addresses them as either *bàhbā* and *màhmā* or, especially in an old-fashioned family, *lóuhyèh* 老爺 and *nàaihnáai* 奶奶. A man calls his wife's parents either by her terms (i.e., *bàhbā* and *màhmā*) or with the proper designatives: *ngoihfú* 外父 and *ngoihmóu* 外母 (lit. external father and external mother), or *ngohkfú* 岳父 and *ngohkmóu* 岳母.[10] For more discussion on these terms, see below.

2.4.4. Spouses: The general designatives for husband and wife are *sīnsāang* 先生 and *taaitáai* 太太, and their vernacular counterparts are *lóuhgūng* 老公 and *lóuhpòh* 老婆. The more literary forms, *jeuhngfū* 丈夫 and *chāijí* 妻子, are rarely used in speech. The vernacular forms may be used as vocatives, but usually not in the public as they carry a sense of intimacy. More commonly a couple would refer to each other by their names or, after they have become parents, by their children's references, namely *bàhbā* and *màhmā*, or their variants. Teknonymy, i.e., the adoption of a child's terminology, is actually a common practice in all languages.

2.4.5. Children: A parent introduces his/her children as *jái* 仔 (s) and *néui* 女 (d) and calls them by their names, usually their pet names. In speaking to the child's siblings, the parent may adopt teknonymy while referring to

---

[10] There are several interpretations on the origin of the term *ngohk* 岳. For a general summary, see Feng (1937), pp. 254–255.

the child. For example, if the child is the younger brother, the parent can refer to him as *sailóu* 細佬 while talking to his older brother. *Sailóu* may eventually become a vocative form which the parent uses to address the younger child.

2.5. Teknonymy

Teknonymy is a denominational device which enables a person to address others in a personable manner but at the same time keeping them at a distance. By adopting a child's naming term, the speaker is in effect withdrawing himself from a direct personal contact with the addressee; he has indirectly transferred the conversation to a discoursal relationship between his child and the addressee. On the other hand, since it is a child's term that is being borrowed, the reference usually comes forth with both respect and affection. Teknonymy is found in all languages as it readily supplies a speaker with terms of address when there is no form available for or appropriate to the occasion.

Teknonymy also accounts for many cases of seemingly anomalous use of kin terms in language. In Chinese, most of the terminologies for in-law relations are derived from teknonymous usages. The term *káuh* 舅, or *jiu* in Mandarin, refers to both "mother's uncle" and "wife's brother," a practice that can be dated back to the 10th century AD.[11] The dual functions, as observed by a Qing scholar, is the obvious result of gradual teknonymy. The initial reference of *káuh* is mother's brother. As wife's brothers are *káuh* to his own children, ego conveniently takes over the term and calls his wife's brothers *kauh*.[12] In other words, the affinal reading is an extension of the original consanguineal designation. Some other teknonymous terms in Chinese are:

---

[11] In his 1936 article "Teknonymy as a Formative Factor in the Chinese Kinship System" (*American Anthropologist*, 38 [1936]: 59–66), H. Y. Feng details the historical development of the teknonymous terms in Chinese. Most of his findings have been incorporated into his 1937 article cited previously. This article owes much of its observation in this regard to Feng's enlightening studies.

[12] Qian Daxin 錢大昕 (1727–1804), *Hengyan lu* 恒言錄, 3.13b.

伯—*bo* (Mandarin), *baak* (Cantonese): father's older brother
→ husband's older brother
叔—*shu* (Mandarin), *sūk* (Cantonese): father's younger brother
→ husband's younger brother
姑—*gu* (Mandarin), *gū* (Cantonese): father's sister
→ husband's sister

The four teknonymous terms, *baak* 伯, *sūk* 叔, *gū* 姑, and *káuh* 舅, are still in use in Cantonese, though with some modification. For example, a generational marker is sometimes attached to differentiate the dual readings of a term. A woman refers to her husband's oldest brother as *daaih baak* 大伯, but her children calls him *daaih baak fuh* 大伯父, *fuh* being the indicator of the first ascending generation. Likewise, the youngest sister in the family is *saigū* 細姑 to her older brother's wife, but *saigūjē* 細姑姐 to their children. Note that -*jē* in this case is a marker for both generation and age. The following table summarizes these terms, plus the words for wife's sister or mother's sister, as they appear at different generational levels. To show an age difference in appellation, three sibling members are assumed to be in the family, ego being the middle son. In the case where there are more siblings, numerical ordering is usually adopted, e.g., *daaih* 大 (the oldest), *yih* 二 (the second), *sàam* 三 (the third), etc.

	To E's spouse	To E's child	To E's grandchild
Male ego			
ego's elder brother	daaihbaak 大伯	daaihbaakfuh 大伯父	daaihbaakgūng 大伯公
ego's younger brother	saisūk 細叔	saisūk 細叔	saisukgūng 細叔公
ego's elder sister	daaihgū 大姑	daaihgūmā 大姑媽	daaihgūpòh 大姑婆
ego's younger sister	saigū 細姑	gūjē 姑姐	saigūpòh 細姑婆
Female ego			
ego's elder brother	daaihkáuh 大舅	daaihkáuhfú 大舅父	daaihkáuhgūng 大舅公
ego's younger brother	saikáuh 細舅	saikáuhfú 細舅父	saikáuhgūng 細舅公
ego's elder sister	daaihyìh 大姨	yìhmā 姨媽	daaihyìhpòh 大姨婆
ego's younger sister	saiyìh 細姨	a-yī 阿姨	saiyìhpòh 細姨婆

With the exception of *baak*, the above teknonymous terms can all be suffixed with *-jái* 仔 to indicate young age. When marriage and child birth take place early in one's life, the junior siblings of one's spouse are usually quite young, possibly in their pre-teen's. Even when children come along, the new junior uncles and aunts may still be very little, both physically and age-wise. Thus, their appellations often carry a diminutive marker *-jái* 仔: *sūkjái* 叔仔, *kūjái* 姑仔, *káuhjái* 舅仔, and *yījái* 姨仔. These terms have now become standard forms to refer to the junior siblings of one's spouse even if they are already in their mid-thirties when the marriage takes place. The *-jái* forms may be used to refer to the uncles and aunts as long as they are very young in age; if not, the regular forms will be used. Hence, *yījái* 姨仔 can refer to both wife's younger sister and mother's child sister. The child sister, however, may grow up with this appellation without ever having it changed to *a-yī* 阿姨.

2.6. Teknonymy in Reverse

In contrast with the teknonymous derivations of *baak*, *sūk*, *gū*, and *káuh*, the semantic extension for *yìh* 姨 is a case of teknonymy in reverse. Historically, *yìh* was used for wife's sisters and its reference to mother's sister was a later practice. In other words, the generational extension of *yìh* was downward, unlike that of *gū*, etc. which was upward from child to adult. Feng (1936) describes the derived function of *yìh* in the following manner:

> Mother's sisters are *yi* 姨 to one's father just as wife's sisters are *yi* to oneself. The son imitates the language of his father, so he calls his father's *yi* also *yi*. (p. 65)

Citing many examples from the literature, he succeeds in demonstrating that the blending of generations in the use of *yi* 姨 is a case of reversed teknonymy. In modern Cantonese, *yìh* preserves these two meanings, although other morphological devices have been employed to clarify the generational ambiguity. As shown in the above section, wife's sisters are called *yìh* with the pertinent ranking word (such as *daaih*, *yih*, . . . *sai*) prefixed, but mother's sisters are marked either with *-ma* 媽 for the older ones or with a high tone for the younger ones, viz., *yìhmā* and *a-yī*.[13]

According to Feng's study, there are many examples of kin teknonymy in the Chinese language, but *yìh* seems to be the only case illustrating a reversed operation. There may, however, be another case in Cantonese of such nature. The words for mother and paternal grandmother are segmentally identical: *a-mā* 阿媽 (m) vs. *a-màh* 阿嬤 (f m), the former with a high-level tone and the latter with low-falling. As most dialects make a deliberate distinction between the two kins lexically, e.g., *mama* 媽媽 vs. *nainai* 奶奶 in Mandarin, the phonological resemblance we witness in Cantonese is indeed quite unusual. However, such an anomaly may be explained as a phenomenon of teknonymy in a reverse direction. Since the mother of ego is the grandmother of ego's child, the child imitates the father's addressing term and calls the grandmother by the same expression. But, unlike the word *yìh* or, for that matter, all the teknonymous terms, whose two references are in reality identical (e.g., the father's *daaihyìh* 大姨 is the same person as the child's *yìhmā* 姨媽), the two referents involved in the present case are two women of different generations quite possibly living under the same roof, caring for the same child. Some kind of a differentiation needs to be made, hence the tonal marking. The suprasegmental distinction is also maintained in the duplicative forms: *màhmā* 媽媽 for (m), but *màhmàh* for (f m). The graphic difference between the two forms is of course an artificial differentiation.

2.7. Generational Downgrading

Since teknonymy is a circumlocutory means of addressing someone when direct naming would be inappropriate, impolite, or embarrassing, Chao (1956) notes that teknonymy plays a greater part in a woman's speech than in a man's. A woman may refer to the third younger brother of

---

[13] In ancient Chinese as well as in modern dialects, *yìh* may be used to refer to a man's other wives, e.g., *yìhtaaitáai* 姨太太 meaning "concubine." This usage is evidently related to the base meaning of the word: "wife's sisters." In feudal China when the sororate was practiced, i.e., two sisters marrying the same man, wife's sister and husband's other wife would be the same woman.

her husband's as *sàamdaih* 三弟 (third brother), but it is deemed more proper for her to call and mention him as *sàamsūk* 三叔 (third uncle). In a traditional Chinese society, a bride is required to play a humble role in her new family; both in deeds and in speech, she needs to show respect to all members of her in-law family. Teknonymy is probably the most convenient and simple way to express such deference. In referring to her husband's *sàamdaih* as *sàamsūk*, the woman has adopted her child's status in discourse, thereby lowering herself, in effect, by one generation. Self-degradation is of course not the underlying cause for the teknonymous practice in language; the application may, however, be interpreted in view of its sociological implication.

One argument in support of this sociological interpretation is that, in Cantonese, the terms for the in-law parents are actually designations for two different generations, *fu* and *móuh* for parents and *gūng* and *pòh* for grandparents, and they are kept apart in use between the married couple. A man refers to his wife's parents as *ngohkfú* 岳父 / *ngohkmóu* 岳母 or *ngoihfú* 外父 / *ngoihmóu* 外母, where *fú/móu* are clear markers of an ascending generation. A woman, on the other hand, refers to her husband's parents as *gāgūng* 家公 and 家婆 *gāpó*, which are teknonymous in origin. As previously noted, *gūng* 公 and *pòh* 婆 are markers of the grandparent generation, hence a generation higher than that of *fú/móuh*. The maternal grandparents are *a-gūng* 阿公 and *a-pòh* 阿婆, which are short forms for *ngoihgūng* 外公 and *ngoihpòh* 外婆. As members of mother's family are considered *ngoih* 外 (external) to ego, her parents are characterized as *gūng/pòh* of a *ngoih* clan. By contrast, ego's paternal grandparents are *gāgūng/gāpòh*, where *gā* stands for "ego's family" as in *gājē* (sister of ego's family). In other words, when a woman refers to her parents-in-law as *gāgūng/gāpó*, she is linguistically lowering herself by one generation, speaking with veneration as if from the standpoint of a grandchild. This teknonymous use of the terms has eventually replaced the original reference to the grandparents. For substitution, *a-yèh* 阿爺 and *a-màh* 阿嫲 are now in use. As a consequence, a child has only one set of grandparents designated by *gūng/pòh*, viz., *ngoihgūng/ngoihpòh*. The non-sib marker, *ngoih*, has become superfluous and is, therefore, dropped, hence *a-gūng* and *a-pòh*.

If there is an askew correspondence between the terms that a married couple use to refer to each other's parents, the sexual inequality is, to a certain extent, redressed by the fact that the parents-in-law also lower themselves by one generation when addressing the bride. They call her *gāsóu* 家嫂, where *sóu* by definition is elder brother's wife. The use is, of course, another case of teknonymy, whereby a parent borrows a younger son's terminology in addressing the wife of an older son. It is a sign of good-natured compromise between the in-laws as the term indicates not only a lowering in generation but also juniority in age. Respect is implied as if, by her right as *sóu*, the woman commands respect from the younger brothers of her husband. In modern Cantonese, *gāsóu* is reserved for "daughter-in-law" whereas a sister-in-law is referred to as *a-sóu* or *sóu* with a numeral prefix such as 三嫂 *sàamsóu* (h b$_{3rd}$ w).

Another even more salient case of generational downgrading in kin terminology is the term that ego uses to refer to father's concubine. The woman is ego's senior by one generation, and yet she is not accorded with a *mā* 媽 nomenclature. To the contrary, she is called *a-jē* 阿姐, an apparent demotion from the parent generation to that of the sibling. The "dishonor" continues even when she becomes a grandmother—she is to be addressed as *a-sám* 阿嬸 (wife of uncle), still one generation lower than her actual status. Only the principal wife has the privilege to enjoy the venerated reference *a-màh* 阿嬤.

2.8. Adoption of Servants Terms of Address

A wife refers to her parents-in-law as *gāgūng* and *gāpó*, but she addresses them in conversation as *lóuhyèh* 老爺 and *nàaihnáai* 奶奶. The latter pair is actually what a servant uses to address the master and mistress of the house. Again, the wife assumes a lowly position in front of her in-laws, an assigned role equivalent to that of a servant. In like manner, she may address every member in her husband's family in the way a servant does. His brothers are *siuyèh* 少爺 (young masters) to her, or simply *siu* 少 with an appropriate ranking prefix as in *sàamsiu* 三少 (the third young master / his third brother). (This reference is of course an alternative to the teknonymous term *sàamsūk* 三叔.) Their wives are *siunāai* 少奶 (young mistress) with an ordinal prefixing, e.g., *sàamsiunāai* 三少奶 for the wife of the third brother. An unmarried younger sister, say, the fifth one, is *ńgh-gūnéuhng* 五姑娘, where *gūnèuhng* 姑娘 means "miss." By analogy, an older sister is *gūnāai* 姑奶 and her husband is *gūyèh* 姑爺. This in-law reference system based on servant's terms is restricted to woman's use. A man either uses teknonymous terminologies or follows his wife's terms of address for her relations.

2.9. Collateral Distinctions

In a kinship system, the collateral lines are often distinguished from the lineal lines in kin terminology. In China, both lineal relations and collateral relations of the same patronym are grouped into one "sib" family, where cousins are considered brothers to each other. Thus, ego may refer to his cousin who is the eldest of his generation in the sib family as *daaihgō* 大哥 (eldest brother). He may address the wife of his third uncle as *sàammā* 三媽 (third mother). In a modern family where few siblings live together after marriage, the sib system of vocatives is no longer prevalent. The first cousins of the sib family are described as *tòhng gājē* 堂家姐 (elder sib sister), *tòhng sailóu* 堂細佬 (younger sib brother), etc. *Tòhng* 堂, as noted earlier, is the marker for descents of father's brother(s). The children of the *tòhng* cousins are *sōtòhng* 疏堂 relations to each other; the literal meaning of *sō* is "sparse and loose," hence "removed."

All non-sib relations are categorized as *bíu* 表, which can be further divided into the following categories:

(1) *yìh-bíu* 姨表: parallel cousins along mother's line, i.e., maternal aunt's children are one's *yìh-bíu* cousins
(2) *gū-bíu* 姑表: cross cousins along father's line, i.e., the paternal aunt's children are one's *gū-bíu* cousins
(3) *káuh-bíu* 舅表: cross cousins along mother's line, i.e., the maternal uncle's children are one's *káuh-bíu* cousins

Gū-bíu and *káuh-bíu* actually refer to the same set of cousins. If A is the child of X and B is the child of Y, and X and Y are brother and sister to each other, then A is B's *káuh-bíu* cousin but B is a *gū-bíu* cousin to A.

In the first and second ascending generations, *gū-bíu* and *yìh-bíu* relations share the same format of denomination; they both refer to sisters of one's father and mother (p).

	1ˢᵗ ascending generation			2ⁿᵈ ascending generation	
	p si>p	p si<p	p si h	p p si	p p si h
kū-bíu 姑表 (F's)	gūmā 姑媽	gūjē 姑姐	gūjéung 姑丈	gūpòh 姑婆	gūjeuhnggūng[14] 姑丈公
yìh-bíu 姨表 (M's)	yìhmā 姨媽	a-yī 阿姨	yìhjéung 姨丈	yìhpòh 姨婆	yìhjeuhnggūng 姨丈公

On the other hand, *kauh-bíu* relations are labeled quite differently from the above as well as from the *tòhng* line. Both *tòhng* and *kauh* refer to the male siblings of the parents.

		p b>p	p b<p	p b>p w	p b<p w
+1 gen.	tòhng (F's)	baahkfuh 伯父	a-sūk 阿叔	baahkneùhng 伯娘	a-sám 阿嬸
	káuh (M's)	káuhfú 舅父		káuhmóuh 舅母	
+2 gen.	tòhng (F's)	baahkgūng 伯公	sukgūng 叔公	baahkpòh 伯婆	sūkpòh 叔婆
	káuh (M's)	káuhgūng 舅公		káuhpòh 舅婆	

As for the first descending generation, male ego's children are *jat* 侄 to both his brother and sister, and female ego's children are *sāng* 甥 to both her brother and sister. In Cantonese, *sang* is also known as *yìhsāng* 姨甥 which, in effect, includes both *yìh-bíu* and *káuh-bíu* relations, as represented by the following diagram. In other words, the collateral marker *yìh* has extended its coverage to include *káuh-bíu* members in the first descending generation. Some older speakers keep a distinction between the two lines, *sang* from the *yìh-bíu* line are referred to as *yìhshāng* 姨甥, but those from the *káuh-bíu* line as *ngoihsāng* 外甥.

---

[14] Both terms can be shortened to *jeuhnggong* 丈公.

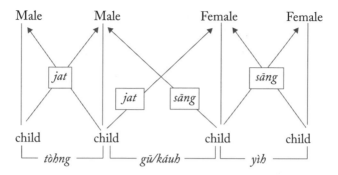

2.10. Modern Trends in Kin Reference

The Cantonese kinship terminology is a complicated system that often poses challenges even for native speakers, old and young alike, who have to distinguish which term is for what relation and which term to use in accordance with the status of the referent and the context of the discourse. As few families still live in the former clan style, with siblings and cousins of several generations all under the same roof, most young people nowadays demonstrate little knowledge of the linguistic differentiations. They may recognize a kin term but they do not necessarily know which relation it represents in a family tree. For example, a *bíugō* is simply an elder male cousin with a different surname. Whether the *bíu* refers to *gū-bíu*, *yìh-bíu*, or *káuh-bíu* is of little importance. More often than not, the cousins mention and call each other by their given names. Teknonymous practice has also become less prevalent for in-law references. Husband and wife refer to each other's family members either directly by names or they may simply borrow each other's terms of address. A wife can call her husband's mother *màhmā* and introduce her as *ngóh sīnsāang ge màhmā* 我先生嘅媽媽 (my husband's mother), without resorting to any of the self-degrading terms described above. A husband can call his wife's sisters, both old and young, by their English names, which, in fact, has become an increasingly popular practice among the young people in addressing their peers and juniors in their own families as well as those connected through affinal relations. English terms such as "uncle," "aunt," "cousin," etc. are gaining ground over the traditional designations. It may be that before long a large number of the kin appellations will disappear in use, thereby replacing a complex network with a much simpler system more in tune with the present day family structure. What has been described above would then become a special branch of learning that would interest only anthropologists, sociologists, historians, linguists, and the like.

3. Social Terms of Address

The most commons terms of address in polite discourse are *sīnsāang* 先生 for male, *taaitáai* 太太 for a married woman, and *síujé* 小姐 for an unmarried woman.

As age is a sensitive issue especially for women, *taaitáai* is now less often used than before, unless one is sure of the marital status of the addressee. It is considered quite proper for a salesperson to greet a middle-aged woman customer as *síujé*. An old-fashioned term of respect, *sī-nāai* 師奶 (lit. "wife of teacher") has disappeared from use.[15] All these titles can be compounded with surnames, e.g., *Wòhng sīnsāang* 王先生 (Mr. Wong), *Léih síujé* 李小姐 (Miss Lee), *Chàhn táai* 陳太 (Mrs. Chan), *Dīng sīnāai* 丁師奶 (Mrs. Ding). Notice that when *taaitáai* is preceded by a surname, the form gets truncated as in the case from *Chàhn taaitáai* to *Chàhn táai*. Similarly, *Wòhng sīnsāang* 王先生 can be shortened to *Wòhng sāang* 王生.

3.1. Colloquial Terms of Address

Colloquial Cantonese displays a conscientious effort in separating vocative terms into various age categories, a phenomenon more salient in terms for male than for female. There are at least six forms for addressing a male, ranging from *a-gō* 阿哥 for a young adolescent to *a-gūng* 阿公 for a real old man, and, in between, *a-sūk* 阿叔 for a young to middle-aged man,

---

[15] Some years ago, a woman in Hong Kong sued her hairstylist for addressing her as *sīnāai*, which she felt was a case of defamation—she was unmarried at the time.

a-baak 阿伯 for someone perhaps in his fifties, and *lóuhbaak* 老伯 for an elderly gentleman. Of course, a male adult can always be referred to as *sīnsāang* regardless of age. A rather informal but affectionate vocative for a young teenager is *gòhgōjái* 哥哥仔; for a small boy, one can use the term *síudîhdí* 小弟弟. For ladies, there are three major age categories: the very young girls are referred to as *síumuihmúi* 小妹妹, the very old ladies as *a-pòh*, and all those in between are *síujé*. The term *taaitáai* may appear when the context justifies its use, for example, when the woman is accompanied by her husband or her children. Terms such as *daaihgū* 大姑 (lit. "big aunt"), *a-sám* (lit. "wife of younger uncle"), and *sī-nāai* are occasionally used to refer to a middle-aged woman, but, to most young people, they represent uncouth "country" talk that should be avoided. A semi-literary form, *síupàhngyáuh* 小朋友 (lit. "little friends"), may be used for young children of both genders.

The most fashionable terms of address now are *a-sèuh* and *mītsih*, both being transliterations from the English words "sir" and "miss." The borrowings probably began in a school context. Since the early 1960s, most students in Hong Kong have been enrolled in Anglo-Chinese schools where the medium of instruction is primarily English. Instead of *sīnsāang*, the traditional form to address one's teacher, "Sir" and "Miss" become terms of daily use in the classroom. Decades after their first introduction, the two forms have finally broken out of the confines of the school context and found acceptance into the social repertoire of address terms. A policeman can be addressed as *a-sèuh*, and a woman office worker may be called *mītsih*. Phonologically, they have been modified to suit the Chinese syllabic pattern: "sir" is now a two-syllable word with an *a*-prefix, and "miss" takes on an extra syllable at the end: *mīt-sih*. There are no standard ways of writing these two terms in characters. The following table summarizes the use of terms of address according to age and the appropriate context.

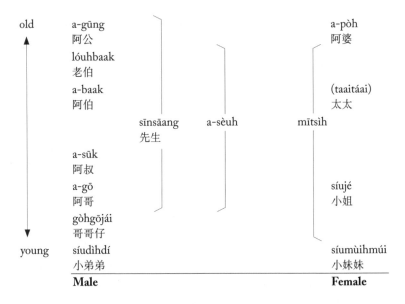

It is interesting to note that, perhaps with the exception of *sīnsāang*, *a-sèuh*, and *mītsìh*, almost all the common social vocatives are direct borrowings from the kinship system. The male set covers three generations from "brother" (0), "uncle" (+1), to "grandfather" (+2), all along a patrilineal line. Again, generational distinctions are on account of age differences. The female set also exhibits a drastic shift from "sister" to "grandmother." In like manner, the greeting terms in a child's language marks the age status with generational features. When a young person sees another child of his age, he uses a term from the sibling category; in front of elderly people, he salutes them as if they were his grandparents. For middle-aged persons, he chooses from words for uncles and aunts. In all cases, he uses reduplication, which is characteristic of child talk.

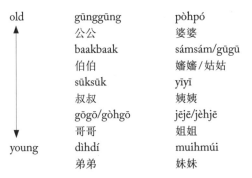

In both gender sets, there is an old/young distinction for the first two "generations": *dìhdí/muihmúi* vs. *gōgō/jèjē*, and *sūksūk/baakbaak* vs. *yīyī/sámsám/gūgū*. Of these nine names, only *yīyī* is from the mother's family; the rest are all members from the father's side. Even *gūnggūng/pòhpó*, as previously argued, are bonafide designatives for the paternal grandparents. In short, the social terms of address are essentially transplants from the patrilineal system. There is a very good reason why there is a seeming intrusion of a matrilineal term, *yīyī*. It has been shown that of the first ascending generation, only the paternal uncles show an age distinction in appellation, a differentiation that has been carried over into the social system. The paternal aunt does not show a denominational sub-division based upon age. Even though Cantonese employs a secondary marking for this purpose, namely the use of suffix as in *gūmā* vs. *gūjē*, it is of no use in this regard since it is the basic relational term *gū* that goes through the phonological reduplication. For the same reason, the affinal term, *sámsám*, is also incapable of reflecting an age discrimination. Thus, to make up for the inadequacy, secondment from the matrilineal system is a necessary move. *Yī* is a logical choice since its modified high tone is an overt marker of youth (cf. *yìhmā* vs. *a-yī*). In its new role, *yīyī* complements with *gūgū* or *sámsám* in a child's language in separating a younger woman from an older one. It should be noted that, in current Cantonese, *āngkòuh* and *āangtìh* are popular terms of address for adults, indiscriminate of age. They are both transliterations from the English words "uncle" and "auntie." Again, there are no standard characters for writing the two terms.

3.2. Tone Change in Compound Vocatives

A person whose surname is *Chàhn* 陳 may be addressed as *Chàhn sīnsāang* by his acquaintances, subordinates, or people he has just been introduced to. To his close friends, he may be known as *A-Chán* 阿陳. With the exception of words with a high-level tone, most surnames go through a tone change in certain vocative compounds, yielding a high-rising reading. Names that are originally high-rising in tone are not affected by the change. Examples are:

Original tone
Mid-level: 鄺 *Kwong*
Low-level: 鄭 *Jehng*
Low-rising: 李 *Léih*
Low-falling: 王 *Wòhng*

Changed tone

A-Kwóng	Kwóng-baak	Kwóng-sūk	Kwóng-jái	Kwóng-sèuh
A-Jéng	Jéng-baak	Jéng-sūk	Jéng-jái	Jéng-sèuh
A-Léi	Léi-baak	Léi-sūk	Léi-jái	Léi-sèuh
A-Wóng	Wóng-baak	Wóng-sūk	Wóng-jái	Wóng-sèuh
阿-X	X-伯	X-叔	X-仔	X-sèuh

The same names, however, appear unaltered in other compound forms like the following:

X-*hīng* 兄   "Brother X": *Chàhn-hīng* 陳兄
X-*sāang* 生   "Mr. X" (*sāang* being a short form for *sīnsāang*): *Jehng-sāang* 鄭生
X-*táai* 太   "Mrs. X" (*táai* being a short form for *taaitáai*): *Léih-táai* 李太

There is one case where the tonal modification, depending on the speakers, is optional:

X-*sóu* 嫂   "Wife of X, a friend": *Chàhn-sóu* or *Chán-sóu* 陳嫂

It is a general impression among native speakers that a changed tone indicates familiarity, informality, and casualness. X-*sāang* and X-*táai* are proper terms of address, thus disallowing tone change. X-*hīng* represents a highly formal style and does not partake in the modification. The tonal modification is appropriate for *A*-X and X-*jái* since they are casual reference terms used only among close friends. X-*baak* and X-*sūk*, or X-*sóu* for that matter, express not only respect for, but also closeness and intimacy with the seniors; they can also be used to address those who are senior in age but lower in social standing, e.g., a doorman, a custodian, a street peddler, etc. The use of a changed tone in these cases is, therefore, a gesture of friendliness. The only violation to this casualness rule is the compound X-*sèuh*, which begins as a respectful term for teachers in school. Incorporated into the daily vocabulary of a city-dweller, the form *sèuh* carries the same weight of social significance as *sīnsāang*. However,

X-*sāng* and X-*sèuh* are different in their susceptibility to this tonal phenomenon. X retains its original tone in X-*sāng*, but takes on a changed tone in X-*sèuh*. The only possible speculation with regard to this difference is that *sèuh* is a borrowed form from English, an ambivalent status that may account for it being some sort of an anomaly. The other loan word, *mītsìh*, is also peculiar in behavior. It is a general practice in Chinese to have the surname come before the title. Even *sèuh* follows this rule. Yet, *mītsìh* invariably appears before the surname, as in *Mītsìh Chán*, an ordering of words that betrays its origin from English. In any case, these two hybrid forms aside, the difference between the two tonal patterns can be accounted for in stylistic terms: changed tone as marker for informality. Tone change is never allowed when the surname is compounded with a two-syllable title, e.g., *Wòhng yīsāng* (Dr. Wong), *Léih síujé* (Miss Lee).

Social terms of address have undergone changes in many ways. It has become more and more common to address each other on a first name basis in recent years, following the practice in English calling friends or even new acquaintances by their English names, e.g., John and Mary. The first name referral has in fact extended its usage to Chinese when a person, say, 張大文, is being called by his given name 大文 instead of his full name. It was actually not too long ago when such an abbreviation was reserved for exchange between parents and children, between spouses and lovers. News media have also adopted the practice to refer to stars of favorite choices simply by their given names. For example, the pop singer Aaron Kwok 郭富城 is often amicably referred to as 富城. It should be noted, however, that in Mandarin, it is an acceptable practice for teachers to call their students by their first names.

4. To conclude: as in all forms of communication, language itself displays changes that reflect new developments in the social and cultural context in which it performs. As the family structure has been pared down from a clan system to a much reduced size of a few immediate members living under the same roof, the kinship system adjusts itself with a process of simplification. Many of the kin terms have made their gradual exits from the daily speech, words that younger speakers may find strange or even foreign to their ears. Likewise, social terms are faced with new waves of changes that speakers from an older generation or of a different dialect may fail to comprehend or get used to their usage. Changes are part of the underlying force that navigates our speech habits as we adapt to a new social milieu with concepts and words unknown of to our parents; and, as we look back, the terms we seem to be accustomed to and comfortable with may already be the labels that date our generation, The reference terms for one's wife have gone through a wide range of choices in social discourse, from 拙荊 to 賤內, from 內人 to 我太太 and 我老婆, each with a different shade of self-deprecation and gender discrimination, and the references are used in different environments by speakers of different age groups and educational background. A very modern denomination, 愛人, a borrowing from mainland Chinese, denotes "a loved one" and applies to both husband and wife. Apparently void of any gender bias, the term has yet to earn its prevalence in the colloquial language. Also, despite the increasing mixing of English and Chinese, the term "wife" does not have a role to play in this context. "Husband" has a Cantonese version, 黑七板凳 *hak-chat-baan-deng*, a transliteration term that no longer enjoys much prevalence in daily speech. When we look back, say, twenty years from now, we will for sure find ourselves facing the same challenges in addressing and renaming our kins. With old terms in reserve for remembering the past, we will be adopting new strategies to meet our cognitive needs, to record a world with different cultural and social changes, and, above all, to reflect and refer to our relations in both familial and communal settings.

References

Aijmer, Göran. 1986. *Atomistic Society in Shatin: Immigrants in a Hong Kong Valley*. Goteberg, Sweden: Acta Universitatis Gothoburgensis.

Chao, Yuen Ren. 1956. "Chinese Terms of Address." *Language*, 32.1: 217–241. Also in his *Aspects of Chinese Sociolinguistics* (Stanford University Press, 1976), pp. 309–342.

Chen, T. S., and J. K. Shryock. 1932. "Chinese Relationship Terms." *American Anthropologist*, 34: 623–664.

Fang, H. Q., and J. H. Heng, 1983. "Social Changes and Changing Address Norms in China." *Language in Society*, 12: 495–507.

Feng, Han-yi. 1936. "Teknonymy as a Formative Factor in the Chinese Kinship System." *American Anthropologist*, 38: 59–66.

———. 1937. "The Chinese Kinship System." *Harvard Journal of Asiatic Studies*, 2.2: 141–275.

Hanyu fangyan cihui 漢語方言詞匯, 1964. Wenzi gaige chubanshe 文字改革出版社.

Hong-Fincher, Beverly, 1987. "Indication of the Changing Status of Women in Modern Standard Chinese Terms of Address." In *A World of Language: Papers Presented to Professor S. A. Wurm on his 65th Birthday* (Pacific Linguistics), ed. D. Laycock and W. Winter, pp. 265–273.

Lin, Mei-rong. 1982. "Morphological Expansion and Semantic Expansion in Chinese Kin Terms." *Bulletin of the Institute of Ethnology*, 52: 33–114.

Morgan, Lewis H. 1987. *System of Consanguinity and Affinity of the Human Family*. Washington: Smithsonian Institution.

Rao Bingcai 饒秉才, Ouyang Jueya 歐陽覺亞, and Zhou Wuji 周無忌. 1981. *Guangzhouhua fangyan cidian* 廣州話方言詞典. Hong Kong: The Commercial Press.

This article originally appeared in *Journal of Chinese Linguistics*, 18.1 (1990): 1–43.

Appendix

This appendix includes four charts describing the kinship terms for the father's clan, the mother's clan, the husband's clan, and the wife's clan. Each chart is followed by a listing of these terms in both descriptive and vocative terms. Please note that changed tones are diacritically marked after the syllable. An asterisk indicates a high-rising reading and a little circle, a high-level.

Cantonese: Since the 19th Century

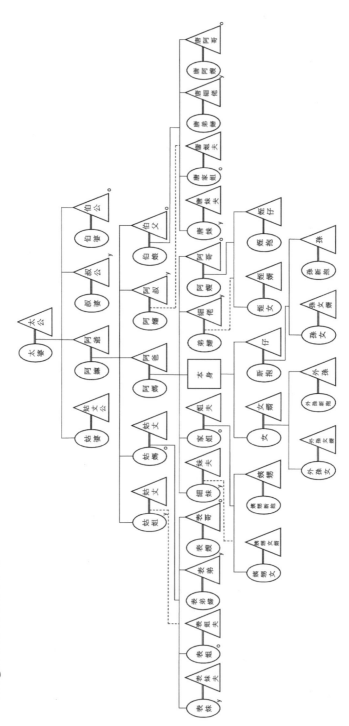

Diagram 1. Father's Clan

		Designative	Vocative
曾祖父	f f f	太公	太公
曾祖母	f f m	太婆	太婆
祖父	f f	祖父、阿爺	阿爺
祖母	f m	祖母、阿嫲	阿嫲
伯祖父	f f b$_o$	伯公	伯公
伯祖母	f f b$_o$ w	伯婆	伯婆
叔祖父	f f b$_y$	叔公	叔公
叔祖母	f f b$_y$ w	叔婆	叔婆
姑祖母	f f s	姑婆	姑婆
姑祖父	f f s h	姑丈公	丈公
舅祖父	f m b	舅公	舅公
舅祖母	f m b w	舅婆	舅婆
姨祖母	f m si	姨婆	姨婆
姨祖父	f m si h	姨丈公	丈公
父	f	爸爸、老竇	爸爸、阿爸、爹哋、阿爹、老竇、老頭子
母	m	媽媽、老母	媽媽、阿媽、媽咪、老媽、老媽子
伯父	f b$_o$	伯父	大伯父、大伯
伯母	f b$_o$ w	伯娘	大伯娘
叔父	f b$_y$	阿叔	阿叔、三叔
叔母	f b$_y$ w	阿嬸	阿嬸、三嬸
姑	f si$_o$	姑媽	姑媽、大姑媽
姑	f si$_y$	姑姐	姑姐°、三姑姐°
姑丈	f si h	姑丈	姑丈*、大姑丈*
妻	w	太太*、老婆	老婆、太太*、名、阿媽
兄	b$_o$	哥哥、阿哥	阿哥、哥哥、大哥、大佬
嫂	b$_o$ w	阿嫂	阿嫂、大嫂
弟	b$_y$	弟弟*、細佬	細佬、阿弟*、名
弟婦	b$_y$ w	弟婦、細佬嘅太太	名
姊	si$_o$	家姐	家姐、姐姐°、大家姐°、家家
姊夫	si$_o$ h	姐夫	姐夫、大姐夫
妹	si$_y$	細妹*、妹妹*	細妹*、阿妹*、三妹*、名
妹夫	si$_y$ h	妹夫	名
堂兄	f b s$_o$	堂阿哥	大哥、名 + 哥
堂嫂	f b s$_o$ w	堂阿嫂	大嫂、名 + 嫂
堂弟	f b s$_y$	堂細佬	名
堂弟婦	f b s$_y$ w	堂細佬嘅太太	名
堂姊	f b d$_o$	堂家姐°	名 + 姐°
堂姊夫	f b d$_o$ h	堂姐夫	名 + 哥
堂妹	f b d$_y$	堂妹*	名
堂妹夫	f b d$_y$ h	堂妹夫	名
表兄	f si s$_o$	表哥	表哥、大表哥、名 + 表哥
表嫂	f si s$_o$ w	表嫂	表嫂、大表嫂、名 + 表嫂

		Designative	**Vocative**
表弟	f si s_y	表弟*	表弟*、名
表弟婦	f si s_y w	表弟*嘅太太	名
表姊	f si d_o	表姐	表姐、大表姐、名+表姐
表姊夫	f si d_o h	表姐夫	名+哥
表妹	f si d_y	表妹*	表妹*、三表妹*、名
表妹夫	f si d_y h	表妹夫	名
子	s	仔	阿仔、名、teknonymy
子婦	s w	新抱、媳婦	家嫂、名
女	d	女*	阿女*、名、teknonymy
女婿	d h	女婿	名
侄	b s	侄*、侄仔	名
侄婦	b s w	侄(新)抱、侄婦	名
侄女	b d	侄女	名
侄女婿	b d h	侄(女)婿	名
外甥	si s	姨甥	名
外甥婦	si s w	姨甥嘅太太、甥媳	名
外甥女	si d	姨甥女*	名
外甥女婿	si d h	姨甥女*嘅先生	名
孫	s s	孫	名
孫婦	s s w	孫新抱、孫媳	名
孫女	s s d	孫女*	名
孫女婿	s s d h	孫女婿	名
外孫	d s	外孫	名
外孫婦	d s w	外孫新抱	名
外孫女	d d	外孫女	名
外孫女婿	d d h	外孫女婿	名

Diagram 2. Mother's Clan

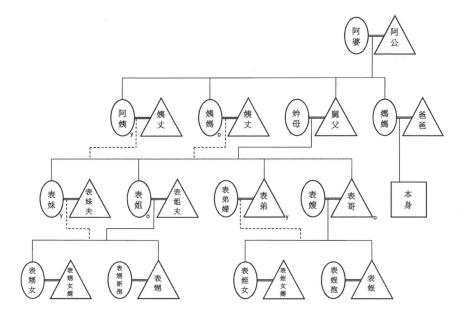

		Designative	**Vocative**
外曾祖父	m f f	太公	太公
外曾祖母	m f m	太婆	太婆
外祖父	m f	阿公	阿公
外祖母	m m	阿婆	阿婆、婆婆*、婆婆
舅父	m b	舅父*	舅父*、大舅父*
舅母	m b w	妗母	妗母、大妗母
姨母	m si$_o$	姨媽	姨媽、大姨媽
姨母	m si$_y$	阿姨°	阿姨°、三姨°、姨°仔
姨父	m si h	姨丈*	姨丈*、大姨丈*
舅表兄	m b s$_o$	表哥	表哥、名 + 表哥
舅表嫂	m b s$_o$ w	表嫂	表嫂、名 + 表嫂
舅表弟	m b s$_y$	表弟*	表弟*、名
舅表弟婦	m b s$_y$ w	表弟婦	名
舅表姊	m b d$_o$	表姐	表姐、大表姐、名 + 表姐
舅表姊夫	m b d$_o$ h	表姐夫	名 + 哥
舅表妹	m b d$_y$	表妹*	表妹*、三表妹*、名
舅表妹夫	m b d$_y$ h	表妹夫	名
姨表稱謂 (m s s) 同舅表			
舅表姪	m b s s	表姪*	名
舅表姪婦	m b s s w	表姪抱	名
舅表姪女	m b s d	表姪女	名
舅表姪婿	m b s d h	表姪女婿	名
舅表外甥	m b d s	表甥	名
舅表外甥婦	m b d s h	表甥新抱、表甥媳	名
舅表外甥女	m b d d	表甥女	名
舅表外甥女婿	m b d d h	表甥女婿	名

Diagram 3. Husband's Clan

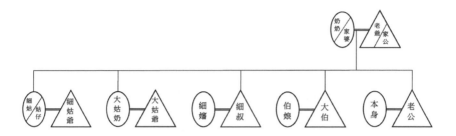

		Designative	**Vocative**
公	h f	家公、老爺	老爺、爸爸
婆	h m	家婆、奶奶*	奶奶*、媽媽
夫	h	丈夫、先生、老公、男人*	名、老公、teknonymy
妻	w	太太、老婆、女人*	名、老婆、teknonymy
伯	h b$_o$	大伯	大伯、大少、大哥
伯婦	h b$_o$ w	伯娘、伯母	大少奶°大嫂
叔	h b$_y$	細叔、叔仔	三叔、三少、名
叔婦	h b$_y$ w	細嬸、嬸娘	三少奶°、三嬸、名
姑	h si$_o$	姑奶°	大姑奶
姑	h si$_y$	細姑、姑仔	三姑娘、名
姑夫	h si h	姑爺	大姑爺

Diagram 4. Wife's Clan

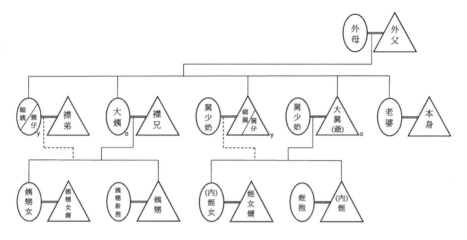

		Designative	**Vocative**
岳父	w f	岳父*、外父*、泰山	爸爸、岳父*
岳母	w m	岳母、外母、泰水	媽媽、岳母
舅兄	w b$_o$	妻舅、大舅、大舅爺	大哥、名
舅嫂	w b w	舅少奶	大嫂、名
舅弟	w b$_y$	細舅、舅仔	名
舅弟婦	w b$_y$ w	舅仔嘅太太	名
姨姊	w s$_o$	大姨	名
姨姊夫	w si$_o$ h	大姨嘅先生、襟兄	名 + 哥
姨妹	w si$_y$	細姨、姨°仔	名
姨妹夫	w si$_y$ h	姨°仔嘅先生、襟弟*	名
內姪	w b s	太太嘅姪*	名
內姪婦	w b s w	太太嘅姪抱	名
內姪女	w b d	太太嘅姪女	名
內姪女婿	w b d h	太太嘅侄女婿	名
姨外甥	w si s	太太嘅姨甥	名
姨外甥婦	w si s w	太太家姐嘅新抱	名
姨外甥女	w si d	太太嘅姨甥女	名
姨外甥女婿	w si d h	太太家姐嘅女婿	名

A Study of *Xiehouyu* Expressions in Cantonese

蘿蔔脂粉，電燈胆，淘古井，大光燈，二世祖，放白鴿，荷蘭水樽，賣剩蔗，盲公竹，大頭蝦爬，十月芥菜，神檯貓屎，棺材蟲，杉木靈牌，烏蠅摟馬尾，亞蘭嫁蒲星公吊頸，生虫拐杖，坭水佬激眼淚，跪倒餵猪乸，老鼠跌落天平扇底燒炮仗，床下底放紙鷂。

Abstract: *Xiehouyu* is a special form of idiomatic expressions in Chinese. It is made up of two segments, the first giving a clue, the second providing an answer, with a slight pause in between. The clue phrase could be in the form of a metaphor, generating a message that may be applied to its immediate narrative context or different general discoursal and social contexts. In more complicated cases, the message thus derived undergoes a second stage of derivation, giving it a new reading that bears no direct relevance to its original story. The derivation involves different linguistic operations, including semantic extension, sound borrowing, compounding, and structural re-organization. This article focuses on the use of Cantonese *xiehouyu* in Hong Kong. And, on the bases of close to four hundred expressions, it examines the structural relationship between the clue phrase and the answer phrase, by looking at various factors, linguistic and pragmatic, involved at every stage of the derivation from the message pointer to the message carrier. As some of the expressions incorporate English and foreign names and objects into their verbal manoeuvers, the analysis also adds to our understanding of the complex nature of the Hong Kong language.

Keywords: Cantonese *xiehouyu*; metaphor; semantic extension; sound borrowing; compounding; structural reorganization; taboo words; commercials

1. Introduction

Language is a symbolic system that assigns meanings to sounds according to various rules of phonological, syntactic, and semantic conventions. The meanings of a combination of words are generally determined by the meanings of their constituent words and the way they are put together. When the meaning of such a combination cannot be inferred or predicted from the conjoined meanings of the words it comprises, it is referred to as an idiom, a complex lexical item whose usage is idiosyncratic and requires a separate entry in a dictionary. All languages are replete with idiomatic expressions, the use of which, when appropriate, often adds color and effect to the way we communicate and express our thoughts; but, on the other hand, since idioms are by and large culturally and socially bound in both meaning and use, they may create problems between speakers coming from different backgrounds.

Xiehouyu 歇後語 is one form of idiomatic expressions in the Chinese language. Like all idioms, a *xiehouyu* expression is concise in form but rich in connotations; its suggestive power far excels that of a straightforward description of the situation to which the expression refers or that of a direct paraphrase of the saying itself. But, unlike other forms of Chinese idiomatic expressions, such as *chengyu* 成語 and *yanyu* 諺語, each constituting an utterance unit all by itself, a *xiehouyu* expression consists of two parts, separated by a pause. Generally speaking, the first part contains certain information, egimatic at times, as a cue leading to the core message in the second part. In other words, the first part is similar to a riddle in function, whereas the second half gives the answer highlighting the message of the expression. The following example from Cantonese illustrates this phraseological device.

(1) 泥菩薩過江 —— 自身難保
Nàih Pòuh-saat gwo gong—Jih-sàn nàahnbóu.[1]
Clay Bodhisattva crossing a river—hardly able to protect himself.

---

[1] All Cantonese examples in this article are romanized according to the Yale system. General terms including names, titles, and technical terms are romanized according to Mandarin.

The saying consists of two halves. The first half draws a picture of a Bodhisattva trying to cross waters while making every effort to preserve his own earthern statue from dissolving in the river. Precarious as it is, the situation finds a parallel between what the clay deity experiences and what a person finds in the real world of danger, a world where he is incapable of getting himself—let alone others—out of troubles. What the narrative sets up is in effect a metaphor, with a warning that is to be delivered in the second half. In four simple words 自身難保, the message of ineptitude and vulnerability is loud and clear. Structurally, there are two parts in the saying, with a slight pause in between when uttered; in essence, however, there is only one focus, and the focus comes after the pause, hence the name of the rhetorical device, *xie-hou-yu* (post-pause expression).

Xiehouyu expressions are to be distinguished from other sayings that also employ the use of metaphor. For example, 泥牛入海 *nàihngàuh yahp hói* (a clay ox entering the sea) is often used metaphorically to describe the disappearance of a person, a person gone forever, never to be heard of or seen again. Evidently, the expression plays with the clay motif too. But, while *nàihngàuh yahp hói* stands as a complete and independent expression with its figurative meaning to be deduced directly from the metaphor, 泥菩薩過江 constitutes only the first half of the *xiehouyu* and is immediately followed by a second half explicitly stating the intended reading of the metaphor. If a metaphor is a message-pointer in function, then a *xiehouyu* expression is made up of a message-pointer and a massage-carrier. It is possible that the message-carrier may disappear altogether from a *xiehouyu* expression when the use is so frequent that the association becomes simply instant and automatic. In that case, the message-pointer becomes an expression all inclusive; and if the pointer is made up of a metaphor, it is a metaphorical saying on its own right.[2] As will be explained later in the discussion, a message-pointer in a *xiehouyu* expression does not always have to be metaphorical in nature. It may pun on any one of the individual components in the message-carrier.

---

[2] 泥牛入海 was given as 泥牛入海，永無消息 *nàihngàuh yahp hói, wíhng mòuh sìusik* (Clay ox entering the sea—Never to be heard of again) in *Jingde chuandeng lu* 景德傳燈錄, an 11th-century collection of Buddhist works. The phrase was, therefore, originally used in the form of a *xiehouyu* expression. See Ning (1980), p. 53.

The term *xiehou* was historically used to refer to a literary device that would cut off the last word or unit from a well-known line and use the crippled version in place of that word/unit. 燕爾 *yin-yíh*, for example, is derived from 燕爾新婚 *yin-yíh sàn-fàn* (you feast your new marriage-kin; Waley's translation), and is often used as a substitute for 新婚 *sànfàn* (newly wed) in classical Chinese. 燕爾 has thus taken on the role of a message-pointer; 新婚, though not stated, is brought out by 燕爾, which otherwise would not have stood as a lexical unit by itself. It is precisely in this regard that the early usage of *xiehou* differs from its later development. 泥菩薩過江 in example (1) legitimately constitutes a well-formed phrase even when not used as part of the *xiehouyu* saying; 燕爾, however, does not, except as an abbreviation of 燕爾新婚. Furthermore, when 自身難保 appears with 泥菩薩過江 in speech, there is always a deliberate pause in between. 燕爾, on the other hand, appears alone, and just in case 新婚 shows up in the immediate context, the two parts would reunite as an unbroken sequence of the original phrase. In its truncated version, the presence of its primary focus, i.e., 新婚, is only hinted at through what is left in the line. To hint through omission is a challenging device, and by virtue of the mechanism, cases like 燕爾 are also known, perhaps more aptly so, as *suojiaoyu* 縮腳語 (foot-hiding expression), a sub-category of *cangci* 藏詞 (word ellipsis).[3]

The use of 縮腳語 was evidently quite a popular practice among scholars in ancient times, a word game in which they could delightfully partake to show off their versatile command of the classical language. However, aside from a few expressions that have become lexical compounds with origins unknown even to most native speakers, 縮腳語 is no longer productive in modern Chinese.[4] Examples from spoken Cantonese are also limited to a handful only.

(2) 佢擰擰吓個酸薑蕎
 Kéuih nihng-nihng-háh go syùn-gēung-kíu.
 He shook his head.

---

[3] Cf. Wang (1980), pp. 137–142.

[4] For example, 下馬威 *xiamawei* in Mandarin from 下馬威風 *xiama weifeng*, "the awe-inspiring look of an official when he dismounts from his horse upon arriving at his new office—intimidation at first encounter."

(3) 我呢次嚟搵你嘅目的係茅根竹
Ngóh nīchi làih wán néih ge muhkdīk haih màauh-gān-jūk.
The purpose of this visit is to ask you for a loan.

酸薑蕎 in (2) is derived from 酸薑蕎頭 *syun-gēung-kíu-tàuh* (pickled ginger and preserved onion bulbs), with 頭 *tàuh* (head) as the hidden word. 茅根竹 in (3) is a short form of 茅根竹蔗水 *màauh-gān jūk-je-séui* (a kind of sugar-cane juice); the abbreviated head 蔗水 *je-séui* is homophonous with 借水 *je-séui*, the Cantonese expression for borrowing money. In both examples, the keywords have been deliberately omitted so as to highlight the intended readings.

It is often noted that the second part of a *xiehouyu* expression is omissible when the context does not permit a literal reading of the first half or any reading other than the intended one.[5] Through repeated use, however, the connection between the message-pointer and the message-carrier may become so familiar and conventionalized that a listener would need no more than the cue itself, say 泥菩薩過江, to arrive at the intended meaning that the speaker has in mind. In other words, the second half of a *xiehouyu* expression may be redundant in function and thus omissible in use. In reality, however, omission of the second part is not a common practice. Depending on the context and the immediate intelligibility of the cue phrase, the message-carrier is more often than not kept in the expression, though there is invariably a pause between the two halves.

Xiehouyu have also come to be known as *qiaopihua* 俏皮話 (witty sayings). Even though play on words is an important and common element in the construction of many *xiehouyu* expressions to effect a sense of humor, jocularity, or even absurdity, it is their unique feature of bipartite composition that readily distinguishes *xiehouyu* from other witty metaphorical remarks such as 俏皮話.[6]

The use of *xiehouyu* is extremely common in colloquial Chinese. Even in literary writings, when there is the necessity to create special effects

---

[5] Cf. Ning (1980), pp. 46–47.

[6] For a detailed discussion on *xiehouyu*, *qiaopihua*, and other forms of verbal games, see Ma and Gao (1979), pp. 7–23.

with colloquialism, *xiehouyu* are employed.[7] Through twists of sounds and words and by means of clever manipulations of images, *xiehouyu* render important messages of various sorts, philosophical and cautionary, or merely descriptive observations in simple and vivid terms that are easy to understand, to remember, and to say. They are vernacular in style and folkloristic in essence. In fact, they represent one of the linguistic inventions based upon the popular understanding of man and nature, sound and meaning. As customs, beliefs, and language habits may vary in each speech community, *xiehouyu* are just as complex in geographical groupings as sounds and grammatical patterns. In the past, Mandarin, in its broadest sense of application, has chiefly been the target language for a systematic investigation.[8] It is the purpose of this article to examine the kind of *xiehouyu* we find in Cantonese, more specifically, in the context of Hong Kong in the early 1980s, with specific emphasis on the linguistic mechanisms reponsible for the operation of *xiehouyu* in the dialect. Sociolinguisitic aspects will be touched upon, though briefly, at the end of the article. The data are primarily collected from Cantonese speakers of various age groups in Hong Kong, recent Hong Kong immigrants now residing in the San Francisco area.[9] Another source of information comes from newspapers published in Hong Kong, many of which have made deliberate efforts to capture, often with great success, the colloquial style in their special columns. The implications of the discussion that follows are by no means limited to Hong Kong Cantonese. It is hoped that the observations presented in this article can be applied to and attested in our further studies of Chinese *xiehouyu*, including those used in other speech communities.

---

[7] For various discussions on this topic, see Zhang (1954); Tori (1970); Ma and Gao (1979), pp. 249–252; and Wang (1980), pp. 169–184.

[8] A representative work of this nature is Ma and Gao (1979).

[9] I wish to thank the following people for contributing interesting examples to this study: 翟志成, 陳勝長, 李曉茵, 梁仲森, 梁東, 廖國輝, and 司徒福華. References have also been made to two collections of Cantonese *xiehouyu*: Qiao (1966) and Tan (1980).

2. Message Pointer and Message Carrier

Cantonese shares some of its *xiehouyu* expressions with Mandarin and other dialects. The above example (1), for instance, is generally considered a borrowing from Mandarin. The majority of Cantonese *xiehouyu* are, however, characterized by a typical local flavor in their use of sounds and words. The following two examples are distinctly Cantonese, which would not have worked with the same popular appeal if they were to be said in another dialect.

(4) 寡母婆死仔 —— 無望
 Gwámóuhpó séi jái—Móuhmohng.
 A widow mother lost her only son—No more hopes.

(5) 關公細佬 —— 翼德 (→ 亦得)
 Gwāan Gūng sailóu—Yihkdāk. (→ yihkdāk)
 The younger brother of Gwāan Yúh—Yihkdāk. (→ That's alright too.)

Following the same general principle of bipartite composition, Cantonese *xiehouyu* expressions are formed with two parts, separated by a pause. The part before the pause is the *cue phrase* which serves as the message-pointer, and the part that comes after it is the *answer phrase* which carries the message of the expression. The way how the two parts are connected is a matter of linguistic association, a fun mechanism where words are given new meanings and images new roles in what they stand for in each of the settings. To be more exact, we may ask: what kind of information is produced in the cue phrase that will lead to the message in the answer phrase? Sentence (4) is a good example to illustrate the associative link. What could be more devastating than a widow mother losing her only son? What better words to describe the suffering and despair that the woman feels than the expression 無望 *mouhmohng* (no more hope) in colloquial Cantonese? The words evoke an emotional response, vivid and strong, by means of a metaphorical comparison; but once removed from that immediate context, the *xiehouyu* with its derived message may be used to characterize any experience of disappointment one feels, not necessarily of the same intensity as losing one's child but also in a situation when hope seems to be beyond reach. (4a), for example, provides a different context in which this expression is used.[10]

(4a) 你咁樣都想追女仔,正一「寡母婆死仔,冇望」。
Néih gámyéung dōu séung jèui néuihjái, jihng yāt ...
Given your condition, you're thinking of chasing after girls? It's truly a case of ...

By comparison, example (5) is much more complicated in its derivation. Unlike (4), it does not involve an analogus association. The cue phrase provides the name of a historical figure, 關公; but, even given all the necessary information of Gwaangung and his younger brother being 張飛 Jēung Fēi, we still would not have any clue how to get to the intended answer—亦得 *yihkdāk*—a casual but reassuring phrase meaning "that's okay too." For those who are familiar with the story of the Three Kingdoms, a saga where Gwaangung and Jeung Fei are exemplary figures of sworn brotherhood, we would remember that the younger brother, 張飛 has a courtesy name 翼德 *Yihkdāk*. The trick to resolve the riddle is to call for a switch in words, or an exchange of characters with the same pronunciations. The name 翼德 and the answer phrase 亦得 are pronounced exactly the same in Cantonese: *yihkdāk*. In other words, the resolution involves two steps of derivation. The first step produces a surface answer on the basis of the clue given in the message-pointer; and the second step is to take this surface answer as an input for the next derivation—a transference to homophous but different characters. Complicated as it may seem to be, especially for those who do not know Cantonese, this second step could sometimes become a daunting task as it requires various linguistic modifications to generate the intended message.

Generally speaking, all examples of *xiehouyu*, whether in Cantonese, Mandarin, or in any other dialect, can be classified into two major categories according to their derivational procedures: (A) those that undergo only one step, and (B) those that go through two steps. Category A includes examples whose answer phrases are related to the cue phrases

---

[10] For a similar discussion on the distinction between the immediate context and the general context of a *xiehouyu* expression in use, see Kroll (1966), p. 298.

by a simple step of derivation, and the answer phrases thus derived are applicable to their individual immediate contexts as well as in other and more general situations. Expressions of Category B follow the same derivation in the first stage to produce answer phrases relating to the cue phrases in their immediate contexts and, in addition, they then reprocess these surface answers through another set of rules to obtain answers in other or general contexts. Because of the ambiguity in meaning impregnated in the answer phrases, *xiehouyu* of the second category are usually more difficult to comprehend than those in the first category.

2.1. Category A

Of the *xiehouyu* expressions that belong to Category A, i.e., those that go through only one stage of derivation, there are two sub-groups that are distinguished from each other in terms of the degree of immediacy that answer phrases carry in relation to their use in a general context. The cue phrases in both groups are basically metaphors; but while the answer phrases of one group are directly applicable to both immediate and general contexts, those in the other group are restricted in their application to an immediate context only—their relevance to a general context is indirect and often by extension. Compare the following two examples:

(6) 蚊髀同牛髀 ——冇得比
Mānbéi tùhng ngàuhbéi—Móuh dāk béi.
The thigh of a mosquito and the thigh of of a cow—Absolutely no comparison.

(6a) 你賺咁少錢想同佢鬥，真係蚊髀同牛髀 ——冇得比
Néih jaahn gam síu chín, séung tòhng kéuih dau, jànhaih ...
You're making so little money and yet you're thinking of competing with him. It's truly ...

(7) 鷯哥命 ——就食就疴
Līugō mehng—Jauh sihk jauh ngò.
The fate of a hill-myna—Discharging as fast as it takes in.

(7a) 佢賺到錢就即刻用晒，唔慌唔係鷯哥命，就食就疴
Kéuih jaahndóu chín jauh jīkhāk yuhngsaai, mhfòng mhhaih ...

He spends all his money as soon as he makes any; it must surely be a case of...

Both expressions employ an animal motif to draw a parallel between what happens in the human world and what one observes in nature. The drastic difference in size between a cattle's thigh and the limb of a tiny insect is all too powerful an image to characterize the absurdity in real life when a poor fellow hopes to beat out someone who is exceedingly rich. The answer phrase in (6), 冇得比, is a conclusion one can easily draw from the cue phrase featuring a cattle and a mosquito; it also acts as a direct comment on the futile competition in a general context as seen in (6a). Please also note that 髀 (thigh) in the cue and 比 (to compete) in the answer are different words but with exactly the same pronunciation, a game of homophony that would for sure add another touch of verbal humor to the saying. By contrast, the answer phrase in (7), 就食就疴, relates only to the eating habit of a bird, and bears no relationship to the unscrupulous spendthrift as shown in (7a). Rather it is by extension of that metaphor of fast eating and the ensuing results that we find a linkage between the speedy relief of a bird and the habit of wasteful extravagance. Example (8) also belongs to this subgroup as (7).

(8)　阿蘭賣豬——一千唔賣賣八百
　　A-Làahn maaih jyū—Yātchìn mhmaaih maaih baatbaak.
　　A-Laahn selling pigs—Not at the price of a thousand but for the price of eight hundred.

This *xiehouyu* expression alludes to a quaint old story which took place in Canton years ago. A peasant woman named A-Laahn, for some strange reasons, sold her livestock for a price lower than what others would have offered.[11] Even though the allusion is no longer familiar to most Cantonese speakers of today, the expression itself is still quite popular in Hong Kong. It is often used to describe someone who drives a hard bargain which, by an ironic twist, turns out to be against his favor. The answer phrase is part of the metaphorical sequence, and, without the

---

[11] See Wu (1922), p. 11.

background sketch in the cue phrase, a saying like "not a thousand but eight hundred" would have made little sense as a comment in a general context.

Notwithstanding their differences in terms of relevane and applicability extending from the immediate to the general contexts, examples (6) to (8) are all cases of metaphor or analogy, drawing parallels between two situations. They do not require any linguistic modification for the answer phrases to arrive at the intended readings. The characteristic feature of a *xiehouyu* expression of Category A is that it involves no play on words. The answer phrase means exactly what it says on the surface. It may be used as a direct comment, or it may continue with the metaphorical narrative in the cue, together with which it casts its say on the general context where it is applied.

2.2. Category B

Xiehouyu expressions of Category B are characterized by the fact that their answer phrases all possess two readings, one for the immediate context and one for the general context. They invariably involve linguistic modification of some sort that will render new readings to the outputs of the first derivation. It may be a simple extension of the meaning of one of the words, or it may be as complicated as restructuring the grammatical elements in the answer phrase. The product of this second derivation, though retaining in some cases the same phonetic representations, has acquired a new semantic reading and is applied to the general context in the capacity of an idiomatic expression. Generally speaking, there are four different kinds of linguistic mechanisms that may be employed for modification.

2.2.1. Semantic Extension

A word may often carry several different meanings that are actually, upon close scrutiny, related by metaphorical extension. They may be considered various manifestations of the same semantic unit, variations that become more noticeable and eventually distinguishable in different contexts. The word 刮 *gwaat*, for example, means "to scrape, to rub smooth" literally, as in 刮面 *gwaat-mihn* (to shave face). Figuratively, however, it can be used to describe an action of extorting money or fleecing. A verbal play is built on this semantic extension in the following *xiehouyu* expression.

(9) 剃頭佬教仔──有得刮就刮
Taitàuhlóu gaau jái—Yáuh dāk gwaat jauh gwaat.
A barber teaching his son—Take in whatever there is to be taken in.

The answer phrase which is used in its immediate context as a piece of professional advice from a barber becomes something entirely different in the following sentence.

(9a) 呢個人貪得無厭，係人都要攞翻啲，正一係剃頭佬教仔，有得刮就刮。
Nīgo yàhn tàamdāk mòuh yim, haih yàhn dōu yiu lóhfāan dī. Jihngyāt haih...
This man is insatiably greedy; he would take advantage of anybody. This is truly a case of...

刮 takes on the pejorative reading of "extorting" and is the meaning intended in the *xiehouyu* expression when applied to a general context describing the avarice of a man without scruples. The cue phrase 剃頭佬教仔 provides a lead to 刮 in its literal sense, which in turn goes through a second derivation that extends its meaning to a figurative reading. Compare this expression with (10), which is an example of Category A.

(10) 光棍佬教仔──便宜莫貪
Gwōnggwanlóu gaau jái—Pìhnyìh mohk tāam.
A hustler teaching his son—Don't covet small advantages.

The answer phrase which characterizes the teaching of a swindler is used as a piece of straightforward warning to people of all walks.

There are some cases where the semantic extension goes in a reverse direction, from figurative to literal. For example,

(11) 出爐鐵──聽打
Chèutlòuh tit—Tihng dá.
Iron just out of the furnace—Waiting to be forged.

In the immediate context of this *xiehouyu* expression, 打 has a specific meaning of "iron forging," which is clearly an extension of the basic meaning of the word, "to beat, to strike." And, it is this original reading that comes to focus in the general application of the expression. For example, when a child is so naughty that it takes a good lesson of spanking to straighten him out, (11) would be an appropriate quote.

The semantic extension of the two uses of 刮 and 打 is easy to understand even to people who do not speak Cantonese. The association is immediate and obvious. There are, however, language-specific associations that would make certain *xiehouyu* expressions incomprehensible to speakers of other dialects. The Cantonese word 掂 *dihm*, for example, carries a basic meaning of "straight in shape" and an extended meaning of "things in order, well-handled." Thus,

(12) 亞駝命———死都唔得掂
A-tó mehng—Séi dōu mhdāk dihm.
The fate of a hunchback—Won't be straight even dead.

It is the literal meaning of 唔掂 *mhdihm* (not straight) that we find in the story of the hunchback—never able to straighten his back; and when the saying refers to a person trapped in deep troubles, the answer phrase underscores the seriousness of the situation, a mess impossible to straighten out even dead. In either case, the use of 掂 is highly Cantonese and the meaning of 唔掂 (not okay) is idiomatic, and to the non-natives, they are simply "foreign" words.

Sometimes, as a result of one switch in the semantic reading of a keyword in the carrier, other words in the same phrase may take on new meanings by extension. Such an extension is triggered off only when the cue is grasped correctly. An example of this additional modification is (13).

(13) 黃皮樹鷯哥———唔熟唔食
Wòhngpèihsyuh līugō—mhsuhk mhsihk.
A hill-myna on a cork tree—Eating only those (drupes) that are ripe.

Through the regular second stage of derivation, 熟 *suhk* extends its reading from the basic meaning of "ripe" to that of "familiar," which then entails another step of modification for 食 *sihk*. From the meaning "to eat," 食 takes on a new reading of "to target," essentially in the sense of "taking advantage of those whom one knows well." 食 in (13) would not have been read this way if 熟 had not gone through its own extension. In example (7) above, however, 食 remains in its literal sense even in the intended reading of the answer phrase. The entire expression 鸚哥命——就食就疴 is a metaphorical comparison with no deliberate play on words.

2.2.2. Sound Borrowing

Another important feature of the *xiehouyu* is their intriguing use of homophonous words for puns. Because of the monosyllabic nature of the Chinese language, there is a huge repertoire of cases where various unrelated semantic units come to share the same phonetic form or even the same graph in the writing system. *Xiehouyu* thrive on phonetic borrowings and operate vigorously on homophony, gaining an even greater flexibility in word play. The answer phrase often contains a keyword, which is transformed into a different word but with the same pronunciation in the cue phrase. To resolve the riddle, the first step is to come up with the surface answer from the cue, and then identify the keyword in the surface, submit it to another round of derivation, and retrieve from a host of possible homophonous candidates the correct form for the final answer. For example,

(14) 蛋家佬打醮——冇壇
Dahnggālóu dájiu—Móuh tàahn.
The boat people performing a sacrificial ritual—No ritual platform.

Since the boat people live on water and confine all activities within their boat, there is practically no extra space where they can build a ritual platform for any religious functions; hence, the literal meaning of the surface answer phrase is 冇壇 *móuh tàahn* (no platform). The word 壇, however, is homophonous with 彈 *tàahn*, here meaning "to attack verbally, to criticize." Appearing in the negative, 冇彈 as a phrase carries the meaning of "no criticism" or "no fault." As used in the following sentence, the message proclaiming "no criticism" is actually a rather welcomed remark of appreciation.

(14a) 佢呢個人咁為得人，真係蛋家佬打醮——冇彈
Kéuih nīgo yàhn gam waihdāk yàhn, jānhaih . . .
He is such a person so eager to help others—he truly is . . .

The two readings of "no platform" and "no criticism" are related only through sound borrowing.

Compare (14) with the following example which shares a similar message-carrier.

(15) 斷線三弦——冇得彈
Tyúhn-sin sàamyìhn—Móuh dāk tàahn.
A three-string lute with broken chords—Nothing to pluck → Nothing to criticize.

The literal meaning of 彈 is "to shoot" or "to pluck" as with a string instrument; the figurative use of it, as found in both (14) and (15), is "to attack verbally" or "to criticize." But, unlike (14) where 彈 is generated through sound borrowing from 壇, (15) is an example of semantic extension where we find the same keyword 彈 in both phrases, with different but related readings.

Example (16) is a case where borrowing happens to homophonous words, which also happen to share the same character in writing.

(16) 海軍鬥水兵——水鬥水
Hóigwān dau séuibīng—Séui dau séui.
The navy fighting against the marines—"Water" against "water."

As the navy and the marines are soldiers at sea, it is obvious why 水 (water) appears in the answer phrase. In colloquial Cantonese, however, the same character 水 is also used as a descriptive word meaning "poor in quality." A common expression to use when speaking of poor performance is 水皮 *séuipèih*, literally "water-skin." Thus, the intended reading in the answer phrase, 水鬥水, is a disapproving remark as is used in the following example about a disappointing match between two ball teams:

(16a) 呢兩隊籃球隊都好曳。今次比賽，好話唔好聽，正一……
Ni léuhng deuih làahmkàuhdéui dōu hóu yáih. Gàmchi béichoi, hou wah mhhóutèng, jihngyāt . . .
These two basketball teams are equally bad. This contest, to put it bluntly, is truly a case of . . .

It is possible to think of the unflattering *séui* as another case of semantic extension in use of the same form for "water." Since water is extremely thin in consistency, it could be viewed as symbolic of insubstantiality (cf. the use of "watery" in English). Such an association, however, is not common in other Chinese dialects.[12]

雞 is another Cantonese form that carries two completely different meanings: "chicken" and "woman" (cf. the use of "chick" in English slangs). For example,

(17) 石罅米——俾雞啄
Sehkla máih—Béi gāi dèung.
Rice in the cracks of stones—To be pecked by chickens.

To speakers who do not know much about Cantonese, this expression would mean little more than a vivid description of chickens pecking rice from crevices in stones. Yet, to a native Cantonese, the saying will draw a knowing look and perhaps a sneering smile. The expression is actually a cynical description of a stingy fellow whose money no one can touch—except for women, usually of an infamous profession. Aside from playing on the two homophonous words, 雞$_1$ (chicken) and 雞$_2$ (woman), the expression also assigns an extended reading to 啄, from "pecking" to "extracting money," a rendering just right for the this new context.

Homophonous borrowing can sometimes operate on more than one word in the same *xiehouyu* expression, making its derivation even more complicated and interesting than usual. 金 *Gām* and 宋 *Sung* in the following example refer to the two dynasties that Kublai Khan overthrew in his ambitious expansion of the Mongol hegemony.

(18) 忽必烈——吞金滅宋
Fatbītliht—Tàn Gām miht Sung.
Kublai Khan—Destroying the Jin and exterminating the Song.

---

[12] 水 *séui* is also used as a metaphorical substitute for money and wealth in Cantonese. Thus, the following *xiehouyu* expression:

蛋家雞——見水唔飲得
Dahnggāgāi—Gin séui mhyámdāk.
A chicken kept by the boat people—Water in sight but not for a sip → Money in sight but not touchable.

Through the second stage of derivation, the dynastic name 金 is converted to its homophonous form 金, meaning "gold, money," and, in a similar manner, the imperial 宋 is changed to 餸, a Cantonese word for "food, groceries." When a servant attempts to make a profit out of the money he is given to buy food, he is described as 吞金 (swallowing money) by 滅餸 (reducing the food). Both verbs 吞 and 滅 have also taken on an extended shade of meaning.

Example (19) is a similar case which involves modification of two elements in the answer phrase.

(19) 樹林菩薩 ―― 蔭夾獨
Syuhlàhm Pòuhsaat—Yàm gaap duhk.
Bodhisattva in the woods—Under the shadows of trees and being alone.

蔭 *yàm* (shade) is homophonous with and often written as 陰. The latter carries a second meaning of "being insidious," a reading that can of course be construed as a semantic extension of "shady." 獨 *duk* (alone), on the other hand, is a true homophonous borrowing for 毒 *duk*, meaning "poison—evil, malicious." The surface reading of the answer phrase 蔭夾獨 is a portrayal, as shown in the cue phrase, of a Buddhist god sitting, all alone, in the shade of trees; its intended reading, however, is a far cry from a calling for religious meditation. Rather, it is to deliver a condemning message pronoucing someone being "insidious and malicious."

The drastic shift in meaning comes from a process that puts the two seemingly innocuous words, 蔭 *yàm* (shade) and 獨 *duhk* (alone), together to form a new compound, *yàmduhk*, which shares the same pronunciation with a very negative word, 陰毒, meaning "sinister, insidious." Graphically different in writing, the new compound paints in heavy strokes the schematic nature of an evil person. As will be taken up in the next section, compounding is one of the major operative mechanisms in the *xiehouyu* language.

It should be added that in some cases sound modification is involved in borrowing. For example, the surface reading of the following *xiehouyu* is 水神 *séuisàhn* (water god).

(20) 龍舟菩薩 —— 水神
Lùhngjāu Pòuhsaat—Séuisàhn.
Bodhisattva on a dragon boat—Water god.

The phonetic form *séuisàhn* is slightly modified when it is borrowed to render the compound 衰神 *sèuisàhn*, meaning "a bad person, bad," as the intended reading. Notice, however, it is the modified version, i.e., *sèui* instead of *séui*, the same syllable but with a different tone, that is used in the second half. In other words, the surface reading *séui* is simply bypassed so as to avoid any unnecessary misunderstanding in communication.[13]

2.2.3. Compounding

Xiehouyu operate on sound similarity, and they pun on the literal meaning of a compound word. The reading of the answer phrase that relates to the immediate context is often a combination of the literal meanings of the individual words that make up that compound phrase. To apply to a general context, the phrase needs to go through a compounding process, which joins all relevant elements together to form a semantic or idiomatic unit. 陰毒 in (19) is an example of compounding, even though 陰 and 毒 could be taken as separate elements as well in the intended reading. In contrast, the yieldings of the first derivation in the next few examples have to be compounded in order to produce the intended readings of the expressions.

(21) 濕柴煲老鴨 —— 夠晒煙韌
Sāpchàaih bōu lóuhngaap—Gousaai yìnngahn.
Cooking an old duck with wet firewood—Smoky and tough, for sure.

---

[13] Another example of sound modification is
東莞佬猜枚 —— 三個四個 → 生個死個
Dùnggúnlóu chàaimúi—Sàamgo seigo → Sàang go sei go.
A Dunggun fellow playing the finger-guessing game—Three or four → One born and one died.

The actual reading of the expression refers to the ill fate of a woman who lost all her babies in infancy. The expression plays on the dialectal pronunciation of 三 and 四 in Dunggun, which is rather close to but not exactly the same as in Cantonese. Again, only 生個死個 is used in speech as the second phrase of the *xiehouyu* expression.

Wet firewood, when lit if at all possible, produces more smoke than fire, hence 煙 *yīn* (smoke); the meat of an old duck, however cooked, will never be tender, hence 韌 (tough). 煙韌, as a compound unit, means neither "smoky" nor "tough"; it is a colloquial term for being "lovey-dovey," as used in the following example.

> (21a)　佢兩個又錫又乘，傍若無人，十足濕柴煲老鴨，夠晒煙韌。
> Kéuih léuhnggo yauh sek yauh sihng, pòhng-yeuk-mòuh-yàhn, sahpjūk . . .
> The two of them kissed and what-not as if there weren't anyone around. It was indeed a case of . . .

The following are a few more examples where compounding adds to the amusing effect of the *xiehouyu* expressions.

> (22)　飛機火燭 —— 燒雲
> Fēigēi fójūk—Sìu wàhn.
> Airplane on fire—Burning the clouds.

燒 is homophonous with 銷 *sìu* meaning "melt," and 雲 is homophonous with 魂 *wàhn* meaning "soul." When an airplane is on fire, 燒雲 *sìu wàhn* (cloud burning) would be literally a description of the flames; yet, through sound borrowing and compounding, "*sìu wàhn*" becomes 銷魂 *sìuwàhn*, a compound word referring to the "soul melting" power or the "coquettish" charm of a woman.

> (23)　彭祖尿壺 —— 老積
> Pàahngjóu niuhwú—Lóuhjīk.
> The urinal pot of Paahngjou—Old stains.

As one may have easily guessed it, the reading of 老 as "old" is apparently derived from the allusion to 彭祖, who allegedly lived for eight hundred years. 積 refers to the dirt and stains that he has left on his urinal pot. The meaning of the new compound, phonetically and graphically unchanged, is not a literal combination of "old" and "stain." Rather, it carries one single meaning: "precocious." In fact, as a semantic unit, the word is not analyzable as is the case of 銷魂 in (22).

The use of the new compound through a second derivation applies to the following context:

(23a)　而家啲細佬哥個個都係彭祖尿壺──老積
　　　　Yìhgā dī sailouhgō gogo dōu haih . . .
　　　　Kids nowadays are all . . .

The next example shows an idiomatization of a Verb-Object phrase, the literal meaning of which serves as the surface reading of the first part of the expression.

(24)　牀下底破柴──撞板
　　　Chòhng hahdái po chàaih—Johng báan.
　　　Chopping wood under the bed—Bumping against the plank.

As a compound, 撞板 means "get blocked by problem." Its idiomatization from "bumping against the plank" finds a close parallel in the English expression "running up against a stone wall." It may be considered a metaphorical compound, and it may allow some structural expansion as in *johng daaih baan* (running into huge problems).

The last example of compounding is a unique case of reverse derivation. Unlike expressions cited above that derive their intended readings from compounding, example (25) demonstrates a process of de-compounding.

(25)　乾隆皇契仔──周日清
　　　Kìhnlùhngwòhng kaijái—Jàu Yahtchìng.
　　　Emperor Kìhnluhng's adopted son—Jau Yaht-ching.

The surface message is a proper noun, the name of an adopted son of the imperial family. The intended reading, however, is to take that proper name 周日清, break it up into its original three component characters, and read them literally: "All-Day-Clean." De-compounding will then give us a new and real message, "spend it all everyday," as applied to a case where a person makes no effort to save even a penny of what he earns.

2.2.4. Structural Reorganization

Compounding, in some cases, is one form of structural reorganization. As elements in the same sequence demonstrate a different grouping relationship before and after compounding, they bear different readings. For example, 老積 in (23), taken literally, is either a coordinate phrase "old and stained" or a subordinate construction "old stain"; as an idiomatic unit meaning "precocious," it is one single disyllabic morpheme. 周日清 in (25) is to be analyzed as 周 + 日清 in the nominal form, i.e., Surname + Given Name; but, when dissected into 周日 + 清, i.e., Head Noun + Verb or Topic + Comment, it becomes a descriptive phrase. None of the elements in the surface message have been moved around, but the re-arrangement of their structural relationships yields a different reading through the second derivation. Generally speaking, restructuring of the immediate constituents is quite common in the *xiehouyu* exercises. The following are a few more examples for illustration.

(26)   抬棺材甩褲 —— 失禮死人
Tòih gūnchòih lāt fu—Sātláih séiyàhn.
While carrying the coffin, one drops one's pants—A disgrace to the dead.

失禮 *sātláih*, which is a Verb-Object compound ("lose-propriety") by itsetf, acts as a transitive verb meaning being "discourteous." In the first reading, it takes on 死人 *séiyàhn* (the deceased) as its object, hence, the translation of the surface message: "a disgrace to the dead." At the idiomatic level, *satlaih* remains as the verb, but *séi* acts as an intensifier for the verb, and *yàhn* (people) alone is the object. In English, the expression is a loud and exclamatory remark, "an utmost disgrace to others." The structural reorganization of the phrase can be diagrammed as below:

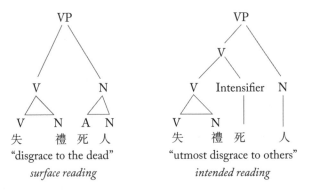

Other examples that require a similar re-adjustment of the grammatical status of 死 include:

(27) 紙紮老虎 —— 嚇死人
Jíjaat lóuhfú—Haak séi yàhn.
Paper-made tiger—Scaring off the dead → Scared to death.

(28) 棺材老鼠 —— 食死人
Gūnchòih lóuhsyú—Sihk séi yàhn.
Rats in a coffin—Feeding on the dead → Incredibly avaricious.

(29) 放路溪錢 —— 引死人
Fong louh kàichìhn—Yáhn séi yàhn.
Paper money placed on the roadside—Leading the way for the dead → extremely alluring. (引 : lead → attract → attractive)

Similarly, in the following examples, 鬼 *gwái* is used in two different meanings:

(30) 閻羅王揸攤 —— 鬼買
Yìhmlòhwòhng jà tāan—Gwái máaih
King Yama is in charge of the gambling den—Ghosts come for bets.

The mention of Yama, King of the Hades, in the cue phrase is an obvious clue that 鬼 *gwái* in the following segment is to be taken literally as meaning "ghosts." And, in that capacity, *gui* serves as the grammatical subject of the following verb 買, forming a sentence "鬼買," meaning "the ghosts would want to come and make bets." Attractive a deal as it may seem to be, the clue is nevertheless a misleading one. 鬼 in Cantonese, also functions as a marker for a rhetorical question, and is indeed the intended usage that gives the answer phrase a new reading—a negative declaration, a rhetorical question, rather than a narrative conclusion: "Who would want to buy it?"

Examples (31) and (32) employ the same trick, playing on the double meanings of the word *gwái*.

(31) 閻羅王嫁女 —— 鬼要
Yìhmlòhwòhng ga néui—Gwái yiu.
King Yama marrying off his daughter—Ghosts want her → Who'd want it?

(32) 閻羅王出告示 —— 鬼睇
Yìhmlòhwòhng chēut gousih—Gwái tái.
King Yama posting a notice—Ghosts look at it → Who's coming to see it?

The following examples feature the use of taboo words, which are to be reprocessed through a seond derivation to become modal particles, adding an extra shade of emphasis and colloquial flavor to the message.

(33) 風吹皇帝褲 ——孤䦉寒
Fūng chèui wòhngdai fulong—Gū-lán-hòhn.
Wind blowing against the crotch of the emperor's trousers—My penis is cold.

The literal reading of the answer phrase contains a subject noun phrase 孤䦉 gū lán and an adjectival predicate 寒 hòhn (cold). By itself, 孤 can function as a first person pronoun used by a king, and 䦉 lán is the colloquial word in Cantonese for the male sexual organ. When strung together, the three-character phrase presents a vivid picture what a sovereign feels under his crotch.

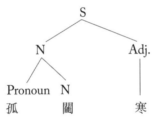

The actual reading of the message has nothing to do with the chill or any part of the imperial body. *Gū-lán-hòhn* is simply an expanded expression of a disyllabic Cantonese compound 孤寒 *gūhòhn* meaning "miserly." And, 䦉 *lán*, like profane words in many other languages, is added, or inserted in this case, for emphasis. Thus, *gu lan han* translates roughly into "f**king stingy."

Example (34) follows a similar mechanism and shifts the intended reading of the message by adding a taboo marker.

(34) 法國大餐 ——多閪魚 → 多閪餘
Faatgwok daaihchāan—Dò gauh yú → Dò-gàu-yùh.
French dinner—Extra piece of fish → Damned superfluous.

Gàu is another word for the male organ in Cantonese and is used similarly as an emphasis particle for insertion in a compound. But, unlike the case in (33), *gàu* is not taken literally as a taboo term in the surface reading. It is modified in tone and is used as a measure word *gauh* (often written with a borrowed character 舊) for 魚 *yú* (fish). It is believed that a French meal serves an extra course of fish than meals of other styles. Hence, 多魚 is a Verb-Object construction, which is then changed through homophonous transformation to a compound word 多餘 *dòyùh* (superfluous). Please note that 魚 carries a high rising tone (*yú*) in its colloquial pronunciation, but its original tone is low-falling, the same as 餘 *yùh*.

Complicated as they may seem, the above examples all share one common feature in their structural reorganization. A functive word is created through modification, which allows a further restructuring of elements. An extreme case of such a restructuring is the following example which literally moves elements around, back and forth, to produce the intended reading.

(35) 裙頭插令——閪出旗 → 出閪奇
Kwàhntàuh chaap lihng—Hāi chēut kèih → Chēut-hāi-kèih.
Banner sticking out at the waist of a skirt—Flag coming out of the vagina → Damned surprising.

Because of the cue of 裙 (skirt, i.e., "what a woman wear"), *hāi* is interpreted as a woman's body part, which is here taken as the place where a banner 旗 is tied to. Again, through homophonous transformation, 出旗 *chut-kèih* turns into 出奇 *chutkèih*, a disyllabic adjective meaning "surprising, curious." The process concludes with the insertion of the taboo word 閪 *hāi* as an emphasis marker. In short, 閪 has changed more than its meaning and function in the sequence. Its placement has also been shifted. The new reading is now "f**king strange."

hāi chēut kèih 閪出旗
↓
hāi chēut kèih 閪出奇
↓
chēut hāi kèih 出閪奇

2.3. Multiple Applications

As illustrated in the above discussion, a *xiehouyu* expression often involves more than one type of linguistic modification as it goes through the second stage of derivation. This is especially true when there is a play on (near-)

homophonous words. When a different word is introduced through sound-borrowing, it is bound to entail new semantic and syntactic relationships with the neighboring elements in the answer phrase. Either compounding or structural reorganization, or both, follow. Here are a few more examples to illustrate the complexities involved for a *xiehouyu* expression to derive its idiomatic reading from the surface answer. The modifications are described in steps and the structural changes are diagrammed.

(36)　火燒旗杆 ——— 長碳
Fó sìu kèihgōn—Chèuhng taan.
"Fire burning a banner-pole."
Surface reading: "Long charcoal"
　　(a) Sound borrowing: 碳 taan (charcoal) → 嘆 taan (enjoy)[14]
　　(b) Semantic extension: 長 chèuhng　　→ chèuhng
　　　　　　　　　　　　　　 "long in shape" "long in time"
　　(c) Restructuring:

Idiomatic reading: "to enjoy for a long time"

(37)　黃腫腳 ——— 不消蹄
Wòhngjúng geuk—Bātsìu tàih.
"A yellow swollen (pig's) leg."
Surface reading: "A leg that shows no signs of subsidence of swelling."
　　(a) Sound borrowing: 蹄 tàih (trotter) → 提 tàih (raise)
　　(b) Compounding: 不消 bāt sìu　　→ 不消 bātsìu
　　　　　　　　　　　 "not subsiding"　 "not necessary"
　　(c) Restructuring:

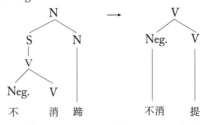

Idiomatic reading: "(the matter is so disheartening that) it is not worth mentioning"

14　　Please notice that 嘆 *taan* is a colloquial word for "to enjoy" in Cantonese.

Please note that the surface message in (37) is a noun phrase with 蹄 as the head modified by a negative verb 不消, whereas the message in the idiomatic reading becomes a verb phrase with 提 as the verb negated by the marker 不消.

(38) 龍舟棍——頂水神
Lùhngjāu gwan—Díng séuisàhn.
A dragon-boat oar—Beating against the water god.

As in example (20), 龍舟 is tied to stories of water deities, hence the presence of a water god, 水神. 頂 *díng* is a verb for "pushing against."

Idiomatic reading: "really bad, worst"

Example (38) also shows that although the linguistic modification of an answer phrase usually follows a certain order of application, i.e., sound-borrowing followed by compounding and/or restructuring, the cycle can be repeated on other elements in the same phrase.

In passing, it should be noted that there is another form of linguistic modification at work in Mandarin *xiehouyu* that is not found in Cantonese. In addition to playing with sounds and meanings, Mandarin can also work on the character representation of a word. The cue phrase provides all the necessary information for constructing the graphic form of the keyword in the answer phrase. For example,

(39) 心字頭上一把刀——你就忍一點兒吧
(Mandarin) Xinzi toushang yiba dao—Ni jiu ren yi-dianr ba.
A knife on top of the character "xin"—Try to endure it.

As described in the cue phrase, the character 忍 is made up of two components, 心 *xin* (heart) and 刃 *ren* (dagger), the latter of which is a close approximation of 刀 *dao* (knife), in meaning as well as in writing. The admonitive message as inscribed in this expression is "to refrain from complaining—endurance requires the will to bear pain." Evidently, graphic conversion is just as challenging a verbal game as punning on sounds and words, but such cases are extremely rare even in Mandarin.[15]

3. Making of a *Xiehouyu* Expression

The above discussion deals primarily with the decoding process of a *xiehouyu* expression, examining the various mechanisms involved in converting the surface reading to an idiomatic reading that is applicable to a general context. The conversion could be a simple step of metaphorical extension or it could require additional steps of linguistic modification. Admittedly, the conversion may appear complex and sometimes even convoluting; it is, nonetheless, a necessary procedure to follow so as to understand how the message pointer is connected to the message carrier. In real life, however, *xiehouyu* expressions are memorized and used as idiomatic units. To those who are familiar with *xiehouyu*, the mention of the message-pointer is a sufficient cue to bring to mind the intended meaning of the expression; the answer phrase calls for no further analysis in order to appreciate its use in the general context. But to speakers less sophisticated with colloquialism, an explanation of the connection and conversion would be a useful guide for understanding the intricate workings at various levels.

As mentioned earlier, *xiehouyu* are very much like riddles: if you have heard of the riddle before, you know the answer immediately even

[15] For other examples, see Ma and Gao (1979), p. 44.

without fully comprehending its content; if not, you need to put all the clues together and play with them until the riddle is solved. And, just like riddles, the cues in the message-pointer of a *xiehouyu* expression are made up according to the answer in the message-carrier. In other words, it is the answer phrase that decides what kind of information is to be provided in the cue phrase. Thus, the making of *xiehouyu* expression reverses the direction of its decoding process: it goes from the message-carrier to the message-pointer.

The two major categories of *xiehouyu* that we have set up in the previous discussion are accordingly quite different in their compositional procedure. On the one hand, a speaker could be faced with a particular overwhelming situation and would want to describe his impression, reaction, or comment in more vivid and concrete terms. He could look back at his own experience in the past, fall back on his understanding of the cultural and folkloristic traditions, or stretch his imagination into the natural and supernatural worlds, and come up with a situational parallel or a metaphorical comparison which would best serve this purpose. This parallel or metaphor, therefore, becomes a message-pointer and the comment, whether descriptive or evaluative in nature, is the message itself. Perhaps, because of the aptness or the humor of the comparison, the entire expression, including both the message-pointer and the message-carrier, is adopted by other speakers in the community and soon becomes part of the colloquial repertoire. When this is the case, the immediate context in which the expression was originally composed is no longer known or relevant; the parallel or the metaphor now becomes its immediate context, and the message phrase is applicable to this new immediate context as well as to other general contexts. I personally witnessed the creation of such a *xiehouyu* expression on television in Hong Kong. A game show host, stunned by an obviously absurd answer from one of the contestants, wanted to make a funny but teasing comment to show his disapproval. He wanted to say *gaamngáanglàih* (try by force), a common colloquial expression which would best characterize the poor attempt but which might sound a bit too harsh or inappropriate for a popular family show. At the spur of the moment, he ingeniously came up with the following comparison, a make-up comical anecdote that instantly brought bursting laughter and resounding applause from the audience including the poor contestant himself.

(40)　沈殿霞試童裝——監硬嚟
　　　　Sám Dihnhàh si tùhngjōng—Gaamngáanglàih.
　　　　Sam Dihnhah trying on the children's wear—Done by force.

沈殿霞 Sam Dihnhah (Lydia Sum) was a famous television comedienne who weighed more than two hundred pounds. What could be more hilarious than imagining a heavy-set funny lady trying her very best to put on petite clothings that wouldn't even fit her chubby limbs? The analogy drew an uprorious parallel that everyone could easily and instantly relate to. And, since that evening, the comic expression has become a popular *xiehouyu* saying that can be freely applied to any situation where there is a desperate attempt to do something or to argue an issue by force.

Whether the *xiehouyu* in (40) was used in its original context on television, or when it relates to the actress trying on clothes as described in the immediate context, or when it is applied to any other related contexts in real life, the association between the message phrase and the cue phrase is always direct and immediate; it requires no linguistic modification to generate a new reading from the cue phrase. This direct derivation, as we have observed above, is an essential characteristic of all *xiehouyu* expressions of Category A.

As for expressions in Category B, the compositional procedure is somewhat different. Instead of merely having a general idea for a message in mind, the speaker could have the exact wording of the entire message (or part of it) already worked out, and is ready to deliver it in a modified form with some additional touch-ups here and there to make it sound more interesting or intriguing. He could pun on the sounds, play with the multiple meanings of the same word, break up a compound or an idiom and toy with the literal meaning of each component, or he could re-adjust the grammatical relationship or positioning among the various elements in the message phrase. Any or all of these modifications are then captured and stated in a cue phrase, now serving as the message-pointer. Thus, the relationship between the cue(s) and the intended reading is indirect. The cue phrase only provides leads to the modified version of the message phrase, and the modified version will need to go through a second stage of derivation to arrive at the correct reading. To take the analogy of riddles one step further, we can describe *xiehouyu* expressions of Category B as conundrums which involve a pun or a similar play on words, and those of Category A as riddles that operate on analogies and comparisons.

The following are a few pairs of examples to demonstrate the distinction between the two categories in clear terms.

(41) 阿婆賴尿 ——— 常慣
A-pòh laaih niuh—Sèuhng gwaan.
An old lady involuntarily discharging urine—Often is the case.

(42) 阿跛上樹 ——— 常躓 → 常慣
A-bāi séuhng syuh—Sèuhng gwaan → Sèuhng gwaan.
The crippled climbing up the tree—Often tumbles and falls → Often is the case.

In (41), 常慣 *sèuhnggwaan* is a direct comment on the unfortunate incontinence problem of an elderly woman, whose involuntary control of urination is taken as a specific example of frequent and habitual happenings. The same message of "repeated occurrences, common phenomenon" is delivered in (42), however, through linguistic modification. 慣 *gwaan* (habitual) is homophonous with 躓 *gwaan* (tumble), and it is the meaning of the latter word that is rendered in a concrete image in the cue phrase. Therefore, (41) belongs to Category A and (42) to Category B.

(43) 落雨擔遮 ——— 顧前唔顧後
Lohk yúh dàam jē—Gu chìhn mhgu hauh.
Holding up an umbrella in the rain—Can't take care of both the front and the back.

(44) 落雨擔遮 ——— 死擋 → 死黨
Lohk yúh dàam jē—Séi dóng → Séi dóng.
Holding up an umbrella in the rain—Fending off the rain as hard as possible → Buddies.

Although both *xiehouyu* expressions share the same cue phrase, they are quite different in operation. (43) is a case of Category A, a parallel of any awkward attempts to take care of things all at the same time; (44), on the other hand, plays on the identical pronunciation between 擋 *dóng* (to fend off) and 黨 *dóng* (a gang). It further re-adjusts the grammatical status of *séi* and *dóng* from a verbal phrase (Adverb-Verb) to a nominal expression (Adjective-Noun), "unswerving buddies." The distinction in the compositional procedure between the two categories is not only reflected in the steps taken to decipher the meanings of the *xiehouyu*; it also explains why certain expressions behave differently from others.

As described above, a *xiehouyu* expression consists of two parts: the message-pointer and the message-carrier, both of which, in most cases, appear in set phrases. Though some slight modification in form is allowed, like the addition of a functive word or a connector, the answer phrase usually remains the same with its basic constituents. There are, however, some expressions which tolerate greater variations or even complete change in the answer phrase. For example,

(45) <u>Message-pointer</u>
趕狗入窮巷
Gón gáu yahp kùhnghohng.
Driving a dog into a dead-end alley.

<u>Message carriers</u>
(a) 反咬一口
Fáan ngáauh yāt háu.
Snaps/attacks in return.
(b) 擰轉頭咬翻啖
Nihngjyuntàuh ngáauhfāan daahm.
It turns around and attacks.
(c) 臨死咬翻啖
Làhm séi ngáauhfāan daahm.
Attacks before it dies.

(45) is clearly a case of metaphorical comparison and falls under Category A. It is the message itself ("retaliation when hard-pressed" in this particular case) and not the wording itself that prompts the creation of the *xiehouyu* expression. Therefore, any phrase can serve as the answer as long as it adequately relates this message. Although one particular form may be preferable to others, they are all acceptable in speech and can be readily

understood. On the other hand, if it is a certain linguistic form in that message phrase that triggers off a pun in the making of a cue phrase, then the answer part, at least the keyword that has been employed in the verbal game, will remain unchanged. For illustration, compare the next example with (36) cited above.

(46) 火燒棺材——大碳 → 大嘆
Fó sìu gūnchòih—Daaih taan → Daaih taan.
Fire burning the coffin—A big charcoal → To enjoy as much as possible.

(36) 火燒旗杆——長碳 → 長嘆
Fó sìu kèihgōn—Chèuhng taan → Chèuhng taan.
Fire burning a banner-pole—A long charcoal → To enjoy for a long time.

While (36) stresses the length of time for enjoyment, (46) emphasizes a "grand" enjoyment, hence 大. 旗杆 and 棺材 are images carefully picked out to render the meanings of "long" and "grand" respectively. Thus, even though (46) and (36) are quite close in connotation, the answer phrases are not interchangeable.

Example (9) from Category B and example (10) from Category A form another pair of contrast.

(9) 剃頭佬教仔——有得刮就刮
Taitàuhlóu gaau jái—Yáuh dāk gwaat jauh gwaat.
A barber teaching his son—Take in whatever there is to be taken in.

(10) 光棍佬教仔——便宜莫貪
Gwōnggwanlóu gaau jái—Pìnyìh mohk tàam.
A swindler teaching his son—Don't covet small advantages.

A paraphrase of the message in (10), such as (10a) or (10b), will adequately take the place of a message phrase.

(10a) 千祈唔好貪心
Chìnkèih mhhóu tàamsàm.
Don't ever be greedy.

(10b) 千祈唔好見到便宜就攞
Chìnkèih mhhóu gindóu pìhnyìh jauh lóh.
Don't ever grab anything that seems profitable.

Changing the message phrase in (9) to (9b), which shares the same meaning of hair-cutting, will not work.

(9b) 有得剪就剪
Yáuh dāk jín jauh jín.
Cut whatever there is to be cut.

Since the *xiehouyu* expression plays on the double meanings of 刮 *gwaat*—"shave" and "take advantage," changing the keyword will make the entire saying inappropriate to apply to a general context. (9c), on the other hand, is acceptable since the keyword 刮 is retained.

(9c) 刮得幾多就幾多
Gwaat dāk géidò jauh géidò.
Scrape however much there is to be scraped.

Modification of the cue phrase is also possible as long as the relevant information contained remains unaffected. For example, (47) is a case of Category B and plays on the double meanings of 點 *dím* ("to light" and "to hint") and of 明 *mìhng* ("bright" and "enlightened").

(47) 牛皮燈籠──點極唔明
Ngàuhpèih dànglùhng—Dímgihk mhmìhng.
A lantern made with cowhide—However hard you try to light it, it is not bright → However hard you try to explain it, he doesn't get it.

It is interesting to note that the cue phrase has undergone some new expansion in Hong Kong and is now often rendered as:

(47a) 牛皮燈籠加黑漆
Ngàuhpèih dànglùhng gà hākchāt.
A lantern made with cowhide and smeared with black paint.

The inclusion of 黑漆 does not undercut the functions of either the "lantern" or the action of 點; in fact, the extra layer of paint provides an additional clue for 唔明.

Cases from Category A can exhibit even greater changes in their cue phrases. (48) and (49) could be considered variations of the same expression since they provide the same cue in different metaphors for the same message.

(48) 雞痾尿 ——— 少有
Gāi ngò niuh—Síu yáuh.
A chicken pees—How rare!

(49) 大蛇痾屎 ——— 少有
Daaih sèh ngò sí—Síu yáuh.
A big snake poos—How rare!

It was mentioned earlier that the message phrases in some *xiehouyu* expressions can be omitted in speech. In fact, it is possible that people do not have to recall or even to know the entire string so as to comprehend the underlying message as applied to a relevant context. Most of these cases are from Category A. Some examples are:

(50) 水過鴨背 ——— 冇晒
Séui gwo ngaapbui—móuh-saai.
Water running through the back of a duck—Nothing left, all gone.

(51) 問師姑攞梳 ——— 實冇
Mahn sīgū lóh sō—Saht móuh.
Asking a buddhist nun for a comb—There isn't any for sure.

(52) 豬籠跌落水 ——— 四圍咁入
Jyūlùhng ditlohk séui—Seiwàih gám yahp.
A bamboo cage for pigs falling into the water—Coming in from all sides ("water" referring to money).

The reason for possible omission of the answer phrases is quite obvious. When the expression is a case of analogy or metaphor, there is a close parallel between the immediate context and the general context. And, because of that parallel, the message in the second half becomes obvious and hence superfluous. Example (53) is a case where the answer phrase is gradually disappearing from use among younger speakers in Hong Kong.

(53) 竹織鴨 ——— 冇心肝
Jūkjīkngáap—Móuh sāmgōn.
A bamboo-made duck—No heart; ungrateful.

To them, 竹織鴨 is now merely a picturesque expression that belongs to a rich repertoire of metaphorical compounds in the Cantonese language; it bears no apparent link to the slightly accusatory remark about someone being heartless.

Category B, on the other hand, does not seem to witness a gradual tendency in deleting the second half of a *xiehouyu* in conversation. One apparent exception is:

(54) 電燈膽 —— 唔通氣
Dihndāngdáam—Mhtùnghei.
A light bulb—Not letting air in → not being considerate.

While 通氣 *tùnghei* literally means "air going through," 唔通氣 is an idiomatic expression with a specific connotation of "being inconsiderate." It is ofter used to refer to an intruder whose presence is not welcomed at a lovers' rendezvous. The *xiehouyu* expression takes the literal meaning of the phrase and repackage it with an image of a vacuumized light bulb in the cue, an extension from the literal "not letting air in" to the idiomatic reference to someone who spoils the fun. The intricate semantic relationship between the cue and the message, however, has undergone a radical change in recent years. Very few people are aware anymore of the original mechanism involved in the creative process; and, instead, they attribute the use of 電燈膽 as a cue for "inconsideration" to the fact that lovers prefer to be in the dark when they get together, an intimate ambience which could be abruptly disrupted when a light bulb is turned on. As it sheds it plays on words, the *xiehouyu* expression offers a metaphorical comparison, a comparison that is so visual and direct that it also sheds its second half of the string, leaving 電燈膽 now as an independent metaphorical compound, often used alone in speech as in (54a).

(54a) 人地兩個想疏扶一下，你無謂去做電燈膽呀。
Yàhndeih léuhnggo séung sòfùh yātháh, néih móuhwaih heui jouh dihndāngdáam a.
The two of them want to have a good time together. Why be a ...

4. Other Issues

The *xiehouyu* represent a form of language art, crude but vivid and humorous. They are strongly characterized by a local color with images and metaphors drawn primarily from the cultural tradition and the social context in which the speakers live. The linguistic features are often peculiar to that dialect alone. But, as social activities develop and linguistic habits change in time, many new expressions are created, and old ones fall out of use when the verbal twists involved have become too subtle or the metaphorical comparison too vague for younger speakers to comprehend. A large number of the Cantonese *xiehouyu* expressions collected for this study originated in Canton before the 1940s. Very often little is now known about the stories to which these expressions alluded decades ago. For example, the following expressions are simply old sayings that young people in Hong Kong today have learned and remember as set phrases; to them, the stories in the immediate context or the figures in the cue-phrase are of no particular concern or relevance to the way they cite them in conversation.

(55) 亞蘭嫁亞瑞──累鬥累
A-Làahn ga A-Suih—Leuih dau leuih.
A-Laahn marrying A-Suih—Giving troubles to each other.

(56) 西南二伯父──教壞後生仔
Sàinàahm yihbaakfuh—Gaauwaaih hauhsàangjái.
The old man in the southwest—Leading the youths astray.

(57) 陸雲廷睇相──唔衰攞嚟衰
Luhk Wahntìhng tái seung—Mhsèui lóhlàih sèui.
Luhk Wahntihng going in for a physiognomy reading—Incurring problems otherwise not called for.

Some older expressions make references to various specific localities in the City of Canton; since the names are virtually unheard of in Hong Kong, the expressions have become obsolete. (58) is an example in which a temple in Canton is mentioned.

(58) 三元宮土地──錫身 → 惜身
Sàamyùhngūng tóuhdéi—Seksān → Sek sān.
The idol of the local god in the Saamyuhn Temple—Statue made of tin → Care for oneself dearly.

Examples (59) to (61) demonstrate an interesting change in the process of updating *xiehouyu* for current use in the speech community.

(59) 鹽倉土地 —— 鹹濕伯父
Yìhmchōng tóuhdéi—Hàahmsāp baakfú.
A local god of the salt despository—Salty and wet old man → A dirty old man.

鹹濕 *haahmsāp* is a Cantonese word for "lustful" and "lascivious." The compound is made up of two constituants, each of which is literally a word of what one physically senses: *hàahm* (salty) and *sāp* (wet). The cue phrase plays with these literal readings as it introduces "the salt depository" as a venue, for sure, salty and possibly wet, and a statue of "a local god," an image of an elderly man. The juxtaposition cleverly pronounces the notion of an old lecher in vernacular terms. Salt depositories, however, are no longer easily found in Hong Kong, and the local gods, though still worshipped on special festival days, have long lost the popularity that they once enjoyed. As the cue phrase may now appears a bit outdated in its use of images, the message word 鹹濕 is still a prevalent term in the colloquial idiom. A new cue phrase has been coined.

(60) 廚房階磚 ——— 鹹濕
Chyùhfóng gāijyūn—Hàahmsāp.
Kitchen floor tiles—Salty and wet → Lascivious.

Because of heavy cooking in a Chinese kitchen, "salty" and "wet" are features one can easily associate with the tiles on its floor, hence an updated replacement for an outdated association. The new version, however, does not stop the witty mind from coming up with still another *xiehouyu*, this time featuring an even more familiar object in a similar mode of logical association.

(61) 豉油樽枳 —— 鹹濕
Sihyàuh jēunjāt—Hàahmsāp.
The cork of a soy sauce bottle—Salty and wet.

(61) has received very wide use in Hong Kong. One might have never set foot in a kitchen, but one surely knows what a cork of a soy sauce bottle is like. The sauce rules the Chinese culinary world as the most important flavoring agent, and its presence, usually in a small bottle, is ubiquitous on all tables in a Chinese restaurant.

Produced all between the early and the late 20th century, examples (59) to (61) provide a rare set of examples that documents the history of the past and present of the *xiehouyu*, attesting to the sociological influence on its process to create and revise.

While our data are exclusively examples of Cantonese, there are quite a few cases that are distinctively of the Hong Kong origin, both in form and in meaning.

A cosmopolitan city which has prospered during the past few decades, Hong Kong has developed its own culture and language, which Cantonese speakers from other parts of the world may have difficulty in appreciating and getting used to. The rule of the British government which requires the learning of English as the major form of official language, the social and business interactions with peoples from all parts of the world, the input of foreign goods which have become part of the daily necessities for the locals, the introduction of foreign customs and festivals which the locals observe and celebrate with enthusiasm, the mingling use of English words and expressions in spoken Cantonese or even in written Chinese—these all contribute to the uniqueness of the Hong Kong culture, a culture some tend to describe as hybrid in nature. Many of these "hybrid" features have, indeed, found their way to *xiehouyu* in Hong Kong.

For example, because of the mixed use of English and Chinese in speech, some *xiehouyu* expressions boldly introduce English words into the phrases and associate them with Chinese meanings, some in a ludicrous fashion, but always with a sense of humor. The following examples, though somewhat vulgar in use, are representative of this practice.

(62)　法國皇帝 —— 費闌事傾
　　　Faatgwok wòhngdai—Failánsih kìng.
　　　King of France—Won't waste (f**king) time talking about it.

The intended reading of the expression, *failansi king* is a close approximation in sound to "France king" in English, and the Chinese translation is given in the cue phrase. The syllable "France" is broken up, according to the structural principle in Chinese phonology, into three parts, with each part assigned a Cantonese sound and meaning. "King" also has its own Chinese rendition, with a Chinese reading.

France → 費 *fai* (waste) + 閪 *lán* (male organ) + 事 *sih* (thing)
King → 傾 *kìng*

費事 *faisih* is a colloquial expression for "why waste time/effort on, why bother." *Lan* is inserted, as previously noted, as an emphatic particle. The word "king" is almost identical in pronunciation with the Cantonese word *kìng* meaning "to talk." Thus, altogether, the new string *fai-lán-sih kìng* would be: "Why bother to talk about it?" or "Don't bother to talk about it!" Please note that it is the pidgin form "France King" and not "King of France" or "French King" that takes part in the word play.

An even more coarse expression, example (63) demonstrates a similar trick on sounds.

(63) 法國公爵 ——費閪事屌
    Faatgwok gūngjeuk—Failánsih díu.
    A French duke—Won't waste time on that.

The form *díu* in the answer phrase is a close transliteration of "duke"—phonotactically, a diphthong in Cantonese is never followed by a consonant. It is also a taboo word, and, like *lán*, its literal meaning of "coition" is lost in its colloquial use as an emphatic particle.

The next example is clearly a case of Category B since the cue is simply created on the basis of the sounds contained in the message phrase.

(64) 澳門風扇 ——麻閪煩
    Ngoumún fungsin—Màhgàufàahn.
    Electric fan from Macau—Damn nuisance.

As used in example (34), *gàu* is another member of the taboo words that often appear in compounds for extra emotive and emphatic effect. 麻煩 *màhfàahn* is a compound word, meaning "troublesome, nuisance." Since the pronunciation of the combination 麻閪煩 *màhgàufàahn* is very much like that of "Macau fan," the Chinese translation is used as a clue in the first phrase. Macau, by the way, does manufacture electric fans.

The next example is an unusual one in the sense that it is not so much a switch between Chinese and English as a play on the English words themselves. The cue 賣魚佬 *maaihyùhlóu* in (65) is based on the reading of the message phrase as "sell fish" rather than "selfish."

(65)　賣魚佬──Selfish（自私）
　　　Maaihyùhlóu—Selfish.
　　　Fishmonger—Selfish ← Sell fish.

Of all the nationalities well-represented in Hong Kong, only Indians and Pakistanis, for some reasons, figure in Cantonese *xiehouyu* expressions. For decades, there has been a good population of South Asian families in Hong Kong. Working in different professions including government, businesses, and education, they are an important, albeit less well-known, part of this metropolitan community. Perhaps a misconception on the part of the Chinese people in Hong Kong, most Indians and Pakistanis do not seem to enjoy the kind of social esteem they deserve in general. Yet, their unusual dark features and bearded faces, their exotic costumes such as saris and turbans, and their esoteric religious practice in mosques, make them all the more mysterious and beguiling at the same time. The following expressions, to a certain extent, reflect some of these personal impressions.

(66)　摩囉叉拜神──睇天
　　　Mōlōchā baai sàhn—Tái tīn.
　　　Indians worshipping god—Looking into the skies → Play by ear.

摩囉叉 is a general term referring to both Indians and Pakistanis.

(67)　摩囉叉騎膊馬──叉上叉 → 差上差
　　　Mōlōchā kèh bokmáh—Chā seuhng chā → Chā seuhng chā.
　　　One Indian carrying another pickaback—Indian on Indian → Worse than bad.

The word 叉 *chā* is an abbreviated form for 摩囉叉, and the word is homophonous with 差 *chā* meaning "bad."

(68)　摩囉叉屙尿──烏séusèuh
　　　Mōlōchā ngò niuh—Wūséusèuh.
　　　When an Indian pees—Dark and gurgling → muddleheaded.

Wūséusèuh is a colloquial compound describing the person being muddleheaded and confused. Taken literally, 烏 *wu* means "dark in color," a reference to 摩囉叉; and *seuseuh*, an onomatopoeic word for the sound of water flowing, thus a reference to 屙尿 *ngò niuh* (to urinate).

Some *xiehouyu* expressions incorporate foreign names and objects in their workings, with great entertaining effects. A most notable example is the following that features the famous American movie star, Elizabeth Taylor:

(69) 伊莉沙白泰萊抱孫 —— 肉嬤夾肉孫 → 肉麻夾肉酸
Yīleihsābaahk taailòih póuh syūn—Yuhkmàh gaap yuhksyùn.
Elizabeth Taylor holding her grandson—The fat grandma holding her fat grandson tightly → Disgusting and repulsive.

肉麻 *yuhkmàh*, a colloquial compound meaning "disgusting," is made up of two phonetic elements, i.e., *yuhk* and *mah*, which could be read separately as 肉 *yuhk* (flesh, hence "fleshy, fat") and 嬤 *mah* in a different character, meaning "grandmother." Similarly, the compound 肉酸 *yuhksyùn* (repulsive) is homophonous with the combination of 肉 *yuhk* (flesh) and 孫 *syūn*, also in a different character, meaning "grandson."[16] Through mechanical transformation, two nominal compounds referring to a world-famous actress and her big, fat baby have come to stand for two descriptive words for qualities not necessarily desirable. Notice that 夾 *gaap* is quite often used as a connector "and" in *xiehouyu* expressions, such as example (19), but only in (69) do we find its literal meaning of "clutch, hold tightly" kept in the cue: a picture of a happy, chubby Liz cuddling her chubby baby grandson.

Example (70) has Christmas as its setting:

(70) 兩仔爺報佳音 —— 代代平安 → 袋袋平安
Léuhng jái-yèh bou gāaiyām—Doihdoih pìhngngòn.
Father and son singing carols on a Christmas Eve—Both generations singing the song of peace → (Money) in the pocket, safe and sound.

The intended message is an idiomatic expression 袋袋平安 (in the pocket, safe and sound), which is taken apart in the surface answer and given a different wording. 袋袋 *doihdoih* (pocket and pocket), is re-casted as 代代 *doihdoih*, a homophonous compound meaning "generation and generation,"

---

[16] Cantonese *xiehouyu* expressions do not reflect the tonal distinction between high-level and high-falling. Some speakers, however, maintain a difference in tone between 孫 *syūn* and 酸 *syùn*, as marked in this article.

hence the choice of 兩仔爺 *léuhng jáiyèh* (father and son) as a clue to 代代 (two generations). On the other hand, 平安夜 *pihngonyeh* (peaceful night) is the Chinese title of "Silent Night," a Christmas carol that the father and son team sets out to sing. The scene is aptly named 代代平安 *doihdoih pìhngngòn*. However, after a homophonous transfer, the festive title becomes 袋袋平安 *doihdoih pìhngngòn*, a colloquial phrase to ensure that "money has been safely pocketed." For comparison, the next example is an expression that also uses the "father and son" image to highlight another religious practice, a Chinese custom of paying homage to the ancestral deceased.

(71) 兩仔爺拜山 —— 一族都齊
Léuhng jái-yèh baai sāan—Yātjuhk dōu chàih.
The father and the son sweeping their ancestral grave—The entire clan is here → All present.

Foreign objects and imported goods also find their presence in the repertoire of Cantonese *xiehouyu*. We have already seen how the extra course of fish in a French meal contributes to the savor of the expression in (34). The following are a few more examples to illustrate such a mixture in the local word game.

(72) 日本郵船 —— 遲早完
Yahtbún yàuhsyùhn—Chìhjóu yùhn.
A Japanese steamer—Will be over sooner or later.

The expression plays on 完 *yuhn* (to finish), which is identical in pronunciation with 丸 *yuhn*, a character that the Japanese often use, pronounced as *maru*, to name their ships. Aside from this sound borrowing, there is no other association between 遲早 *chihjou* (sooner or later) with Japanese steamers.

(73) 冇柄士巴拿 —— 得把牙
Móuhbeng sihbālá—Dāk bá ngàh.
A spanner without handle—Teeth only → Bragging and blustering.

牙 *ngàh* is used as a short form for 牙刷刷 *ngàhchaatchaat*, a colloquial expression meaning "bragging and swaggering." Please note that the transliteration of "spanner" as *sihbāla* renders the English nasal *n-* with a lateral *l-*. The substitution reflects a phonological change that merges *n-*

with /- in Cantonese. a change that is quite common among Hong Kong speakers especially of the younger generation.

 (74) 啞仔飲沙示
   Ngájái yám sāsí.
   The mute drinking Sarsaparilla.

This is an interesting example with two different answer phrases. Sarsaparilla is a beverage similar to root-beer and was quite popular in Hong Kong in the late 1960s. The carbonated drink produces a lot of gas in the stomach, but a mute person cannot describe such a sensation in words. Thus, the first answer phrase of the expression is:

 (74a) 有氣講唔出
   Yáuh hei góngmhchēut.
   There is gas, but not able to tell.

氣 is also a word with a derived meaning of "anger." Thus, the intended reading is "unable to describe or let out one's anger." On the other hand, even a mute person can utter the sound *geuh* when the accumulated air is let out. *Geuh*, written as 噱, has also an extended meaning of "a sense of relief or satisfaction." Thus, the second answer phrase of the expression is again a case of double entendre.

 (74b) 噱晒
   Gèuhsaai.
   A complete relief of gas → Fully contented.

 (75) 新澤西 ── 食水深
   Sànjaaksāi—Sihk séui sàm.
   New Jersey—Taking in / displacing large volume of water.

New Jersey is an American submarine that was unable to come into the harbor of Hong Kong because of water displacement problems. As explained earlier, 水 is another form used for "money." Thus, 食水深 is an idiomatic saying describing "a deal that requires huge investment" or "a person who draws great profits from deals." In some derogatory cases, it could even be used to describe a woman with demanding sexual needs.

(76) 日本鬧鐘 —— 大聲夾冇準
Yahtbún naauhjūng—Daaihsēng gaap móuhjéun.
Japanese alarm clock—Loud but not accurate.

In the early 1960s, while the Japanese were trying to sell their products to the Hong Kong market, local customers had little faith in what they had to offer—"pretty but not always reliable" was the general feedback. The answer phrase in this *xiehouyu*, however, is making a critical remark of an entirely different nature; by metaphorical extension, it describes a person who talks loud but without substance.

(77) 日本膏藥 —— 脫苦海
Yahtbūún gōyeuhk—Tyutfúhói.
Japanese medical plasters—Tokuhon.

脫苦海 is the trade name of a medical plaster for fast pain relief produced by Suziki Nippondo Medical Company in Japan. The literal meaning of the name 脫苦海, "released from the sea of pain," is a powerful catch phrase, advertising its fast healing effects. In the *xiehouyu* expression, however, it is the literal reading that is restored in the intended message: "suffering—all over!" What a relief!

Commercial advertisements play quite an important role in producing some of the best *xiehouyu* expressions in Cantonese. Good advertisements, written in concise, vivid, and often witty language, attract instant attention and welcomed approvals from thousands of customers through all forms of media. People like what they hear and may in turn use them, though perhaps unwittingly in the beginning, as active set phrases in their speech and apply them to other contexts by extension. They may later incorporate them into *xiehouyu* expressions by simply providing the brand names of the commodities as the cues. One such case is (78).

(78) 樂聲牌電唱機 —— 聲音兩邊走
Lohksìngpàaih dihncheunggēi—Sīngyām léuhngbin jáu.
National stereo record player—Sound travelling from side to side.

The answer phrase, originally a National advertisement statement, is now used to ridicule a busy person or a busybody who hurries from one place to another.

The next expression also originated from a commercial advertisment for a merchandise that has now long been discontinued in the market.

(79)　梁新記牙刷 —— 一毛不拔
　　　Lèuhnsàngēi ngàhchaat—Yātmòuh bāt baht.
　　　Leuhngsangei toothbrush—Not even a hair/bristle can be pulled out.

A quotation from the classics 一毛不拔 now functions as an idiomatic expression criticizing an extremely selfish person who is unwilling to give up even one hair for the good of the world. More specifically, it refers to an act of parsimony. Taken literally, however, the phrase about "inability to pluck out even a hair" serves as a most appropriate slogan for selling toothbrushes, an expression that the manufacturer, the Leuhngsangei Company, readily adopted in its advertisements. The locals evidently loved the ad, and played with it. They reversed the pun and used the name of the manufacturer as the cue for the idiomatic reading.

A most recent *xiehouyu* expression that has come to use since 1980 is (80).

(80)　南紅賣洗衣粉 —— 乜都冇晒
　　　Nàahm Hùhng maaih sáiyīfán—Māt dōu móuhsaai.
　　　Naahm Hung selling detergent—Everything is gone.

南紅, a popular television actress, did a commercial for a detergent, in which she emphatically claimed that all stains, whether made by soy sauce or ketchup, would all be gone after a wash with the cleansing powder. Her final words in the ad, which she delivered with conviction, was 乜都冇晒 *māt dōu móuhsaai* (everything is gone). It was either her charm or the charm of the phrase that soon made these four simple words a popular household expression. And, a *xiehouyu* saying has been created featuring her in the cue, but to everyone's pleasant surprise, it gives a rather twisted and discouraging reading: "everything all gone" with the connotation of "to have lost everything."

5. Conclusion

The above discussion of the social factors that account for making, revising, and perhaps even dismissing certain *xiehouyu* expressions in Hong Kong provides us with but a glimpse of the great complexities involved in a sociolinguistic investigation of what we use to communicate and express our thoughts. The use of *xiehouyu*, or for that matter any particular style of speech, is a social phenomenon characterized essentially by its function in a communicative context. Because of their witty use of words and images, *xiehouyu* lend both color and vigor to the language and, as a result, enhance and enliven exchange of ideas. As illustrated in some of the above examples, a *xiehouyu* expression is often used as a comment on something we bring up in a conversation. It may be a brief statement, but it is an incredibly effective way to render in vivid and concrete terms what a speaker may have already formed, perhaps only vaguely, in his mind. At the same time, as the expression is rich in connotations, it may allow the other party to draw various associations as he stretches his imagination. The words could be emotionally bold and expressive, but as they are phrased in the form of a quotation, the expression conveniently removes any feelings of obtrusiveness from an otherwise abrupt statement. Indeed, *xiehouyu* function much like classical quotations in an elevated style of speech.

Classical quotations and *xiehouyu* expressions do not often mix in the same speech, since they belong to different stylistic registers. As the social contexts change and the relationships among speakers vary, the speech style of the same speaker shifts from one register to another. Despite their communicative effectiveness, *xiehouyu* are generally not considered a form of prestige language, and are, thus, seldom used in formal occasions. *Xiehouyu* expressions are more often used in the marketplace than in a church, more in a narrative description than in a philosophical discussion, more among close friends than with strangers. They thrive in chit-chats, gossips, and curses. The vulgar and ribald ones are used, as expected, less by females than males. It should be noted, however, that people of the younger generation in Hong Kong are less familar with *xiehouyu* than their parents and grandparents. Teenagers who study in Anglicized schools are less exposed to, and thus less conversant in, the use of *xiehouyu* than members of the same age group who work, say, in factories. It requires, in short, an in-depth and systematic examination of the use of *xiehouyu* in Hong Kong in order to identify all the relevant social factors and evaluate their correlations with the frequency and distribution in use, a task admittedly not included in this project. This study has restricted itself to an analysis of the *xiehouyu* expressions themselves, examining their operations from a linguistic perspective. The data, primarily drawn from Cantonese as spoken in Hotog Kong, are given in the appendix for reference.

References

Chao, Yuen Ren. 1968. *A Grammar of Spoken Chinese*. Berkeley, CA: University of California Press.

Chen Wangdao 陳望道. 1955. *Xiucixue fafan* 修辭學發凡. Shanghai: Xinwenyi chubanshe 新文藝出版社.

Cheng Daming 程達明, and Li Yunhan 黎運漢. 1963. "Shilun xiehouyu" 試論歇後語. *Zhongshan daxue xuebao* 中山大學學報, 1.2: 28–31.

Cheung Hung-nin Samuel 張洪年. 1972. *Xianggang Yueyu yufa de yanjiu* 香港粵語語法的研究 (Studies on Cantonese grammar as spoken in Hong Kong). Hong Kong: The Chinese University of Hong Kong.

He Mingyan 何明延. 1957. *Tan xiehouyu* 談歇後語. Shanghai: Xinzhishi chubanshe 新知識出版社.

Kono, Michikazu 河野通一. 1925. *Zhina xienüeyu yanjiu* 支那諧謔語研究. Beijing: Yanchenshe 燕塵社.

Kosaka, Jun'ichi 香坂順一. 1974. *Guangdongyu de yanjiu* 廣東語の研究. Taiwan: Guting shuwu 古亭書屋. Reprinted.

Kroll, J. L. 1966. "A Tentative Classification and Description of the Structure of Peking Common Sayings (*hsieh-hou-yu*)." *Journal of American Oriental Society*, 68: 267–273.

Li Mengbei 李孟北. 1980. *Yanyu xiehouyu qianzhu* 諺語歇後語淺注. Yunnan chubanshe 雲南出版社.

Li Shoupeng 李壽彭. 1936. *Xieyouyu lunji* 歇後語論集. Beiping: Jingshan shushe 景山書社.

Ma Guofan 馬國凡, and Gao Gedong 高歌東. 1979. *Xiehouyu* 歇後語. Neimenggu renmin chubanshe 內蒙古人民出版社.

Mao Dun 茅盾. 1959. "Guanyu xiehouyu" 關於歇後語. In *Guchui ji* 鼓吹集, pp. 71–76. Beijing: Zuojia chubanshe 作家出版社.

Moshi Xiangzhu 墨室香主. 1980. "Yueyu jigu" 粵語稽古, *Oriental Daily* 東方日報.

Ning Ju 寧榘. 1980. *Yanyu, geyan, xiehouyu* 諺語、格言、歇後語. Hubei renmin chubanshe 湖北人民出版社.

Qiao Yannong 喬硯農. 1966. *Guangzhou kouyuci de yanjiu* 廣州話口語詞的研究. Hong Kong: Huaqiao yuwen chubanshe 華僑語文出版社.

Tan Daxian 譚達先. 1980. "Xiehouyu—Zhongguo minjian wenxue de zhubao" 歇後語——中國民間文學的珠寶. *Wide Angle* 廣角鏡, 92 (May 1980): 70–75.

Tori, Hishayasu 鳥居久靖. 1970. "Mingdai xiehouyu de xingge" 明代歇後語の性格. *Zhongwen yanjiu* 中文研究, 11: 1–7. Japan: Tianli daxue Zhongguo xueke yanjiushi 天理大學中國學科研究室.

Wan Er 莞爾. 1969–1970. "Guangdong suyu jie" 廣東俗語解. *Hong Kong Commercial Daily* 香港商報.

Wang Qin 王勤. 1980. *Yanyu xiehouyu gailun* 諺語歇後語概論. Hunan renmin chubanshe 湖南人民出版社.

Wu Qingshi 鄔慶時. 1922. *Panyu yinyu* 番禺隱語.

Yang Guangzhong 楊光中. 1978. *Miaoyan miaoyu* 妙言妙語. Taiwan: Linbai chubanshe 林白出版社.

Yu Fei 于飛. 1929. "Guanyu xiehouyu yu geyao de yanjiu" 關於歇後語與歌謠的研究. *Minsu zhoukan* 民俗週刊, 84. Guangzhou: Zhongshan daxue yuyan lishixue yanjiusuo 中山大學語言歷史學研究所.

Zhang Shoukang 張壽康. 1954. "Xiehouyu shibushi wenxue yuyan?" 歇後語是不是文學語言？. *Zhongguo yuwen* 中國語文 (May 1954): 8–9.

Zhao Rongguang 趙榮光. 1972. *Xiandai yueyu* 現代粵語. Hong Kong: Yunhua yuwen xueyuan 雲華語文學苑.

Zhu Boshi 朱伯石. 1954. "Xiehouyu shi yuyan youxi ma?" 歇後語是語言遊戲嗎？. *Zhongguo yuwen* 中國語文 (May 1954): 7.

This article originally appeared in *Tsing Hua Journal of Chinese Studies* 清華學報, 14.1–2 (1982): 51–103.

Appendix: Common Cantonese *Xiehouyu* Expressions Used in Hong Kong

All compound words are spelled with a hyphen between syllables. The romanization follows that of the Yale system, with tone marks placed on top of the main vowels, e.g., *ā* for level, *á* for rising, and *à* for falling. Tones of the low register are marked with an *h* after the vowels. The negative marker 唔 is a syllabic [m], with a low-falling tone, and is here simply marked as *mh*.

1. 亞崩吹簫 ——— 嘥聲壞氣
   A-bāng chèui sīu—Sàai sēng waaih hei
2. 亞崩叫狗 ——— 越叫越走
   A-bāng giu gáu—Yuht giu yuht jáu
3. 亞崩咬狗虱 ——— 唔死有排慌
   A-bāng ngáauh gáu sāt—Mh-séi yáuh pàaih fòng
3a. 亞崩咬狗虱 ——— 咬嚟咬去咬唔到
   A-bāng ngáauh gáu-sāt—Ngáauh làih ngáauh-heui ngáauh-mh-dóu
4. 亞崩劏羊 ——— 咩都冇得咩
   A-bāng tòng yèuhng—Miē dòu móuh dāk miē
5. 亞崩養狗 ——— 轉性
   A-bāng yéung gáu—Jyún sing
6. 亞超著褲 ——— 焗住
   A-chīu jeuk fu—Guhk-jyuh
7. 亞單睇榜 ——— 一眼睇晒
   A-dān tái bóng—Yāt ngáahn tái saai
8. 亞蘭嫁亞瑞 ——— 累鬥累
   A-Làahn ga A-Seuih—Leuih dau leuih
9. 亞蘭賣豬 ——— 一千唔賣賣八百
   A-Làahn maaih jyū—Yāt-chìn mh-maaih maaih baat-baak
10. 亞聾送殯 ——— 唔聽你枝死人笛
    A-lùhng sung ban—Mh-tèng néih jì séi-yàhn dék
11. 亞跛上樹 ——— 常慣(← 常躓)
    A-bāi séuhng syuh—Sèuhng gwaan
12. 亞婆拉尿 ——— 常慣
    A-pòh laaih niuh—Sèuhng gwaan

13. 亞陀賣蝦米 —— 人唔掂貨都唔掂
    A-tó maaih hā-mái—Yàhn mh-dihm fo dōu mh-dihm
14. 亞陀命 —— 死都唔得掂
    A-tó mehng—Séi dōu mh-dāk-dihm
15. 亞陀行路 —— 中中哋（中 ← 躦）
    A-tó hàahng louh—Jùng-jùng-déi
16. 白鼻哥考試 —— 陪人
    Baahk-beih-gō háau-sí—Pùih-yàhn
17. 白鼻哥抽褲 —— 好嘢，好嘢
    Baahk-beih-gō yàu fu—Hóu-yéh, hóu-yéh
18. 白撞雨 —— 讚壞人（讚 ← 潀）
    Baahk-johng-yúh—Jaan-waaih yàhn
19. 白蟮上沙灘 —— 唔死一身潺
    Baahk-síhn séuhng sā-tāan—Mh-séi yāt-sàn sàahn
20. 扮豬食老虎 —— 詐傻扮懵
    Baahn jyū sihk lóu-fú—Ja sòh baahn múng
22. 班鳩唔食米 —— 死咕咕
    Bāan-gāu mh-sihk máih—Séi-gùh-gùh
22. 八十歲番頭嫁 —— 攞路行（路 ← 佬）
    Baat-sahp-seui fàan-tàuh ga—Lóh láu hàahng
23. 八仙過海 —— 各顯神通
    Baat sīn gwo hói—Gok hín sàhn-tung
24. 崩牙成賣藥 —— 一口齊晒
    Bāng-ngàh Síng maaih-yeuhk—Yāt-háu chàih-saai
25. 玻璃甲萬 —— 有得睇冇得使
    Bō-lēi gaap-maahn—Yáuh dāk tái, móuh dāk sái
26. 玻璃棺材 —— 睇通晒
    Bō-lēi gūn-chòih—Tái-tùng-saai
27. 波羅雞 —— 靠黐
    Bō-lòh gāi—Kaau chī
28. 煲冇米粥 —— 水汪汪
    Bòu móuh máih jūk—Séui-wòng-wòng
29. 半夜食黃瓜 —— 貪口爽
    Bun-yeh sihk wòhng-gwā—Tāam háu-sóng
30. 半夜食黃瓜 —— 唔知頭共尾
    Bun-yeh sihk wòhng-gwā—Mh-jì tàuh gohng méih
31. 叉燒包掟狗 —— 有去無回
    Chā-sīu-bāau deng gáu—Yáuh heui móuh wùih

32. 茶瓜送飯——好人有限
    Chàh-gwā sung faahn—Hóu-yàhn yáuh haahn
33. 賊過興兵——無濟於事
    Chaahk gwo hìng bīng—Móuh jai yù sih
34. 杉木靈牌——唔做得主
    Chaam-muhk lìhng-pàaih—Mh-jouh-dāk jyú
35. 蠶蟲師爺——自困自
    Chàahm-chúng sī-yèh—Jih kwan jih
36. 趁墟買魚尾——一定要搭咀
    Chan-hui máaih yùh-méi—Yāt-dihng yiu daap jéui
37. 秋後扇——冇人吼
    Chāu hauh sin—Móuh yàhn hàu
38. 牆頭草——隨風倒
    Chèuhng-tàuh chóu—Chùih fūng dóu
39. 出爐鐵——非打不可
    Chēut-lòuh tit—Fēi dá bāt hó
39a. 出爐鐵——聽打
    Chēut-lòuh tit—Ting dá
40. 匙羹都揮唔起——削到極
    Chìh-gàng dōu bāt-mh-héi—Seuk dou gihk
41. 青磚沙梨——咬唔入（重蝕啖口水）
    Chìng-jyūn sā-léi—Ngáauh-mh-yahp (juhng siht daahm háu-séui)
42. 青山古寺——煙都冇陣
    Chìng-sāan gú-jí—Yīn dōu móuh jahn
43. 潮州佬煲粥——呢鑊杰
    Chìuh-jàu-lóu bòu jūk—Nī wohk giht
44. 潮州音樂——自己顧自己
    Chìuh-jàu yàm-ngohk—Gih-gī guh gih-gī
45. 床板跳上蓆——相差有限
    Chòhng-báan tiu-séuhng jek—Sèung chà yáuh haahn
46. 床下底破柴——（包）撞扳
    Chòhng-hah-dái po chàaih—(Bàau) johng-báan
47. 床下底踢毽——大家咁高
    Chòhng-hah-dái tek yín—Daaih-gā gam gòu
47a. 床下底踢毽——一樣高低
    Chòhng-hah-dái tek yín—Yāt-yeuhng gòu dài
48. 床下底放紙鷂——高極有限
    Chòhng-hah-dái fong jí-yíu—Gòu gihk yáuh haahn

49. 廚房楷磚 —— 鹹濕
    Chyùh-fóng gāai-jyūn—Hàahm-sāp
50. 打齋鶴 —— 渡人昇仙
    Dá-jàai hók—Douh yàhn sìng sīn
51. 大花面叫母親 —— 無錢 (← 母親)
    Daaih-fā-mín giu móuh-chàn—Mòuh-chìhn
52. 大花面抹眼淚 —— 離行離列
    Daaih-fā-mín mut ngáahn-leuih—Lèih-hòhng-lèih-laaht
53. 大光燈 —— 噓噓聲
    Daaih-gwōng-dāng—Hèuh-héu-sēng
54. 大良亞斗官 —— 敗家仔
    Daaih-lèuhng a-dáu-gūn—Baaih-gā-jái
55. 大碌墨打鑼 —— 烏噹噹
    Daaih-lūk-mahk dá lòh—Wū-dēung-dēung
56. 大碌藕抬色 —— 好少理
    Daaih-lūk-ngáuh tòih-sīk—Hóu síu léih
56a. 大碌藕抬色 —— 盡地快活
    Daaih-lūk-ngáuh tòih sīk—Jeuhn-deih faai-wuht
57. 大蛇疴屎 —— 少有
    Daaih sèh ngò sí—Síu yáuh
58. 單筷子挾豆腐 —— 搞禍晒
    Dàan faai-jí gihp dauh-fuh—Gáau-wó-saai
59. 單料銅煲 —— 一滾就熟
    Dàan-líu tùhng-bōu—Yāt gwán jauh suhk
60. 單眼佬睇老婆 —— 一眼睇晒
    Dàan-ngáahn-lóu tái lóuh-pòh—Yāt-ngáahn tái-saai
61. 單眼佬睇榜 —— 一眼見晒
    Dàan-ngáahn-lóu tai póng—Yāt-ngáahn gin-saai
62. 蛋花湯 —— 水汪汪
    Daahn-fā-tōng—Séui-wōng-wōng
63. 第一津對上 —— 冇譜 (← 冇甫)
    Daih-yāt-jēun deui-séuhng—Móuh-póu
64. 蛋家雞 —— 見水冇得飲
    Dahng-gā-gāi—Gin séui móuh dāk yám
65. 蛋家佬打醮 —— 冇彈 (← 冇壇)
    Dahng-gā-lóu dá-jiu—Móuh tàahn
66. 蛋家婆攞蜆 —— 第二世 (← 遞篩)
    Dahng-gā-pó lóh hín—Daih-(yih)-sai

67. 電燈膽 ── 唔通氣
    Dihn-dāng-dáam—Mh-tùng-hei
68. 吊頸鬼搽粉 ── 死要面
    Diu-géng-gwái chàh fán—Séi yiu mín
69. 倒吊臘鴨 ── 一咀油
    Dóu-diu laahp-ngáap—Yāt-jéui yàuh
70. 冬前臘鴨 ── (一)隻賴(一)隻
    Dùng-chìhn laahp-ngaap—(Yāt)-jek laai (yāt)-jek
71. 東莞佬猜牧 ── 害晒(→開晒)
    Dùng-gún-lóu chàai-múi—Hòi-saai
72. 東莞佬猜枚 ── 生個死個(←三個四個)
    Dùng-gún-lóu chàai-múi—Sàang go séi go
73. 凍水冲茶 ── 冇味
    Dung-séui chùng chàh—Móuh meih
74. 董永失妻 ── 問天攞
    Dúng Wíhng sāt chài—Mahn tīn lóh
75. 花旦梳頭 ── 唔駛計←唔使髻
    Fā-dáan sò tàuh—Mh-sái gai
76. 花被冚雞籠 ── 外邊好睇裡邊臭
    Fā-péi kám gài-lùhng—Ngoih-bihn hóu-tái léuih-bihn chau
77. 幡杆燈籠 ── 照遠唔照近
    Fāan-gōn dàng-lùhng—Jiu yúhn mh-jiu gahn
78. 番鬼佬睇榜 ── 倒數第一
    Fàan-gwái-lóu tái póng—Dóu-sóu daih-yāt
79. 犯神公仔 ── 唔係你都係你
    Faahn-sàhn gōng-jái—Mh-haih néih dōu haih néih
80. 法國大餐 ── 多閪餘(←多舊魚)
    Faat-gwok daaih-chāan—Dò gāu yùh
81. 法國公爵 ── 費闌事屌(←France duke)
    Faat-gwok gùng-jeuk—Fai-lán-sih díu
82. 法國皇帝 ── 費闌事傾(←France king)
    Faat-gwok wòhng-dai—Fai-lán-sih kìng
83. 墳頭耍大刀 ── 嚇鬼
    Fàhn-tàuh sá daaih-dōu—Haak gwái
84. 佛山孝子 ── 包有眼淚
    Faht-sāan haau-jí—Bàau yáuh ngáahn-leuih
85. 忽必烈 ── 吞金滅艇(←吞金滅宋)
    Fāt-bīt-liht—Tān gām miht song

86. 飛機火燭──銷魂(←燒雲)
    Fēi-gēi fó-jūk—Sìu-wàhn
87. 肥婆坐塔──塌塌冚
    Fèih-pòh chóh taap—Tāp-tāp-hahm
88. 火麒麟──週身癮
    Fó-kèih-léun—Jàu-sàn-yáhn
89. 火燒旗杆──長歎(←長炭)
    Fó sìu kèih-gōn—Chèuhng taan
90. 火燒棺材──大歎(←大炭)
    Fó sìu gūn-chòih—Daaih taan
91. 桄榔樹──一條心
    Fóng-lòhng-syuh—Yāt-tìuh sàm
92. 放路溪錢──引死人
    Fong louh kài-chìhn—Yáhn séi yàhn
93. 苦瓜煮鴨──苦過弟弟
    Fú-gwā jyu ngaap—Fú gwo dìh-dí
94. 苦瓜撈牛肉──越撈越縮
    Fú-gwā lòu ngàuh-yuhk—Yuht lòu yuht sūk
95. 風吹雞蛋殼──財散人安樂
    Fūng chèui gāi-daahn-hok—Chòih saan yàhn ngòn-lohk
96. 風吹皇帝褲──孤闌寒
    Fūng chèui wòhng-dai fu-lohng—Gù lán hòhn
97. 隔夜茶──一天光就賭(←一天光就倒)
    Gaak-yeh chàh—Yāt tīn-gwòng jauh dóu
97a. 隔夜茶──唔賭唔安樂(←唔倒唔安樂)
    Gaak-yeh chàh—Mh-dóu mh-ngòn-lohk
98. 隔夜餸鉢──食精(←食蒸)
    Gaak-yeh song-buht—Sihk jīng
99. 隔夜油炸鬼──冇(厘)火氣
    Gaak-yeh yàuh-ja-gwái—Móuh (lèih) fó-hei
100. 交通燈──點紅點綠
    Gàau-tùng-dàng—Dím hùhng dím luhk
101. 雞疴尿──少有
    Gāi ngò niuh—Síu yáuh
102. 雞食放光蟲──心知肚明
    Gāi sihk fong-gwōng-chùhng—Sām jì tóuh mìhng
103. 韭菜命──一長就割
    Gáu-choi mehng—Yāt chèuhng jauh got

104. 狗咬呂洞賓 ── 不識好人心
 Gáu ngáauh Léuih Duhng-bān—Bāt sīk hóu-yàhn sām
105. 狗上瓦坑 ── 有條路
 Gáu séuhng ngáh-hāang—Yáuh tìuh louh
106. 狗食月 ── 一肚明
 Gáu sihk yuht—Yāt-tóuh mìhng
107. 姜太公釣魚 ── 願者上釣
 Gèung taai-gūng diu yú—Yuhn-jé séuhng diu
108. 姜太公封神 ── 封人唔封（自）己
 Gèung taai-gūng fùng sàhn—Fùng yàhn mh-fùng (jih)-géi
109. 趕狗入窮巷 ── 反咬一口
 Gón gáu yahp kùhng-hohng—Fáan ngáauh yāt-háu
109a. 趕狗入窮巷 ── 擰轉頭咬番啖
 Gán gáu yahp kùhng-hohng—Ning-jyun tàuh ngáauh fàan daahm
109b. 趕狗入窮巷 ── 臨死咬番啖
 Gán gáu yahp kùhng-hohng—Làhm séi ngáauh fáan daahm
110. 乾糕餅 ── 咪制（← 米製）
 Gòn gōu-béng—Máih jai
111. 缸瓦佬打老虎 ── 盡地一煲
 Gōng-ngáh lóu dá lóuh-fú—Jeuhn deih yāt-bōu
112. 棺材老鼠 ── 躝屍
 Gūn-chòih lóuh-syú—Lāan si
113. 棺材老鼠 ── 食死人
 Gūn-chòih lóuh-syú—Sihk séi yàhn
114. 棺材鋪執笠 ── 死得人少
 Gūn-chòih-póu jāp-lāp—Séi-dāk yàhn síu
115. 寡母婆死仔 ── 冇望
 Gwá-móuh-pó séi jái—Móuh mohng
116. 桂姐買布 ── 一疋還一疋
 Gwai-je máaih bou—Yāt-pāt wàahn yāt-pāt
117. 跪地餵豬乸 ── 睇錢份上
 Gwaih-deih wai jyū-ná—Tai chín fahn seuhng
118. 關公細佬 ── 亦得（← 翼德）
 Gwāan-gūng saih-lóu—Yihk-dāk
119. 滾水淥豬腸 ── 兩頭縮
 Gwán-séui luhk jyū-chéung—Léuhng-tàuh sūk
120. 掘尾龍拜山 ── 攪風攪雨
 Gwaht-méih-lúng baai sāan—Gáau fūng gáau yúh

121. 過路溪錢 —— 引死人
    Gwo-louh kài-chìhn—Yáhn séi yàhn
122. 光棍佬教仔 —— 便宜莫貪
    Gwōng-gwan-lóu gaau jái—Pìhn-yìh mohk tàam
122a. 光棍佬教仔 —— 唔好貪便宜
    Gwōng-gwan lóu gaau jái—Mh-hóu tàam pìhn-yí(~yìh)
123. 光頭佬擔遮 —— 無法無天 (← 無髮無天)
    Gwōng-tàu-lóu dàam jē—Mòuh faat mòuh tīn
124. 鞋底沙 —— 抌乾淨先至安樂
    Hàaih-dái sā—Dan gòn-jehng sìn-ji ngòn-lohk
125. 客家佬彈琵琶 —— 顧得上唔顧得下
    Haak-gā-lóu tàahn pèih-pá—Gu-dāk-seuhng mh-gu-dāk-hah
126. 鹹蛋煲湯 —— 心實
    Hàahm-dáan bòu tōng—Sām-saht
127. 鹹魚臘肉 —— 見火就熟
    Hàahm-yùh laahp-yuhk—Gin fó jauh suhk
128. 戲棚仔 —— 好快大
    Hei-pàahng jái—Hóu faai daaih
129. 戲棚竹 —— 死頂
    Hei-pàahng jūk—Séi-díng
130. 河南對面 —— 成 (← 城)
    Hòh-nàahm deui-mihn—Sèhng
131. 海軍鬥水兵 —— 水鬥水
    Hói-gwān dau séui-bīng—Séui dau séui
132. 好柴燒爛竈 —— 好心唔得好報
    Hóu-chàaih sìu laahn-jou—Hóu-sām mh-dāk hóu-bou
132a. 好柴燒爛竈 —— 好佬戴爛帽
    Hóu-chàaih sìu laahn-jou—Hóu lóu daaih laahn móu
133. 祭灶鯉魚 —— 瞌埋雙眼亂噏
    Jai jou léih-yú—Hāp-màaih sèung ngáahn lyuhn ngāp
134. 砧板蟻 —— 為食鬼
    Jàm-báan ngáih—Waih-sihk-gwái
135. 著瓦靴 —— 唔落得台
    Jeuk ngáh-hēu—Mh-lohk-dāk-tòih
136. 張飛打李逵 —— 黑鬥黑
    Jēung Fēi dá Léih Kwái—Hāak dau hāak
137. 紙紮下巴 —— 口輕輕
    Jí-jaat hah-pàh—Háu-hēng-hēng

138. 紙紮老虎 —— 嚇死人
     Jí-jaat lóuh-fú—Haak séi yàhn
139. 趙匡胤 —— 大餸王（← 大宋王）
     Jiuh Hōng-yahn—Daaih-song-wòhng
140. 竈君老爺 —— 黑口黑面
     Jou-gwān lóuh-yèh—Hāak-háu hāak-mihn
141. 灶君上天 —— 有句講句
     Jou-gwān séuhng tīn—Yáuh geui góng geui
142. 竹織鴨 —— 冇心肝
     Jūk-jīk-ngáap—Móuh sām-gōn
143. 竹絲燈籠 —— 心眼多
     Jūk-sī dāng-lùhng—Sām-ngáahn dò
144. 竹樹尾甲由 —— 歎風涼
     Jūk-syuh méih gaaht-jáat—Taan fùng-lèuhng
145. 竹樹尾甲由 —— 又想風流身又餲
     Jūk-syuh méih gaaht-jáat—Yauh séung fùng-làuh sān yauh ngaat
146. 豬欄報數 —— 又一隻
     Jyū-lāan bou sou—Yauh yāt-jek
147. 豬籠跌落水 —— 四圍咁入
     Jyū-lùhng dit-lohk séui—Sei-wàih gam yahp
148. 豬嫲噍螺殼 —— 貪口爽
     Jyū-ná jiuh ló-hok—Tàam háu sóng
149. 豬嫲賣仔 —— 大覺嚛
     Jyū-ná maaih jái—Daaih gaau gèuh
150. 朱義盛 —— 永不脫色
     Jyū Yih-sing—Wíng bāt tyut sīk
151. 豬腰煲杜仲 —— 唔好有餐送
     Jyū-yīu bòu douh-juhng—Mh-hóu yáuh chàan song
152. 旗下佬叫狗 —— 越叫越走
     Kèih-hah-lóu giu gáu—Yuht giu yuht jáu
153. 旗尾風 —— 兩頭擺
     Kèih-méih fūng—Léuhng-tàuh báai
154. 乾隆皇契仔 —— 周日清
     Kìhn-lùhng-wòhng kai-jái—Jàu-yaht-chīng
155. 裙頭插令 —— 出閪奇（← 閪出旗）
     Kwàhn-tàuh chaap lihng—Chēut-hāi-kèih（← hāi chēut kèih）
156. 懶婆娘紮腳帶 —— 又長又臭
     Láahn-pòh-nèuhng jaat-geuk-dáai—Yauh chèuhng yauh chau

157. 爛紗燈 —— 得個架
     Laahn sā-dāng—Dāk go gá
158. 冷巷擔竹竿 —— 直出直入
     Láahng-hóng dàam jūk-gōn—Jihk chēut jihk yahp
159. 褸蓑衣救火 —— 燒埋自己
     Làu sō-yī gau fó—Sìu-màaih jih-géi
159a. 褸蓑衣救火 —— 惹禍上身
     Làu sō-yī gau fó—Yéh woh séuhng sān
160. 劉備借荊州 —— 有借冇回頭
     Làuh Béi je Gīng-jāu—Yáuh je móuh wùih-tàuh
161. 漏氣橡皮波 —— 吹唔賬，掹唔長
     Lauh-hei jeuhng-pèih-bō—Chèui-mh-jeung, màng-mh-chèuhng
162. 琉璃油 —— 浮（上）面
     Làuhlèih-yàuh—Fàuh-(séuhng)-mín
163. 雷公打交 —— 爭天共地
     Lèuih-gūng dá-gāau—Jàang tīn guhng deih
164. 兩個啞仔嗌交 —— 唔知邊個著
     Léuhng-go ngáh-jái ngaai-gàau—Mh-jì bīn-go jeuhk
165. 兩個人考試 —— 最低第二
     Léuhng-go yàhn háau-sí—Jeui dài daih-yih
166. 兩公婆見鬼 —— 唔係你，就係我
     Léuhng gūng-pó gin gwái—Mh-haih néih, jauh haih ngóh
167. 兩仔爺拜山 —— 一族都齊
     Léuhng jái-yèh baai-sāan—Yāt juhk dōu chàih
168. 兩仔爺報佳音 —— 袋袋平安（← 代代平安）
     Léuhng jái-yèh bou gāai-yām—Doih-doih pìhng-ngòn
169. 梁新記牙刷 —— 一毛不拔
     Lèuhng-sàn-gei ngàh-cháat—Yāt mòuh bāt baht
170. 靈前酒壺 —— 斟親都滴眼淚
     Lìhng-chìhn jáu-wú—Jàm-chàn dōu dihk ngáahn-leuih
171. 鷯哥命 —— 就食就疴
     Līu-gō-mehng—Jauh sihk jauh ngò
172. 駱駝牌（暖）水壺 —— 一味靠滾
     Lohk-tòh-pàaih (nyúhn-)séui-wú—Yāt-méi kaau gwán
173. 樂聲牌電唱機 —— 聲音兩邊走
     Lohk-sīng-pàaih dihn-cheung-gēi—Sīng-yām léuhng-bin jáu
174. 樂聲牌電飯煲 —— 大飯桶
     Lohk-sīng-pàaih dihn-faahn-bōu—Daaih-faahn-túng

175. 落雨擔遮 —— 顧前唔顧後
Lohk-yúh dàam jē—Gu chìhn mh-gu hauh

175a. 落雨擔遮 —— 死黨（← 死擋）
Lohk-yúh dàam jē—Séi-dóng

176. 落雨賣風爐 —— 越擔越重
Lóhk-yúh maaih fùng-lóu—Yuht dàam yuht chúhng

177. 䏸住屎弗吊頸 —— 穩陣
Long-jyuh sí-fãt diu-géng—Wán-jahn

178. 老虎屙蛋 —— 一次過
Lóuh-fú díu hāi—Yāt-chi gwo

179. 老公撥扇 —— 凄涼（← 妻涼）
Lóuh-gūng put sin—Chài-lèuhng

180. 老鼠跌落天秤 —— 自（己）稱自（己）
Lóuh-syú dit-lohk tīn-pihng—Jih(-géi) chihng jih(-géi)

181. 老鼠拉龜 —— 無從入手
Lóuh-syú làai gwāi—Mòuh chùhng yahp sáu

181a. 老鼠拉龜 —— 冇揰埋手
Lóuh-syú làai gwāi—Mòuh dehng màaih sáu

182. 老鼠尾生瘡 —— 大極有限
Louh-syú méih sàang-chōng—Daaih gihk yáuh haahn

182a. 老鼠尾生瘡 —— 問你有幾多膿血
Lóuh-syú méih sàang-chōng—Mahn néih yáuh géi-dò nùhng-hyut

183. 六點鐘 —— 指天篤地
Luhk-dím-jūng—Ji tīn dūk deih

184. 陸魂廷睇相 —— 唔衰攞嚟衰
Luhk Wàhn-tìhng tái-seung—Mh-sèui lóh-làih sèui

185. 龍舟棍 —— 頂衰神（← 頂水神）
Lùhng-jāu gwan—Díng sèui-sàhn (← Díng séui-sàhn)

186. 龍舟菩薩 —— 衰神（← 水神）
Lùhng-jāu Pòuh-saat—Sèui-sàhn (← séui-sàhn)

187. 籠裡雞 —— 作反
Lùhng-léuih gāi—Jok-fáan

188. 聾佬拜年 —— 大家咁話
Lùhng-lóu baai-nìhn—Daaih-gā gám wah

189. 聾佬放花炮 —— 靜幽幽散晒
Lùhng-lóu fong fā-paau—Jihng-yāu-yāu sáan-saai

190. 龍船裝狗屎 —— 又長又臭
Lùhng-syùhn jòng gáu-sí—Yauh chèuhng yauh chau

191. 馬尾紮豆腐 —— 不堪提
　　 Máh-méih jaat dauh-fuh—Bāt-hàm tàih
192. 賣魚佬 —— Selfish
　　 Maaih-yùh-lóu—Selfish (← Sell fish)
193. 買鹹魚放生 —— 不顧死活
　　 Maaih hàahm-yú fong-sāang—Bāt gu séi wuht
194. 賣魚佬洗身 —— 冇(晒)聲氣 (← 冇腥氣)
　　 Maaih-yùh-lóu sái sān—Móuh (saai) sēng-hei
195. 擘大眼拉屎 —— 眼光光做錯
　　 Māak-daaih ngáahn laaih-niuh—Ngáahn-gwōng-gwōng jouh-cho
196. 猛火煎堆 —— 皮老心唔老
　　 Máahng-fó jìn-dēui—Pèih lóuh sām mh-lóuh
197. 盲公開眼 —— 酸嘟嘟
　　 Màahng-gūng hòi ngáahn—Syùn-dū-dū
198. 盲公占卦 —— 搵丁
　　 Màahng-gūng jìm-gwa—Wán-dīng
199. 盲公竹 —— 督人唔督自己
　　 Màahng-gūng jūk—Dūk yàhn mh-dūk jih-géi
200. 盲公貼符 —— 倒貼
　　 Màahng-gūng tip fùh—Dou tip
201. 盲佬生仔 —— 冇眼睇
　　 Màahng-lóu sàang jái—Móuh ngáahn tái
202. 盲佬食湯丸 —— 心中有數
　　 Màahng-lóu sihk tōng-yún—Sām-jung yáuh sou
203. 盲頭烏蠅 —— 亂飛亂撞
　　 Màahng-tàuh wū-yīng—Lyuhn fèi lyuhn johng
204. 貓哭老鼠 —— 假慈悲
　　 Māau hūk lóuh-syú—Gá chìh-bèi
205. 茅根竹 —— 借水 (← 蔗水)
　　 Màauh-gān-jūk—Je séui
206. 麥攔街口 —— 關人
　　 Mahk-lāan gāai-háu—Gwàan yàhn
207. 問師姑攞梳 —— 實冇
　　 Mahn sī-gū lóh sō—Saht móuh
208. 蚊髀同牛髀 —— 冇得比
　　 Mān-béi tùhng ngàuh-béi—Móuh dāk béi
209. 密底算盤 —— 冇漏罅
　　 Maht-dái syun-pùhn—Móuh lauh-la

210. 密實姑娘 ── 假正經
 Maht-saht gū-nèuhng—Gá jing-gìng
211. 摩囉叉拜神 ── 睇天
 Mō-lō-chā baai sàhn—Tái tīn
212. 摩囉叉騎膊馬 ── 差上差
 Mō-lō-chā kèh bok-máh—Chā seuhng chā
213. 摩囉叉疴尿 ── 烏□□
 Mō-lō-chā ngò-niuh—Wù-séu-sèuh
214. 冇鼻佬戴眼鏡 ── 你緊佢唔緊
 Móuh-beih-lóu daai ngáahn-géng—Néih gán kéuih mh-gán
215. 冇柄士巴拿 ── 得把牙
 Móuh-beng sih-bā-lá—Dāk bá ngàh
216. 冇柄剃刀 ── 冇用夾整損手
 Móuh-beng tai-dōu—Móuh-yuhng gaap jíng-syún sáu
217. 冇尾飛陀 ── 唔見影
 Móuh-méih fèi-tòh—Mh-gin-yíng
218. 無聲狗 ── 咬死人
 Mòuh-sèng gáu—Ngáauh-séi yàhn
219. 無事獻殷勤 ── 非奸即盜
 Mòuh sih hin yàn-kàhn—Fèi gàan jīk douh
220. 冇頭烏蠅 ── 亂咁舂
 Móuh tàuh wū-yīng—Lyuhn gám jùng
221. 冇耳藤喼 ── 靠托
 Móuh yíh tàhng-gīp—Kaau tok
222. 冇掩雞籠 ── 自出自入
 Móuh yím gāi-lùhng—Jih chēut jih yahp
223. 奶媽抱仔 ── 人家物
 Náaih-mā póuh jái—Yàhn-gā maht
224. 南紅賣洗衣粉 ── 乜都冇晒
 Nàahm Hùhng maaih sái-yī-fán—Māt dōu móuh-saai
225. 泥菩薩過江 ── 自身難保
 Nàih Pòuh-saat gwo gōng—Jih sān nàahn bóu
226. 泥水佬開門口 ── 過得自己過得人
 Nàih-séui-lóu hòi mùhn-háu—Gwo-dāk jih-géi gwo-dāk yàhn
227. 啞仔飲沙示 ── 有氣講唔出
 Ngá-jái yám sā-sí—Yáuh hei góng-mh-chēut
227a. 啞仔飲沙示 ── 噱晒
 Ngá-jái yám sā-sí—Gèuh-saai

228. 啞仔食湯丸 —— 心裡有數
 Ngá-jái sihk tōng-yún—Sām-léuih yáuh sou
229. 啞子食黃蓮 —— 有苦難言
 Ngá-jí sihk wòhng-lìhn—Yáuh fú nàahn yìn
230. 啞蟬跌落地 —— 冇聲出
 Ngá-sìhm dit lohk déi—Móuh sēng chēut
231. 牙簽大少 —— 撩完就掉
 Ngàh-chīm daaih-siu—Lìu-yùhn jauh diuh
232. 瓦風領 —— 包頂頸
 Ngáh-fūng-léhng—Bàu díng-géng
233. 瓦荷包 —— 有兩個錢就噹噹聲
 Ngáh hòh-bāau—Yáuh léuhng-go chìhn jauh dōng-dōng-sēng
234. 瓦簷獅子 —— 叻到炆
 Ngáh-sìhm sì-jí—Lèk dou man
235. 矮仔上樓梯 —— 步步高陞（← 步步高升）
 Ngái-jái séuhng làuh-tāi—Bouh-bouh gòu-sìng
236. 歐家全藥水 —— 一掃光
 Ngàu-gā-chyùhn yeuhk-séui—Yāt-sou gwōng
237. 牛嚼牡丹 —— 唔知香共臭
 Ngàuh jiuh máauh-dāan—Mh-jì hèung guhng chau
238. 牛皮燈籠（加黑漆）—— 點極唔明
 Ngàuh-pèih dāng-lùhng (gà hāk-chāt)—Dím gihk mh-mìhng
239. 疴尿遞草紙 —— 徒勞無功（← 徒勞無恭）
 Ngò-niuh daih chóu-jí—Tòuh lòuh mòuh gūng
240. 疴屎瞌眼瞓 —— 眼開眼閉
 Ngò-sí hāp ngáahn-fan—Ngáahn hòi ngáahn bai
241. 外江佬打死馬騮 —— 唔還得
 Ngoih-gōng-lóu dá-séi má-lāu—Mh-wàahn-dāk hèung
242. 澳門風扇 —— 麻閔煩（← Macau fan）
 Ngo-mún fung-sin—Màh-gāu-fàahn
243. 年初一拜年 —— 大家咁話
 Nìhn-chō-yāt baai-nìhn—Daaih-gā gám wah
244. 年晚煎堆 —— 人有我有
 Nìhn-máahn jīn-dēui—Yàhn yáuh ngóh yáuh
245. 彭祖尿壺 —— 老積（← 老漬）
 Pàahng-jóu niuh-wú—Lóuh-jīk
246. 炮仗頸 —— 爆完至安樂
 Paau-jéung-géng—Baau-yùhn ji ngòn-lohk

247. 皮鞋筋 —— 扯到衡
Pèih-hàaih-gān—Ché dou hàhng

248. 平洲奶媽 —— 賺個肚
Pìhng-jāu náaih-mā—Jaahn go tóuh

249. 撒穀落田 —— 聽殃（← 聽秧）
Sá gūk lohk tìhn—Tīhng yèung

250. 沙灣燈籠 —— 何苦（← 何府）
Sā-wāan dàng-lùhng—Hòh-fú

251. 三條狗 —— 咪郁手
Sàam-tìuh gáu—Máih yūk sáu

252. 三元宮土地 —— 惜身（← 錫身）
Sàam-yùhn-gūng tóu-déi—Sek sān

253. 三水佬食麵 —— 照辦煮碗
Sàam-séui-lóu sihk mihn—Jiu báan jyú wún

254. 三水佬睇走馬燈 —— 陸續有嚟
Sàam-séui-lóu tái jáu-máh-dāng—Luhk-juhk yáuh làih

255. 山頂屎 —— 通天臭
Sāan-déng sí—Tùng tīn chau

256. 生白果 —— 腥夾悶
Sàang baahk-gwó—Sèng gaap muhn

257. 生蟲枴杖 —— 靠唔住
Sàang-chùhng gwáai-jéung—Kaau-mh-jyuh

257a. 生蟲拐杖 —— 躓人
Sàang-chùhng gwáai-jéung—Gwaan yàhn

258. 生蟣貓入眼 —— 死追
Sàang-jī-māau yahp ngáahn—Séi jèui

259. 生骨大頭菜 —— 縱壞（← 種壞）
Sàang-gwāt daaih-tàuh-choi—Jung-waaih

260. 洗腳唔抹腳 —— 猛咁捹
Sái geuk mh-muht geuk—Máahng gám fing

261. 西瓜皮 —— 踎到直
Sài-gwā pèih—Sin dou jihk

262. 西南二伯父 —— 教壞後生仔
Sài- nàahm yih-baak-fuh—Gaau-waaih hauh-sàang-jái

263. 細佬哥剃頭 —— 快嘞快嘞
Sai-louh-gō tai-tàuh—Faai lak faai lak

264. 沈殿霞試童裝 —— 監硬嚟
Sám Dihn-hàh si tùhng-jōng—Gaam-ngáang-làih

265. 新澤西 —— 食水深
     Sàn-jaahk-sài—Sihk séui sàm
266. 神前桔 —— 陰乾
     Sàhn chìhn gāt—Yàm gòn
267. 神枱貓屎 —— 神憎鬼厭
     Sàhn-tòih māau-sí—Sàhn jàng gwái yim
268. 神仙屎 —— 唔臭米氣
     Sàhn-sīn sí—Mh-chau máih-hei
269. 濕柴煲老鴨 —— 夠晒煙韌
     Sāp-chàaih bòu lóuh-ngaap—Gau-saai yìn-ngahn
270. 濕水欖核 —— 兩頭□
     Sāp-séui láam-waht—Léuhng-tàuh bīt
270a. 濕水欖核 —— 又尖又滑
      Sāp-séui láam-waht—Yauh jìm yauh waaht
271. 十幾人食一分煙 —— 冇釐癮頭
     Sahp-géi yàhn sihk yāt-fahn yīn—Móuh lèih yáhn-tàuh
272. 十個瓦罉九個蓋 —— 抌嚟抌去抌唔冚
     Sahp-go ngáh-chāang gáu-go goi—Kám làih kám heui kám-mh-hahm
273. 十五隻吊桶 —— 七上八落
     Sahp-mh-jek diu-túng—Chāt séuhng baat lohk
274. 十月芥菜 —— 起（晒）心
     Sahp-yuht gaai-choi—Héi(-saai)-sām
275. 秀才手巾 —— 包輸（← 包書）
     Sau-chòih sáu-gān—Bàau syù
276. 秀才遇著兵 —— 有理說不清
     Sau-chòih yuh-jeuhk bīng—Yáuh-léih syut-bāt-chìng
277. 秀才遇老虎 —— 吟詩都吟唔甩
     Sau-chòih yuh lóuh-fú—Yàhm sī dōu yàhm-mh-lāt
278. 綉花枕頭 —— 一肚草
     Sau-fā jám-tàuh—Yāt-tóuh chóu
279. 壽星公吊頸 —— 嫌命長
     Sau-síng-gūng diu-géng—Yìhm mehng chèuhng
280. 四方木 —— 踢都唔郁
     Sei-fòng-muhk—Tek dōu mh-yūk
280a. 四方木 —— 踢一踢郁一郁
      Sei-fòng-muhk—Tek yāt tek, yūk yāt yūk
281. 死牛龜 —— 一便頸
     Séi-ngàuh-gwāi—Yāt-bihn géng

282. 死人燈籠 —— 報大數
　　 Séi-yàhn dāng-lùhng—Bou daaih-sou

283. 石地堂鐵掃把 —— 硬打硬
　　 Sehk deih-tòhng tit sou-bá—Ngaahng dá ngaahng

284. 石灰籮 —— 到處留痕
　　 Sehk-fūi lòh—Dou-chyu làuh hàhn

285. 石罅米 —— (俾)雞啄
　　 Sehk-la máih—(Béi) gāi dèung

286. 水草綁豆腐 —— 不堪提
　　 Séui-chóu bóng dauh-fuh—Bāt-hàm-tàih

287. 水浸眼眉 —— 唔知死
　　 Séui jam ngáahn-mèih—Mh-jī séi

288. 水瓜打狗 —— 唔見一橛
　　 Séui-gwā dá gáu—Mh-gin yāt-gyuht

289. 水過鴨背 —— 冇晒
　　 Séui gwo ngaap-bui—Móuh-saai

290. 水銀瀉地 —— 無孔不入
　　 Séui-ngàhn se deih—Mòuh húng bāt yahp

291. 水上扒龍船 —— 好醜有人見
　　 Séui-seuhng pàh lùhng-syùhn—Hóu-chóu yáuh yàhn gin

292. 順風屎艇 —— 快夾臭
　　 Seuhn-fūng sí-téng—Faai gaap chau

293. 雙天單地 —— 走人
　　 Sèung-tīn dāan-deih—Jáu yàhn

294. 屎窟掛牌 —— 撞大板
　　 Sí-fāt gwa páai—Johng daaih báan

295. 屎坑竹枝 —— 枒楂夾臭
　　 Sí-hāang jūk-jī—Ngah-jah gaap chau

296. 屎坑買草紙 —— 問心
　　 Sí-hāang máaih chóu-jí—Mahn sām

297. 屎坑石 —— 又臭又硬
　　 Sí-hāang sehk—Yauh chau yauh ngaahng

298. 屎坑關刀 —— 文唔文得，武唔武得 (文 ← 聞，武 ← 舞)
　　 Sí hāang gwāan-dōu—Màhn mh-màhn-dāk, móuh mh-móuh-dāk

298a. 屎蘸關刀 —— 文唔文得，武唔武得 (文 ← 聞，武 ← 舞)
　　 Sí yáahm gwāan-dōu—Màhn mh-màhn-dāak, móuh mh-móuh-dāk

299. 市橋蠟燭 —— 假細心
　　 Síh-kiuh laahp-jūk—Gá sai-sām

300. 豉油樽枳 ── 鹹濕
　　 Sih-yàuh-jēun jāt—Hàahm-sāp
301. 豉油撈飯 ── 整色（整）水
　　 Sih-yàuh lòu faahn—Jíng sīk (jíng) séui
302. 食屎食著豆 ── 撞彩數
　　 Sihk sí sihk-jeuhk dáu—Johng chói-sou
303. 燒豬耳 ── 免吵（← 免炒）
　　 Sìu jyū-yíh—Míhn cháau
304. 燒壞瓦 ── 唔入劄
　　 Sìu-waaih ngáh—Mh-yahp-daahp
305. 肇興荷包 ── 扡衰人
　　 Siu-hing hòh-bāau—Tòh sèui yàhn
306. 樹林菩薩 ── 陰夾毒（陰 ← 蔭，毒 ← 獨）
　　 Syuh-làhm Pòuh-saat—Yàm gaap duhk
307. 酸姜竹 ── 篤完掉
　　 Syun-gèung-jūk—Dūk yùhn diuh
308. 酸薑蕎 ── 頭
　　 Syùn-gèung kíu—Tàuh
309. 剃頭佬教仔 ── 有得刮就刮
　　 Tai-tàuh-lóu gaau jái—Yáuh dāk gwaat jauh gwaat
310. 剃頭佬走警報 ── 懶刮
　　 Tai-tàuh-lóu jáu gíng-bou—Láahn gwaat
311. 剃頭唔濕水 ── 乾刮
　　 Tai-tàuh mh-sāp-séui—Gòn gwaat
312. 天上雷公，地下舅公 ── 惡到極
　　 Tīn-seuhng lèuih-gūng, deih hah káuh-gūng—Ngok dou gihk
313. 鐵咀雞 ── 牙尖咀利
　　 Tit-jéui-gāi—Ngàh jìm jéui leih
314. 抬棺材甩褲 ── 失禮死人
　　 Tòih gūn-chòih lāt fu—Sāt-láih-séi yàhn
315. 鐵沙梨 ── 咬唔入
　　 Tit sā-lei—Ngáauh-mh-yahp
316. 塘底突 ── 水乾就見
　　 Tòhng-dái daht—Séui gòn jauh gin
317. 蜻蜓咬尾 ── 自己食自己
　　 Tòhng-mēi ngáauh méih—Jih-géi sihk jih-géi
318. 土地燈籠 ── 夜不收
　　 Tóu-deih dàng-lùhng—Yeh-bāt-sàu

319. 銅銀買病豬 ── 你笑我又笑
Tùhng-ngàhn máaih behng jyū—Néih siu ngóh yauh siu

320. 斷線紙鳶 ── 無牽無掛
Tyúhn-sin jí-yíu—Mòuh hìn móuh gwa

320a. 斷線紙鳶 ── 一去無蹤
Tyúhn-sin jí-yíu—Yāt-heui mòuh jūng

321. 斷線三弦 ── 冇得彈
Tyùhn-sin sàam-yìhn—Móuh-dāk-tàahn

322. 禾叉跌落井 ── 差到底 (差 ← 叉)
Wòh-chā dit-lohk jéng—Chà dou dái

323. 禾草穿針 ── 唔過得眼
Wòh-chóu chyùn jàm—Mh-gwo-dāk ngáahn

324. 和尚仔念經 ── 有口無心
Wòh-séung-jái nihm-gīng—Yáuh háu mòuh sām

325. 皇帝道白 ── 寡人
Wòhng-dai douh-baahk—Gwá-yàhn

326. 皇帝女 ── 唔憂嫁 (嫁 → 價)
Wòhng-dai-néui—Mh-yàu ga

327. 黃大仙 ── 有求必應
Wòhng-daaih-sīn—Yáuh kàuh bīt ying

328. 黃腫腳 ── 不消提 (提 ← 蹄)
Wòhng-júng-geuk—Bāt-sìu tàih

329. 黃蓮樹下彈琴 ── 苦中作樂
Wòhng-lìhn-syuh-hah tàahn kàhm—Fú-jūng jok lohk

330. 黃牛落水 ── 各顧各 (各 ← 角)
Wòhng-ngàuh lohk séui—Gok gu gok

331. 黃皮樹鷯哥 ── 唔熟唔食
Wòhng-pèih-syuh līu-gō—Mh-suhk mh-sihk

331a. 黃皮樹鷯哥 ── 熟嗰個食嗰個
Wòhng-pèih-syuh līu-gō—Suhk gó-go sihk gó-go

332. 黃生醫眼 ── 有突
Wòhng sēng yì ngáahn—Yáuh daht

333. 黃蕭養燈籠 ── 終須有日
Wòhng Sìu-yéuhng dāng-lūhng—Jùng sèui yáuh yaht

334. 王小二過年 ── 一年不如一年
Wòhng-síu-yih gwo-nìhn—Yāt-nìhn bāt-yùh yāt-nìhn

335. 烏蠅摟馬尾 ── 一拍兩散
Wū-yīng làu máh-méih—Yāt paak léuhng saan

336. 烏蠅頭上生瘡仔 —— 冇乜膿血
　　 Wū-yīng tàuh-seuhng sàang chōng-jái—Móuh māat nùhng-hyut
337. 芋頭煲糖水 —— 心淡
　　 Wuh-táu bòu tòhng-séui—Sām táahm
338. 人在江湖 —— 身不由己
　　 Yàhn joih gōng-wùh—Sān bāt yàuh géi
339. 日本膏藥 —— 脫苦海
　　 Yaht-bún gōu-yeuhk—Tyut fú hói
340. 日本鬧鐘 —— 聲大夾冇準
　　 Yaht-bún naauh-jōng—Sèng daaih gaap móuh jéun
341. 幽飽餡 —— 冇料
　　 Yàu-bāau háam—Móuh líu
342. 伊莉沙白泰萊抱孫 —— 肉麻夾肉酸（麻 ← 嫲，酸 ← 孫）
　　 Yī-leih-sā-baahk-taai-lòih póuh syūn—Yuhk-màh gaap yuhk-syūn
343. 二仔底 —— 死跟
　　 Yih-jái-dái—Séi gàn
344. 二四六八單 —— 冇得變
　　 Yih-sei-luhk-baat-dàan—Móuh dāk bin
345. 二叔公割禾 —— 望下截
　　 Yih-sūk-gūng got wòh—Mohng hah-jiht
346. 二叔婆揼心口 —— 自有分數
　　 Yih-sūk-pó dám sām-háu—Jih yáuh fàn-sou
347. 鹽倉土地 —— 鹹濕伯父
　　 Yìhm-chōng tóuh-déi—Hàahm-sāp baak-fú
348. 閻羅王出告示 —— 鬼睇
　　 Yìhm-lòh-wòhng chēut gou-sih—Gwái-tái
349. 閻羅王揸攤 —— 鬼買
　　 Yìhm-lòh-wòhng jà tāan—Gwái máaih
350. 閻羅王嫁女 —— 鬼要
　　 Yìhm-lòh-wòhng ga néui—Gwái yiu
351. 熱火棒 —— 唔掉得翻轉頭
　　 Yiht-fó-páahng—Mh-diuh-dāk-fàan-jyun-tàuh
352. 原子火柴 —— 一擦就著火
　　 Yùhn-jí fó-chàaih—Yāt chaat jauh jeuk-fó

Appendix: Chinese Abstracts

一語兩制：1888年兩本粵語教科書的語音研究
One Language, Two Systems: A Phonological Study of
Two Cantonese Language Manuals of 1888 (page 1)

提要：1888年有兩本粵語教科書同時面世，一本是居港英國人J. Dyer Ball編寫的 *Cantonese Made Easy*（CME），一本是美國人T. L. Stedman和李桂攀在紐約合編出版的 *A Chinese and English Phrase Book in the Canton Dialect*（PB）。兩書採取羅馬拼音教學，每字每句都一一註明聲韻調，是研究早期粵語音韻史的寶貴材料。兩書在前言中都說明粵語以廣州話為準。但是細較之下，兩書音系頗有出入。本文排比兩書記音材料，歸納出CME有22聲母、56韻母、9聲調，與今日標準粵語系統大致相同；而PB則有19聲母、51韻母、8聲調，顯然不屬於廣州音系。PB紀錄的究竟是哪一種粵方言？本文翻查當日其他粵音材料，又與今日珠江三角洲方言比較，以為PB音系與中山方言有頗多相似之處，而PB的作者李桂攀正是中山人。

關鍵詞：早期粵語；歷史音韻；方言語音；語言教科書；*Cantonese Made Easy*；*A Chinese and English Phrase Book in the Canton Dialect* 英語不求人

從粵語歌曲中押韻的現象來看音韻擬構的一些問題
Cantonese Phonology as Reconstructed from Popular Songs (page 33)

提要：研究古韻分部大都根據古人詩歌押韻的用字，歸納類推而得。材料中用韻分合有異，往往會視作音韻變化的痕跡。然而古人用韻是否一定從嚴？兩字相押，是否一定韻母相同？本文試就香港粵語歌曲中押韻的情形，對這問題作一探索。研究材料包括四百多首流行歌曲，押韻的字數以千計。韻腳可以利用系聯的原則歸納成24韻部，而現代粵語共有53個韻母，兩者之間相距甚大。細究其因，粵語歌曲除韻母相同的字可以互相押韻以外，更有其他兩種通押的現象。一種是凡元音相同的字皆可互押，所以陽聲韻本 -m、-n、-ng 三分，詩歌中可以通叶，而且陰陽入三聲通押的例子也不乏其例。另一種情形是歷史遺留下來的押韻成規。江陽不分，文微通叶，這是從詞曲以來已有的現象，今人填詞，雖是發音不同，但仍照通叶無礙。據此而言，詩歌用韻和實際語音並不完全相符合，研究古音，對於材料運用，不得不嚴加謹慎。香港粵語歌曲中又有中西語言互相押韻的現象，文中也一併陳述。

關鍵詞：粵語歌曲押韻；粵語聲調；中英押韻；系聯

早期粵語中的完成體貌
Completing the Completive:
Reconstructing Early Cantonese Grammar (page 75)

提要：標準粵語的完成體詞尾是「咗」。但早期粵語語料中除「咗」以外，還有「曉」，語法功能和表現和「咗」相同。而且有的文本，「曉」和「咗」並存，而且可以互用。本文參考1841年至1946年間編寫的六套粵語教學語料，排比「曉」、「咗」出現的頻率，並分析其使用場合，推定「曉」的使用大概在1930年代消失。材料中頗有一些使用變調標完成體貌的例子，對我們如何解釋「曉」的消失或能提供一些線索。「曉」、「咗」二詞源自何來，本文亦試勾勒出其歷史演變的痕跡。

關鍵詞：完成體；早期粵語；曉；咗；了；變調

早期粵語中的疑問句式
The Interrogative Construction:
(Re-)constructing Early Cantonese Grammar (page 109)

提要：漢語提問有各種句式，每種句式皆有自己組成的規則和演變的軌跡。反複問又稱正反問，基本句式是把動詞語的肯定形式和否定形式並列，提供選擇作答。本文試從歷時角度探討粵語反複問的變化規則。反複問以正反並列，句式中必然有重複的部分，可以省略從簡。省略可以向前省略，從否定句中削去重複部分，承前省後；也可以向後從肯定句中進行省略，省前存後；至於省略部分，亦可多可少，不盡相同。省略方向不同，省略部分多寡，因而疑問也呈現不同的句式。我們翻檢粵語歷時語料，從1828年的口語教材到二十世紀中期的記載，羅列有關例句，對比其間省略的方向以及省略多寡，歸納成六種句式。從時代上言，六種句式出現前後不一致，但細究之下，亦可發現其間發展相承繼，前後有序。從發展趨勢來看，十九世紀到二十世紀三十年代是一大突破，承前省後的句式都變成省前存後的新局面，大幅度的省略後可以只留下否定詞「唔」作為標誌。材料中亦顯現新句式中保留下來的「唔」[m]可以和句末助詞「呀」[a]語音複合，產生「嗎」[ma]。後起的「嗎」字句是否從此而來，亦可備為一說。

關鍵詞：早期粵語疑問句；反複問；省略方向；雙音節詞；嗎字句

將字句：粵語中的前及物句式
The Pretransitive in Cantonese (page 151)

提要：現代漢語的動賓句，可以利用「把」字為標誌，使賓語前置，組成[主+把-賓+動]，一般稱為「把」字句。漢語各地方言均有「把」字句式，但標誌不一，粵語的標誌是「將」。將字句和把字句的用法相近似，但使用條件寬嚴有別。本文參考多種香港粵語語料，分析將字句出現的場合，並對比現代漢語中把字句的相關例句，從動詞配搭、使用條件、語用闡釋等各層面切入，討論其間異同，進一步了解方言對處置式的要求和應用，從而突出粵語本身的使用特點。

關鍵詞：粵語將字句；現代漢語把字句；處置式；動賓結構；主題話語

地圖地名考：十九世紀香港粵語的多元性
Naming the City: Language Complexity in the Making of an 1866 Map of Hong Kong (page 209)

提要：地名是一種地域指稱。人們聚居或外出，總是劃地命名，以便記憶，也便於交談。但是地名不僅是一個地方的名稱，地名背後往往也包含一定的社會、歷史、文化訊息，反映人們對當地的認識和關注。為地方命名，以語言文字為標誌，所以地名本身也記錄當時的語言實況。香港位處珠江三角洲，本屬粵語地區。但是香港百多年來，華洋雜處，南北共居，地方命名究竟是以什麼語言為依據？是漢語還是其他民族語言？是粵語還是別的方言？學者一直未有確實的論證。

我們試從一幅十九世紀的香港地圖來看當年各地各區的名稱，嘗試作初步的探索。地圖上的地名用漢字標寫，並附有英文拼音。我們根據拼音可以擬構這些地名當時的發音，進一步考究這些地名是否根源於粵語。同時，由於這些地名的漢字和拼音跟今日地圖上的標寫不盡相同，這些不同究竟是反映粵語本身語音的變化？還是由於方言混雜而有所差異？書面材料是我們研究語言歷時變遷的基本依據。然而，這些書面語料所記錄的語音，是否和地圖上所呈現的相同或相類似？我們希望能通過一手的歷時材料，進一步考察十九世紀香港語言的實況。

關鍵詞：Fr. S. Volonteri；《新安縣全圖》；香港地名；十九世紀語言；粵語；客家話

粵語中的稱謂用語
Terms of Address in Cantonese (page 247)

提要：稱謂是語言研究的一大課題。本文試從香港粵語取材，研究稱謂系統中的語音、構詞、語義各層面的表現。重點在親屬稱謂，包括所謂的面稱及背稱。至於社交稱謂，用法多從親屬稱謂延伸而來，文中亦略略提及。文末並附稱謂圖表，列明父母夫妻各系親屬稱謂。

關鍵詞：香港粵語；親屬稱謂詞；社交稱謂；親從子名稱謂；面稱；背稱

粵語中的歇後語現象
A Study of *Xiehouyu* Expressions in Cantonese (page 287)

提要：歇後語是中國語言中一種特別的熟語類型，由前後兩個語言片段組成。前段設譬，後段作解，中間稍具停頓。解語針對譬語而言，所以譬語是解語的直接語境；而歇後語在一般話語中是充當話題的說明部分，借譬來表達自己對話題的看法，所以話題是解語的應用語境。大體而言，歇後語可分兩類，一類是解語因譬語而生，既可用於直接語境，亦可用於應用語境，用法容或伸縮有異，但其義本一。另一類是解語由譬語而發，但只可用於直接語境，再諧音轉意，或望文生義，轉折而另有所指，然後適用於應用語境，所以用法不同，意義亦各有別。屬第一類的歇後語，以意為主，所以解語部分，唯大意不傷，則文字盡可有所更改，而且語義既明，解語部分亦可省去。屬第二類的歇後語，一音多義，一字數解，所以雙關部分，一字不得更易。而且由譬至解，由解而至他指，其間雙重轉折，非一目瞭然，所以解語多不可省。

　　本文搜集香港粵語中流行的歇後語數百條，研究譬解之間的關係，從語音、語意、構詞、造句各方面來看解語本身意義轉折的關鍵。香港是一個華洋雜處的社會，歇後語中亦多有中英語文夾雜的現象。同時，商用廣告、電視用語、舶來貨品、洋人異俗，亦雜見於歇後語中，中西並容，亦一時一地之特色。

關鍵詞：粵語歇後語；譬喻；語義延伸；聲音假借；詞語複合；語法重組；禁忌語；廣告語言